PINXTON'S HEROES

by J Taylor, S Berrill, J Meredith, D Pryor ARPS

*This book is dedicated
to all the men and women
of Pinxton who have served
their Country*

With Special Thanks to

For sponsoring the printing of this book

The Authors are:

Jennie Taylor (née Freeman)

Stanley Berrill

John Meredith

Donald Pryor ARPS

Published by J Taylor

Copyright © J Taylor

ISBN 978 0 9560945 0 6

Contents

Greater love hath no man than this, that a man lay down his life for his friends
(John 15:13)

Foreword

Acknowledgements

Introduction

The Pinxton They Knew

The Pinxton War Memorial, WW I

Pinxton War Memorial Plaques

The Pinxton War Memorial, WW II

Rededication of the Memorial, 2006

Military Medals

Crich Memorial Tower

The Ypres Memorial, Menin Gate

The Unknown Soldier

War Memorials and Casualties

The Royal British Legion

PINXTON'S HEROES

World War One

World War Two

Those who returned

Index of those remembered

Foreword

Why should four ordinary people dedicate several years of their lives to researching 103 names taken from a dusty war memorial and then go to the bother of writing a book about them? Why knock on doors, write letters, make phone calls, visit museums, leave notices in local shops, and spend hours on the internet searching through regimental records? Surely they are just names - the men were not relatives or even known to them - they were just strangers from another time.
 Why go to all the trouble?

For those who dwell for any length of time on war, soldiering and death in the 20th century, whatever they come to think, their hearts become filled with a mixture of inspiration, awe and profound sadness: inspiration at the courage and fortitude of groups of men who stood face-to-face with death and did not turn away; awe at the sheer rate of mechanised death and destruction wrought in the name of 'God and Country', and profound sadness at the shock waves of grief and loss that ran through whole communities when the men never returned. Ultimately those who begin to ask 'why' become haunted by the names of such places as the Marne, Vimy Ridge, the Somme, Passchendaele and Normandy.

It is easy to become overwhelmed by the sheer incomprehensible scale of it all. But an antidote to this feeling of numbness and disbelief is to narrow down the focus of enquiry to something that is altogether more comprehensible and more recognisably human in scale. In fact, it makes perfect sense to narrow the search for understanding down to a small group of real 'local' men and their stories.

Soldiers may fight for their country but individual men invariably die for the love of the comrades who stand beside them. Shakespeare got it right when he said,
> *We few, we happy few, we band of brothers;*
> *For he to-day that sheds his blood with me*
> *Shall be my brother…*
> *(Henry V Act 4, Scene3)*

Here then, we have four individuals from Pinxton whose struggle to understand and come to terms with war, suffering and all of its insanity has developed a camaraderie all of its own and led them to focus on the fallen soldiers of their own village. Their bond with these names etched on a cold war memorial is not difficult to understand. The researchers and the remembered are the sons and daughters of Pinxton and share a common heritage. They walked its lanes, roamed its fields, courted by its canals, and worked in its offices, pits and workshops. But, an accident of fate meant that these 'Heroes of Pinxton' were born at a time of war, which meant they left and never came back. For all four writers, the strap line of this book could easily have been John Bradford's famous phrase, 'There but for the grace of God go I'.

Their determination as writers and researchers is that from this moment onwards and for always the names on the Pinxton War Memorial will be more than 'just names'. They will be people, and where time has been kind they will have faces and families and histories. Their hope is that it will stimulate others to further the research and breathe yet more life into these heroic men who died so that we may live and have the freedom to seek the truth on their behalves. As one of Pinxton's sons myself, it has been a privilege and a pleasure to edit what I know will become a unique and important testimony to a village's pride and gratitude. As memories and living links fade for ever, their efforts are timely and despite its humble intent, I believe this book will become a document of profound personal, social and emotional significance for years to come.

Mike Berrill   August 2008

Acknowledgements

We would like to thank the following for their help with information, without which the compiling of this book would not have been possible.

Commonwealth War Graves Commission……..……......Mrs. Jackie Withers
Imperial War Museum………………….….....................Ian Proctor
Royal Air Force Museum……………….….….………..Nina Burls
Air Historical Branch RAF……………….…….……….Alan Thomas
RN Second Sea Lord and Naval Home Command…….Mrs. Ann Nowak
Fortrose Assistant Registrar………………….……......Muriel M. Macleman
Highland Council Archive……………….…….……….Alison Brown
Historian, Sherwood Foresters…………………..….…..Mel Siddons
Manor Kingdom (Widmerpool Hall)……………..…..Janice Giles
Graphic Design (Cover and Inserts)………………..…..Trevor Gibson
I.T………………………………………….……...........Adrian Toon
Pinxton Church Burial Register…………………….…..Tracie Noad
Rededication photographs……....................………….Phil Handley
Sutton in Ashfield Library (Free Press Archive)…….Janet Simmons
Mike Berrill (Foreword and Introduction)
Chesterfield Library (Derbyshire Times)
North Notts Newspapers [Chad] (Rededication photographs)
The Queen's Royal Regimental Museum
The Royal British Legion

We are indebted to the families and friends of the Pinxton men and women remembered in this book that have helped by providing information, treasured memorabilia and photographs.

The authors would also like to thank their partners for their patience and support throughout the many years this book has been in preparation.

Introduction

As the number of people who remember the individuals behind the names on the Pinxton War Memorial begins to dwindle and disappears forever, and these men become transformed from 'friends' and 'relatives' into anonymous historical figures, four of us have come together to keep their memories alive both as soldiers and people. The book has taken several years to research and write, and it is our own personal monument to Pinxton's sons who made the ultimate sacrifice and laid down their lives so that we might live and be free.

Every effort has been made to gain accurate information and we are grateful to the many people who have helped with stories, photos and documents. However, gathering this has often proved difficult. The names on the Pinxton Memorial did not always match the spellings of the names at the Commonwealth War Graves Commission (CWGC) or in local newspapers. During the First World War many in the community could not read or write and when deaths were notified mistakes were sometimes made. For some of the names, we had difficulty finding any information at all as families have moved away from the area and there is no record of where they went. We have nevertheless tried to piece together what evidence we can and draw assumptions from it; where this proves to be wrong we accept full responsibility and apologise in advance for any inaccuracies you might find.

The World at War.

The 20th Century was a period of separation and conflict, and no corner of the globe was left unaffected by it. Strong national and imperial identities forged in the 19th Century reached their peak in the early years of the 20th, and as the major players on the world stage vied with each other for power and supremacy the die was cast for 100 years of war. As one unresolved conflict gave way to the next, the struggle for imperial supremacy gave way at the mid-point of the century to the ideological intrigues of the 'Cold War', where only the threat of 'mutually assured destruction' prevented a repetition of the scale of carnage from the first 50 years. Still there were the human tragedies of Korea and Vietnam to come, and as the century began to draw to its close there were wars in the Falklands, Iraq and Kosovo, just in case anyone thought the world might have learned lessons from a century of conflict and death.

Recruitment Poster for 1st World War

The two wars that most overshadowed the lives of those who lived in the village of Pinxton, however, were the First and the Second World Wars. It is thought that 65 million men fought in the 1st World War. It began as a war of movement in 1914, as the German Army swept through Belgium, but on the Western Front it soon became a lethal stalemate with the Germans and the Allies facing each other across a trench line that stretched 230 miles across Belgium and France. At first the trenches were shallow pits, but with machine guns and artillery scything whole units of men down, they soon became a maze of zigzagging channels over six feet deep, which left opposing armies 'dug in' often separated by no more than 100 yards of barbed wire.

Heavy rain quickly turned the trenches in to drainage ditches, despite the use of wooden 'duck boards'. Added to this were regular artillery barrages, deadly accurate sniper fire for anyone raising their heads above the parapet, and the use of poisonous gases like chlorine and mustard gas. The conditions for fighting men were often grim and deadly. In the first ever gas attack in 1915, 15,000 cylinders of gas were released to blow across the Allied trenches with a military gain of only 200 yards. In 1917, mustard gas, which eats away the lining of the lungs, caused 160,000 British casualties.

Major frontal assaults on each others trench lines were often preceded by days of lethal artillery barrages and huge mines were often exploded underneath enemy positions as preludes to major battles. Tunnelling under enemy trench systems and laying massive explosive charges became a new aspect of war and one that involved Pinxton miners. In 1917 at Messines near the Belgian town of Ypres, the British blew the top off a long ridge and 10,000 German soldiers were killed within minutes. In the series of battles in the days that followed 600,000 men lost their lives. To stop soldiers becoming inactive or complacent during the lulls between major battles, at night trench raids would be mounted where small groups of men would crawl into the opposition trenches and try to capture enemy personnel to gain intelligence. There was little rest and no escape other than death or serious injury.

It was in conditions such as those described above that many Pinxton men lost their lives. In a way those who were given proper burials were lucky. Many of the dead were simply placed in shell holes because of the difficulty of burial under fire. Some were blown apart or buried under falling earth. The monuments at Thiepval on the Somme and at the Menin Gate in Ypres commemorate over 120,000 men whose bodies were never found. It is difficult to know exactly how many were killed in the First World War, estimates put it between 8 and 9 million killed and a further 21 to 22 million wounded. In all over 60 million soldiers were mobilised world wide and many who were not physically scarred by its bullets and shells were left emotionally crippled in the aftermath.

Slaughter on this vast and industrial scale could not, however, prevent a second world conflagration 20 years later. Punitive and humiliating reparations against Germany sowed the seeds for a demagogue who would rise and restore this once proud imperial power to what they saw as being their rightful position in the world. When Hitler's Wehrmacht launched its invasion of Poland in September 1939, England and France had no real option but to declare war.

The Second World War was very different; it was a war of swift movement and 'Blitzkrieg', and given a new and more deadly dimension by airpower. Over 100 million soldiers were mobilised and it is estimated that over 72 million people died, two thirds of them being civilians, which makes it the worst and most deadly military conflict the world has ever known. It saw the beginning of 'Total War' where there was no longer a distinction between civilians and the military. The whole of each nation's economic, industrial and scientific resources were mobilized for war and consequently everyone and everything was a potential target.

As a consequence death in the Second World War came in different ways. Rather than gas attacks, it was air raids; rather than just static artillery fire, it was swift moving tank warfare, and the air proved a new and lethal battle ground - over 300,000 British R.A.F. personnel were killed alone. Despite early successes by the German and Japanese forces, the overwhelming power of the armies ranged against them led to their eventual defeat, but only at an even greater cost in human life than the First World War. In this conflict civilians shared the misery of death and destruction - victims of bombing, genocide, mass starvation and finally atomic weapons. Whereas the First World War was characterised by certain innocence in those who signed-up and went off to fight, by the time of the Second World War, conflict on this scale was understood for what it was – ruthless and bloody.

Debt of Honour

Though the numbers of those killed world-wide during two World Wars will never be known, we can be a little more accurate about the death toll for Britain and the Commonwealth. The 'Debt of Honour Register' is a database listing 1.7 million men and women of the Commonwealth forces who died during the two World Wars. They are either buried or commemorated in 23,000 cemeteries or memorials world-wide, as are 67,000 Commonwealth civilians who died as a result of enemy action in the Second World War.

There are no words that can adequately summarise the effect of a century of conflict on those who have come after. Our simple aim has been to ensure that as we move into a new century already scarred with war and international conflict we do not forget those of Pinxton's sons who gave their lives during the 20th century. Visiting war graves in Flanders in 1922 King George V said,

> *We can truly say that the whole circuit of the earth is grilled with the graves of our dead…And, in the course of my pilgrimage, I have many times asked myself whether there can be more potent advocates of peace upon earth through the years to come, than this massed multitude of silent witnesses to the desolation of war.*

We hope our humble record is just one more 'potent advocate of peace upon earth'. If the 20th century was a period of separation and conflict, we hope that the 21st century will become one where we come together and embrace human diversity in all its many forms as richness and strength, and not a source of discord and conflict. We also hope that you may be inspired to make a pilgrimage yourself to one of these 'corners of a foreign field' to pay your own respects and say a personal word of thanks for what they gave.

The Pinxton They Knew

No. 2 Pit

Pinxton Coke Ovens

Brookhill Colliery

Green Engine - this was near
to where the motorway bridge now stands
on Kirkby Lane

Shady Pit Somercotes, an early photograph

The building of Langton Colliery

Park Lane where many soldiers lived

Kirkstead School

King Street School

Longwood School, Wharf Chapel and Alexander Terrace

Parade collecting money for victims' families

Methodist Outing in the charabanc owned by Ernest Spiers

Pinxton Midland Station

Pinxton Wharf Station

Hospital parade on Victoria Road

Hospital parade on Wakes Ground

Booth's Department Store where
most Pinxton people shopped

Pinxton Football Club
between the wars

The War Memorial, St Helen's Church, Pinxton

The village of Pinxton lies in the Erewash Valley on the border of Nottinghamshire and Derbyshire. St Helen's Church is situated at the top of Park Lane on the summit of a hill, with good views all round. Records show the church was built on the ruins of an ancient castle, parts of which date back to the 13th Century. The war memorial is sited on the east side of the church.

Pinxton Church

Major George Coke Robertson

Widmerpool Hall

UNVEILING AND DEDICATION OF PINXTON WAR MEMORIAL

The war memorial was originally dedicated on 8th October 1920, less than two years after the end of the Great War. There was a large congregation at the unveiling and dedication ceremony. Major Robertson, of Widmerpool Hall, Nottinghamshire, formally with the 17th Lancers, carried out the unveiling ceremony, referring to the heroic deeds of the 46th Division on September 29th 1918, and the important part played by the Derbyshire men.

1914 - 1918 War Memorial, dedicated 1920

Mr. and Mrs. Hancock, who were at the dedication

Other speakers at the dedication included Mr. H. Hancock, JP, Mr. W. Sansome and Mr. H. Stevenson. The service was conducted by the Rector, The Rev. S. Coke, and the Bishop of Derby. Many beautiful floral tributes were placed at the base of the monument by relatives and friends of the fallen. The monument, on which is inscribed the names of 68 men of the parish who fell in the Great War, has been erected at a cost of between £500 and £600.

It was stated that the monument was blown over and had to be re-erected in 1922.

Report from Local Paper

We are pleased to note that Pinxton's imposing War Memorial has now been fully restored, and all traces of its rough passage during the gale of last April are entirely obliterated.
It will be remembered that the 12 foot Cornish granite shaft was dislodged and broken. A recurrence of such a disaster seems almost impossible now despite the very exposed position the monument occupies.

Pinxton War Memorial

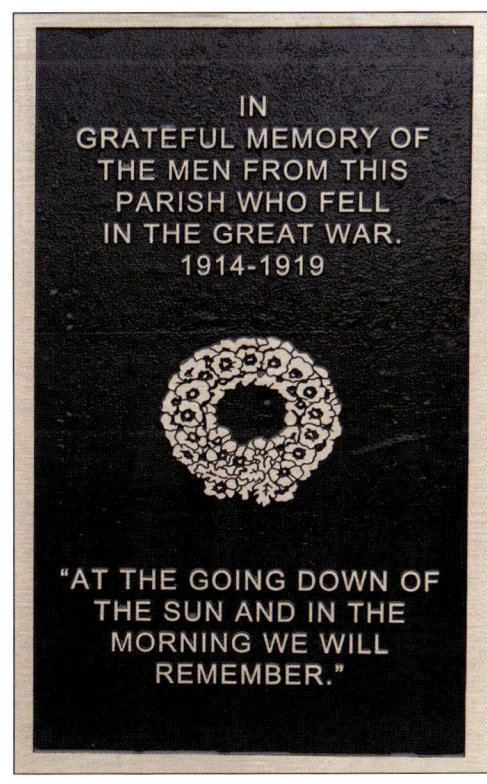

IN GRATEFUL MEMORY OF THE MEN FROM THIS PARISH WHO FELL IN THE GREAT WAR.
1914-1919

"AT THE GOING DOWN OF THE SUN AND IN THE MORNING WE WILL REMEMBER."

IRISH GUARDS

Lt. L.S. COKE.

GRENADIER GUARDS

Pte. W. LANE.
Pte. J.H. UPTON.
Pte. J.W. GREGORY.

ROYAL ENGINEERS

Cpl. W. BARKER.
Spr. P. NAYLOR.

Cpl. N. ANTHONY. R.A.M.C.
Pte. S.M. BINGLEY. M.C.C.
Pte. J. BUTLER. K.S.L.I.
Pte. H. CLARIDGE. O & B.L.I.
Pte. A.E. DONNELLY. SCOT. R.
Pte. T.L. FAULKNER. R.A.F.
Pte. H. LINES. N.S.R.
Pte. T. NOAKES. K.O.Y.L.I.
Pte. J. SEARSON. Y.W.R.I.
Pte. B. SMITH. A.P.C.
Pte. R. WILSON. R.M.L.I.
C. DUTTON. R.N.

ROYAL WARWICKS

Sgt. R.H. LANE. M. Medal.
Pte. W.E. SLATER.

ROYAL FIELD ARTILLERY

Dvr. R. JESSOP. M. Medal.
Dvr. J. PRITCHETT.
Dvr. F.E. SHAWCROFT.

CANADIANS

Pte. H.H. BINGHAM.
Pte. F. HILL.

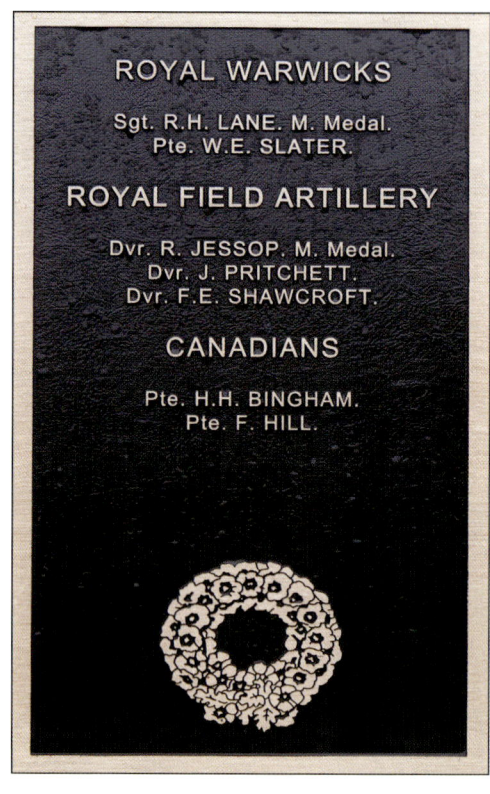

ROYAL FUSILIERS

2nd. Lt. H. MARSH.
Pte. A. HOTEN.

NORTHUMBERLAND FUSILIERS

Sgt. S. WINFIELD. M. Medal
Cpl. S. MATKIN.
L.Cpl. R. STREET.
Pte. G.W. DAY.

KINGS ROYAL RIFLES

Pte. E.C. LEATHERLAND.
Pte. F. SHARMAN.

ROYAL WELSH FUSILIERS

Sgt. W. RIGBY.
Sgt. E. ROHUN.
Sgt. B. TAYLOR.
Pte. A. DYE.
Pte. D. EDSON.
Pte. A. GELL.
Pte. A. HOTEN.
Pte. W.E. LUDLAM
Pte. H. PARNHAM.
Pte. J. PRITCHARD.
Pte. F. RODGERS.
Pte. B. STOCKS.
Pte. H. WATSON.

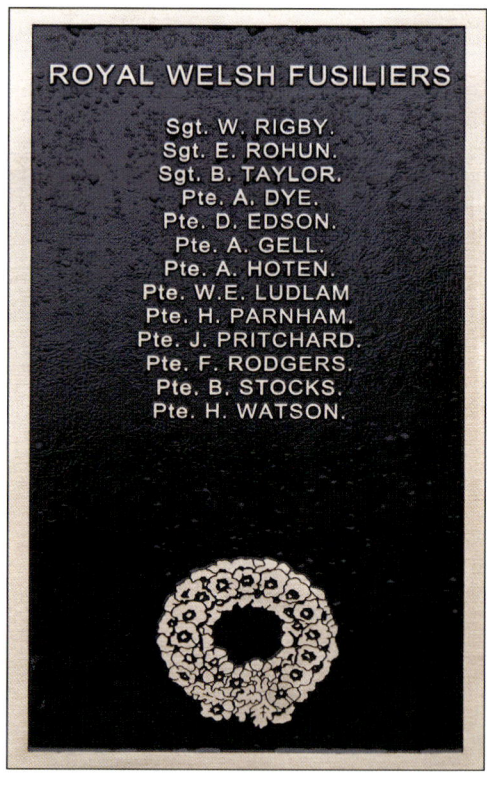

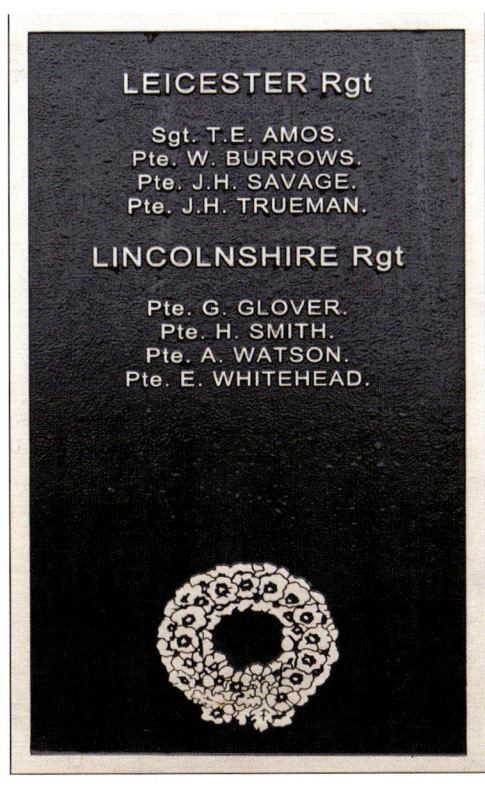
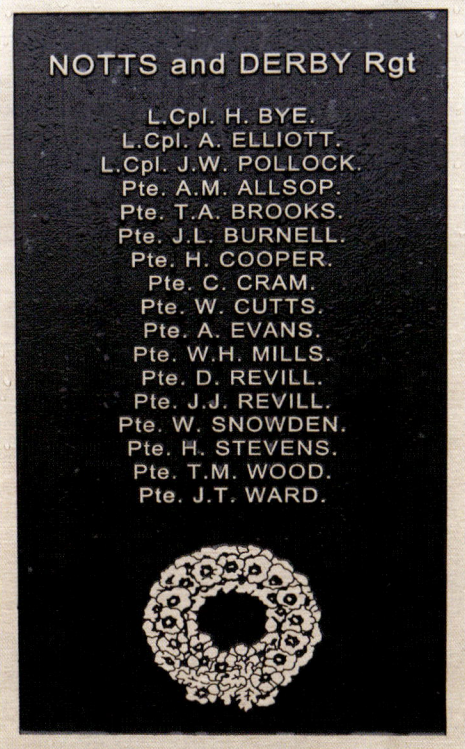

The Memorial with World War Two Plaques

The War Memorial with the wall and the Second World War names added

In 1965 a stone wall was erected surrounding the Memorial Cross. Upon it was a plaque to commemorate the fallen of the Second World War, 1939 – 1945. Originally there were teak seats by the wall, but these have long since disappeared.

In October 1965 Reverend Gwyther officiated at the dedication service of the new plaque. Mrs. Nicholson from the District Royal British Legion and Mrs. Millington unveiled the plaque.

Mrs. Nicholson and Mrs. Millington unveiling the plaque

The Wall was built by Mr. Alan Tomlin and his son Andrew, their time and labour being freely given. Mr. Tomlin was a British Legion member and had served in the Royal Artillery during World War Two.

**Alan Thomlin (left) with friends
(photo taken on South Coast 1942)**

Alan Thomlin who built the wall

Remembrance Day after the wall was built

Rededication of the Memorial, October 2006

Pinxton Church with the flagpole and flag given by the Berrill Family

Pinxton Memorial with new brass plaques   **Congregation on rededication day**

Major Richard Preece of the 1st Battalion, Worcester and Sherwood Foresters salutes the new name plates on the memorial at a special rededication service at St. Helen's Church, Pinxton.

Major Richard Preece saluting and laying a wreath

More than 140 locals attended the church service led by The Rev. Leslie Harris to remember the soldiers who died fighting for their country since 1914.

After the service, the congregation gathered outside for the unveiling and blessing of the new brass plaques, containing the names of the war dead and their regiments.
Also attending were representatives of the Royal Air Force, Army and Navy.

The Royal British Legion representatives were Bob Willmer, Pinxton Chairman and Bernard Page, County Chairman.

Representatives of the Parish Council were Mary Dooley, Richard Street, Joan Morley, Philip Handley, Anne Wright, Paul Wilson and Laura West, Clerk to the Council. The Council paid for the plaques at a cost of £7,000.

Remembrance

The new plaques with poppies placed at the base

Taking the Salute
Bob Willmer of the British Legion (centre)

The Military Medal

The Military Medal was established in wartime Britain by King George V on the 25th March 1916.

The medal was awarded to personnel below commissioned rank for bravery in battle on land on the recommendation of the Commander-in-Chief in the field.

A silver laurelled bar was awarded for subsequent acts of bravery and devotion to duty under fire.

Recipients of the medal, which is silver, 36 mm diameter and features the head of the monarch, were allowed to use the letters MM after their name.

Pinxton had three recipients of the medal; we should be proud of them.

Sergeant Richard H. Lane MM
Driver Richard Jessop MM
Sergeant Samuel Winfield MM

The Distinguished Service Medal

This is awarded to Navy personnel for acts of extreme bravery. We have one recipient, who saved many lives whilst risking his own:

Stoker First Class Joseph Ellis DSM

The Distinguished Service Medal

"Pip, Squeak and Wilfred"
The medals presented to soldiers who fought throughout the First World War

**The Sherwood Foresters (Notts and Derby Regiment)
Memorial Tower, Crich, Derbyshire**

In the early stages of the First World War around 300 men joined the colours from Pinxton and many of them joined the Notts and Derby Regiment. At Crich a memorial tower was completed in 1923 and was officially opened on Monday 6th August 1923, the ceremony being carried out by the Colonel of the Regiment, General Sir Horace L. Smith-Dorrien, His Grace the Duke of Portland, His Grace the Duke of Devonshire, Admiral Salmon and the Bishop of Southwell. It was dedicated to the memory of 11,409 men who fell in the First World War.

In August 1930 General Smith-Dorrien was tragically killed in a motoring accident. In 1931 a memorial was erected in his memory in front of the tower with the words:

GENTLEMEN WE WILL STAND AND FIGHT

which he said at the Battle of Le Cateau on 26th August 1914.

In 1952, a dedication to the memory of 1,520 Sherwood Foresters who died during the Second World War took place. For many years the light had a range of 38 miles and revolved, it being visible over several counties. Now a much smaller light is used.

The plaque at the front of the tower is the memorial to Smith-Dorrien

The Menin Gate Memorial

The Menin Gate is perhaps the most visited war memorial on the Western Front. It stands in Belgium in the ancient town of Ypres. Once a centre of the Flanders wool trade, it became one of the most important European city-states of the 13th century. In 1260 it had a population of 40,000 - far more than it does today - whereas during the same period the city of Oxford in England had only 4,200 residents.

The area has been fought over down the centuries by the English, the Dutch, the French and the Spanish, and was called "The Cockpit of Europe". It took the Great War however, to cause the wholesale destruction of the town, and the loss of its priceless medieval architecture.

The Menin Gate prior to the Great War

Prior to the war, Ypres had an exit road leading north towards the town of Menin. There had been a gate on the road once as part of the original medieval fortifications but it had been demolished long before the war to widen the road into the town, leaving only two raised mounds on either side.

The Menin Gate Memorial is one of four memorials to the missing in Flanders, and covers the area known as the Ypres Salient. The battle ground was formed during the First Battle of Ypres in October and November 1914, when a small British Expeditionary Force succeeded in securing the town and pushing the German forces back to the Passchendaele Ridge. The Second Battle of Ypres took place in 1915 when the Germans released poison gas into the Allied lines north of the town. This forced an Allied withdrawal, but Ypres was never held by the Germans. However the cost in terms of human life of holding on to the area was immense.

Almost as soon as the war was over, there were plans to build a memorial in the Ypres area. The Menin Gate was chosen and it was decided that it should commemorate the "missing", those members of the British and Empire armies who had died in the fighting around Ypres, but whose bodies were never found. The Memorial was designed by Sir Reginald Blomfield and was opened in 1927, ten years after the terrible Third Battle of Ypres, a campaign that ended with the capture of the village of Passchendaele by Canadian troops.

Blomfield's memorial combines the architectural images of a classical victory arch and a mausoleum, and contains huge panels into which are carved the names of 54,896 officers and men of the Commonwealth Forces who died in the Ypres Salient area and who have no known graves. Immense though it is, it was found that the Menin Gate was not large enough to hold the names of all the missing. The names recorded on the panels are therefore those of the men who died in the area between 1914 and 15th August 1917. The names of a further 34,984 missing soldiers who died between 16th August and the end of the war are recorded on carved panels at the Tyne Cot Cemetery, on the slopes just below Passchendaele ridge.

The Menin Gate is not a memorial tucked away in some remote part of the town remembered now and then; it is still an important thoroughfare, and both traffic and pedestrians pass under the arch as part of the daily life of Ypres. In this respect alone, remembrance is kept alive in the town, but in tribute to the men from around the world who came to defend their town, every night of the year without exception, policemen close the road to traffic at 8.00 p.m., while buglers from the Ypres Fire Brigade play "The Last Post". During the Second World War the Germans banned this ceremony but as soon as the war ended in 1945 it was reinstated by the town.

The Last Post

That there were 89,880 men whose bodies were never found in the Ypres salient– many blown to bits or drowned in the mud - gives some idea of the carnage and suffering of the troops in the surrounding area. Lieutenant Coke was one of the first men from Pinxton to die in the First World War. He was buried in the garden of a small farmhouse on the Zillebeke Road near Ypres but his body was never recovered. In the months to come, where the Menin road crossed the Zillebeke Road, the area became known as Hell Fire Corner. There was a particularly corny joke about the area in vogue in 1917: "Tell the last man in the line to close the Menin Gate". For all of those families, like the Coke family, with no grave to visit to pay their respects, the Menin Gate Memorial with its simple grandeur and its daily act of remembrance is a fitting place to honour those that died; especially since it is along that road that so many travelled north to the front line, never to return.

As Field Marshal Plumer said on the unveiling of the Menin Gate:
A memorial has been erected which, in its simple grandeur, fulfils this object, and now it can be said of each one in whose honour we are assembled here today:

HE IS NOT MISSING; HE IS HERE

The Menin Gate Memorial

**Who will remember, passing through this Gate,
The unheroic Dead who fed the guns?**

Siegfried Sassoon

22

The Tomb of the Unknown Soldier

The idea of an unknown man being buried with honours is a comparatively recent idea. It sprang from the imagination of an Army Chaplain, the Reverend Railton MC, who during the First World War noticed a grave bearing a pencilled inscription: "An Unknown Soldier in the Black Watch". This gave him the idea for what was to become a National Memorial, but it was not until 1920 that he was able to put into action his plan. He approached the Dean of Westminster Abbey, who persuaded the Government to accept his idea.

A Committee headed by the Foreign Minister, Lord Curzon, recommended that his office should arrange for an unknown soldier to be disinterred in France and brought to Westminster Abbey. It further recommended that the re-burial should be on Armistice Day of that year and that King George V should be asked if, after he had unveiled the Cenotaph, he would allow the Gun Carriage to bear the body to the Abbey.

Instructions were given that the body of a British Soldier, whom it would be impossible to identify, should be bought in from each of the six battle areas – Aisne, Cambrai, Somme, Arras, Marne and Ypres – on the night of the 7th November. The bodies were taken to an army hut not far from Ypres where they were received by the Reverend George Kendall OBE.

Later that night the Brigadier-General in charge of the troops in France and Flanders, Brigadier-General L.J.Wyatt, entered the hut. The bodies had been placed on a row of stretchers, each covered with a Union Jack. The Brigadier was blind-folded and picked one of the bodies, which was placed in the shell of a coffin which had been sent from England to receive the remains. The lid was screwed down; the other bodies were buried in the Military Cemetery at St. Pol.

Following mixed services which were held the following morning, the body was sent to Boulogne under escort. A French Company furnished the guard through the night on French soil.

At noon the next day the rough wooden shell was placed in a plain oak coffin which had wrought-iron bands, through one of which was passed a 16th Century Crusader's sword from the Tower of London's collection. On the coffin was inscribed:

"A British Warrior who fell in the Great War 1914-1918 for King and Country".

The coffin was taken into Boulogne where the destroyer H.M.S. Verdun was waiting to carry it to England, together with six barrels of soil taken from the Ypres salient, which was to be placed in the tomb in Westminster Abbey so that the body should rest in soil on which so many troops had given up their lives.

As the destroyer steamed into Dover Harbour a 19 gun salute was fired from the Castle. After the body had been bought ashore it was carried to the Marine Railway Station and put aboard a London bound train. The coffin, covered by a Union Jack, with a steel helmet, side arms and a webbing placed upon it, remained on the train overnight.

On its arrival in London, the coffin was put onto a gun carriage and slowly made its way to the Cenotaph. Troops from all the Services followed. As the gun carriage drew-up at the Cenotaph King George stepped forward and placed a wreath of red roses and bay leaves on the coffin. After the silence the gun carriage moved off with King George, as chief mourner, taking his place behind it.

At the Abbey the coffin passed through two lines of 100 holders of the Victoria Cross. Behind were the widows and mothers of the fallen. The Service was conducted by the Dean of Westminster and during the singing of Lead Kindly Light the bearers removed the helmet and side arms and lowered the coffin into the tomb. At the committal the King scattered earth from the battlefields from a silver shell. After a roll of drums the poignant notes of the Last Post rang out, followed by Reveille. Finally, the two lines of VC holders filed past. The honours paid were those due to a Field Marshal.

To the surprise of the organisers, in the week after the burial an estimated 1,250,000 people visited the Abbey. The site is now one of the most visited War Graves.

The Cenotaph, London

King George placing a wreath on the coffin

The Tomb, Westminster Abbey

BENEATH THIS STONE RESTS THE BODY
OF A BRITISH WARRIOR
UNKNOWN BY NAME OR RANK
BROUGHT FROM FRANCE TO LIE AMONG
THE MOST ILLUSTRIOUS OF THE LAND
AND BURIED ON ARMISTICE DAY
11 NOV. 1920, IN THE PRESENCE OF
HIS MAJESTY KING GEORGE V
HIS MINISTERS OF STATE
THE CHIEFS OF HIS FORCES
AND A VAST CONCOURSE OF THE NATION

THUS ARE COMMEMORATED THE MANY
MULTITUDES WHO DURING THE GREAT
WAR OF 1914-1918 GAVE THE MOST THAT
MAN CAN GIVE LIFE ITSELF
FOR GOD
FOR KING AND COUNTRY
FOR LOVED ONES HOME AND EMPIRE
FOR THE SACRED CAUSE OF JUSTICE AND
THE FREEDOM OF THE WORLD

THEY BURIED HIM AMONG THE KINGS BECAUSE HE
HAD DONE GOOD TOWARD GOD AND TOWARD
HIS HOUSE

War Memorials and Casualties

World War One

For most of human history War Memorials were erected to commemorate great victories.
Remembering the dead of wars was a secondary concern; indeed, in Napoleon's day the dead were simply shovelled into mass unmarked graves.
It was after the First World War that commemoration took centre stage because of the great losses, and most communities erected a War Memorial listing those men and women who had gone to war and not returned. Pinxton built an impressive memorial in the churchyard out of Cornish granite, in the shape of a cross.
Massive memorials, such as The Menin Gate at Ypres and Thiepval on the Somme, were built commemorating the thousands of dead with no identified grave.

Casualties

The number of men who fought and the number of casualties were unimaginable. Below is an approximation of the main combatants. 52% of all the Allies mobilised were killed, wounded or missing.

Country	Mobilised	Killed	Wounded	POWs + Missing	Total Casualties
Russia	12.0 m	1.7 m	4.9 m	2.5 m	9.15 million
France	8.4 m	1.3 m	4.2 m	537,000	6.1 million
Britain and the Empire	8.9 m	908,000	2.0 m	191,000	3.1 million
Italy	5.5 m	650,000	947,000	600,000	2.1 million
U.S.A.	4.3 m	126,000	234,000	4,500	350,000
Total Allies with smaller nations added	42.0 m	5.0 m	13.0 m	4.0 m	22.0 million
Germany, Austria, Turkey and Bulgaria	22.8 m	3.3 m	8.35 m	3.6 m	15.3 million

World War Two

During World War Two, many nations saw massive devastation and loss of life of civilians as well as military and most cities and towns involved in the conflict erected memorials, many listing the names of each local soldier killed. Some extended the First World War Memorials, as did Pinxton.

Total population involved	Military Deaths	Civilian Deaths	Jewish Deaths	Total Deaths
1,961 million	25.2 million	41.7 million	5.75 million	72.7 million

Casualties by Country

Soviet Union 23.1 m; China 20.0 m; Nazi Germany 7.3 m; Poland 5.6 m; Dutch East Indies 4.0 m; Japan 2.7 m; India 1.58 m; Yugoslavia 1.0 m; United Kingdom 450,000.

The Royal British Legion

The Royal British Legion was founded in 1921 from four separate ex-service organizations. The first official Legion poppy day was held in Britain on the 11th November 1921 (The First World War ended at the 11th hour of the 11th day of the 11th month in 1918). Millions had died with many more injured and scarred by their horrific experiences. Civilians wanted to remember the service personnel who had given their lives so they could live in freedom.

An American War Secretary, Moira Bell Michael was so inspired by John McCrae's poem "In Flanders' Fields" that she became the first person to wear a poppy for remembrance. She sold poppies to her friends throughout the United States to raise money for ex-servicemen. And so the tradition began. Her French colleague, Madam Guerin, took up the idea and made artificial poppies for war orphans. In 1922 Major George Howson MC founded a small factory in Bermondsey where ex-servicemen could make artificial poppies. In 1926 the factory moved to Richmond, Surrey and became the Royal British Legion Poppy Factory.

The British Legion Memorial Parade in the 1950's with Arthur Kirkwood and Mavis Seals carrying the flags. The mother of Ernest Smith, who was killed in an aeroplane crash in 1947, is seen carrying the wreath in the centre of the three ladies.

**Mavis Seals and Dennis Etherington at a
British Legion Parade, Chatsworth**

Pinxton British Legion Woman's Section

Pinxton British Legion Members

Eddie Ward representing The British Legion at a Remembrance Day Service

Eddie was in the Royal Navy, serving from 1958 in H.M.S. Pembroke, H.M.S. Vangard, H.M.S. Albion, H.M.S. Ganges, H.M.S. Seahawk, H.M.S. Hermes, H.M.S. Bellerophon, H.M.S. Sheffield, H.M.S. Tarter, H.M.S. Dido and H.M.S. Victory. He loved the Navy and travelled all over the world.
After leaving the Navy he threw himself into the British Legion and worked very hard to help service families in their times of need; he was awarded a statue of a Standard Bearer for meritorious service. He went to local schools to tell the children all about poppy day because, as he put it, "It was my duty to the men who's names were on the Roll of Honour". He died in 2003, and it was said at his passing that he was a gentleman who carried out his duty with pride and dignity.

WORLD WAR ONE

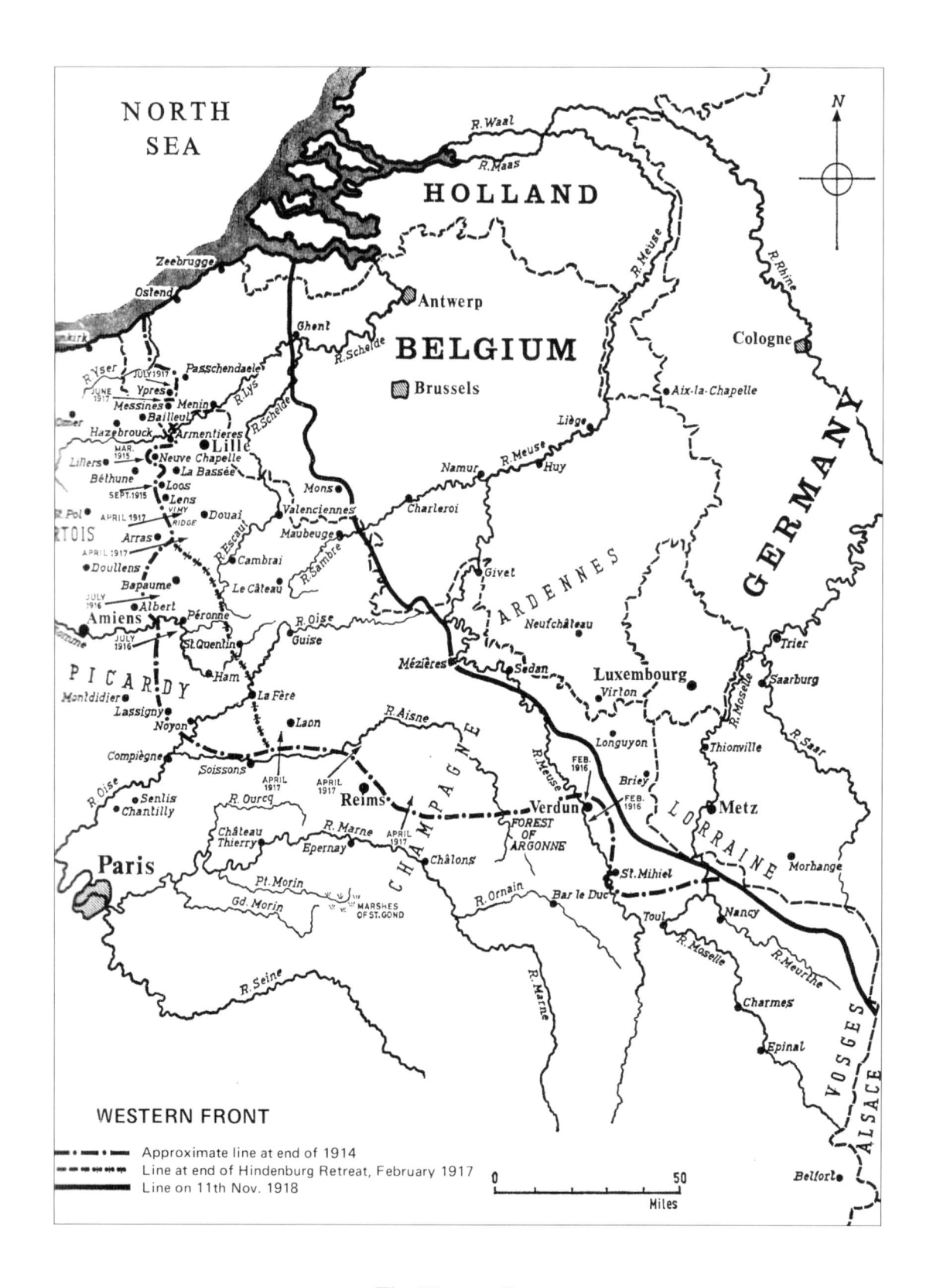

The Western Front

A.M. Allsop.

Rank.	Private
Regiment.	Sherwood Foresters (Notts and Derby Regiment)
Unit.	17th Battalion (Welbeck Rangers)
Service No.	30677
Date of Death.	7th July 1916
Cemetery.	Le Touret Cemetery
Grave.	III. J. 18.

A. Allsop enlisted at Worksop, Notts. He was born in Hucknall, Notts.
Killed in action when serving in the trenches near Givenchy, France.
He is also commemorated on a plaque in Underwood Church, Notts.

Showing the trenches and the desolation of the Somme

1st Battle of the Somme

Fought 1st July 1916 to 13th November 1916

This was a costly and largely unsuccessful Allied offensive on the Western Front during World War 1.
The Germans were securely entrenched and strategically located when the British and French launched their frontal attack on a 34 kilometre front, north of the Somme River.
A week-long artillery bombardment preceded the British infantry's going over the top into the so called no-man's land with barbed wire and stakes stopping fast progress. The Allies were mowed down as they assaulted the virtually impregnable German positions. The Allies suffered nearly 60,000 casualties on the first day of the attack.
The Somme offensive gradually deteriorated into a battle of attrition. Later, torrential rains turned the Battlefield into an impassable sea of mud, and by November the Allies had advanced only 8 kilometres.
Although the figures have been much disputed the battle resulted in 650,000 German, 195,000 French and 420,000 British casualties.
The Battle of the Somme became a metaphor for futile and indiscriminate slaughter.
   A. Allsop was in the area and probably died in the early stages of this Battle.

> What passing-bells for these who die as cattle?
> Only the monstrous anger of the guns.
> Only the stuttering rifles' rapid rattle
> Can patter out their hasty orisons.
> No mockeries now for them; no prayers nor bells;
> Nor any voice of mourning save the choirs,-
> The shrill, demented choirs of wailing shells;
> And bugles calling for them from sad shires.
>
>   Wilfred Owen

Le Touret Cemetery. France.

Cecil (T E) Amos.
    Rank.   Sergeant
    Regiment.   Leicestershire Regiment
    Unit.   7th Battalion
    Service No.   12080
    Date of Death.   14th July 1916
    Age.   31
    Memorial.   Thiepval Memorial
                               Pier and Face 2C and 3A.   No Known Grave

Cecil was the son of Mrs. Anne Amos of North Street, Pinxton, Derbyshire. He was born at Great Gonerby, Lincolnshire about 1885.
Enlisted Mansfield, Nov 1914.

Cecil Amos

Harold, Cecil's brother 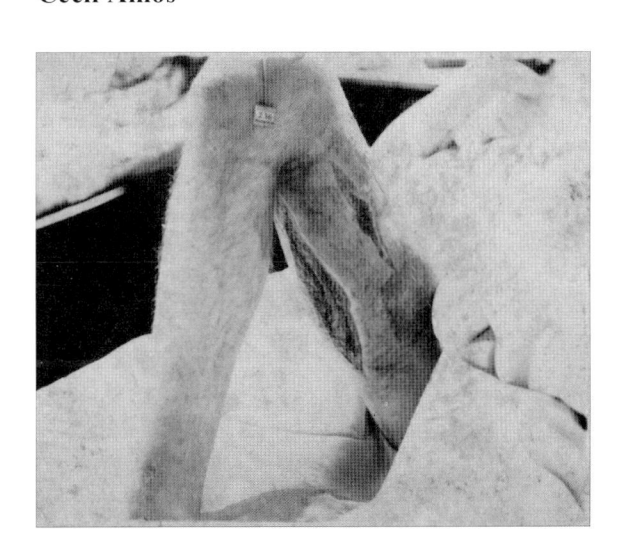   **Harold's leg wound**

You could say Cecil's brother Harold was more fortunate than Cecil because he received the shrapnel injury, shown above, in his right leg, which got him a "Blighty" back home. He sustained this injury in 1918 which invalided him out of the army. Without this injury the odds are that he would have been killed like Cecil.

The Battle of the Somme.

On July 1st 1916 the Allies, with 13 divisions, supported by a French attack to the south, launched an offensive on a line from North of Gommecourt to Maricourt. Despite a preliminary bombardment lasting seven days, the German defences were barely touched, and the attack met unexpectedly fierce resistance. Losses were catastrophic and with only minimal advances on the southern flank, the initial attack was a failure. In the following weeks huge resources of manpower and equipment were deployed in an attempt to exploit the modest success of the first day. However, the German Army resisted tenaciously and repeated attacks and counter attacks meant a major battle for every village, copse and farmhouse gained. At the end of September Thiepval was finally captured. The village had been the original objective of 1st July. Attacks on the north and east continued into November, but eventually the weather, with the onset of winter, halted the Battle.

The Thiepval Memorial, the Memorial to the Missing of the Somme, bears the names of 72,000 officers and men of the United Kingdom and South African forces who died in the Somme sector before 20th March 1918 and have no known grave. Over 90% of those commemorated died between July and November 1916. Sergeant C. Amos was probably one of these.

The Memorial, designed by Sir Edwin Lutyens, was built between 1928 and 1932 and unveiled by the Prince of Wales in the presence of the President of France on 31st July 1932.

Cecil Amos's Death Plaque

Thiepval Memorial. France.

Noah Anthony.

Rank.	Corporal
Regiment.	Royal Army Medical Corps
Unit.	1st (London) Sanitary Company
Service No.	527336
Date of Death.	24th February 1919
Cemetery.	Cambrai East Military Cemetery
Grave.	IV. A. 22.

Noah Anthony
Husband of Harriett Stemp, they were married at Hanover Square, London in early 1918. Noah was the son of Noah and Hannah Anthony of Pinxton, Derbyshire.

Noah's cap badge  **Christmas card sent to his family**

Noah enlisted in 1914 in the Royal Army Medical Corps. He was shipped out to France and was involved in operations around Lille and the siege of Antwerp. In 1915 he was on his way to the Dardanelles, but did not know it. At that time he sent a card home saying "I am at Malta but I do not know where I am going". He eventually landed at Kum Kale Sedd-el-Bahr on the Turkish Peninsula. The full landing was at Cape Helles on 5 beaches S,V,W,X,Y. Noah landed on Y beach and was unopposed. The village of Krithia nearby was deserted. There was no more advance and Y beach was eventually evacuated on May 15-16th. Noah was

35

then at Gaba - Tepe and Anzac Cove under constant fire. The only success of the campaign was the evacuation in December 1915. By 1916 he was back in France at the front which continued well into 1918. After his marriage to Harriett and a spell of leave he returned to France again in late 1918 to Cambrai. Here Noah developed pneumonia which may have been brought on by the influenza virus which was sweeping the world at this time. He was admitted to a casualty clearing station where he subsequently died. Noah had been in just about all the theatres of war and came through unscathed only to be cruelty taken by a virus.

Noah married Harriett Stemp who was a companion to Mary, wife of Colonel Coke, the father of Sacheverell Coke of Brookhill Hall Pinxton.

Noah's wife Harriett    **Noah in Civvies**    **Noah's sister Miriam**

The ship Minnewaska owned by the Atlantic Transport Line Company, on which Noah sailed on the 4th March 1915 to Kumkale Sedd el - Bahr.

Noah's Badge    **Noah back row R/H side**

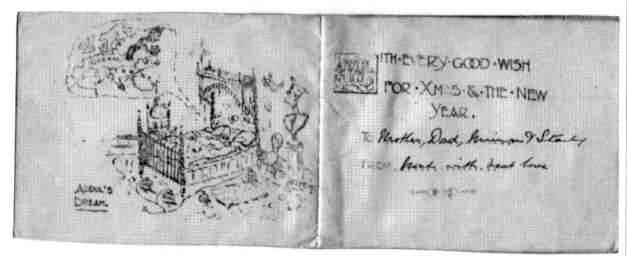

Christmas cards sent from Gallipoli

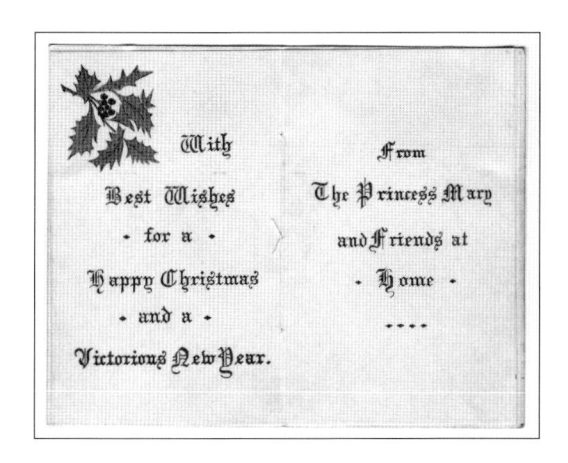

Princess Mary's Christmas card and tobacco tin

Cambrai East Military Cemetery. France.

Fredrick Barker.

Rank.	Private
Regiment.	Coldstream Guards
Unit.	3rd Battalion
Service No.	16044
Date of Death.	2nd April 1916
Cemetery.	Essex Farm Cemetery, Belgium
Grave.	II. H. 16.

Fredrick was born in Eckington, Derby and lived in Pinxton, Derbyshire.

Fredrick Barker was the brother of Walter Barker

The land south of Essex Farm was used as a dressing station and cemetery from April 1915 to August 1917 so Fred Barker could have been injured and died at the dressing station. The burials were made without a definite plan, and some of the divisions which occupied this sector may be traced in almost every part of the cemetery.

The cemetery was designed by Sir Reginald Blomfield. It is in this dressing station that Lieutenant-Colonel John McCrae of the Canadian Army Medical Corps wrote the poem "In Flanders Fields" in May 1915.

In Flanders fields the poppies blow
Between the crosses, row on row,
That mark our place; and in the sky
The larks, still bravely singing, fly
Scarce heard amid the guns below.

We are the Dead. Short days ago
We lived, felt dawn, saw sunset glow,
Loved and were loved, and now we lie
In Flanders fields.
Take up our quarrel with the foe:
To you from failing hands we throw
The torch; be yours to hold it high.
If ye break faith with us who die
We shall not sleep, though poppies grow
In Flanders fields.

John McCrae

Essex Farm Cemetery. Belgium.

Walter Barker.

Rank.	Lance Corporal
Regiment.	Royal Engineers
Unit.	180th Tunnelling Company
Service No.	139120
Date of Death.	31st July 1916
Age.	35
Memorial.	Thiepval Memorial
	Pier and Face 8A and 8D No Known Grave

Walter Barker

Walter was born in Sharlston Yorkshire in 1881. After his marriage to Mary, he moved to Pinxton and lived on Park Lane where their daughter was born on the 3rd October 1905. He enlisted at Sutton in Ashfield to the Notts and Derby Regiment, later being transferred to the Royal Engineers in the 180th Tunnelling Company which was formed in the autumn of 1915 at Labuissiere. He then entered the Vermelles Sector and was engaged in constructing saps and trenches in addition to much carrying work. They were then moved into the Givenchy area in 1916, all the time working under arduous and dangerous conditions.

The Royal Engineers were the backbone of the Army; without the Engineers there would be no supplies to the Armies. They maintained the railways, roads, water supplies, bridges, transport, communications, telephones, wireless, guns and signalling. They also dug the tunnels under the enemy lines in which explosives were placed.

Report from local paper.

Lance Corporal Walter Barker of the Royal Engineers a native of Pinxton has been killed in France by a mine explosion. He was 35 years old and leaves a wife and five children, who reside at Park Lane Pinxton.

He worked at the Langton Colliery up to the time of enlisting. He was only promoted three weeks before his death. He has been with the forces since 1914. He had a brother Private Fred Barker who was in the Coldstream Guards and was killed on the 2nd of April.

Walter Barker with wife Mary and two children

Sappers in digging party

Thiepval Memorial. France.

Herbert North Bingham.

        Rank.   Private
        Regiment.   Canadian Infantry (Quebec Regiment)
        Unit.   14th Battalion
        Service No.   440278
        Date of Death.   30th April 1917
        Age.   39
        Memorial.   Vimy Memorial   No Known Grave

Herbert was the son of Joseph and Emma Bingham who had 8 children.
He was the husband of Annie Bingham of 25 Chaucer Street, Mansfield.

In 1872 Emma Bingham acquired the George Inn at Pinxton from her father John North who built the inn in 1869. The inn appears to have been in Joseph Bingham's name until 6 years after his death when it was conveyed to Emma Bingham and her son Herbert North Bingham.

The Bingham Family Grave in Pinxton Churchyard

Emma lived until 4th February 1912. Her obituary described her as a kind and generous person to those in need. The graves of the North's and Bingham's in Pinxton Churchyard are very impressive. Herbert Bingham was in Canada at the time of Emma's death. Herbert North Bingham was born on the 28th August 1878, and as a young man he set sail to Canada to become a Pool Room Proprietor. He enlisted on the 20th April 1915 at the age of 36. His wife Annie was still living in England at the time. He embarked for England on the S.S. Empress of Britain on the 29th March 1916 and arrived on the 9th April 1916 at Liverpool. He was then admitted to hospital with tonsillitis on the 11th April 1916 and discharged on the

21st April 1916. He embarked to France on the 8th June and was wounded on the 9th October and taken to Boulogne Hospital with wounds to his neck, right knee and left hand. He was discharged to rest camp on 23rd November 1916, rejoined his unit on the 13th December and took part in the action on Vimy Ridge in April. Three weeks later he was killed in action by a 5.9 mm shell which hit the dug-out he was in. The location was west of Arleux-en-Gohelle.

Local Report.

Pinxton residents will learn with regret of the death of Private Herbert North Bingham, who was killed in action on April 30th. A son of the late Mr. and Mrs. Bingham, who kept the George Inn for so many years, Private Bingham emigrated to Canada in 1911, and when war broke out he joined the forces in the Dominion. After training in Winnipeg he came to England where he passed through a further period of training before being drafted to France in 1916. Through many actions including the taking of Vimy Ridge he passed successfully, but was eventually killed in action. He was 39 years old and leaves a wife and three children.

The Vimy Memorial stands on Hill 145 overlooking the battlefield, once so hotly contested. On soil offered by France in 1922 for the use of Canada, the Memorial took 11 years to build and was unveiled by King Edward VII on July 26th 1936. Vimy Ridge was a formidable fortress, many thought it invincible. Finally, at daybreak on April 9th, 1917, Easter Monday, in rain, sleet and falling temperatures, the Canadians attacked, sheltering closely behind a moving curtain of artillery. By mid-afternoon the Canadians had taken most of the Ridge and by the 12th of April victory was complete.
The Memorial is adorned with 11,285 Canadian trees and shrubs, to reflect the number of names on the Monument to the Missing.

Vimy Memorial. France.

Stephen Murray Bingley.

Rank.	Private
Regiment.	Machine Gun Corps
Unit.	36th Battalion
Service No.	117143
Date of Death.	5th April 1918
Age.	30
Cemetery.	Senlis Communal Cemetery Extension
Grave.	I.D.16.

Stephen was the son of Mrs Agnes Bingley and husband of
Ethel May Bingley of 5 Council House, Church Street, Pinxton, Derbyshire.
He was the father of 7 children.

Photographs of Stephen Bingley

Stephen Bingley's Machine Gun Corps badge

Stephen Bingley is remembered at the base of his in-laws' Burial Cross in Pinxton Churchyard

Article from local paper.

Official information was received by Mrs. Bingley, Wilson Street, Pinxton on Saturday that her husband Stephen M. Bingley was killed in action on 5th April. He was amongst the first to volunteer on August the 6th 1914 in the Notts and Derby Regiment, but was discharged through having an operation in April 1915. In June 1917 he was recalled under the Review of Exceptions Act, and after training as a machine gunner was despatched to France on December 3rd 1917. The deceased was one of three brothers conducting a bakery and grocery business in Pinxton. He leaves a widow and seven children. Another brother is now serving with the South Notts Hussars in Egypt. The following letter, received by Mrs. Bingley, shows how commendably the deceased carried out his allotted duty.

Letter to Mrs. Bingley.

I am writing this letter to tell you how much I sympathise with you at the loss of your husband. He was killed in action on 5th April while on duty near his gun. A shell landed about one yard from him, so that he must have been killed instantly. I have been his section officer since he joined the company just before Christmas, and though such a short time with us he had proved himself a good comrade both in and out of action. The Company Commander himself had commented on his efficiency in action during the big attacks a few days previously. All his friends in this section join with me in expressing our sorrow at his loss both to you and to his country at a time when every month we have fresh comrades to mourn, who have fallen for the sake of defending their country………Lieutenant W. Stevens.

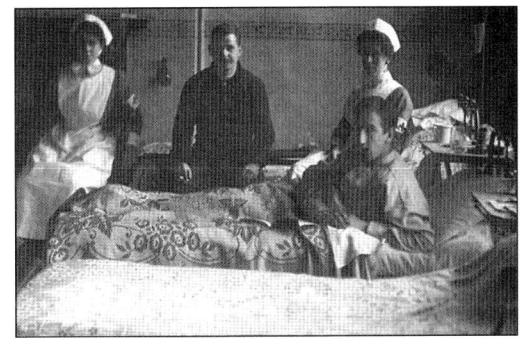

Bakery shop owned by the family   **Stephen visiting a friend in hospital**

The extension to the communal cemetery began in April 1918, after the fall of Albert, by the 12th (Eastern) and 38th (Welsh) Divisions. It was used until the following August but was enlarged after the Armistice when bodies were brought in from the battlefields of the Somme. The Senlis Communal Cemetery Extension now contains 104 First World War Graves.

Senlis Communal Cemetery Extension, Somme. France.

Thomas Brooks.

Rank.   Private
Regiment.   Sherwood Foresters (Notts and Derby Regiment)
Unit.   11th Battalion
Service No.   17700
Date of Death.   1st October 1916
Age.   28
Memorial.   Thiepval Memorial
                 Pier and Face 10C, 10D and 11A. No Known Grave

Thomas was the son of Charles and Mary Jane Brooks of 77 Park Lane, Pinxton. He was born in 1888 at 41 Cross Street, Clay Cross, Derbyshire. He enlisted at Ripley. Thomas Brooks' father originated from Buckinghamshire.

Thomas Brooks in Dress uniform   **Thomas in Army uniform**

On the 1st of October 1916 in the area of Martinpuich the 11th Battalion formed part of a force consisting of the 23rd and 50th Divisions to capture the Flers-Le Sars line on a front of over a mile to the right of the Albert-Bapaume road. The battalion moved up under a covering barrage, the objective for the battalion was two lines of hostile trenches in the Flers-Le Sars line. The barrage lifted off the objective at 3.15 p.m.; the battalion moved forward, took the position and consolidated it. The battalion was relieved from the line during the evening of the 2nd and came to bivouacs at Lozenge Wood. The losses on these two days were: Three officers killed, 12 other ranks killed; two officers wounded and 137 other ranks wounded; one officer missing, 13 other ranks missing. Sadly Thomas Brooks was one of the missing. The G.O.C. wrote the following letter to the Officer Commanding: "Will you please tell all ranks of your battalion how very pleased I am at their behaviour on October 1st. I congratulate them most heartily on their complete success which was due to their gallantry and the fine spirit they showed. Good luck to you all". Signed J.M.Babington. 11th Battalion.

Crater caused by explosives set under the German lines on the Somme, 1st July, at Hawthorn Ridge, Beaumont Hamel. This alerted the Germans to the forthcoming attack.

Thiepval Memorial. France.

John L. Burnell.

Rank.	Lance Corporal
Regiment.	Sherwood Foresters (Notts and Derby Regiment)
Unit.	2nd Battalion, "C" Company, 9th Platoon
Service No.	15240
Date of Death.	23rd March 1918
Memorial.	Arras Memorial
	Bay 7. No Known Grave

Shown in Red Cross Lists as missing on 21st March 1918.
Killed in action during the German offensive near the Maricourt Road, France.
John was born at 76 Nottingham Road, Somercotes, Derbyshire. He went to France on the 29th June 1915.

The battalion was holding the line along the River Somme, the centre being at the village of St. Christie. About noon the enemy were observed advancing on the ridge in front. During the day they contented themselves with digging in, out of effective rifle range. At 9 p.m. the enemy attempted to cross the St. Christie Bridge which had been blown up but only partially demolished. By 10 p.m. the enemy had succeeded in gaining a footing on the other side but was unable to progress further into the village owing to our machine gun and rifle fire and the stubborn resistance of our men. Soon after midnight a counter-attack was organised and carried out. The enemy was driven back across the river leaving behind many dead. Sadly, during this action J. L. Burnell was killed.

"Good-morning, good-morning!" the General said
When we met him last week on our way to the line.
Now the soldiers he smiled at are most of 'em dead,
And we're cursing his staff for incompetent swine.

"He's a cheery old card", grunted Harry to Jack
As they slogged up to Arras with rifle and pack.
. . . . . .
But he did for them both by his plan of attack.
                    Siegfried Sassoon   April 1917

Arras Memorial. France.

John William Burrows.

Rank.	Private
Regiment.	Leicestershire Regiment
Unit.	7th Battalion
Service No.	49127
Date of Death.	8th October 1918
Age.	24
Cemetery.	Marcoing British Cemetery
Grave.	I. A. 15.

John was the son of Mr. and Mrs. Burrows, Church Street, Pinxton. Born Brampton.

Report from paper

Official news has been received of the death, on October 8th last, of Private John William Burrows of Church Street, Pinxton. He was 24 years old and had been out in France only two months. Before joining the army he had worked at the New Pinxton Colliery. In a letter sent to his mother the chaplain says:

It is with deep regret that I am writing to tell you of the death of your gallant son, Private John William Burrows 49127, who was wounded on October 8th. and died the same day at the 53rd Field Ambulance. I know you will be glad to know that he practically suffered nothing whilst he was here. I buried him on October 9th. You should write for particulars of his grave to the Director of Graves Registration, Winchester House, St James Square, London.

I pray our heavenly Father that he may console and comfort you and yours in your great and deep sorrow.

Marcoing British Cemetery. France.

Joseph Butler.

Rank.	Private
Regiment.	King's Shropshire Light Infantry
Unit.	5th Battalion
Service No.	17296
Date of Death.	3rd August 1915
Age.	21
Cemetery.	Etaples Military Cemetery
Grave.	II. A. 32.

Joseph Butler

The Regimental Badge

Article from the local paper.

Official intimation has now been received of the death of another of Pinxton's Soldier sons, Private Joseph Butler, of the 5th Shropshire Light Infantry, whilst on active service. A telegram was received on Bank Holiday Monday stating that he was laying dangerously ill in hospital at Etaples, and this was followed on Friday by an announcement of his death on August the 3rd. The message stated that he was wounded in the head, back and shoulder, but no information to the date or place was given. Private Butler, who resided at West End Pinxton, was 21 years of age, and leaves a widow and one child. He enlisted in February and went out with the Expeditionary Force to France on June 7th.

After training at Aldershot, the Shropshire Light Infantry 5th Battalion landed at Boulogne in May 1915 and served entirely on the Western front. The Shropshires moved into the line to relieve the Princess Patricia's Canadian Light Infantry after they had been in the line for twelve days under heavy shell fire from the enemy that had the range down to the inch. The shallow trenches crumbled beneath the onslaught with heavy causalities. The Shropshires had very little time to settle in because they had to shore up the defences as best they could as the shrapnel shells rained down. The Shropshire Light Infantry saw some of the worst fighting of the war in the Ypres Salient in 1915, in the area of Polygon Wood and sustained many casualties. Helmets did not become standard issue till 1916 and any head wounds very often were fatal. Joseph Butler was wounded around this time and was transported to one of the 16 hospitals at Etaples where he later died. Towards the end of the war there were twenty three hospitals at Etaples. This area was also known for its notorious Bull Ring where the training of soldiers took place. Here attempts were made to prepare men for the front ready for the trenches among the sand dunes. On any given day 100,000 soldiers were milling around. The cemetery at Etaples contains 10,773 burials of the First World War.

The cemetery was designed by Sir Edwin Lutyens.

Etaples Military Cemetery. France.

Etaples is a town about 27 kilometres south of Boulogne. The Military Cemetery is to the north of the town, on the west side of the road to Boulogne. It is the largest Commission cemetery in France.

Harry Bye.

Rank. Lance Corporal
Regiment. Sherwood Foresters (Notts and Derby Regiment)
Unit. 1st Battalion
Service No. 32472
Date of Death. 4th March 1917
Memorial. Thiepval Memorial
Pier and Face 10 C, 10 D and 11A   No Known Grave

Harry was born at Wood Dinton, Cambridgeshire. One of seven children, he was the youngest son of Charles and Letha Bye.
He joined the battalion on the 14th December 1916 and served with B Company before being transferred to A Company 5th Platoon. Harry was reported killed in action at Andover Trench when the objective to be obtained was the capture of the ridge immediately south of St. Pierre Vaast Wood.

At 5.15 a.m. on the 4th of March 1917 a barrage began and within 3 minutes the enemy got his counter barrage down, practically before all the men could move forward. Nine men were hit by a shell. Sgt. Kemp, showing great courage, rallied his men when they were shaken. He reorganised the remainder of the platoon and by example lead them forward through enemy fire. During this time "A" and "B" Company were mopping-up, carrying ammunition and material from the original front line and crossing over no-man's land continuously through enemy fire. It was in this action that Harry Bye was killed.

Thiepval Memorial. France.

Harry Claridge.

        Rank.   Private
        Regiment.   Oxford and Buckinghamshire Light Infantry
        Service No.   7897
        Date of Death.   31st October 1914
        Memorial.   Menin Gate, Ypres, Belgium
                                 Panel 37 and 39   No Known Grave

Harry was born in Charlbury in Oxfordshire. Enlisted in Oxford. Resided in Pinxton.

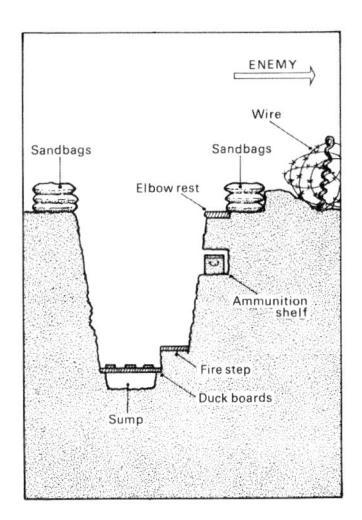

Illustration of a trench

<u>The First Battle of Ypres.</u>

The Oxford and Buckinghamshire Light Infantry arrived in Boulogne on Aug 14th after being on board the SS Michigan over sixteen hours waiting half the night in Southampton Water for the order to sail, then waiting half the morning outside the port of Boulogne for a berth. The camp was four miles away, marching with full kit over cobblestones was no easy task. The next day they were transported eastwards towards Mons, the British Expeditionary Force fanning out across the countryside around Mons by August 23rd. By August 24th they were dug in near the village of Frameries. The shells were coming thick and fast and they were ordered to retire. With the enemy hard on their heels, without any casualties, fighting as they withdrew, they were tired, hungry and thirsty. They did not stop until just on the outskirts of Paris, where they halted the German advance at the battle of the Marne on the 5th to 9th September. Later they took part in all subsidiary battles of the first battle of Ypres, 19th October to 22nd November, which saw the heart ripped out of the regular army.

As winter was setting in, the battle was almost over. The German Army had made small attacks but by November 11th serious fighting had ended. It was another four years to the day before the fighting would be over, but not before Ypres was reduced to rubble. Even so the line held and the Germans never took

Ypres. Hard battles lay ahead but the regulars (Old Contemptibles) had finished as a fighting force. The battles of Mons, Le Cateau, Aisne, Marne and Ypres had all passed into history and the men that had fought them were dead and gone. By the end of 1914 the army had suffered 90% casualties, taken prisoner, wounded, missing or killed. Sadly, Harry was one of those killed.

With the failure of the Germans in the battle of the Marne, both of the armies began a movement towards the North Sea. As they went each Army constructed a series of trench lines which came to characterise the Western Front.
The Allies had reached the North Sea at Niuwport, Belgium and the Germans ended up near Ypres.

How proud the British lion sits
Enthroned above the Menin Gate,
Eyes fixed upon the Menin Road,
Alert and watchful for his sons
Who, countless, marched
To feed the mouth of Hell. Long will he wait
For their return, not knowing that the waiting guns,
Long silent now had triumphed then,
To cheat them of a final resting place.
They have no "corner of a foreign field"
Where ordered plots can testify.
Their only epitaphs are names and ranks
Engraved in piers on each stone face.
For what they gave, remember them,
And ask not where and how they died, but only why.

How proud the British Lion sits,
Symbolic of the unity and pride
Of British arms that stood and fought
Their desperate battles here.
At each and every setting of the sun
He sits in witness to preside
That timeless homage of the "Last Post" sound
Unbroken year by year.
This simple tribute shall endure.
Our Flemish friends have recognised
The struggles here
Were not like other Nations' wars.
Much more, this is a tragic, hallowed place
Where Britain sacrificed
A generation of her sons for no good cause.

C. M. Berrill   1985

Ypres Menin Gate Memorial. Belgium.

Langton Sacheverell Coke.

Rank.	Lieutenant
Regiment.	Irish Guards
Unit.	1st Battalion
Date of Death.	31st October 1914
Age.	36
Memorial.	Menin Gate, Ypres, Belgium
	Panel 11 No Known Grave

Son of Colonel W.L. Coke JP, DL and Mary Coke. Born 25th January 1878.
Husband of Dorothy Maye Huntingford. Father of Elizabeth Joan (Betty) and Roger George Sacheverell of Brookhill Hall, Pinxton, Derbyshire. Roger was a famous musician and composer and played at the Wigmore Hall, London. Sacheverell went to France on the 13th September 1914.

Sacheverell Coke in Irish Guards Uniform

The Irish Guards was formed in 1900 at the request of Queen Victoria in recognition of the bravery of Irish Soldiers in the Boer War. Lt. Sacheverell Coke (known to his family as Chev) was a founding officer of the regiment. On his marriage to Dorothy Maye Huntingford in 1908 the Regiment gave them a silver bowl with the names of the founding officers engraved on it. This was returned to the regiment in 1973.

The following is an extract from the diary of Major the Hon J. F. Trefusis of the 1st Battalion of the Irish Guards on the day Lt. Coke was killed.

At about 2.30 p.m. we were ordered to fall in, and go to the assistance of the 7th Division at Klein Zillebeke. We had a march of about three or four miles, and were then sent to reinforce the cavalry. We came up to them in a perfect hail of shrapnel and big gun fire, and took up a line behind them. No sooner had we come than a good many, thinking we were relieving them, went away, and the consequence was that we found a very big gap in the line between our left and right of the next Battalion, so we had to send for the Grenadiers, and we eventually got the line straightened out, and had to dig ourselves in starting about 11 p.m. We managed to get the men up some food.

Our line was fairly dug in, and at 7 a.m. the enemy began the most terrific bombardment with guns of every calibre. Not a house within range of four miles was left untouched, and the incessant roar went on all day, shells dropping within a very few yards of our dugout. We had many casualties, amongst them

Lieutenant Coke. I think this was one of the worst days I have ever spent. No one in the front line could put their heads up over the trenches without a bullet coming at it. Casualties I think about four officers and 50 to 60 men. L. S. Coke was buried in the garden of a farm near to the Zillebeke Road. His grave was never found. Nearby, where the Zillebeke Road crosses the Menin Road, was later to be known as "Hell Fire Corner".

Brookhill Hall, the Coke family home

Chev Coke and friend playing Diablo

L. S. Coke and Dorothy on their engagement

Girl Guides with Elizabeth (Betty), back row centre

The Coke family have lived in Pinxton from about 1600, being Lords of the Pinxton Manor. The family owned a large amount of Pinxton, including Brookhill Hall, Langton Hall, Longwood Hall and Red Hall. They owned several coal mines before Privatisation in 1947; No.1 Pit to the west, up to No.7 Pit in the east of Pinxton. Also the Pinxton China Works with its famous pottery.

The Coke family lived in Pinxton until the death of Roger Coke in the early 1970s. The Hall then passed on to his nephew Christopher Darwin. Sacheverell's army duties prevented him from living at Brookhill Hall, and because he died before his father, he never became the Lord of the Manor.

Elizabeth, Sacheverell's daughter, married Gilbert William Lloyd Darwin of Elston Hall, Newark-on-Trent, Nottinghamshire and went to live at Oxton, Notts.

After Sacheverell's death Dorothy came to live at Brookhill Hall with her husband's family.
Dorothy, Sacheverell's widow, died in 1957 aged 76 years and her ashes are interred in front of the east window of Pinxton Church.

Members of Pinxton Cricket Club. Roger 3rd from left.

Sacheverell's son Roger

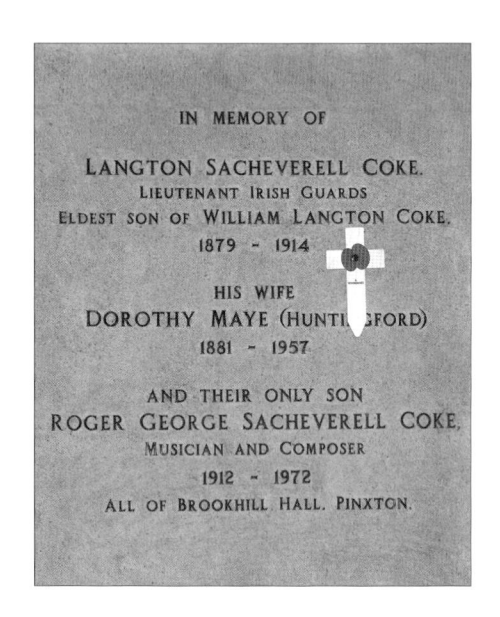

Coke Memorial in Pinxton
Church

Roger Coke's grave
in Pinxton churchyard

Ypres Memorial (Menin Gate). Belgium.

Harold Cooper.

Rank.	Private
Regiment.	Sherwood Foresters (Notts and Derby Regiment)
Unit.	2/7 Battalion
Service No.	266853
Date of Death.	26th September 1917
Age.	21
Memorial.	Tyne Cot Memorial

Panel 99 to 102 and 162 to 162A. No Known Grave

Harold was the son of George Cooper, Home Cottage, Birches Lane, Oakerthorpe, Derbyshire. He enlisted at Alfreton, Derbyshire.

The Third Battle of Ypres

The Allies launched the Battle on the 31st of July 1917. It was meticulously planned and continued until the fall of Passchendaele village on 6th November. The Allied Commanders were at last trying to make a final break through and break the will of the German Army; a similar view to that held at the height of the Somme offensive in 1916.

On the evening of the 24th the battalion moved up and took over from the 6th North Staffordshire Regiment, the line running roughly from Schuler Farm to Schuler Galleries, Loos, west of Ypres. On the morning of the 25th the enemy put down a heavy barrage on the front line and on the line at Fort Hill. This barrage lasted about two and a half hours. A practice barrage was put down by our own guns at 6 p.m. which was replied by the enemy in a barrage lasting two hours, on the same lines as above. From observations made, this practice barrage seemed very effective. By 3.30 a.m. on the morning of the 26th September the battalion formed up in two waves on 2 Company frontages, on lines which had been previously taped under cover of darkness. During the night orders were received that zero hour would be 5.50 a.m. At about 4 a.m. a bombardment by our guns was put down on the enemy lines, which apparently proved effective. The battalion advanced and the barrage was lifted according to the time-table. The first wave suffered a fair number of casualties through machine gun fire. The first objective was then consolidated by the first wave, the 2nd wave leapfrogging over. From here little opposition was met by the 2nd wave onto their 2nd objective, most of the casualties being caused by enemy shells. At 7.30 a.m. the 2nd objective was captured and consolidated. It was in this action that Harold was reported missing, feared killed. At 2 p.m. the enemy launched a counter-attack which was broken-up by our artillery fire. The battalion was under constant enemy shelling on the 27th - 28th and was relieved on the 29th by the 2nd Canterbury Regiment. The battalion then marched back to Vlamertinghe No. 2 Area, via Ypres.

Tyne Cot Memorial. Belgium.

Charles Cram.

Rank.	Private
Regiment.	Sherwood Foresters (Notts and Derby Regiment)
Unit.	15th Battalion (Bantams)
Service No.	23794
Date of Death.	25th February 1917
Age.	29
Cemetery.	Fouquescourt British Cemetery
Grave.	I. D. 2.

Charles was born Alfreton, Derbyshire. He resided in Pinxton and enlisted at Alfreton, Derbyshire. He was killed in action in the trenches near St. Vaast-en-Chaussée, France and leaves a wife and two children.
The Medal Roll shows Charles was entitled to the BWM and VM.

On the 21st February at 12 noon the 15th Battalion proceeded to take over the line from the French in the Chilly sector. The Deux Cimetieres communication trench was entered at 4.30 p.m., but was found almost impassable owing to mud; this greatly delayed the taking over of the front line trenches. The relief was not completed until 11.30 a.m. on the 22nd February. The line was held by X company on the right and Y on the left with Z company in support and W company in reserve. Trenches were found to be in a water-logged condition, with no revetments of any description and communication between platoon and Company Headquarters was impossible except over the top. From the 25th to the 28th the battalion was clearing out the communication trenches towards the front line. Sadly Charles was killed at this time.

Report from local paper.

News has been received that Private Chas Cram, of the Notts and Derbys, whose home was at Pinxton was killed in action on February 25th. The deceased soldier enlisted in March 1915. He was formerly employed at the Pinxton Coke Ovens. He was 29 years of age, and leaves a wife and two children.

The following letter has been received by Mrs. Cram from the deceased's Officer:

It is with deepest regret that I write to inform you of the death in action of your husband on the night of the 25th. I should have written to you at once to apprise you of the sad event, but a telegram, which came just after his death, informed me that you were very ill and I thought it better not to write.

Your husband was in my platoon, and we went into the trenches on the night of 21st February and they where knee deep in mud. To add to the awfulness of it all, the Germans opened a heavy bombardment on our lines, and on the night of the 24th of February, one shell bursting in the firing bay where your husband was at his post, was responsible for his death and that of one of his comrades, Private Gill. I may assure you that we all grieve over his loss; my brother officers, my men and myself extend to you and yours our heartfelt sympathy in this your deep sorrow. Your husband was a good soldier and comrade, always willing to do his share of work and duty, and like a true British Soldier he stood to his post, despite the awful rain of shell splinters and bullets, ready for the expected onslaught of the Huns. This will perhaps be some consolation to you, and also to know that he gave his life for his God, his King, his Country and his home. Your husband's few belongings I collected together and handed over to our adjutant for sending on to you. I might tell you that, with Private Gill, your husband was buried to the rear of the trench where he fell. It was absolutely impossible to have him carried right away to the rear, owing to the frightful state of the communication trenches. A small wooden cross marks the grave and bears the following inscription: "In memory of 23794 Private C Cram, 31352 Private W Gill, 15th Sherwood Foresters, killed in action 25th Feburary1917." May God, who is our father and without whose knowledge not even a sparrow falls to the ground, sustain and comfort you in your hour of sorrow.

Fouquescourt British Cemetery. France.

Fouquescourt is a village located on the Somme and is 35 kilometres east of Amien and 8 kilometres due north of Roye.
The village was captured by the Canadian Infantry on August 10th 1918.

William Cutts.

Rank.	Rifleman
Regiment.	Sherwood Foresters (Notts and Derby Regiment)
Unit.	16th Battalion (Chatsworth Rifles)
Service No.	65620
Date of Death.	10th August 1917
Age.	27
Cemetery.	Mont Huon Military Cemetery
Grave.	III. A. 3A.

William was the son of James and Mary Cutts of Pinxton, Derbyshire.
He was in the 19th Battalion, which was a training Battalion, and then transferred to the 16th Battalion (Chatsworth Rifles) Notts and Derby Regiment.

Notts and Derby men marching to the front

The battle in which William was wounded and subsequently died took place at St. Julien on the 1st/2nd August 1917. At about 6 p.m. orders were received for the 117th Infantry Brigade to take over the Divisional front. The 16th Battalion Sherwood Foresters relieved the 13th Royal Sussex Regiment in and behind St. Julien to the right of the Brigade front. The Battalion Headquarters were at Vanheule Farm and the relief was completed by 9.30 p.m. During the process of the relief, a high velocity shell entered Vanheule Farm, killing and injuring 30, including 3 officers.
"A" and "B" Companies were heavily shelled in their "dug-in" positions, and suffered heavy casualties. Their positions became untenable and at 6 p.m. on August 3rd the company had to withdraw and were sent up to reinforce the St. Julien defences.

4th August: The enemy bombarded the positions steadily the whole day, and at night placed a heavy barrage on Vanheule Farm and the approaches to St. Julien.

5th August: St. Julien again had a steady bombardment of the defences, making supplies a great difficulty. At 11.20 p.m. the battalion was relieved by the 1/5 Gloucester Regiment. Owing to a lull of enemy shelling, the relief was carried out speedily and with few casualties.

It was in this period of action that William was wounded and transported to Le Treport Military hospital were he later died.

He is also remembered on his parents' headstone in Pinxton churchyard.

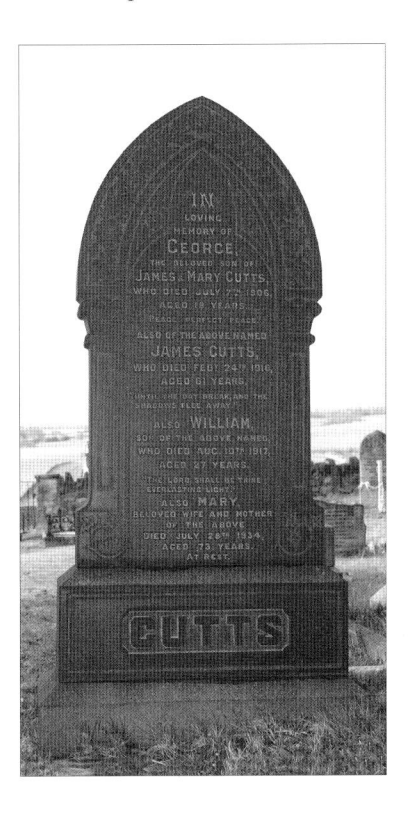

William Cutts parents' headstone in Pinxton churchyard

Mont Huon Military Cemetery, Le Treport. France.

Le Treport is a small sea port 25 kilometres north east of Dieppe and was an important Hospital Centre

George William Day.

Rank.	Private
Regiment.	Northumberland Fusiliers
Unit.	24th (Tyneside Irish) Battalion
Service No.	238057
Date of Death.	28th April 1917
Age.	27
Cemetery.	Bailleul Road East Cemetery, St Laurent-Blangy
Grave.	I. B. 37.

George is also commemorated on his parents' grave in Pinxton Churchyard

George's parents were George Henry Day and Elizabeth (Chappell) Day. They lived originally in Wakefield but, with several members of their family, walked to Pinxton to find work. His parents resided at 87 Park Lane in 1925, moving to 14 Kirkstead in 1928. They moved again to 2 North Street, then to 242 Wharf Road and finally into Station Road. George married Mary Scholey and they had two daughters, Mary, who was born in 1912 and Nora, born in 1914. Mary married Jim Poole and Nora married Frank Cooper.

George was wounded on September 15th 1916, returning to France on March 4th 1917.

The Commonwealth War Graves Commission gives George's date of death as 28th April 1917 but on his parents' grave it states that he died on 9th April.

Local Report. 26th May 1917.
Pinxton Man Killed.
We publish herewith a portrait of Private George William Day, of Pinxton.

News has come to hand that he was killed on Easter Monday. Deceased was 27 years old and the son of Mr. and Mrs. George Day of Station Road. He joined the Northumberland Fusiliers on the 4th of January 1915, and later became a signaller in the King's Yorkshire Light Infantry. In his earlier school days he joined the Boys' Brigade. From this he entered the Volunteers and later became a Territorial, in which he served about seven years.

When he left Yorkshire and came over to Pinxton he transferred to the National Reserve. Up to some five years ago his work lay in the Yorkshire Coalfield, and then along with his family he came to reside at Pinxton and started work in the Low Main seam at the Brookhill Colliery of the Pinxton Collieries. Inheriting his progressive element from his father, a close attention to duty gained him a promotion to the status of deputy, which post he relinquished to serve his King and Country, and the loss of a good official is keenly felt by the company whom he had so well served.

His fellow workmen showed respect in this letter:

I was requested by the Pinxton United Committee to state that this meeting of the Pinxton Collieries workmen do hear with deep regret of the death in action of your dear son, and to convey to yourself, wife and family our deepest sympathy. I can assure you that the constant inquiries relating to your son's safety since the first intimation you had goes to prove how highly he was respected by all who knew him. In the sorrowing moments, hours and days, believe me when I say we all feel grieved and shall remember you and yours in this hour of trial.
C.H. Wilson Secretary.

George W. Day's parents' grave in Pinxton churchyard, east side.
He is commemorated at the base.

Bailleul Road East Cemetery, St. Laurent-Blangy. France.

Albert Edward Donnelly.

Rank.	Private
Regiment.	Cameronians (Scottish Rifles)
Unit.	3rd Battalion
Service No.	17784
Date of Death.	18th November 1915
Age.	28
Born.	19th March 1887. Pinxton
Cemetery.	Cromarty Gaelic Chapel Cemetery Ross and Cromarty, Scotland
Grave.	K. North East. 24.

Cromarty Gaelic Chapel where A. E. Donnelly is buried.

Private Donnelly is buried in the Cromarty Gaelic Chapel Churchyard which is situated in the county of Ross and Cromarty, Scotland.

There was a Military Hospital in Cromarty, so he may have been wounded and sent to the Cromarty Hospital for treatment, where he later died.

The Churchyard holds 74 burials of the 1914 – 18 War.

A. E. Donnelly's grave in Cromarty Churchyard. Scotland.

Clifford Henry Dutton.

Rank.	Stoker 1st Class
Service.	Royal Navy
	H.M.S. Dartmouth
Service No.	K/29892
Date of Death.	8th October 1917
Age.	21
Cemetery.	Carrington St John Churchyard, Nottingham
Grave.	Old. 5-2.

Clifford was the son of Thomas and Lucy Dutton of 7, Nantmelyn Terrace, Tonyrefail, Glamorgan.

H.M.S. Dartmouth

H.M.S. Dartmouth was involved in a surface action on May 1917, and then torpedoed by the German Submarine U.C. 25 when homeward bound from the Adriatic.

The damage was severe and the Cruiser was abandoned for a time. 7 Ratings were killed in the surface action and 4 in the engine house from the torpedo. It is possible that Clifford Dutton was wounded in the action, and died at Nottingham. It is a mystery why he is buried at Nottingham, as there are relations in Pinxton. It was perhaps not practical to bring the body to Pinxton.

> Rain, midnight rain, nothing but the wild rain
> On this bleak hut, and solitude, and me
> Remembering again that I shall die
> And neither hear the rain nor give it thanks
> For washing me cleaner than I have been
> Since I was born into this solitude.
> Blessed are the dead that the rain rains upon:
> But here I pray that none whom once I loved
> Is dying to-night or laying still awake
> Solitary, listening to the rain,
> Either in pain or thus in sympathy
> Helpless among the living and the dead,
> Like a cold water among broken reeds,
> Myriads of broken reeds all still and stiff,
> Like me who have no love which this wild rain
> Has not dissolved except the love of death,
> If love it be for what is perfect and
> Cannot, the tempest tells me, disappoint.
>
> Edward Thomas.

St. John's Church

Plaque inside church showing C. Dutton's name

C. Dutton's headstone.

68

Arthur Dye.

Rank.	Private
Regiment.	Northumberland Fusiliers
Unit.	2nd Battalion
Service No.	16608
Date of Death.	8th May 1915
Age.	25
Memorial.	Menin Gate, Ypres, Belgium
	Panel 8 and 12. No Known Grave

Arthur was the son of William and Elizabeth Dye. Husband of Elizabeth Dye, (formerly Dedson), of 61 Talbot Street Pinxton, Derbyshire.
Initially in the Royal Welsh Fusiliers, but transferred to the Northumberland Fusiliers.

Article from local paper.

After a period of something like five months during which relatives of Private Arthur Dye of Pinxton have anxiously awaited official news, confirmation of his death was received on the 22nd October. Arthur was one of three brothers serving with the colours and leaves a widow and three children. He joined the Northumberland Fusiliers in February 1915, and crossed to France with the Expeditionary Force nine weeks later. Early in May this year, the wife and relatives received information from his chums that he had been killed in action, and it now transpires that this actually occurred in the same engagement as that in which his brother Horace was wounded. Previously to enlisting Private Arthur Dye was a Deputy at the No. 2 Pit of the Pinxton Collieries. He was also a member of Sutton Harriers and a very successful Ambulance student.

Menin Gate Memorial Ypres. Belgium.

George Edson.

Rank.	Private
Regiment.	Royal Welsh Fusiliers
Unit.	2nd Battalion
Service No.	19624
Date of Death.	22nd June 1916
Age.	27
Memorial.	Loos Memorial
	Panel 50 to 52 No Known Grave

George was the husband of Annie Edson. Father of Ada and Harry of 19 Park Lane, Pinxton, Derbyshire.

Article announcing his death.

From local paper.

Another Pinxton man to be added to the Roll of Honour is Private George Edson of 19 Park Lane, of the Royal Welsh Fusiliers. He was first officially reported as missing on the 22nd of June, but his wife has received a letter through the British Red Cross, which left little room for doubt that he is killed. It stated on the day in question the whole front line of the deceased's company was blown up by a German mine, and it is believed that Private Edson was killed. Nothing has since been heard of this soldier, which points to the accuracy of the Red Cross report. Private Edson, who was 27 years old, leaves a wife and two children. He enlisted in January 1915, previous to which he worked at the Brookhill Colliery.

Letter of condolence from Pinxton Workman's Relief Fund.

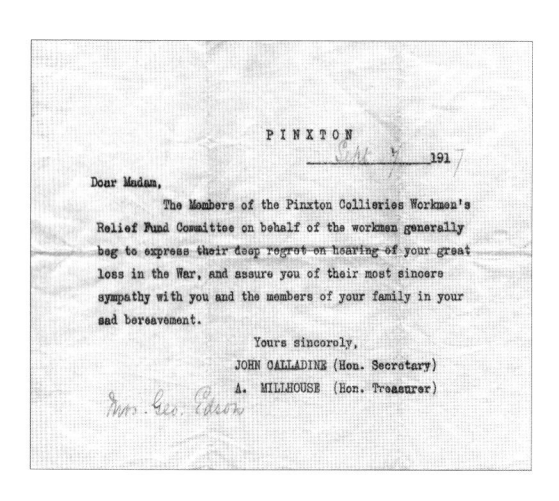

> PINXTON
> _____ 191_
>
> Dear Madam,
>
> The Members of the Pinxton Collieries Workmen's Relief Fund Committee on behalf of the workmen generally beg to express their deep regret on hearing of your great loss in the War, and assure you of their most sincere sympathy with you and the members of your family in your sad bereavement.
>
> Yours sincerely,
> JOHN CALLADINE (Hon. Secretary)
> A. MILLHOUSE (Hon. Treasurer)

Excerpt of letter written to his wife and children a few days before his death.

Dear Annie,

I write to you again in answer to your kind and welcomed letter. I had just come from the trenches, and was having dinner when I got your letter. Well, pleased to let you know I am keeping well. I have sent our Harry and Ada a letter. Well Annie love, tell George thank you for the shilling he sent. Can you send me some more of those long fags you sent? I will let you know when my name goes in for leave, hoping it is in the beginning of August. I know you are feeling lonely but your soldier boy will soon be coming to see you. I often think of those bygone happy days. Can you remember when you ran over me with your bike? We have it a bit rough some times, and I may tell you it seems marvellous we keep dodging those shells. My pal got wounded last time in the trenches, he was bringing up the tea when a grenade came over killing a fellow in front of him. Dear wife, I hope you enjoyed yourself at Whitsun, but never mind, it is better to be the wife of a soldier who is willing to fight for you, than the wife of a shirker. Dear Annie, it is a sad affair about Kitchener's death, we felt a great loss. We had a good Christmas in a French Barn (tray bon) as the French say. The officers paid for barrels of beer. After dinner we supped the beer and I sang a few songs, several of the boys asked me if I had been a comedian. So dear wife you say you will get a job delivering letters in the trenches, well love I don't think you would stop long when the shells start to come over, but I would not mind seeing you anyway. You say that the fireside is the best place in the bad weather, but the fireside here seems a long way off. But keep the home fires burning until your boys come home.

Good night dear one and God bless you and the little ones and keep you safe until I return.

Your loving husband George.

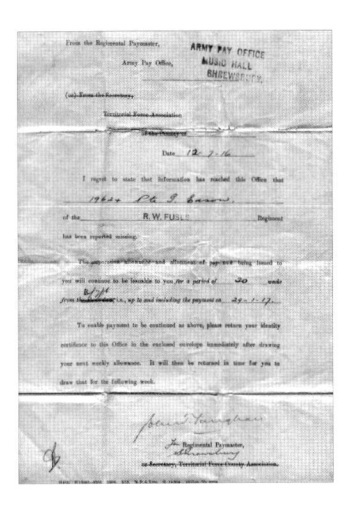

Letter from the Army announcing G. Edson missing

Loos Memorial. France.

Albert Elliott.

Rank.	Lance Corporal
Regiment.	Sherwood Foresters (Notts and Derby Regiment)
Unit.	11th Battalion
Service No.	15393
Date of Death.	10th February 1916
Age.	24
Cemetery.	Rue-David Military Cemetery
Grave.	I. H. 31.

Son of Mr. and Mrs. William Elliott of 57 Park Lane, Pinxton.
Albert enlisted at Mansfield, Notts, shortly after the war commenced. He was born in Pinxton, Derbyshire. Prior to enlisting Albert was a miner at Pinxton Collieries.

Albert had been in France six months when he was killed. The 11th Battalion on the 9th of February were preparing to take over the trenches from the 8th Battalion, K.O.Y.L. I. and was accompanied into the trenches by the 27th Battalion Northumberland Fusiliers. This was completed by the 11th of February. It was during this time, on the 10th February, in the change-over, that Albert was killed, 3 miles south-west of Armentières.

Report from local paper.

The serious side of the present conflict is indeed being brought home to us in a most convincing manner, and Pinxton's gradually increasing death toll, now 17 we believe, goes to show that the lads are now in the thick of the fray. Very few weeks now pass without reference in these columns to one or another from Pinxton, and it is regrettable that the list must be further supplemented by the name of Albert Elliott, of 57 Park Lane who was killed in action on the 10th February, the sad news reaching home on the following Monday.
Private Elliott joined the Notts and Derby shortly after the war commenced, and had been in France about six months. Prior to joining the colours, he was a miner at Pinxton's Collieries. The following letter has been received from Sergeant E. Boyle:

No doubt you have heard the bad news about your son Albert before this letter, and I know he will be a great loss to you. As an outsider there is no one who is as sorry to lose such a bright and intelligent youth. Believe me he was a good soldier and always did his duty cheerfully, and was very interested in Soldiering. As a man he always did his share of work. But unfortunately he is like many others, on the roll of honour. May he rest in peace.

Another letter was received from Private L Drakeford 11th Service Battalion Sherwood Foresters.

I regret to add to the sad news of the death of your son Albert who was killed on the 10th February whilst doing his duty. I was not there when it happened, but his friends told me he was shot through the head and did not suffer. He was my biggest chum and well regarded by all the boys in the platoon, and I am sure we will all miss him. All the boys send their deepest sympathy and the same from me.

> A man's destination is not his destiny,
> Every country is home to one man
> And exile to another. Where a man dies bravely
> At one with his destiny, that soil is his.
> Let his village remember.
>
> T. S. Eliot

Rue-David Military Cemetery. France.

Archibald Evans.

Rank.　　　　　Private
Regiment.　　　Sherwood Foresters (Notts and Derby Regiment)
Unit.　　　　　10th Battalion
Service No.　　116650
Date of Death.　4th November 1918
Age.　　　　　24
Cemetery.　　　Caudry British Cemetery
Grave.　　　　IV. G. 9.

Archibald lived on Wharf Road, Pinxton. He was born in Ripley, Derbyshire and enlisted at Mansfield. At 5.30 a.m. the 10th Battalion moved off from Poix-du-Nord in damp and mist through a mass of heavy German artillery where numerous casualties were sustained: 4 officers and 98 other ranks. This was to be the last battle the 10th Sherwood Foresters would fight and their last action of the war.

How unfortunate that was for Archie, so close to the end of the war, as he was one of the 98 other ranks. He later died of his wounds.

Report from local paper.

Pinxton people generally, and the football going public especially, will hear with regret of the death of Private Archie Evans of Wharf Road Pinxton, official intimation of which has recently come to hand. About a fortnight ago Mr. and Mrs. Evans heard the sad news from the Chaplain of the 10th Battalion Notts and Derbys, and the official document states that death occurred on November 4th at the Casualty Clearing Station, France, from gunshot wounds. Prior to joining up Archie, who was 24 years of age, was employed as a weigh clerk at Langton Colliery, and for several years a distinguished player with the Pinxton Reds in which capacity his moral character was truly reflected as being unobtrusive, clean and straight.

Caudry British Cemetery. France.

T. L. Faulkner.

Rank.	Private. First Class
Service.	Royal Air Force
Unit.	14th Balloon Section
Service No.	76068
Date of Death.	2nd November 1918
Cemetery.	Busigny Communal Cemetery Extension
Grave.	II. A. 26.

Private Faulkner died of Bronchial Pneumonia.

In the spring of 1918 large numbers of soldiers in the trenches on the Western front became ill. The soldiers complained of a sore throat, headaches and loss of appetite. Although it appeared to be highly infectious, recovery was rapid and doctors give it the name of "three day fever". At first the doctors were unable to identify the illness but eventfully they decided it was a new strain of influenza. However, in the summer of 1918, symptoms became much more severe. About a fifth of the victims developed bronchial pneumonia or septicaemia. A large percentage of these men died. Unfortunately this was the fate of T.L. Faulkner, so close to the end of the war. By the end of the summer it had spread to the German lines and created serious problems for the German military. The first cases appeared in Britain in Glasgow in May 1918 and soon spread to other towns and cities.

Photo shows R.A.F. Kite Balloon Company topping up with gas

Observation balloons were used in World War 1 as the trench warfare was an ideal environment for the observation balloon and both the Germans and Allies used them to check what the opposition was doing behind the lines. Balloons had company in the skies because airplanes were starting to appear, but anti-aircraft guns usually gave them a hot reception.

Balloons were susceptible because they were filled with hydrogen which is very inflammable. The inert gas helium had been discovered earlier but was difficult to obtain. Being in an observation balloon was a very dangerous job if shot at by the enemy as the parachute was not invented until 1919.

T.L. Faulkner's job was working with these balloons.

T. Faulkner's Casualty Card

Busigny Communal Cemetery. France.

Busigny is a village about 10 kilometres south west of Le Cateau and 24 kilometres north east of St Quentin. The Cemetery is a short distance west of the village.

76

Albert Henry Gell.

Rank.	Private
Regiment.	Royal Welsh Fusiliers
Unit.	8th Battalion
Service No.	19942
Date of Death.	7th August 1915
Age.	22
Memorial.	Helles Memorial
	Panel 77 to 80. No Known Grave

Albert was born in Wales and moved to Pinxton in his early years to work in the local mines.

Local Report.

Reported as missing on August 7th 1915 the parents, wife and relatives of Private Albert Henry Gell, 19942 Royal Welsh Fusiliers, have now received the sad news that he was killed in action in the Dardanelles on that date. The deceased, who was 22 years of age, leaves a wife and one child. Previous to joining the colours early on in the campaign, the deceased was a miner.

Helles Memorial. Turkey.    **Trenches in Gallipoli**

Gerald Gilbourne.

Rank.	Private
Regiment.	King's Own Yorkshire Light Infantry
Unit.	51st Battalion
Service No.	TR/5/222468
Date of Death.	20th November 1918
Age.	18
Cemetery.	St Helen's Churchyard, Pinxton
Grave.	Plot 5. Row 19. Grave 00. (North-east of the church)

Gerald was the son of William Gilbourne of 23 Park Lane, Pinxton. He was a blacksmith striker with the 51st Battalion. He was at Doncaster in January 1918, then on to Welbeck in May 1918 and to Clipstone in August 1918. The battalion was waiting in reserve, but Gerald died in the flu epidemic of 1918.

It is stated that the flu epidemic was very virulent and it killed more people in the world than the First World War.

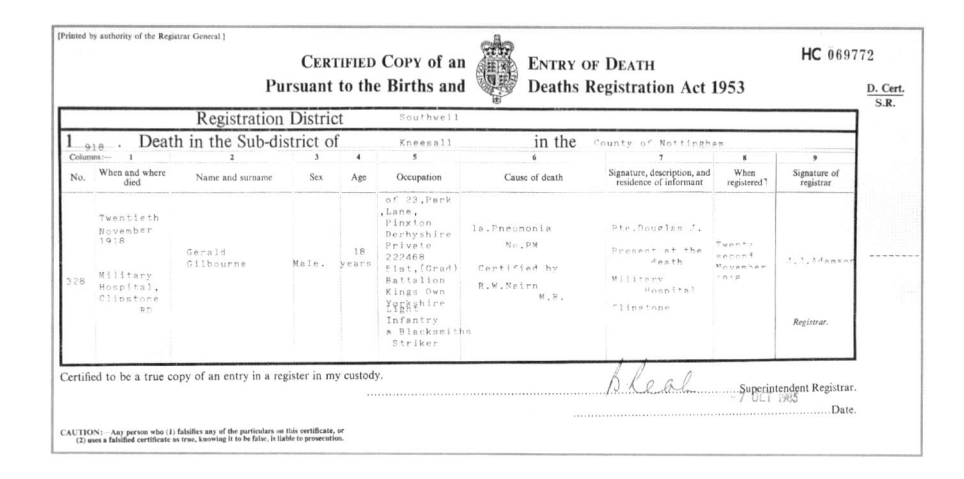

Gerald's Death Certificate

Gerald's grave in Pinxton churchyard

George Glover.

Rank.	Private
Regiment.	Lincolnshire Regiment
Unit.	1st Battalion
Service No.	38726
Date of Death.	21st March 1918
Age.	19
Memorial.	Pozieres Memorial
	Panel 23 and 24. No Known Grave

George was the son of William and Martha Glover of Pool Close, Pinxton.

Second Battle of the Somme. Codenamed "Michael" by the Germans.

Preceded by an artillery bombardment using 6,000 guns, the Germans advanced in early morning fog on the 21st March 1918, which hid the German advance from the Allied observation posts. The British were taken by surprise, but it did not develop as the Germans had foreseen. Whilst they achieved a complete breakthrough south of the Somme, the major attack to the north was held up, mainly by the concentration of strength at Arras. For a whole week the Germans could not exploit the success they had in the south, where they had advanced 40 miles. The Allies eventually halted the German drive east of Amiens and so the offensive was halted. This was the battle which G. Glover probably lost his life as he was in the area at the time.

> Splendid you passed, the great surrender made;
> Into the light that nevermore shall fade;
> Deep your contentment in that blest abode,
> Who wait the last clear trumpet call of God.

Pozieres Memorial. France.

James William Gregory.

Rank.	Private
Regiment.	Grenadier Guards
Unit.	2nd Battalion
Service No.	12972
Date of Death.	24th December 1914
Memorial.	Le Touret Memorial
	Panel 2 No Known Grave

James William Gregory worked at Blackwell Colliery.

J. W. Gregory   **J. W. Gregory's memorial plaque**

James William Gregory was born in Morrison, Jefferson County, Colorado, USA on the 13th April 1883. Morrison is a small town just outside of Denver. His parents were Felicia and John William Gregory. John was born at New Brinsley and Felicia at Westwood, Selston, Nottinghamshire. They were married at Greasley Parish Church on 7th November 1881. Shortly after their marriage the couple sailed to the USA with Felicia's sister and her family, finally settling in Colorado where James was born.

When James was about two years old his father, John, died. Felicia returned to England with her infant son and eventually remarried and settled in Riddings. James, as most other boys in the vicinity, became a coalminer but in November 1906 he enlisted in the Grenadier Guards at Alfreton. He served in the regiment until 1909 when he was placed in the reserve.

At the outbreak of war in 1914 James was mobilised on the 4th August at Chelsea barracks in the 2nd Bat, 1st Company. The regiment was shipped to France as part of the Guards Brigade on the 22nd November and was billeted at Meteren until the 22nd December. They then marched to Bethune, a distance of about 10 miles, where they billeted for the night. They were to relieve an Indian Corps which had been heavily attacked and driven from its trenches between La Bassée Canal and Richebourg. On the 23rd December the Battalion marched to a field at Essarts and in the evening took over the line at Rue de Cailoux from the Royal Sussex Regiment. This was near the village of Festubert where there was to be a greater battle the following spring.

The area around the village of Festubert is, as is most of the Ypres area, just above sea level and it was not the best area in which to dig trenches. The weather had been very bad, with heavy rain, and the trenches were filled with water and liquefying mud which could very easily suck a man down. The section of the front line that the battalion was to occupy had been hastily improvised from dykes because the Germans had captured the British line trenches a few days before. In some places the German trenches were only 25 yards from the British. As the German trenches were higher and overlooked the British line, water drained into the British trenches. The water was knee deep and in some places waist deep. Men got stuck and had to be dug out. At the same time they had to contend with German snipers who were very active, so the relief took 6 hours to complete. The next day, Christmas Eve, was bitterly cold and the enemy was very active with trench mortars and hand grenades as well as there being much sniper action. At many parts of the front-line spontaneous truces occurred and both sides exchanged Christmas gifts, played football and fraternised in other ways, but several hundred yards away the war went on. This was the case on the section of the front where the Grenadier Guards were. The enemy mined to within 10 yards of the Guard's trench and the end of No.2's trench was blown in. The No.1 company commander and several other officers were killed. It was in this action that James Gregory also died.

His platoon sergeant reported that at about 3 o'clock in the afternoon they were given the order to retire. They were up to their waists in water and Sergeant Pownall said that James never came out of the trench. A victim of sniper fire after just one day in the front line.

British Red Cross report on wounded and missing. 15th October 1915.

I regret to say that all the information we have been able to obtain about James Gregory is of the most meagre and unsatisfactory nature.

Sergeant Pownall, 15143, now in hospital abroad (place unknown) says that Private Gregory was with his platoon in the trenches at Festubert last December, and about 3 p.m. in the afternoon they had to retire. In the trenches they were up to their waists in water, and Sergeant Pownall was of the opinion that Private Gregory never came out of the trench.

REPORT FROM DIARY OF MAJOR JEFFREYS   24th Dec 1914

I went round the trenches early, the water up to my waist in places; our trenches were badly sited being full of water and mud. The country is quite flat and featureless being intersected with dykes. A ridge, about 6,000 yards eastward, whence the Germans can overlook us, and about 1.5 miles to the right we can see Givenchy Hill held by our 1st Division. It took me 2 hours getting along the line and found the enemy had sapped up 10 yards of our front trench, and his snipers were very active. Also he was using trench mortars (minenwerfer), which throw heavy bombs. One can usually see them coming but it is impossible to move quickly to avoid them with the mud.

I had just got to the supply line when the enemy blew in No.2 trench, and rushed in behind the explosion. There was a general scramble from Nos.2 and 3 trenches into the second line which the Germans then attacked, but were driven back with heavy losses. But we took losses too: 15 killed, 29 wounded and 9 missing, of whom 5 known to be wounded. We ought never to have held such a line with conditions being so bad. There was continuous firing for the rest of the day and a good deal of bombing from the minewerfers. No.1 Company on the right had remained in position when No.2 came back, and we could get no communication from them. We decided to dig a new line in a better position and finish it by daylight, but it was a ticklish job as the ground was getting frosted and the Germans kept sending flares up, and each time we had to throw ourselves flat, but by daylight we had done and so withdrew into it.

Le Touret Memorial. France.

F. Hill.

Rank. Private
Regiment. Canadian Infantry

After an intensive search, which included contacting Mr. Jim Abbott, the Minister for the Interior, Canada, we have been unable to find any information relating to the Private F. Hill whose name appears on the Pinxton War Memorial.

**The Canadian Memorial
Vancouver Corner**

Although we have no information about this soldier…

His name liveth for evermore.

Albert Hoten.

Rank.	Private
Regiment.	Royal Welsh Fusiliers
Unit.	8th Battalion
Service No.	33184
Date of Death.	11th April 1917
Age.	23
Memorial.	Basra Memorial
	Panel 15. No Known Grave

Albert was the son of William and Harriet Hoten of Spring Cottages, Wharf Road, Pinxton, Derbyshire.

Report from local paper.
The parents of Private Albert Roland Hoten have received the news that their third son Albert has been killed in Mesopotamia. He was 23 years of age and enlisted 1st August 1914. He went to Mesopotamia in August 1916 and knew something of the arduous conditions in the Eastern Campaign.

Proudly you gathered, rank on rank, to war
As who had heard God's message from afar;
All you had hoped for, all you had, you gave,
To save mankind – yourselves you scorned to save.

Soldiers remembering at the Basra Memorial. Mesopotamia (now Iraq).

Algie Hoten.

Rank.	Private
Regiment.	Royal Fusiliers
Unit.	24th Battalion
Service No.	G/100194
Date of Death.	3rd October 1918
Age.	24
Cemetery.	St. Sever Cemetery Extension, Rouen
Grave.	R. III. I. 17

Algie was the son of George and Charlotte Hoten, of Town Street, Pinxton, Derbyshire. He was born at Pinxton 8th April 1894.

News from local paper.

Official news has now been received by Mr. and Mrs. G. Hoten of Town Street, Pinxton, of the death of their son Private Algie Hoten Royal Fusiliers. He was severely wounded in both thighs and sustained a fractured arm on September 11th. He was received into No. 6 Field Dressing Station and then conveyed to the 46th Casualty Clearing Station, afterwards being taken by ambulance train to No.5 General Hospital Rouen. Here he was operated on and progressed favourably for a time, but he had a severe hemorrhage in the left thigh, from which he never rallied. The sad news of his death was received by the bereaved parents by telegram from the War Office on Saturday 5th October, to the effect that Private Hoten died of wounds on 3rd October.

On October the 6th the following letter was received from the Chaplain:

I expect that you have heard that your dear son has passed away this morning. I was often with him, and saw him three hours off the end, or rather the great beginning. My heart is too heavy to find words to express my sympathy. I think I feel something of what you do, but if we think of his dear young spirit, glad in the presence of God, we shall not grieve over his peace and joy. I cannot help but quote these words:

Oh! If the sonless mothers weeping,
And widowed girls, could look inside
The glory that hath them in keeping
Who went to the Great War and died,
They would rise and put their mourning off,
And say: "Thank God, he has enough".

May God console and bless you all.
G. J. Day.

The sister in charge of No.7 ward also wrote the following:

I am very sorry to tell you that your son Private Algie Hoten passed away on 3rd October at 4.30 a.m. We are all so grieved for you and his father, as we know what a terrible loss it will be to you. He was always bright and cheery and so patient and good. Please accept our deepest sympathy in your trouble.
Margaret Browne.

From the relatives.

The Chaplain and Sister have been so kind in informing his parents day to day of his condition.
Private Hoten joined the forces on May 20th 1916, and was attached to the 1st Northern Cyclist Battalion (North Fusiliers), and went to France on 13th April 1918, when he was transferred to the Royal Fusiliers.
The deceased has three brothers also serving their Country:
Private Walter Hoten. Sherwoods in France.
Air Mechanic Ralph Hoten. R. A. F.
Corporal Harold Hoten. A. P. C.

St. Sever Cemetery Extension, Rouen. France.

Richard Jessop. MM.

Rank.	Driver
Regiment.	Royal Field Artillery
Unit.	"B" Battery, 95th Brigade
Service No.	63727
Awards.	Military Medal
Date of Death.	27th May 1918
Age.	38
Memorial.	Soissons Memorial No Known Grave

Richard lived in Pinxton and was the husband of Lily Jessop who, after the war, resided at 4 Byron Street, East Kirkby, Nottinghamshire. He went to France on the 9th September 1915.

Richard Jessop was awarded the Military Medal. This was only awarded for an act of extreme bravery. The recipients were allowed to use the letters MM after their name.

The Military Medal

The Third Battle of Aisne.

The attack was launched on 27th May with a ferocious heavy bombardment of 4,000 guns across a 40 kilometre front, against four divisions of British IX Corps. Casualties from the bombardment were severe as it was also accompanied with a gas attack.

17 divisions of German infantry began their advance through a 40 kilometre gap in the Allied line. The Germans made rapid progress and captured 50,000 Allied soldiers and 800 guns, arriving within 90 kilometres of Paris.

A German victory seemed a possibility but problems with supplies, reserves and troop fatigue and the Allied counter attacks made the Germans run out of steam.

French casualties were heavy numbering 90,000, with the British 29,000.

At the end of April, 5 Divisions of Commonwealth forces were posted to the French 6th Army. Towards the end of May the Germans made a ferocious attack which pushed the Allies over the river Aisne to the River Marne.

Driver Richard Jessop was probably killed in this battle and is remembered on Soissons Memorial.

Richard Jessop was a driver; his job involved leading a team of 6 horses which pulled a heavy gun carriage and ammunition to different areas on the Western Front.

When the road's all blocked with transport
Taking rations to the dump,
And they're shelling Dawson's Corner
With shrapnel and with crump,
When the word comes down the column,
"A stretcher bearer, quick!"
Then your mouth goes kind of dry boys,
And your stomach's awful sick.

When you hear a sort of whistle
That swells into a roar,
And yer ducks, yer ducks like Hell boys!
'Cos you've heard that sound before.
There's a crash that echoes skywards,
And a scream of mortal pain,
Then you curse the blasted Kaiser,
And just march on again.　　　　　　　Anon.

Illustration showing Richard's job as a driver

Soissons Memorial. France.

Richard Harold Lane. MM.

Rank.	Sergeant
Regiment.	Royal Warwickshire
Unit.	1st / 6th Battalion
Service No.	242148
Date of Death.	27th August 1917
Age.	29
Awards.	Military Medal

Awarded 26th February 1917 for outstanding bravery in rescuing a wounded officer

Cemetery.	New Irish Farm Cemetery
Grave.	XXV.H.13.

Photo from Blackwell Colliery book

Richard was born in Lowton Leigh, Lancashire and was the husband of Mary Ann Lane of 109 West End, Pinxton

The Military Medal

Richard enlisted 9th October 1914 into the Sherwood Foresters as a private and saw action in the Arras Sector. On the 22nd March 1916 he was wounded at La Folie (Vimy Ridge). He crawled out of trenches to rescue a wounded officer whilst under enemy fire. Richard was promoted to sergeant with distinction. He was later transferred to the Royal Warwickshire Regiment. Richard was killed in action.

The Military Medal was awarded for acts of gallantry and devotion to duty under fire. The Military Medal was only awarded for bravery in the field. Recipients were allowed to use MM after their name.

Showing the desolation of the trenches

New Irish Farm Cemetery. Belgium.

William Lane.

Rank.　　　　　　Private
Regiment.　　　　Grenadier Guards
Unit.　　　　　　2nd Battalion
Service No.　　　11814
Date of Death.　　24th September 1914
Age.　　　　　　27
Memorial.　　　　Special Memorial
　　　　　　　　Bouilly Cross Roads Military Cemetery

Private William Lane

William, the son of Mr. A. Lane of 54 Beech Road Dartford, Kent and Mrs. H Lane of 51 Park Lane, Pinxton, Derbyshire was born at Glosher Horfield. Eldest of 2 sons, William enlisted at Alfreton Derbyshire in 1904 and was with the British Expeditionary Force in 1914.

Report from local paper.
Pinxton man dies for his country.

The grim consequences of war have now been brought home to Pinxton by the receipt of news announcing that Private William Lane has been killed in action on 24th September. The deceased was the eldest of two Soldier sons of Mr. and Mrs. A Lane of 51 Park Lane, Pinxton and leaves a widow and three children. In 1904 he enlisted in the 3rd Grenadier Guards in which he served a period of seven years. Immediately on the declaration of war he responded to the call of his country, and was quickly despatched to the front. A recent communication stating "All's Well" was received from James Henry, the other brother, who is serving in the Sherwood Foresters.

Mons to the Aisne

On 23rd of August 1914 the British Expeditionary Force held the Germans in front of Mons with rapid accurate gun fire of 15 rounds a minute although out numbered by 3 to1. The Germans long after the war thought they had been held back by machine gun fire. The Kaiser referred to them as "that small contemptible little army" which stuck with the soldiers of 1914. But due to superior numbers, the decision was taken to withdraw. The British losses for that day amounted to 1,600. The general withdrawal continued and on 26th August a stand was made at Le Cateau. The commander of II Corps, Horace Smith-Dorrien, said "Gentlemen, we will stand and fight". The stand gave the British force much needed time to withdraw in good order but losses during this period of heavy fighting amounted to 7,812. As August turned to September the Germans had to be stopped as they were just 35 miles from Paris. At the forest of Villers-Cotterets the 2nd battalion Grenadier Guards had a costly struggle to protect the withdrawal of the 2nd division through the forest and was surrounded and fought to the end. The Germans were stopped at the battle of the Marne 6th-12th September. The British Expeditionary Force was heavily out numbered but pushed the Germans back over the Aisne where they began to dig in. This was the start of trench warfare We do not know exactly where William Lane was killed but the battalion was in the area of the village of Soupir which was active with German snipers. He certainly was involved in some of the fiercest fighting of the war. He was buried in Chavonne church yard, but unfortunately his body was never recovered. He is remembered in Bouilly cemetery with a special memorial headstone along with four other United Kingdom soldiers.

Bouilly Cross Roads Military Cemetery. Marne, France.

The cemetery was created in 1918 by the French Forces to contain British, French, Italian and German soldiers who had fallen in the vicinity. After the Armistice all the other nationalities were removed and the cemetery was used for the concentration of British graves from the surrounding area. Most of the casualties who are buried there fell in the battle of the Marne. There are now over 200 1914-18 casualties commemorated in the site. Of these, over half are unidentified. The cemetery covers an area of 890 square metres and is enclosed by a rubble wall.

Ernest Clarke Leatherland.

Rank.	Rifleman
Regiment.	King's Royal Rifle Corps
Unit.	7th Battalion
Service No.	R/8006
Date of Death.	14th December 1915
Age.	21
Cemetery.	La Brique Military Cemetery No.2
Grave.	I. A. 21.

Ernest was the son of Samuel and Sarah Elizabeth Leatherland of Lyndisfarne, Victoria Road, Pinxton. He enlisted on the 9th December 1914 at Nottingham.

PINXTON SOLDIER'S DEATH.

A tribute of respect and appreciation.

Sir, Please allow me to remember one of Pinxton's honoured dead, through the medium of your paper. I refer to the late Ernest Clarke Leatherland of the 7th King's Royal Rifles who enlisted on the December 9th 1914 and was killed by a shell on December 14th 1915, aged 21 years. He was the eldest son of Mr. and Mrs. Samuel Leatherland of Victoria Road, Pinxton, to whom the sympathy of all village people will be extended in their sad bereavement.

As I have been privileged to know the subject of the letter E.C. Leatherland and the part he played in the less strenuous days prior to the war, and as I have received many communications from him on active service, I can testify to the fact of his being a true patriot and a very worthy citizen of a great empire.

In my capacity of Adult School Secretary, I have known him to be true to the aims of the movement, one of the chief of which is to teach the true responsibility of citizenship. His comrades in arms (Rifleman James Milward and T. T. Smith) first communicated the distressing news and in letters bore testimony to his solid qualities. One of his dearest friends has written a letter from the headquarters of his battalion to his distressed but honoured parents which I have been privileged to read, and which has prompted me to write this, in which he assures them that their son is one of whom to be truly proud.

A few of the statements in the said letter are worthy of repetition. He looked always cheerful and always did his duty; he never turned a hair, no matter how great the danger he was in. He always acted only as an Englishman.

Pinxton ought to be proud of all such sons. Speaking for all the members of the Pinxton Adult School, I may add we are proud to have counted him in the list of our members, and we much deplore his having finished activities with us. In having given his life for his country we sincerely hope a result of his noble sacrifice our members will be inspired to resolve that his dying shall not be in vain.

I am yours etc. Eric Hancock, Redgate Street, Pinxton.

La Brique Military Cemetery No 2. Belgium.

Harry Lines.

Rank.	Private
Regiment.	South Staffordshire Regiment
Unit.	2nd Battalion
Service No.	43520
Date of Death.	30th August 1918
Cemetery.	Orival Wood Cemetery, Flesquieres
Grave.	I. B. 32.

Harry was born at Sibford Ferris, Nr. Banbury, Oxfordshire.
He enlisted at Hucknall and lived in Pinxton.

In 1918 the Germans came to the conclusion that they must beat the British before the Americans led by General Pershing were strong enough to intervene. The Germans attacked on 21st of March 1918 in the area of St Quentin, code named "Michael", and advanced in thick fog, allowing the stormtroopers leading the attack to penetrate deep into the British positions undetected. Between 21st March and 5th April the attack advanced some 40 miles in areas in the hope of capturing Amiens. But by this time their supply lines were dangerously stretched - stretched, moreover, across the shattered terrain of the old Somme battlefield, an area of 25 miles, which they had deliberately laid waste themselves the previous spring. On April the 5th Ludendorff, the German Commander, called off the operation.

In July the Germans launched another attack in Champagne causing a bulge in the lines, but the French made a counter-attack with masses of light tanks, forcing the Germans into a hasty retreat in that section.

Having recovered the initiative, the British, Australian and Canadian forces attacked with 450 tanks, striking the Germans with maximum surprise on August 8th and overwhelming the German divisions who had failed to entrench themselves since the recent occupation of the Michael Bulge. The 4th Army advanced steadily taking 21,000 prisoners, halting only when reaching the old battlefields of 1916. Several German divisions simply collapsed, fleeing or surrendering. Lundendorff stated that this was a black day for Germany and the war should be ended. The British suffered 20,000 casualties and Harry Lines was possibly one of them.

Those long uneven lines
Standing as patiently
As if they were stretched outside
The Oval or Villa Park
The crowns of hats, the sun
On moustached archaic faces
Grinning as if it were all
An August Bank Holiday lark;
And the shut shops, the bleached
Established names on the sunblinds,
The farthings and sovereigns,
And dark-clothed children at play
Called after kings and queens,
The tin advertisements
For cocoa and twist, and the pubs
Wide open all day;

And the countryside not caring
The place-names all hazed over
With flowering grasses, and fields
Shadowing Domesday lines
Under wheats' restless silence;
The differently-dressed servants
With tiny rooms in huge houses,
The dust behind limousines;
Never such innocence,
Never before or since,
As changed itself to past
Without a word - the men
Leaving the gardens tidy,
The thousands of marriages
Lasting a little while longer:
Never such innocence again.

Philip Larkin

Orival Wood Cemetery Flesquieres. France.

This is a small cemetery holding 300 graves with 20 German graves at the rear

Walter Elijah Ludlam.

Rank.	Private
Regiment.	Royal Welsh Fusiliers
Unit.	1st Battalion
Service No.	19458
Date of Death.	25th September 1915
Age.	21
Memorial.	Loos Memorial
	Panel 50 to 52. No Known Grave

The Battle of Loos

Walter was in the area of the battle when he died.

The battle was conducted by the French and British in 1915 and was a major offensive on the Western Front. The attack began on 25th September when 250,000 shells were fired. The Allies had supremacy of numbers of men but the terrain was difficult to cross and the men were fatigued. Once the bombardment had finished 5,100 cylinders of chlorine gas were to be used. Unfortunately the release of the gas had mixed results, in places the wind blew the gas back resulting in 2,632 British casualties.

The first day saw significant progress capturing Loos and moving on towards Lens. Supply and reserve problems brought the attack to a halt. The Germans poured in reserves and the British forces were decimated by machine guns as they tried to further advance, and after a renewed attack with heavy losses the offensive was called off.

During the battle the British suffered 50,000 casualties, and the Germans 25,000. Such losses without gain are hard to imagine.

Loos Memorial. France.

Harold Marsh.

Rank.	Second Lieutenant
Regiment.	Royal Fusiliers
Unit.	5th Battalion. Attached to 3rd Battalion
Date of Death.	4th October 1918
Age.	21
Cemetery.	Prospect Hill Cemetery, Gouy
Grave.	II. D. 13.

Harold was the son of Mr. and Mrs. Richard Marsh of 131, The Marsh, Blythe Bridge, Stoke on Trent. He started Army life as a private and worked his way up to Second Lieutenant.

<u>The Western Front at the time of Harold's death.</u>

The 4th day of October 1918 was the date of Harold's death. This was near the end of the war and he was probably killed in the Battle of Hindenburg. In March 1918 the Germans launched a massive attack using 6,000 guns; the attack was called the Second Battle of the Somme. The Germans advanced 40 miles in places but eventually came to a halt. Further attacks were made but were checked by counter attacks. The Germans were to end up with casualties of 800,000 men. Meanwhile the Allies were now receiving U.S. Troops at a rate of 300,000 men per month.

The Germans then attacked again in July but it came to nothing. The Allies attacked in August taking 21,000 prisoners and inflicting as many casualties, with only 20,000 casualties to itself. Several German divisions simply collapsed. The German commander Ludendorff stated that the war now must end. The Germans made a defensive line called the Hindenburg Line, which was heavily fortified with barbed wire with many concrete bunkers and pillboxes with machine guns all along; a last line of defence. The Battle of Hindenburg was against this line and it was not breached until late 1918. It was probably in this battle where Harold died.

Was not a time to send a man to die.
Of course, to go on any day is sad
But when the working week is done
And lads at home are having fun
Without a care, in summer sun, on Saturday
          - that's bad.

Long after summer's radiant bloom
Has given way to winter gloom
And earth lies frozen under snow,
When larks no longer sing on high,
Is time enough for men to die.
But on the day that heralds in October - pray, no.

Amidst the weekday toil and strife
Would seem an ideal time to quit this life.
Perhaps on Sundays when the dawn breaks grey
Or as the shades of darkness fall,
God may decide to make his call,
But not to soldiers who are young -
         ……….in sunshine on a Saturday

         Cedric Berrill   1986

Prospect Hill. France.

Samuel Matkin.

Rank.	Corporal
Regiment.	Northumberland Fusiliers
Unit.	2nd Battalion
Service No.	16605
Date of Death.	10th September 1916
Cemetery.	Struma Military Cemetery
Grave.	V.E.3.

Samuel was born in Derby.

The 2nd Battalion, Northumberland Fusiliers was involved in the Salonika Campaign which was regarded as a side-show compared to the Western Front. It is possible that Samuel was wounded or killed during this campaign and brought to the Casualty Clearing Station at Struma as he is buried in the Military Cemetery there.

The Struma Heights and Valley were prime locations. The area had a large amount of barbed wire laid down and was known as "The Birdcage". Many of the smaller countries, such as Austria, Bulgaria, Rumania and Turkey, together with Russia, tried to gain influence here.

To save your world you asked this man to die;
Would this man, could he see you now, ask why?

W. H. Auden

Struma Military Cemetery. Greece.

William Henry Mills.

Rank.	Private
Regiment.	Sherwood Foresters (Notts and Derby Regiment)
Unit.	1st Battalion
Service No.	6338
Date of Death.	9th December 1915
Age.	35
Cemetery.	Sailly-sur-la-Lys Canadian Cemetery
Grave.	II. C. 76.

William was the husband of Odessa Mills and lived at 9 Sleights Lane, Pinxton.
He enlisted at Derby.

William died on the 9th December 1915 when the enemy shelled trenches near Erquinhem.

Report from local paper.

Following intimations from several sources, the wife and relations of Private W. H. Mills, 1st Battalion Sherwood Foresters, who lived at No 9 Sleights Lane, Pinxton, have now received official information confirming his death. Private Mills was 35 years old and joined the British Expeditionary Force shortly after the war commenced. He had been home once on leave in August last and it was very singular that his last letter home stating that all was well should bear the very date on which he was killed.

In a letter to his widow dated December 1915, Private C. Keyes states: I am writing a few lines to inform you that your husband was wounded by a shell. He was at once sent to the hospital, and I much regret to say that in spite of every attention he died about six o-clock in the evening the same day. I cannot say how grieved myself and the whole of his company are. He was held in great esteem by all the officers and men of the Brigade's Headquarters staff and I can assure you we have felt the blow greatly. We realize that nothing we can say can lessen your grief, but it may comfort you to know that he died respected by his comrades and on my own and my comrade's behalf please accept our heartfelt sympathy.

Private Mills enlisted when he was 18 years old, serving in the Boer War of 1899-1902 with the No. 4 Company 28th Mounted Infantry.
William was present at the action at Boschbult 31st March 1902, South Africa.
Transferred from H Company WEF 1st October 1902, when serving in Hong Kong he was awarded the clasps Cape Colony and Orange Free State, Transvaal.

Sailly-sur-La-Lys Canadian Cemetery. France.

The Village of Sailly-sur-La-Lys lies 7 kilometres west of Armentières

Peter Naylor.

Rank.	Sapper
Regiment.	Royal Engineers
Unit.	172nd Company
Service No.	112859
Date of Death.	24th October 1916
Age.	37
Cemetery.	Ecoivres Military Cemetery, Mont-St.Eloi
Grave.	III. H. 14.

Peter Naylor enlisted in Nottingham. He was born at 5 Kirkstead Row Pinxton the son of William and Mary Naylor and brother to John. Peter's wife Eliza had eight children: Mary, Elizabeth, Reuben, Peter, Lilian, Esther, Rose and Joseph.

Article from the local paper announcing his death.

I have to announce that official information has been received of the death on which had been rumoured of Private Peter Naylor of the Royal Engineers "British Expeditionary Force". The deceased was previously a worker at Pinxton Colliery. Several letters had been received by his wife including one from Sergeant A. Guest on behalf of his N.C.O. and company.
Prior to enlistment the deceased was employed at the Pinxton Colliery.

The war on the Western Front bogged down into siege conditions by November 1914 and both sides needed a breakthrough. It was not long before the ancient art of mining was remembered and used effectively.
Sir Henry Rawlinson requested a special Battalion to assist in mining. Therefore the "Clay Kickers" who had been employed in mining the London Underground were seconded, and suitable personnel i.e. miners were recruited.
The 172nd Tunnelling Company was first employed in the Bluff / St Eloi area at Ypres, Hill 60 in 1915 and later to various areas along the front line before being moved to Vimy where it was attached to the Royal Canadian Regiment. The Germans held the high ground of the ridge which was known as Hill 145. The first battle of Vimy Ridge took place in 1915. The French 10th Army began a slow stubborn year long advance up the Ridge which ended in February 1916 when the French troops were urgently needed to stop the German slaughter at Verdun. It was then relieved by the British Army. No sooner had they settled

in, needing to brave the hardship of the cold, wet spring, when they were faced with a hurricane of mine explosions which were carefully, violently and successfully orchestrated by the German defenders to throw the newly arrived force back down the slope of the ridge. It was October 1916, at the base of the ridge, that the British were relieved by the Canadian Corps. The Germans kept up the pressure with relentless attacks and the morale of the soldiers plummeted. The psychological impact by the mining was devastating; the soldiers in the front line could hear the Germans coming at them, the noise from the picks and shovels being carried long distances underground, as did the placing of explosive charges under the front line.

By the autumn of 1916, 33 Companies could field 24,000 miner soldiers and Peter Naylor was one of them, and would have been instrumental in the digging of the Grange Tunnel at Vimy. Peter was killed in the early stages of tunnelling and most probably his body was brought in from the front line by the French Military Tramway to be buried at Ecoivres Military Cemetery, where many French and British soldiers were buried. After this time very ferocious fighting took place around Vimy Ridge. Eventually the ridge was taken by the Canadians on Easter Monday 1917 in a famous battle where many Canadians were killed.

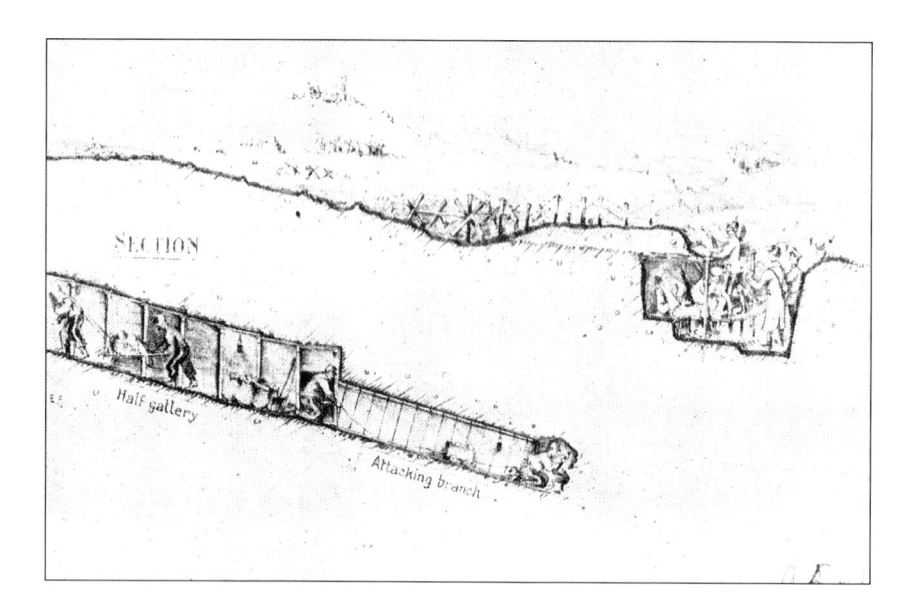

Sappers digging under enemy lines to set explosives

Ecoivres Military Cemetery. Mont-St.Eloi. France.

Lionel Nicholls.

Rank.	Private
Regiment.	Canadian Infantry (Manitoba Regiment)
Unit.	78th Battalion
Service No.	288218.
Date of Death.	10th August 1918
Memorial.	Vimy Memorial No Known Grave

Report from local paper.

The sad news has just been officially conveyed to Mrs. Clara Blundell of Albany House, Pinxton of her son Private Lionel Nicholls 288218, 78th Battalion Canadians whose death in action in France occurred on the 10th August. Amongst his many friends he was held in high esteem, and the following extract from his officer's letter emphasises the facts that the true qualities of manhood he possessed endured him to his associates whilst on service.

Lieutenant J.P. Ryan, 16th platoon writes from France: We can hardly realize that he has left our midst. He was one of the best boys I have ever had to work with me, a gentleman and a favourite with all. Regarding his end, it may be some comfort to know that he died instantly. I was quite close to him at the time. He was carefully buried, a cross erected and the location recorded. It was an inspiring sight to see him lead his section over the top, keeping in the lead all the time until he fell. He is a boy to be proud of and a credit to everyone. With regards to his work, nothing but good words can I say. When things were blue he always kept up a smile, which soon won over the admiration of the other boys. My intentions were to make him an N.C.O. but I believe he would rather be one of the boys.

Vimy Memorial. France.

Thomas Noakes.

Rank.	Private
Regiment.	King's Own Yorkshire Light Infantry
Unit.	1st / 4th Battalion
Service No.	3557
Date of Death.	7th July 1916
Memorial.	Thiepval Memorial

Pier and Face 11 C and 12 A. No Known Grave

A history of the battle in which Thomas died

G. Palmer was put in command when the K.O.Y.L.I. took over the Nab Valley sub. sector from the 6th Buffs where the shelling was very heavy, especially in Authuille Wood. There had been 4 men killed and 48 wounded.

The 4th K.O.Y.L.I. arrived in their assembly trenches in Aveluy Wood at 3 a.m. on the morning of the 1st July. The 49th division being in reserve that day did not participate in the first great advance, but at 6 p.m. orders were received which placed the 4th and 5th Battalions at the disposal of the 96 Infantry Brigade in their attack on Thiepval. By 8.15 next morning they were left holding trenches in Thiepval Wood, a position that had been won within the first line of the enemy trenches (known as the A line) on the previous day. They were then shelled heavily in this position until 5 a.m. the next morning. During the night companies of the 4th K.O.Y.L.I. were sent forward to relieve the 5th.
On the 4th July there was a bombardment, followed by rapid fire and under cover of a thunderstorm the enemy launched an attack. The 4th had Captain H. C. Fraser and 45 other ranks wounded. The 5th July was occupied in bombing attacks on both sides. After an attack, Captain Plackett, who had been leading, was reported missing; 3 other ranks were killed and 20 wounded.

On the 6th July the 4th relieved the 5th in the A line trenches. At 12.30 on the 7th July the enemy opened an intense bombardment of the British front line and the A line. A furious fight with bombs ensued till 6.30 a.m. Casualties were numerous. Major Moorhouse, who already had won the D.S.O., was in command of the sector. He was wounded at 4a.m., but held on until he was forced by loss of blood to retire. Captain Fraser took command and continued the fight, when at 6.30 a.m., having no more bombs, he was forced to retire his men to the communicating trenches, which he continued to hold with the 4th and 5th. He had only 35 men left of the two companies. The casualties numbered 20 killed and 181 wounded. The battalion was relieved at 9a.m.

Over the Top: Attacking out of the trenches.

Thiepval Memorial. France.

Henry Parnham.

Rank.	Private
Regiment.	Royal Welsh Fusiliers
Unit.	1st Battalion
Service No.	19622
Date of Death.	4th November 1915
Age.	22
Cemetery.	Boulogne Eastern Cemetery
Grave.	VIII. C. 54.

Henry Parnham

Henry was the son of Hezekiah and Emily Parnham of Town Street, Pinxton, Derbyshire. Henry's father originated from Cropwell Bishop and his mother from Collingham. Henry had a brother Frederick. He was a native of Clay Cross Derbyshire.

Article from local paper.

After a period of six weeks intense suffering Private Henry Parnham of Pinxton, aged 22, succumbed to wounds on Thursday November 4th. Along with a number of chums he enlisted in the Royal Welsh Fusiliers on January 5th this year, joining the regiment on January 9th and crossing to France on June 22nd. Events proved quite satisfactory up to the never to be forgotten day of September 25th when he was wounded at Loos. Although wounded on the Saturday he lay on the battlefield until Monday morning and it was Tuesday before his uniform was removed revealing wounds caused by an explosive bullet.
The father and Miss Baxter visited him at No. 11 General Hospital at Boulogne on Sunday October 3rd, and not withstanding the fact that he had both thigh bones broken a favourable prognosis was reported and he entertained hopes of being home at Christmas.

On October 14th Mr. Parnham received a letter stating that another operation had been performed, which had not proved satisfactory and news of his death was received from the Records Office Shrewsbury on Friday last. This was followed by a letter from the Matron of the hospital, stating that Henry had been more or less unconscious since the operation through the poisonous condition of his wounds that had left him in a poorly state. The interment took place at the English Cemetery Boulogne on Friday November 5th.

Letter to Miss Baxter, Henry's fiancée, from the Army Chaplain, dated November 5th:

Please accept my deepest sympathy to you and his family in your greatest trouble. May God help you to bear it bravely and proudly, for pride in the noble sacrifice which he has made for his country is sadly right, and may, I hope in part, soften the blow. I am not very sorry that you did not cross over again, for you would have seen him only when he was sinking gradually, and you will like to remember as you knew him in happier days, in the vigour of manhood.
The funeral was attended by a guard of honour from a British Regiment, and everything was done with simple reverence. The grave is marked by a simple cross, which will be replaced by another of polished wood, with his name and regiment. All the graves are similarly marked and are looked after. The number of the grave is 2750 and can easily be identified after the war.

Other letters of condolence were received by Miss Baxter from Mr. H. Morley, Army Scripture Reader and Ensign Mary Booth of the Salvation Army.

> The firefly haunts were lighted yet,
> As we scaled the top of the parapet;
> But the east grew pale to another fire,
> As our bayonets gleamed by the foeman's wire;
> And the sky was tinged with gold and grey,
> And under our feet the dead men lay,
> Stiff by the loop-holed barricade;
> Food of the bomb and the hand-grenade;
> Still the slushy pool and mud –
> Ah, the path we came was a path of blood,
> When we went to Loos in the morning.
>   Patrick MacGill

Boulogne Eastern Cemetery. France.

James William Pollock.

Rank.	Lance Corporal
Regiment.	Sherwood Foresters (Notts and Derby Regiment)
Unit.	7th Battalion (Robin Hood Rifles)
Service No.	268780
Date of Death.	18th October 1918
Age.	36
Cemetery.	Hamburg Cemetery, Germany
Grave.	I. B. 12

James was the son of Mrs. M. E. Pollock of King Street, Pinxton, Derbyshire and James Neth Pollock of Skibbereen, County Cork. Born Buttevant, County Cork.

Lance Corporal Pollock died as a prisoner of war

O valiant hearts who to your glory came
Through dust of conflict and through battle flame;
Tranquil you lie, your knightly virtue proved,
Your memory hallowed in the land you loved.

Hamburg Cemetery. Germany.

Joseph Pritchard.

Rank.	Private
Regiment.	Royal Welsh Fusiliers
Unit.	8th Battalion
Service No.	19459
Date of Death.	17th August 1915
Age.	19
Memorial.	Helles Memorial
	Panel 77 to 80. No Known Grave

Joseph was the son of Joseph and Elizabeth Pritchard of Pevril House, Pinxton, Derbyshire. He worked at the local colliery.

Report from local paper.

Pinxton Athlete Killed in Action.

Member of the Sutton Harriers

Unhappily the fears which were entertained for the late Private Joseph Pritchard of Pinxton have proved to be well founded, for the official intimation was received by his parents on Friday evening last to the effect that he was killed in action in the Dardanelles on August 17th. He was 19 years of age and the second son of Mr. and Mrs. Joseph Pritchard of Pevril House, Pinxton. He enlisted in the Royal Welsh Fusiliers on January 2nd and commenced training at Wrexham, going out with the Mediterranean Expeditionary Force on June 28th. About a month prior to the date he was killed in action he was slightly wounded, and had just sufficiently recovered to be able to take part in operations again, only to meet death in a bayonet charge.

Previous to enlisting he was a miner and his practical interest in athletics generally had welded a circle of friends by no means limited to the parish boundary, who where most keenly interested in the welfare of the lad, and the sad news came as a heavy blow to all. Equally successful with the gloves, on the turf and at football, Joe was prominent amongst the local lads as a scholar.

His sprint racing collected for him over 100 prizes, and just previous to joining the colours he established good records in the one mile flat. Whilst at Wrexham, his club, Sutton Harriers, conferred the honour of selecting him to represent the Harriers in the Novice Championship run at Yardley in March but unfortunately illness prevented his appearance. During a training period Pritchard created quite a sensation in the camp where his abilities as an all-round athlete were quickly recognised by the officers and men. Each of the contests he entered whilst at camp brought further credit to the lad.

On Easter Monday he came in first in the 220 yards and the 440 yards and one mile flat race. He also ran in the relay race being one of the winning team and came off with the much coveted medal for the best all round athlete. These successes found for him a place in the Invitation races organized by the officers and held at Pirbright and Wrexham where he again came in first in the half and one mile.

That a lad of this stamp should desire to do service in the army can easily be understood; he enjoyed the life, the accompanying danger acting as a tonic rather than exercising a deterrent influence and it is deeply regrettable that a promising career should be cut off so short.

Helles Memorial. Turkey.

James Pritchett.

Rank.	Driver
Regiment.	Royal Field Artillery
Unit.	66th Division. Ammunition Col.
Service No.	219135
Date of Death.	26th July 1917
Age.	33
Cemetery.	Coxyde Military Cemetery
Grave.	III. A. 24.

James was born at Aslockton, Notts. in 1883 and was the second son of William and Mary Pritchett.

James had two brothers, Henry and Walter, and two sisters, Emma and Lois.
At the age of 18 James was working as a farm servant at The White House, Scarrington. He then resided at Pinxton and worked at the local colliery.

Killed in Action. Flanders.

Local Report.

Official information has now been received of the death whilst in action of Driver Jas Pritchett R. F. A. aged 33, which occurred on July 26th. Deceased, who before joining up was employed at the Pinxton Collieries, leaves a widow and five children. Amongst the several letters of sympathy received was one from his Captain and one from the Rev. A Walters, Chaplain.

> HE whom this scroll commemorates was numbered among those who, at the call of King and Country, left all that was dear to them, endured hardness, faced danger, and finally passed out of the sight of men by the path of duty and self-sacrifice, giving up their own lives that others might live in freedom. Let those who come after see to it that his name be not forgotten.
>
> 219135, DVR., James PRITCHETT
>
> Royal Horse Artillery and Royal Field Artillery
> Killed in action, France & Flanders, 26/07/17
> Born: Aslockton, Notts, Enlisted: Nottingham.

J. Pritchett's Death Scroll

Coxyde Military Cemetery. Belgium.

Dennis Revill.

Rank.	Private
Regiment.	Sherwood Foresters (Notts and Derby Regiment)
Unit.	1st Battalion
Service No.	16413
Date of Death.	5th March 1917
Age.	24
Memorial.	Thiepval Memorial
	Pier and Face 10C, 10D and 11A No Known Grave

Dennis was the son of Mr. and Mrs. M. Revill of 48 Kirkstead Row, Pinxton.
He enlisted at Mansfield, Notts and joined the battalion on the 28th April 1915. He was wounded on the 29th May 1916.

Dennis was killed in an attack on an enemy trench near Andover.

An account of the battle in which Dennis Revill died

At 5.15 a.m. our barrage opened up. Within 3 minutes the enemy got his counter barrage down, practically before all of our men were able to move forward; 9 men of one platoon where hit by one shell. The remainder of the platoon reorganized and the sergeant led them forward through the enemy fire into the front trenches.

Our men entered the enemy's trenches as the Germans were scrambling to get out. The assaulting battalions went straight onto the Pallas Trench, and our moppers-up remained behind to clear up. The enemy had prepared several bombing posts and these were obstacles that had to be overcome. In several cases there was hand to hand fighting for these posts, causing the loss of 1 officer and 7 men. Dennis, sadly, was one of the men killed. Seven Germans were taken by surprise and when ordered to surrender, they immediately did so.

Thiepval Memorial. France.

John James Revill.

Rank.	Private
Regiment.	Sherwood Foresters (Notts and Derby Regiment)
Unit.	1st Battalion
Service No.	9816
Date of Death.	29th April 1915
Age.	24
Cemetery.	Rue-Petillon Military Cemetery
Grave.	I. D. 45.

John was the son of Matthew and Mary Revill and lived at 24 Kirkstead Row, Pinxton.
He was the husband of Elizabeth Ann Revill. John enlisted on the 6th August 1914.
Killed in action by German shellfire when in reserve billets.

Report from local paper.

Although it is barely four months since Private J. J. Revill No 9816 of the Notts and Derbyshire Regiment returned to the trenches, official intimation has now been received by his family, who reside in the Kirkstead Row, Pinxton, that he was killed in action on the 29th April. Apart from his enforced inaction through a damaged shoulder about six weeks prior to Christmas, Private Revill has been in the thick of the fighting since the war commenced. The information was first received from his brother Dennis, who was with him in the trenches at Ypres at the time. Private Revill, who was the eldest son of Mr. Matthew and Mrs. Mary Revill, of Kirkstead Row, Pinxton, leaves a widow and one child.

William Rigby.

Rank.	Sergeant
Regiment.	Royal Welsh Fusiliers
Unit.	8th Battalion
Service No.	19461
Date of Death.	9th September 1916
Age.	20
Cemetery.	Amara War Cemetery
Grave.	IX. F. 18.

William was the son of William and Annie Rigby of Park Lane, Pinxton, Derbyshire.
He had two brothers Wilfred and Alfred and sister Hena - all born in Bolton.

Now virtually forgotten, the British Army also fought in Mesopotamia (now Iraq) against the Turks, originally with the intention of defending British oil interests. It was another disease – ridden campaign where many died from dysentery, beriberi and diarrhoea.

A description of the battle of Amara and Kut where William Rigby probably died:

The capture of the important Turkish Base of Amara was a remarkable triumph for the British. Amara was a commercial centre situated on the Tigris River. At the British base in Basra, Iraq, there was assembled a fleet of 500 flat bottomed boats for the expedition, each craft bore as much artillery as it could safely bear, machine guns and mounted guns amongst them. The attack on Amara was won by an advance force of 100 men that persuaded the garrison of 2,000 Turkish soldiers to surrender.

The commanders decided to push further up the Tigris in spite of tightly stretched supply lines, which caused disaster through to 1917. Eventually 10,000 men had to surrender to the Turks. Reinforcements of Anglo and Indian troops brought up the strength to 150,000 men, and better supply lines were made. The Allies attacked in the battle of Kut on two fronts and were successful in pushing the Turks back some 100km past Kut and onto Baghdad, which fell the following month.

The Soldier
If I should die, think only this of me:
That there's some corner of a foreign field
That is for ever England. There shall be
In that rich earth a richer dust concealed;
A dust whom England bore, shaped, made aware,
Gave once her flowers to love, her ways to roam,
A body of England's, breathing English air,
Washed by the rivers, blest by suns of home.   Rupert Brooke

Amara War Cemetery Mesopotamia (now Iraq).

RUE DU BOIS.

25th.   Weather fine. Artillery on both sides fairly active. Battalion in billets.

26th.   Weather fine. Artillery on both sides fairly active. Battalion in billets. Nothing to report. One casualty accidentally wounded.

27th.   * Casualties, 7 previously reported missing now reported wounded. 1 previously reported missing now in hospital. Weather fine, enemy shelled "C" Coy billet about 5 p.m. Billet rather badly knocked about and a fire started but was soon extinguished by our men.
Casualties, 3 men in R.I.R. who were passing wounded.
6 p.m. Battalion relieved the 2nd Northamptonshire Regt. in No.2 Section trenches. Quick relief. Pte. LIMERICK was killed at CELLAR FARM.
* 1 previously reported missing now reported killed.

NO. 2 SECTION TRENCHES.

28th.   Weather perfect. About 10.30 a.m. four hostile aeroplanes flew over our lines. Artillery on both sides very active all day. 2nd Lieut. STOTT and 194 other ranks joined the battalion in the trenches. Out of these 194, 105 were men who had been out here before.

29th.   Weather perfect. Enemy shelled our Reserve Company's billets about 3.30 p.m. Roughly 20 shells fell in batches of three. 1 killed and 1 wounded.
2nd Lieut. E.F. MILLAR and 2nd Lieut. R.P. STONEHAM joined the battalion.

Report from Notts and Derby's War Diary

Rue-Petillon Military Cemetery, Fleurbaix. France.

The village of Fleurbaix lies 5 kilometres south west of Armentières

Frank Rodgers.

Rank.	Private
Regiment.	Royal Welsh Fusiliers
Unit.	9th Battalion
Service No.	19969
Date of Death.	22nd August 1917
Age.	30
Cemetery.	Coulomby Churchyard, France
Grave.	South-East corner of churchyard

Frank Rodgers

Born North Wingfield, Derbyshire.
Resided at 105 Park Lane, Pinxton, Derbyshire.
Enlisted at Mansfield.

Report from local paper.

Mrs. E. Rodgers of 105 Park Lane, Pinxton, has been informed of the death of her husband Private Frank Rodgers. He enlisted in the Royal Welsh Fusiliers in January 1915, and was drafted to France in the following August. In November 1915 he was wounded in the head, but did not return to England. From February 1916 he had been attached to the Trench Mortar Battery and according to the letter received from the chaplain, it was whilst in training behind the firing line that he was accidentally killed, one of the shells bursting prematurely on leaving the mortar. He was hit by a fragment and killed immediately. Private Rodgers, who was 30 years old, leaves a widow and two children.

The accident must have happened near to the Coulomby Roman Catholic Church in France, as he is the only British soldier to be buried there. The monument in the churchyard only shows the names of French Troops.

Coulomby Church. France.

Coulomby Church is in the centre of the village which is situated 15 kilometres west of St. Omer, just south of the N42 to Boulogne and contains one Commonwealth burial, that of Frank Rodgers.

Edward Rohun.

Rank.	Sergeant
Regiment.	Royal Welsh Fusiliers
Unit.	24th (Denbighshire Yeomanry) Battalion
Service No.	19466
Date of Death.	15th April 1917
Age.	24
Memorial.	Mikra Memorial Lost at Sea

Edward was at born at Broomhill, Hucknall. He lived in Park Lane Pinxton, enlisting at Mansfield.

He was on board the troopship SS Arcadian 26 miles NE from Milo in the Mediterranean when it was torpedoed by Submarine UC74 without warning and sank, and as a result he was drowned. 35 lives were lost. He had a brother and two sisters.

Report from local paper.

Information has just been received by Mrs. Rohun of Park Lane Pinxton of her husband Sergeant Edward Rohun to be missing and presumed drowned. He was 24 years of age, and his wife has one child. He enlisted in January 1915 and early distinguished himself gaining confidence and promotion rapidly and soon became a 1st Sergeant. He went out to France months ago and has been wounded twice.

His father is at present in France and his brother has been there 2 years.

Sergeant Rohun was in the Royal Welsh Fusiliers and was very popular in the Army and civilian life.

S.S. Arcadian

Edward in uniform

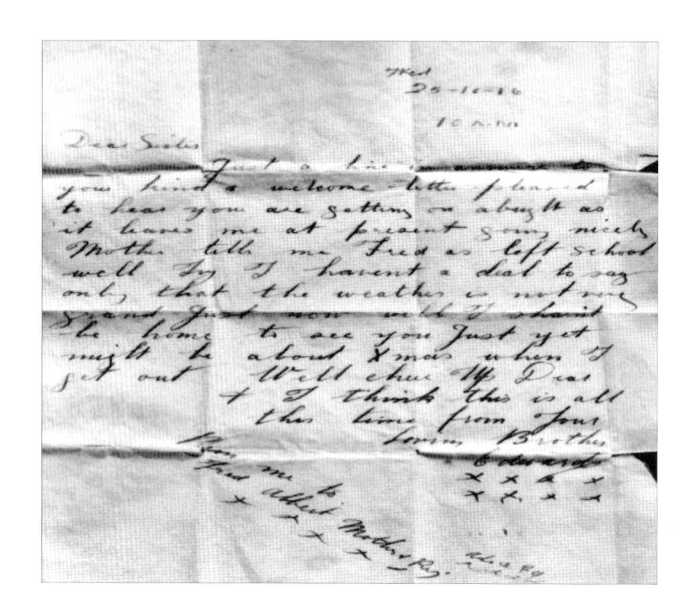

Letter from Edward to his sister

Mikra Memorial. Greece.

120

John Henry Savage.

Rank.	Private
Regiment.	Leicestershire Regiment
Unit.	2nd Battalion
Service No.	22899
Date of Death.	17th August 1916
Age.	23
Cemetery.	Amara War Cemetery
Grave.	III. B. 1.

John was the son of Henry and Julia Savage of Arthur Street, Pinxton, Derbyshire.

Born 20th April 1893. Died of dysentery in Mesopotamia.
John was one of six children and worked at Brookhill Colliery in the wood yard. He enlisted at Sutton in Ashfield.

J. Savage with his girl friend and her mother

Alec Street, John and Harry Savage

121

The Savage family   **J. Savage with his brother**

Family: Henry Father, Harry, Minnie, Mary Ann, John, Mother Julia, Charles on knee
Emily centre front.

Report from local paper.

The death took place on August 17th of Private John Henry Savage of Arthur Street, Pinxton. The deceased was 23 years old and single, and prior to enlisting was employed in the wood yard at Brookhill Colliery.

The news of his death was contained in the following letter from the Rev. J. H. H. MacNeill, Church of Scotland Chaplain with the Mesopotamian Expeditionary Force.

It is with the deepest sympathy and sorrow that I write to tell you of the death in hospital here of your son, Private John Savage. The news will have reached you by cable long before this letter gets home, but I know you wish to hear all that those who have been about him can tell you of him in the last days. He came down from the front very ill with dysentery. I got from the hospital a note that his condition was critical on the night of the 15th, and I went round and saw him that night about half past nine. He was sick and restless and weary after his journey, but he could talk all right, and he gave me your address and told me to send his love to you. We had a short prayer together, into which he entered with full understanding and feeling, as we asked the Great Father to spare him if it might be his will, and to take him into his great keeping and care. I saw your son again on the morning of the 16th. He was in much the same condition, and we knew he was very ill. I could only once more speak a blessing to him as I left him. He passed away that night about nine-o-clock. All the doctors, nurses and orderlies did their best, and I know it will comfort you to hear that at the end he was in kind and skilful hands, seeking to ease and help and heal him.

We had his funeral the following afternoon. He was buried in the cemetery at Amara, and he was laid to rest with all reverence and honour. After the service, in which we remembered the friends far away in their home of loss and mourning, a party of soldiers from the garrison here presented arms in a last salute to him, and the bugle sounded the Last Post over another soldier's grave. He lies not alone, but is one of a very noble company who have given their lives, like him, in the service of their country and of humanity. It is sad to lose our soldiers by sickness, but I know that the spirit of their service has been the same as that of those who have fallen in battle, and their memory is equally worthy of our honour and pride. It is with the greatest of sympathy that I write to you, and I pray that, He, who gave his own son to die for us all, may be with you as a present help while you are mourning for the son you gave to die for his country and his fellow men.

J. Savage's grave

Amara War Cemetery. Mesopotamia (now Iraq).

John Searson.

Rank.	Private
Regiment.	Duke of Wellington's (West Riding Regiment)
Unit.	2nd Battalion
Service No.	25510
Date of Death.	24th October 1918
Age.	35
Cemetery.	Verchain British Cemetery, Verchain-Maugre
Grave.	B.14.

John was the son of Mrs. S. Keeling of 88 Park Lane, Pinxton. He enlisted at Pontefract.

Report from the local paper.

After being in the army nearly three years news has been received that Private John Searson of 88 Park Lane, Pinxton, was killed in action on October 24th. He was 35 years of age. His mother Mrs. Keeling has received the following letter:

"Allow me to express my deepest sympathy in informing you that your son, Private John Searson, was killed in action on October the 24th. We had occupied a quarry in our advance when your son was shot in the head. He died at once. He was one of the best of men and soldiers we had in the company. All his comrades and myself deeply feel for you in your great sorrow. We miss him greatly and we only have the consolation of knowing that he died in the great cause and doing his duty to the last".

Verchain British Cemetery is in the village of Verchain-Maugre in the Department of the Nord about 13 kilometres South of Valenciennes, and 1.5 kilometres North-west of the village on the north side of the road to Monchaux and Thiant.

The British Cemetery was made by the fighting units of the 4th Division in the period 24th October to the 1st November, 1918. There are now over 100 1914-18 war casualties commemorated in this cemetery which covers an area of 344 square metres and is enclosed by a stone rubble wall.

Verchain Cemetery. France.

F. Sharman.

Rank.	Rifleman
Regiment.	King's Royal Rifle Corps
Unit.	25th Battalion
Service No.	R/58025
Date of Death.	29th October 1918
Age.	27
Cemetery.	Estaires Communal Cemetery Extension
Grave.	V.F.8.

Son of James and Charlotte. He was born in Luffenham, Rutland then moved to Pinxton.
First enlisted at Mansfield into the Notts and Derby Regiment.
Transferred to Labour Corps. Service No 406052. Later transferred to the King's Royal Rifle Corps.
Estaires, where F. Sharman was buried, is a town and commune in the Department of the Nord, about 11 kilometres west of Armentières The cemetery is on the eastern outskirts of the town.
Estaires town was occupied by French cavalry on 15th October 1914, and passed at once into British hands.
In April 1918 the Germans on their last great attack, "Michael", along the Western Front captured the town on the 10 April after obstinate defence by the 50th Northumbrian Division.
The town was finally retaken by British troops in the autumn and it is probable that F.Sharman died in this action.
The Town of Estaires was a Field Ambulance centre then an Australian Casualty Clearing Station.
Estaires Communal Extension Cemetery was used for British burials from 1914 to June 1917 and two burials from the British attack in 1918.

> Futility
> Move him into the sun-
> Gently its touch awoke him once,
> At home, whispering of fields half-sown.
> Always it woke him, even in France,
> Until this morning and this snow.
> If anything might rouse him now
> The kind old sun will know.
>
> Wilfred Owen

Estaires Communal Cemetery Extension. France.

Frederick Edward Shawcroft.

Rank.	Driver
Regiment.	Royal Field Artillery
Unit.	"C" Battalion 152nd Brigade
Service No.	8253
Date of Death.	26th July 1918
Age.	22
Cemetery.	Vauxbuin French National Cemetery
Grave.	I. D. 15.

Frederick was the son of Mrs. Emma Shawcroft, of 42 Wharf Road, Pinxton, Derbyshire. He was born at Worksop. Enlisted at Mansfield.

Local Report.

Mr. and Mrs. G Shawcroft 42 Wharf Road Pinxton, have received official intimation of the death on the 26th July of their youngest son Driver Frederick Edward Shawcroft, aged 22 years. Mr. and Mrs. Shawcroft have previously lost a son in the war, another has been wounded and discharged, and two others are still serving. Driver F.E. Shawcroft enlisted three years ago, and has been out in France about two years.

The following letter has been received from the Chaplain:

I regret to say your son was killed in his sleep by a shell on July 26th, in the early hours of the morning with another soldier who had been sleeping beside him. It was my sad duty to lay them both to rest side by side.
I am afraid I am not allowed to tell you where but you can find out by writing to the Director of Graves Registration, and enquiries to War Office, Winchester House, St James Square, London. S.W. If you want a photograph of the grave you can get one, probably by applying at the same address.
The news coming so suddenly must be a terrible blow. You must remember the Lord's Words. I am he that liveth, and have powers of hell and death. He is caring for your boy, He is caring for you, and will bring you both together at the last, never again to be parted.

Frederick Shawcroft was at the second battle of Marne, which was a large German offensive in France. The battle was designed to draw the Allies from Belgium.

The battle was launched on July 15th 1918. The attack to the west of Rheims was eventually halted on 17th July. The Allies launched a counter offensive on 18th July, advancing 5 miles on the first day. On the 20th July the Germans ordered a retreat and were back at the River Aisne by the 3rd August.

Frederick Shawcroft was killed in this area in this period. He is buried at the cemetery which is 4 miles south of the River Aisne.

No further large scale attempt was undertaken by the Germans to win the war.

A scene that would have been familiar to Driver Shawcroft

Vauxbuin French National Cemetery.

W.E. Slater.

Rank.	Private
Regiment.	Royal Warwickshire
Unit.	16th Battalion
Service No.	52219
Date of Death.	1st September 1918
Age.	19
Cemetery.	Favreuil British Cemetery
Grave.	I. B. 14.

Private Slater was the son of Thomas and Annie Maud Slater of 29 Kirkstead Rows, Pinxton.

Subsequent to the official intimation received by Mrs. Slater of 29 Kirkstead Rows of the death of her son, Private W. E. Slater, aged 19, the following letter was received from his officer:
"It is with the deepest regret that I have to inform you of the death of your son Private W. E. Slater 52219 who was killed in action during the recent advance. He was well liked by us all and in offering you my sincerest sympathy may I hope that you will be partly consoled by the fact that your boy died a soldier's death for his King and Country".
Prior to joining up the deceased was employed as an Engineer at Messrs Oakes.

An addition from the same local paper report.

To augment the funds for Christmas Parcels despatched to the Pinxton men serving with the colours, some £4 has been raised by the scholars of the girls' school by the sale of necklaces and spill holders made by the children. The money has been handed over to the Pinxton Nursing Association under whose auspices parcels have been dispatched each Christmas since the war started. Very valuable assistance has been rendered by Miss Hawley (headmistress), her staff and the scholars at the Pinxton Girls' School on many occasions on behalf of the soldiers and sailors. The many letters of thanks and appreciation received from the boys are evidence that their labours have not been in vain.

Favreuil British Cemetery. France.

Benjamin Smith.

Rank.	Private
Regiment.	Army Pay Corps
Unit.	Blackheath
Service No.	18548
Date of Death.	20th May 1918
Age.	38
Cemetery.	Rolleston-on-Dove, St Mary Churchyard, Staffordshire
Grave.	At south side of the church
Resided.	Cutts Street, Pinxton

Benjamin was the husband of Mary Lizzie and father of Sydney Arthur. Sydney, the son, died 27th August 1924, aged 9 years. Mary, his wife, died aged 79. All 3 are buried in St Mary's Rolleston in the same plot.

Benjamin was killed during an air raid over London by German Zeppelins dropping bombs on Sunday night 19/20th May 1918. He was an insurance agent before the war.

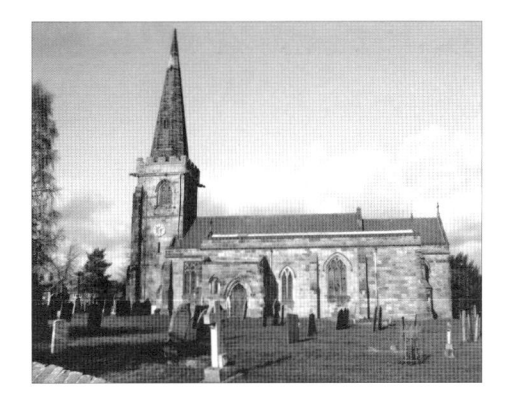

Rolleston-on-Dove Church

Benjamin Smith's headstone.

Henry Smith.

Rank.	Private
Regiment.	Lincolnshire Regiment
Unit.	8th Battalion
Service No.	16170
Date of Death.	20th October 1918
Age.	39
Cemetery.	Caudry British Cemetery
Grave.	Row F, No. 34.

Henry was born at Grantham in 1878. He married Jane Elizabeth Cundy in 1909. Jane was born at Arnold, Nottingham in 1879. They had three girls and four boys and resided at Pinxton. Henry enlisted at Ilkeston.
Killed in action in Flanders.

Jane Elizabeth Smith died on the 23rd November 1918, just 35 days after Henry. It is stated that she died of a broken heart. The girls went to live with an Auntie in Arnold, whilst the boys stayed in Pinxton with their Auntie Annie Smith who lived at the bottom end of Pinxton, near No. 2 Pit Lane. Auntie Annie, a devout Methodist, never married.

Jane Elizabeth's grave in Pinxton Churchyard

Jane Elizabeth Smith's grave, with an inscription on the side of the gravestone: Private Henry Smith Killed in Action 20th October 1918

Caudry was a German centre for medical units and a German cemetery extension until the 10th October 1918 when it was captured by the 37th division. Henry was probably involved in this battle. The cemetery was begun by the New Zealand division and was completed after the Armistice, when the bodies of two French and one Italian soldier were removed to other burial grounds. There are now over 700 war casualties commemorated in this site. Of these, over 50 are unidentified and 650 identified. Special memorials are erected to four soldiers and one airman from the United Kingdom known to be buried there. The cemetery covers an area of 2,770 square metres and is enclosed partly by a rubble wall.

Caudry is a town 10 kilometres east of Cambrai on the south side of the main road to Le Cateau, the cemetery being on the outskirts of the town. Caudry was in German hands from the 26th August 1914 until the 10th October 1918.

Caudry British Cemetery. France.

William Snowden.

Rank.	Private
Regiment.	Sherwood Foresters (Notts and Derby Regiment)
Unit.	1st Battalion
Service No.	13597
Date of Death.	14th January 1915
Age.	20
Memorial.	Le Touret Memorial
	Panel 26 and 27. No Known Grave

William was the son of Henry and Charlotte Snowden who resided at 7 Kirkstead Rows, Pinxton. He was born in Woodborough, Notts and enlisted on the 23rd December 1914.
Killed in action when serving in the line at La Gorgue, France.

Local report.

Pinxton mourns the loss of another of its soldier sons, for on Monday morning the brother of Private William Snowden residing at No.7 Kirkstead Row Pinxton received official intimation that he had been killed in action on January 14th. Soon after the outbreak of the war W. Snowden enlisted, joining the Notts and Derby C. Company, and found his way into the fighting line a fortnight before Christmas. In a communication from him a fortnight ago, he stated that he had been in the trenches for eight days, but he was quite well and hoped the war would soon be over so that he would be able to rejoin his Pinxton friends. He would have reached his 21st birthday had he lived until the 26th of February. Since leaving England his destination had not been made known to his brother. The letter heading simply giving his No. 13597 and the Company, Expeditionary Force, neither is it known in what engagement or at what place he was killed.

Le Touret Memorial. France.

Henry Stevens.

Rank.	Private
Regiment.	Sherwood Foresters (Notts and Derby Regiment)
Unit.	15th Battalion (Bantams)
Service No.	6457
Date of Death.	2nd September 1917
Age.	32
Cemetery.	Templeux-le-Guerard British Cemetery
Grave.	II. G. 2.

Templeux-le-Guerard is a Cemetery near the Belgian Border used for the casualties of the Battles of the Somme.

Henry was the son of William and Mary Ann Stevens of Marehay, Derby. Henry could not have been very tall as he had joined the Notts and Derby 15th Battalion, which took recruits below the service height of 5 foot 3 inches and was nicknamed the Bantams. It was formed at the end of 1914.
The battalion moved to France with the 35th Division in 1916, where it fought with great distinction and with heavy casualties in 1916 at the first battle of the Somme.
However, at the end of 1916 problems arose when trying to recruit men of a shorter stature, there were insufficient numbers to fill the demand.
The 15th Battalion was redesignated to a normal "service" battalion and fought as such until the end of the war. There can hardly be a Notts or Derby street or village that did not produce men to serve in the Notts and Derby, to eventually be called the Sherwood Foresters, 11,409 of whom did not return.

The activities of the 15th Battalion in the last month of Henry Stevens' life were as follows:
August 1917: In the early part of the month, spent at a camp near Lempire, the time was spent in training for an attack on the German lines called the Knoll.
August 19th: After a successful attack near Lempire they took enemy trenches, consolidated and built a bombing block. Casualties on that day were - 25 killed, 53 wounded, 5 missing.
August 20th: Relieved by the Gloucesters, moved to St Emilie.
August 24th: Relieved by the Cheshires at The Knoll; very heavy fighting and shelling-
19 killed, 44 wounded.
September 1st: Relieved the 17th Royal Scots in the Lempire sector, remaining in the front line trenches until 6th September. It was during this period that Henry was killed. The battalion was relieved by the 15th Cheshires and moved to billets in Lempire and Sand Bag Alley.

They lay there in their thousands
The last rays of sunlight
Catching the white of the gravestones
Lending a poignancy to the moment
Numbering in their thousands they lay
Deserving remembrance
And yet the scarred green fields are empty
Nothing remains here
The processions of people vanished with the years
Their sacrifice all but forgotten.

She stands there alone
At the edge of the silent place
And she is shocked
New wars brew and these forgotten men
Will play no part in them
The dead silence warn no ears but hers
In great halls in moments of great decision
What they fought for is forsaken
And by days end new gravestones
Appear on the blood red ground

A poem by a young girl visiting a War Cemetery in France in 2006

Templeux-le-Guerard British Cemetery. France.

Templeux-le-Guerard is a village 26 kilometres east of Peronne

Ben Stocks.
- Rank. Private
- Regiment. Royal Welsh Fusiliers
- Unit. 8th Battalion
- Service No. 19677
- Date of Death. 11th August 1915
- Age. 20
- Memorial. Helles Memorial
  Panel 77 to 80   No Known Grave

Soldiers at the front in Gallipoli

On the 6th August 1915, in Turkey, the Battle of Sari Bair commenced which was crucial to gain control of the central heights of the peninsular. Five divisions were entrusted to the battle; the objective was to take command of the Dardanelle Straights.

Diversionary attacks continued and seven Victoria Crosses were won with hand to hand fighting at Lone Pine. The Allied operation at Sari Bair had depended upon rapid advance to the ridge in order to consolidate the summits. In the event they were denied the opportunity following a series of confused delays.

Fighting petered out at the end of August with both sides suffering from exhaustion. The undisputed victors, however, were the Turkish forces, although they suffered a heavier burden of casualties, namely up to 20,000, with the Allies 12,000.

The Allies had not achieved any of their stated aims. Furthermore, the failure of the operation brought to an end Allied plans to break out of Anzac Cove.

Ben Stocks was in the area and probably died in this battle.

"Damn the Dardanelles – they will be our grave"   Admiral Fisher

It is midday; the deep trench glares…
A buzz and blaze of flies…
The hot wind puffs the giddy airs…
The great sun rakes the skies.

No sound in all the stagnant trench
Where forty standing men
Endure the sweat and grit and stench,
Like cattle in a pen.

Robert Nichols

Helles Memorial. Turkey.

Robert Street.

Rank.	Lance Corporal
Regiment.	Northumberland Fusiliers
Unit.	1st Battalion
Service No.	201234
Date of Death.	29th March 1918
Age.	25
Memorial.	Arras Memorial
	Bay 2 and 3. No Known Grave

Son of James and Lucy Street of Alfreton Road, Pinxton, Derbyshire.

Photograph showing water logged trenches, barbed wire and desolation on the Somme.

Robert was probably in the second Battle of the Somme. It was fought between March 21st and April 5th and was a partially successful German offensive against Allied forces on the Western Front during the latter part of the war. The German Commander believed that it was essential for Germany to use the troops freed from the Russian Front to try to achieve a victory on the Western Front in early 1918, before American Troops arrived in sufficient numbers to reinforce the war weary Allies. The German offensive was directed against the British armies north of the River Somme, between Arras and La Fere. The British trenches were shelled and gassed before a massive morning attack in dense fog. This took the British by surprise, their lines quickly fell and by March 22nd the British 5th Army was in retreat and lost contact with the French to the south. The attack moved swiftly forward, trying to drive a permanent wedge between the British and the French, but by March 28th the Allies had assembled fresh troops that checked the German advance east of Amiens. The offensive had advanced 40 miles and had taken 70,000 prisoners, but in spite of these gains the Allied lines were only bent but not broken.

British casualties amounted to 300,000 during these battles, one of which was Robert Street.

Arras Memorial. France.

Bernard Taylor.

Rank.	Sergeant
Regiment.	Royal Welsh Fusiliers
Unit.	14th Battalion
Service No.	21031
Date of Death.	30th January 1916
Cemetery.	Le Touret Military Cemetery, Richebourg-L'Avoue.
Grave.	III. D. 2.

Report from local paper.

We regret to announce that official intimation has now reached Mr. and Mrs. Edward Taylor, Victoria Street, Pinxton, that their son Sergeant B. Taylor, 14th Battalion Royal Welsh Fusiliers, has been killed in action. Sergeant Taylor was a well known and highly respected Pinxtonian; for several years he was on the staff of Messrs Booth Brothers and was very prominently connected with the Primitive Methodist body. It is apparent from the following correspondence received by his father, Mr. Taylor, that the same esteem of their son was shown in military circles as in civilian life.

Letters of Condolence.

Allow me to tender to you all my deepest sympathy with your sad bereavement in the loss of your dear son Sergeant Taylor, who was killed in action on the 30th of January. I may say that he was one of the most popular N.C.O. s in the unit, and was highly respected and loved by all, being one of the most sincere young men in the Battalion. He could demand respect because of his beautiful character and deep religious convictions. Poor boy, he laid his life down for King and Country, and I pray that the sacrifice which he, together with thousands of his dear comrades, having made may bring forth the fruits of liberty and righteousness. The dear remains were laid to rest at 11 a.m. on Monday 31st January in a British Cemetery alongside hundreds of his comrades who had laid down their lives for the same cause. It was my sad duty to conduct the service over his remains which was done with reverence and intense feeling in the presence of several of his friends and many of his comrades. It was a most pathetic service and to

conduct same was one of the most difficult duties I was called to perform since I have been in France. I could hardly control my feelings as I was thinking of you, his dear parents who are bereaved on one hand, on the other hand knowing that I was burying a young man cut down in the prime of life, a friend, a comrade, yes and thank God, I believe a Christian, a brother of Jesus Christ and I look forward to the glorious day when we shall meet again on the other side, when all our sorrows and troubles are over.
With sincere sympathy,
 Yours faithfully,

H. Jones, Nonconformist Chaplain.

Kindly accept my sincere and deepest sympathy in your sad bereavement. You have lost a kind and soldier-like son. He was shot while out on patrol and died about 4 minutes from the time he was shot, and was happily saved much pain. It's God's way and what I have seen the best are taken first. I have lost a bosom friend, as we have been the best of pals since the day I joined. He was buried in an English Cemetery here very respectfully. Four of us wheeled him down in an ambulance coach. The Reverend H. Jones took the service. There were two officers and a good many soldiers present. A cross has been put on his grave with the inscription: In Loving Memory of Sergeant B.Taylor 21031, who was killed in action January 30th 1916. His cap is nailed to the cross. If I am spared to visit England I hope to have the pleasure of calling on you and giving all the details. We are sending all his things, including his ring, home.

With Kind regards and sympathy,
Yours Sincerely,
A. Rowland Williams. Sergeant.

Le Touret Military Cemetery. France.

Joseph Harold Trueman.

Rank.	Private
Regiment.	Leicestershire Regiment
Unit.	2nd 5th Battalion
Service No.	34435
Date of Death.	26th September 1917
Age.	19
Memorial.	Tyne Cot Memorial
	Panel 50 to 51. No Known Grave

Joseph was the son of Joseph and Caroline Ann Trueman.
He was born at West Hallam, enlisted at Ilkeston and lived in Pinxton.

The Third Battle of Ypres

The first and second battles of Ypres were launched by the Germans. The third was launched by the Allied forces to try and break through Flanders. This battle, referred simply as Passchendaele, though controversial, was the final great battle of attrition of the war and was fought along a line of great distance. The main aim was to be the destruction of German submarine bases on the Belgian coast which were causing large shipping losses. As was the norm, a heavy artillery bombardment was effected for ten days before the attack, with 3,000 guns which used 4-5 million shells. This caused the Germans to expect an attack; the element of surprise was entirely absent. There were only small gains in the French and Allied lines, and the attempt to renew the offensive was severely hampered by the onset of heavy rains, the heaviest for 40 years, which churned the soil into thick muddy swamp. Tanks were stuck fast in the mud. Similarly, the infantry found their mobility severely limited. Ironically the previous bombardment had destroyed the drainage system. After several attacks the Allies were nearing exhaustion as German reserves from the Eastern Front were pouring in. To aid their defence the Germans made use of Mustard Gas which resulted in chemical burns. Unwilling to concede failure, the Allies pressed on with three more assaults with the eventual capture of Passchendaele. British and Canadian forces gave an excuse to call off the offensive, having reasons to claim success. The battle incurred some 310,000 Allied casualties and 260,000 Germans; that is half a million men for a salient widening of only several kilometres.
Joseph was in the area and probably died in this battle; his body was never found.

Tyne Cot Memorial. Belgium.

J. H. Upton.

Rank.	Private
Regiment.	Grenadier Guards
Unit.	3rd Battalion
Service No.	22397
Date of Death.	22nd November 1915
Age.	28
Cemetery.	Royal Irish Rifles Graveyard, Laventie
Grave.	VI. B. 1.
Enlisted.	Nottingham
Born.	Pinxton

The place and manner of Private Upton's death is unknown but given the date and place of his burial it is likely that he died during the build up to the battle of Loos. He died on the 22nd November. The British Loos offensive under the direction of General Haig began on the 25th of September, following a 4-day artillery bombardment in which 250,000 shells were fired. The British committed 6 Army Divisions to the battle.

Though the British had supremacy against the Germans, in places 7 to 1, there were concerns about the difficult terrain that had to be crossed. Once the bombardment had concluded the plans called for the release of 5,100 cylinders of chlorine gas from the British front line. Unfortunately the release had mixed results as in places the wind blew the gas back into the British trenches, resulting in 2,632 British casualties, although only seven died.

There was significant progress on the first day resulting in the capture of Loos with the Army then moving onwards towards the town of Lens, but a failure in supplies and reserves brought the advance to a halt. Meanwhile, north of the road which ran across the battlefield less progress was being made, with the British gas attack being less effective. The delay in getting reserves and supplies to the front was, however, crucial.

No more we'll share the same old barn,
The same old dug out, same old yarn,
No more a tin of bully share,
Nor split our rum by star-shell's flare,
So long old lad.

What times we've had, both good and bad,
We've shared what shelter could be had,
The same crump-hole when the whizz bangs shrieked,
The same old billet that always leaked,
And now- you've "stopped one".

We'd weathered the storm two winters long,
We'd managed to grin when all went wrong,
Because together we fought and fed,
Our hearts were light; but now you're dead
And I am Mateless.

Anon.

Royal Irish Rifles Graveyard Laventie. France.

John Thomas Ward.

Rank.	Private
Regiment.	Sherwood Foresters (Notts and Derby Regiment)
Unit.	17th Battalion (Welbeck Rangers)
Service No.	19552
Date of Death.	1st August 1916
Age.	35
Cemetery.	Gorre British and Indian Cemetery
Grave.	II. E. 23.

John was born at Hawsworth in Nottinghamshire and resided at Station Road Pinxton, Derbyshire. He was married to Edith Wilkinson (formerly Ward) of Staunton-in-the-Vale, near Orston, Notts. He enlisted on the 16th November 1914, was subsequently wounded at Ypres on the 13th April 1916 and was killed during an enemy raid on the German trenches whilst with the 17th Battalion. He was 35 years of age.

On the evening of July 31st 1916, near Duck's Bill crater, a raiding party of the battalion assembled in no-man's land near Givenchy and advanced under cover of our artillery. Three men were hit by their own shells during the advance. The objective of the raiding party was to enter the German trenches, take prisoners and locate two mine shafts. It was here that the party came under heavy machine gun fire from the rear of the crater whilst trying to break through the enemy wire. The mine shaft was eventually located and four German prisoners were taken, the mine shaft being dealt with by the Royal Engineers. The casualties sustained at the end of the operation were 2 officers killed and 4 wounded, 3 other ranks killed with 47 missing. It is believed John Thomas Ward was killed in this action.

Gorre British and Indian Cemetery. France.

Albert Watson.

Rank.	Private
Regiment.	Lincolnshire Regiment
Unit.	2nd Battalion
Service No.	40229
Date of Death.	16th August 1917
Age.	26
Memorial.	Tyne Cot Memorial
	Panel 35 to 37 and 162 to 162A No Known Grave

Albert Watson front right with relatives Mary and Elizabeth either side

The Tyne Cot Cemetery is the resting place of nearly 12,000 soldiers of the Commonwealth Forces, of these 70% are unidentified, the largest number of burials of any Commonwealth Cemetery of either World War.

The Tyne Cot Memorial commemorates a total of 34,888 men who died in the Ypres Salient from the 16th August 1917 to the end of the war and have no known grave. The memorial lies amid peaceful farmland which slopes gently up to the village of Passchendaele. Visiting the memorial today it is almost impossible to believe that in the summer and autumn of 1917 it was a morass of shell holes, mud, scattered equipment and littered with the corpses of soldiers. The bodies of many of those killed would never be found but their names were carved into the panels of the memorial which stands there today. In front of the memorial is Tyne Cot Cemetery, still guarded in peace, as it was in war, by brooding shapes of German Pillboxes. The Cross of Sacrifice in the centre of the cemetery was built on top of one of these. After the Armistice the battlefields were cleared and the bodies found during the clearances, together with those from smaller cemeteries nearby, were concentrated in the Tyne Cot Cemetery. Although Albert's body was never found he is remembered on the memorial.

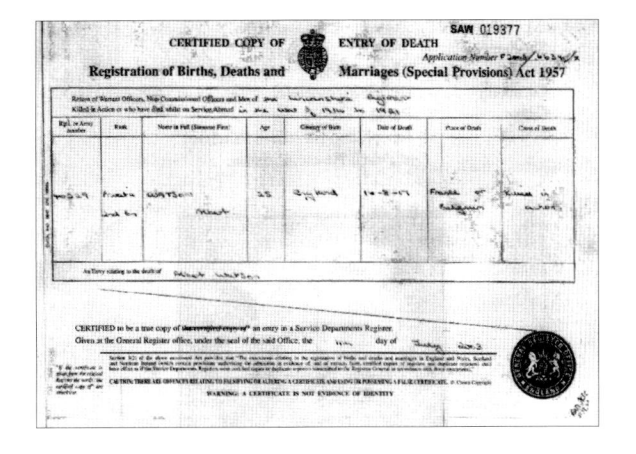

Albert Watson's Death Certificate

Albert Watson's family grave in Pinxton churchyard where he is remembered at the base

Tyne Cot Cemetery and Memorial. Belgium.

Harry Watson.

Rank.	Private
Regiment.	Royal Welsh Fusiliers
Unit.	1st Battalion
Service No.	19464
Date of Death.	5th July 1916
Memorial.	Thiepval Memorial
	Pier and Face 4A. No Known Grave

Harry Watson almost certainly died on the Somme. The 1st Battalion formed part of the 38th Welsh Division whose names will always be synonymous with the courage of the Welsh soldier at Mametz Wood.

The capture of this piece of dense woodland was described by Llewelyn Wyn Griffith, one of many outstanding writers who served in the regiment, as:

"The horror of our way of life and death and of crucifixion of youth."

Its capture can be attributed wholly to the 38th Division. It should be remembered that not one man in the division had been trained to fight in thick woodland and for the majority this was their first experience of battle. The wood was strongly defended by German infantry and artillery; successive assaults failed and the advancing troops were cut down while crossing open ground.

Harry was in good company with the likes of the poet Siegfried Sassoon, who was also in the regiment.

The Welsh Dragon at Mametz Wood

The Welsh Dragon looking towards Mametz Wood down Death Valley

Aftermath

HAVE you forgotten yet?...
For the world's events have rumbled on since those gagged days,
Like traffic checked while at the crossing of city-ways:
And the haunted gap in your mind has filled with thoughts that flow
Like clouds in the lit heaven of life; and you're a man reprieved to go,
Taking your peaceful share of Time, with joy to spare.
But the past is just the same - and War's a bloody game…
Have you forgotten yet?...
Look down, and swear by the slain of the War that you'll never
forget.

Do you remember the dark months you held the sector at
 Mametz -
The nights you watched and wired and dug and piled sandbags on
 parapets?
Do you remember the rats; and the stench
Of corpses rotting in front of the front-line trench -
And dawn coming, dirty-white, and chill with a hopeless rain?
Do you ever stop and ask, "Is it all going to happen again?"

Do you remember that hour of din before the attack -
And the anger, the blind compassion that seized and shook you then
As you peered at the doomed and haggard faces of your men?
Do you remember the stretcher-cases lurching back
With dying eyes and lolling heads - those ashen-grey
Masks of the lads who once were keen and kind and gay?

Have you forgotten yet?...
Look up, and swear by the green of the spring that you'll never forget.

Siegfried Sassoon   March 1919

Thiepval Memorial. France.

Edward Whitehead.

Rank.	Private
Regiment.	Lincolnshire Regiment
Unit.	8th Battalion
Service No.	16165
Date of Death.	28th April 1917
Age.	37
Memorial.	Arras Memorial
	Bay 3 and 4. No Known Grave

Lived at Talbot Street, Pinxton Derbyshire. Leaves a widow and four children.

Edward in uniform

Report from local paper.

Official news of the death in action of Private E Whitehead, aged 37 years, of Talbot Street, Pinxton, has now been received. He joined the Lincolns some two years ago, went out to France on June 28th 1916, and was killed on April 28th 1917. Prior to joining the forces he was employed at the Pinxton Colliery. The deceased leaves a widow and four children.

Arras Memorial. France.

Rennie Wilson.

Rank.	Private
Regiment.	Royal Marine Light Infantry
Service No.	CH/156 (S.)
Date of Death.	17th February 1917
Cemetery.	Queens Cemetery Bucquoy Pas de Calais France
Grave.	I. K. 10.

Rennie in dress uniform

Should you forget 'twas I
That went out under that foreign sky years ago to try
To try and right this world one final once with others same
Not heroes that were once upon a time
Nor fools that this days youth would have us be
But youth of our time, who on that given day
Fought and died for freedom and our way.

Brian Wilson 2006

Death report.

Pinxton people will be sorry to hear of the death of Private Rennie Wilson of Pinxton, who was killed in action on February 17th 1917. He joined the Sherwood Foresters on the 10th September, 1914 and was afterwards transferred to the Royal Marines. Private Wilson had a somewhat unlucky time. He was dispatched to the Dardanelles, and landed at Gaba Tepe on April 28th 1915. On May 1st he was wounded and taken to a hospital at Alexandria. He was again back in the trenches on June 22nd, but only for a short time, as on July 12th he received a nasty wound in the thigh. The unfortunate lad was invalided home and taken to Haslan Hospital, Gosport, later being transferred to Queen Mary's Royal Naval Hospital, Southend on Sea.

During the time spent in England he acquired a good knowledge of the Lewis Gun and went to France in September 1916 as a first-class Lewis Gunner. In a letter, his pal writes: "Rennie moved off in the advance of February 17th in charge of a Lewis Gun, and was then in the best of health and spirits. He was reported missing for some time afterwards, but his body has since been found and buried with all honours that circumstances would permit, and you will be proud to know that he was found only a few yards from the objective. The Lewis Gunners and myself send their deepest sympathy".

Private Wilson's loss is very keenly felt by his father, sister and brothers, two of whom, Horace and William, are on active service, and his many friends.

Rennie convalescing

Rennie at Brighton

Divisional Engineers with Rennie 2nd from left, 2nd from back

Rennie's Headstone

Queens Cemetery Bucquoy. France.

Samuel Winfield. MM.

Rank.	Sergeant
Regiment.	Northumberland Fusiliers
Unit.	12th/13th Battalion
Service No.	16604
Date of Death.	27th May 1918
Age.	21
Awards.	Military Medal
Memorial.	Soissons Memorial No Known Grave

Son of Mrs. Mary Crampton (formally Winfield) of The Toll Bar, Pinxton, Derby.

Samuel Winfield MM

Toll Bar Cottages where Samuel lived

The Military Medal

Sergeant Samuel Winfield was awarded the Military Medal, which was only awarded for extreme bravery, as the local report shows.

Report from local paper.

Writing home to his parents who live at the Toll Bar Pinxton, Lance Corporal Sam Winfield Northumberland Fusiliers states that he has been awarded the Military Medal. In the course of his letter he writes: "Talk about fire and water we have not half been through it. We have had it a bit rough lately. No doubt you will be pleased to know that I have been awarded the Military Medal for bravery in the field on October 4th. I was presented with the ribbon by Major Eddleman D.S.O. yesterday November 1st and I am going to have a Public Presentation made by our Army Commander.

When we made the attack on Polygon Wood we were held up by a machine gun. I fired rifle grenades into the place and my officer and myself rushed forward, there were about 30 Germans in the concrete emplacement. I killed 6 of the gunners, then the others began to run away. I dropped behind the machine gun and fired a bolt of bullets into them, and I can tell you not many got back.

We captured 10 prisoners and our lads came up and we held the position. The officer got the MC and I got the MM. I have had some warm congratulations from my mates. It was the biggest victory there has been on the front, and I am proud to have been in it. We are out of it now for a rest".

After this engagement he was promoted to Sergeant.

Lance Corporal Winfield, who had previously been employed at Langton Colliery, joined up soon after the war commenced and was in the Dardanelles where upon landing he was wounded in the leg and invalided home. On recovery he was sent to France and again wounded in the arm but was not out of action long. A few years ago Pinxton people will remember the all but fatal cycle accident which befell him within an ace depriving him of the honour which he has now won. Lance Corporal Winfield's only brother Arthur, aged 23, also joined in the early months of the campaign but has recently been discharged. He received a wound in the left arm which has left it practically useless from the elbow.

Listen reader, while I tell you
Stirring deeds both old and new,
Tales of battles during which we
-Chits received from Batt. H.Q.

Fought we had a losing battle,
All the day and all the night.
All communications broken,
Never was there such a plight.
Now the Hun comes o'er the sandbags
In one long unbroken mass –
Just in time – the welcome message,
"Indent now for helmets gas".

Shelled they'd been for three days solid,
In a trench just two feet high,
Couldn't get retaliation,
Matter not how they might try.
Binks' men had held the trenches
(Binks is not his proper name)
Savagely he sent the message,
"Carn't you stop their purple game?"
Anxiously they wait the answer,
What a brave but serried band,
Here it comes – Binks grabs the paper,
"Deficiencies not yet to hand!"

           Anon.

Soissons Memorial. France.

Thomas Mathew Wood.

Rank.	Private
Regiment.	Sherwood Foresters (Notts and Derby Regiment)
Unit.	2nd Battalion, "B" Company
Service No.	22782
Date of Death.	3rd March 1916
Age.	22
Cemetery.	Lijssenthoek Military Cemetery
Grave.	II. B. 47.

Thomas Mathew Wood

Thomas was the son of James and Mary Wood of Mill Lane, Pinxton, Derbyshire.
They later moved to 58 Talbot Street, Pinxton.
Thomas enlisted at Mansfield in February 1915, trained at North Shields and Whitley Bay, before embarking for France in August 1915.

Extract from the War Diary

1st March: Considerable artillery activity on our part all day. From 5 p.m. to 5.30 p.m. our guns bombarded enemy trenches from Well Cottage to Canadian Farm. Enemy did not retaliate much on our trenches. "Gas Alert" was cancelled during the afternoon but was ordered again about 5.30 p.m. All working parties were cancelled.

2nd March: We were ordered to open machine gun fire on enemy trenches at 4.32 a.m. for 10 minutes. The 9th Norfolks on our right also opened fire, and the 18 pounders fired too. At the same time our guns opened a heavy bombardment on what appeared to be from Hill 60 way. The Germans must have thought we were going to attack from between Wieltje and Cross Roads Farm for they opened a slow barrage and crumped B12 rather badly. They also used a lot of rifle fire. However, after about half an hour all was quiet again in front of the battalion.

3rd March: The battalion was relieved by the 1st Leicesters at 1.30 p.m.
Sadly, it was during this relief that Thomas was killed.

Local report.

The official announcement has just been received by Mr. and Mrs. James Wood, of 58 Talbot Street, Pinxton of the death of their eldest son Private Thomas Mathew Wood of the 2nd Sherwoods, whilst on active service. He was home on leave a few weeks ago, and had barely got back when the sad but unconfirmed news was sent on March the 3rd.

Private Wood enlisted early in February last year and after some 6 months training at North Shields Backworth Camp, and Whitley Bay, was dispatched to France. At present his father and another brother, who has been at the Dardanelles, are serving with the colours.

Lijssenthoek Military Cemetery. Belgium.

Lijssenthoek Military Cemetery is located 12 kilometres west of Ieper (Ypres) town centre on the road to Poperinge. It is the second largest Commonwealth Cemetery in Belgium.

THE ARMISTICE

The Allies and Germany signed the Armistice to end hostilities on the "eleventh hour of the eleventh day of the eleventh month" 1918, after four long years of war.

The guns fell silent on the Western Front.

Photograph taken after reaching an agreement for the Armistice that ended World War One. Admiral Wemyss is flanked by Général Weygand (left) and Maréchal Foch, The Allied Supreme Commander, (right). They are seen in front of Foch's own railway carriage in the Forest of Compiègne.

WORLD WAR татTWO

St. Paul's Cathedral, London 1940.   Britain stood alone.

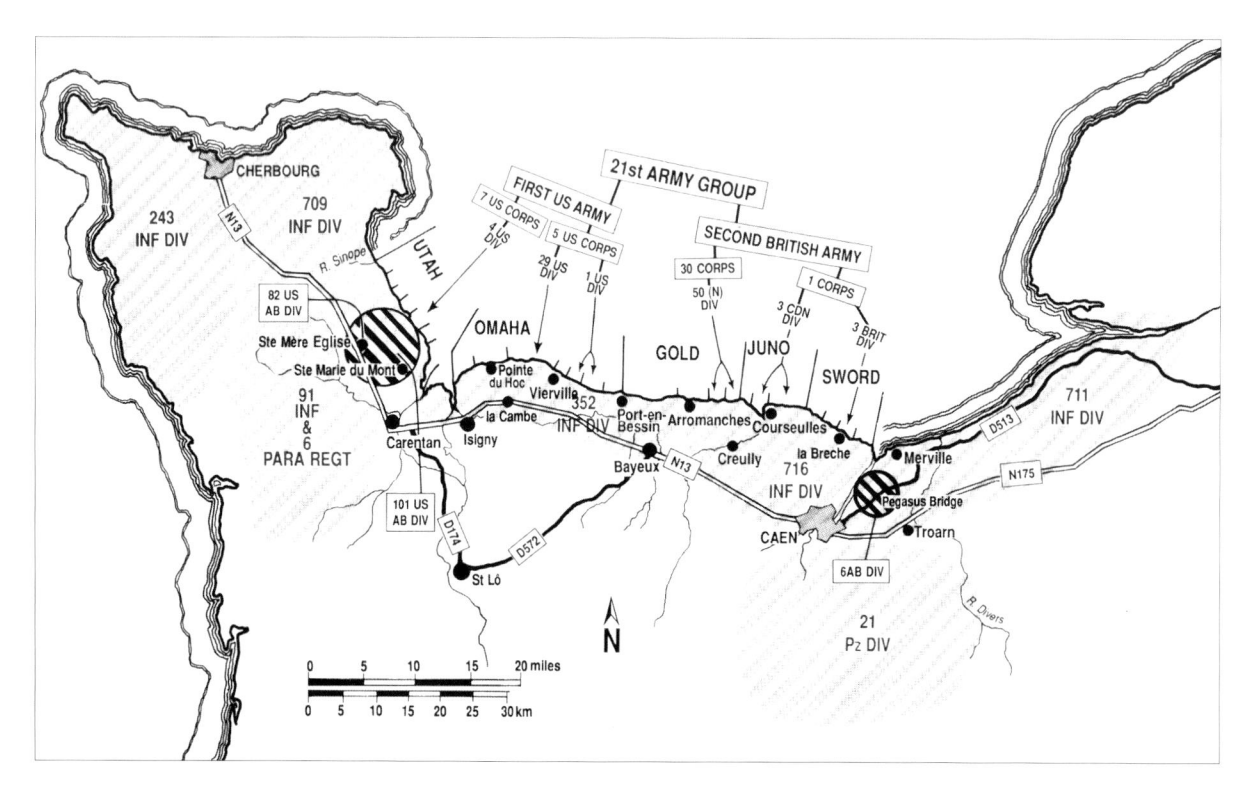

The D-Day beaches and German coastal defensive positions June 6th 1944

Colin Anthony.

Rank.	Able Seaman
Service.	Royal Navy
	H.M.S. Cardiff
Service No.	JX 169083
Date of Death.	23rd March 1946
Age.	25
Cemetery.	St Helen's Churchyard, Pinxton
Grave.	Row 14. Plot 13.

His trade before enlisting: Pony Driver at Brookhill Colliery.

Colin enlisted at Skegness in November 1939, joining H.M.S. Royal Arthur, training and assessment centre acquired by the Royal Navy in 1939, which prior to the war was Butlin's Holiday Camp. Here the new recruits were assessed, kitted out then sent to various depots. On the 15th December 1939 Colin was transferred to H.M.S. Drake shore base, on 22nd February 1940 he was transferred to H.M.S. Cardiff, saw action at Dunkirk then deployed on patrol duty in the North Sea in the event of an invasion. He was also on convoy defence and patrol in home waters. In 1942 H.M.S. Cardiff became a training ship, in 1944 it was used for gunnery training duties and during this period the ship was also used for Air Ministry bombing trials and exercises. In 1945 H.M.S. Cardiff was laid-up in Gareloch, eventually being sold for demolition in 1946. Colin was invalided out of the service on the 15th July 1944 with T B and died on the 23rd March 1946 aged 25. He is buried in Pinxton churchyard.

Brothers Colin (left) and Enoch

Enoch Anthony served on H.M.S. Teviot in the Far East and was the telegraph operator; when the ship was at action stations he operated the depth charges.

Colin's ship H.M.S. Cardiff

Colin with his mother

H.M.S. CARDIFF

Report from local paper.

The internment took place in St Helen's Churchyard on Friday of Mr. Colin Anthony aged 25, son of Mr. and Mrs. H. Anthony of 224 Wharf Road. Mr. Anthony was invalided out of the Navy after serving four and a half years on H.M.S. Cardiff.
The bearers were personal friends: Messrs Lal Taylor; Baden Hill; Arthur Shepherd; J. Hardy; Aubrey Brittain and Ken Hancock.

Colin 1st left back row with H.M.S. Cardiff shipmates

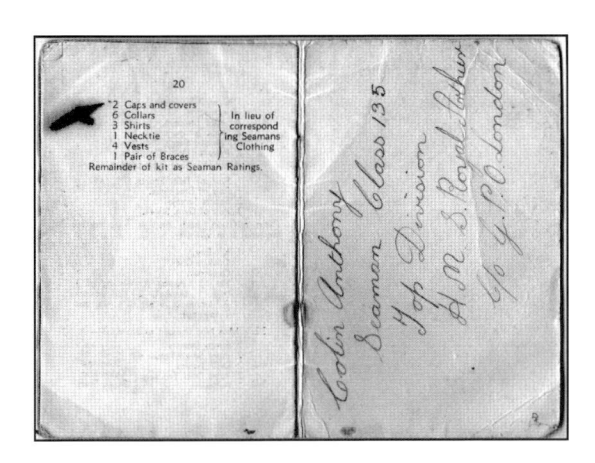

Colin's Handbook   Colin Anthony's Discharge Papers

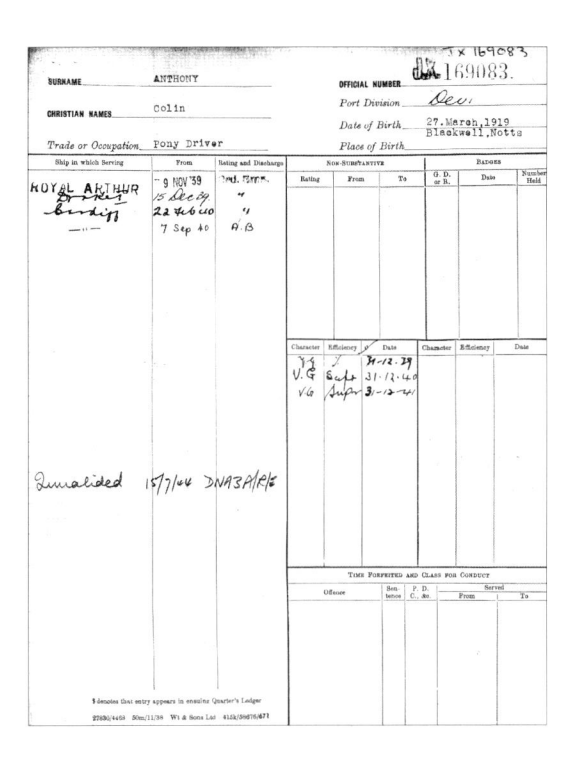

The cross shows the position of Colin Anthony's Grave in Pinxton churchyard

George Bretton.

Rank.	Engineman
Service.	Royal Naval Patrol Service
	Trawler Franc Tireur
Service No.	LT/KX 113682
Date of Death.	25th September 1943.
Age.	27
Memorial.	Lowestoft Naval Memorial
	Panel 12, Column 2. Lost at Sea

Joyce with brother George Bretton. Joyce served in the Land Army.

Report from Free Press dated 15th October 1943.

Mr. and Mrs. J. Bretton of 115 Wharf Road, Pinxton received official news on Friday that their son Petty Officer George Bretton has been killed through enemy action. Petty Officer Bretton was 27 years old, and was born locally. He joined the Royal Navy three years ago, and previously worked at Brookhill Colliery.

Report from Coastal Command.

George Bretton was on the Franc Tireur, one of the two trawlers which were patrolling the waters 12 miles north of Harwich, when they came upon a group of three E- Boats laying mines. The trawlers immediately noticed the presence of the E-Boats and turned to face them. The first burst of torpedoes missed the trawlers by about six feet. However, the second set of torpedoes hit the Trawler Franc Tireur amidships and she sank within a few seconds. These torpedoes were fired from the E-Boat SS.89 commanded by Oberleutnant Ritter von Geog.
Some of the crew were saved by the H.M.S. Stella Rigel, but sadly George Bretton was not one of them.

Peter Scott, the famous naturalist, who was in charge of the battle with the E-Boats, stated afterwards: When a war comes to a country there is only one course for its people to take, and that is to fight as hard as they can until it is won or lost. It is necessary for the sacrifice, the unselfish and continuing effort and the heroism of deliberate courage to be recorded so that it cannot ever be forgotten. The strain, discomfort and boredom which are the three predominant factors in modern warfare cannot be brought into their true perspective in a book of this kind, or it would be so long and dull that nobody would read it. There is no glory to be had out of war that cannot be had out of some greater and more creative enterprise. Nothing will ever compensate us for the men that we have lost, not even the way so many of them died. They were ready to die because they wanted to save their children and children's children from future wars. The least and the most that any of us can do is to devote ourselves to finding a complete and lasting peace, and then to maintain it with all our energy.

Trawler Franc Tireur

Lowestoft Naval Memorial. England.

Thomas Allen Butler.

Rank.	Fusilier
Regiment.	Royal Inniskilling Fusiliers
Unit.	1st Battalion
Service No.	6981827
Date of Death.	18th February 1943
Age.	29
Memorial.	Rangoon Memorial
	Face 11. No Known Grave

Fusilier Thomas Butler

Thomas was born in Selston, the son of Thomas Walter and Mary Ann Butler. Husband of Nora Maisie Butler, from Selston. Resided at 30 Town Street, Pinxton, Derbyshire.
Thomas was educated at the local schools. He worked at The Pinxton Coke Ovens and No.2 Colliery. Thomas and Nora were married on March 27th 1937.

Thomas and Nora Butler on their wedding day

Thomas was conscripted and after training was sent to Belfast to make up the numbers for the 1st Battalion, Royal Inniskilling Fusiliers.

The battalion was sent to Karachi were he was seconded to join Wingate's Chindits. They were fighting behind the Japanese lines in the Assam Valley when Thomas was killed.

Lieutenant Colonel Orde Wingate was a proven guerrilla expert and arrived in Burma with the task of organising guerrilla operations in Burma, and in order to do so he created the Chindits, a special force to fight behind enemy lines.

The first expedition took place on the 8th February 1943. They went into Burma from Imphal. The expedition, code named "Operation Long Cloth", consisted of three thousand offices and men, along with eight hundred and fifty mules. They marched over a thousand miles, blowing up bridges, communication lines and railways etc., whilst living on starvation rations. Supplies should have been air-dropped but it was not always possible. The men were facing two enemies, the Japanese and the jungle. Of the three thousand men who went on the operation, only two thousand one hundred and eighty two came back after twelve weeks in the jungle. Orde Wingate was killed in an air crash on March 24th 1944, just after the start of the second expedition codenamed "Thursday".

The Chindit badge illustrates a Chinthe, a mythical creature half lion, half dragon. They are the guardians of Burmese pagodas.

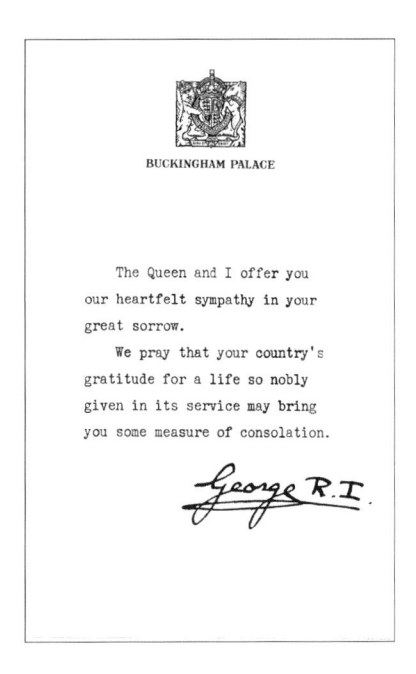

Letter from King George V

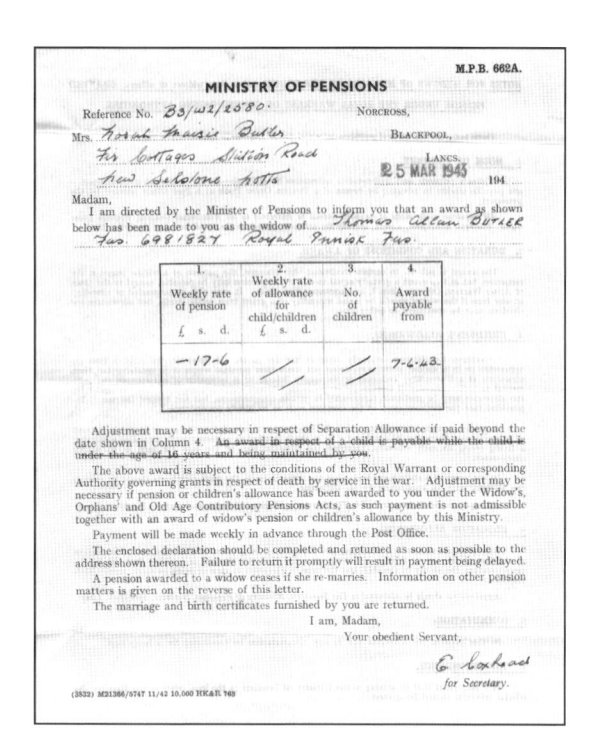

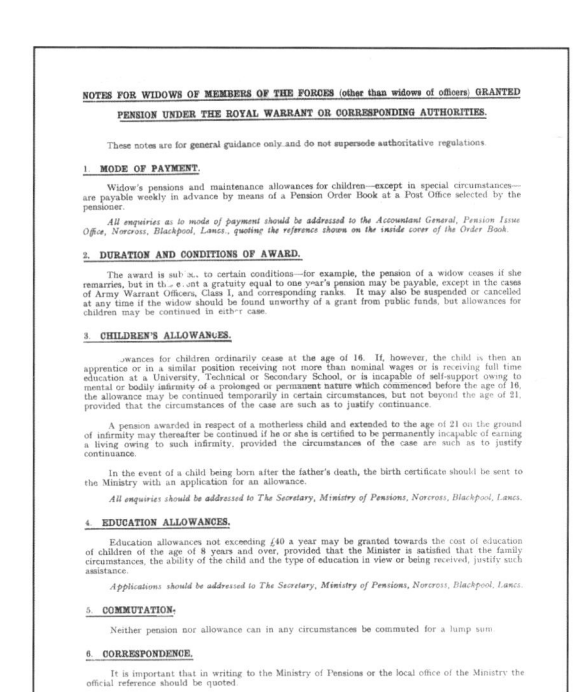

Letters from the Ministry of Pensions

Rangoon Memorial. Myanmar (Burma).

William Clarke.

Rank.	Gunner
Regiment.	Royal Artillery
Unit.	12th Battalion 6 H.A.A. Regiment
Service No.	402224
Date of Death.	6th December 1942
Age.	33
Memorial.	Yokohama Cremation Memorial
	Panel 2. No Known Grave

William was the son of Henry and Mary Hannah Clarke and the husband of Olive Mary Clarke of South Normanton, Derbyshire.

William Clarke

William Clarke was born in Pinxton, one of eleven children comprising of seven sons and four daughters. The family lived at 67 Poole Close, Pinxton. William married Olive and they had four children, two sons and two daughters. He worked at Brookhill Colliery prior to enlisting in the army on the 19th of August 1929. He was in the reserves at the Army School, Colchester. During that time he was transferred to the 2nd Dragoon Guards and into the Cavalry of the Line for 249 days. This was known as 3 years on and 9 years off. He was recalled for service on 14th August 1939 and joined the Royal Artillery, mobilised 2nd September 1939 and sent with the B.E.F. to Northern France. He saw action in France before being evacuated off the beach at Dunkirk. After army leave he was shipped out to Malaya on the 11th November 1941 and was at the fall of Singapore, where he was captured and transported to a Prisoner of War camp on the Island of Moji were he later died. His length of service was 13 years 110 days.

Prime Minister Winston Churchill made a statement before the fall of Singapore saying "The defenders must outnumber the advancing Japanese forces" and telling the officers in Singapore to die with their troops and to fight to the bitter end. "The honour of the British Empire and Army is at stake". The invading Japanese attacked down the Malayan Peninsula with 65,000 troops on Dec 8th 1941, some on bicycles. The infantry advanced 500 miles in 55 days. The onslaught took everyone by surprise; speed was of the essence for the Japanese, who came through the jungle and mangrove swamps, never allowing the British forces to regroup. The British confidently predicted that the Japanese would attack from the sea but by the 11th February, after fierce fighting by the 23,000 Japanese, their supplies were running perilously low. Yamashita, in charge of the Japanese forces, decided on a bluff and sent a message to Lieutenant General Percival "To give up the meaningless resistance" and it worked. The Allies capitulated on Feb 15th 1942. It was the biggest disaster of the British Army; 100,000 men were taken prisoner, some had not even fired a shot. The defeat ushered in three years of appalling treatment and savagery of Allied P.O.W.s who were caught up in Singapore; 9,000 of these were to die building the Burma – Thailand Railway. Winston Churchill called the ignominious fall of Singapore to the Japanese "the worst disaster and the largest capitulation in the history of Britain".

Yokohama Cremation Memorial. Japan.

Horace Oscar Cooper.

Rank.	Gunner
Regiment.	Royal Artillery
Unit.	222 Battalion 10 H.A.A. Regiment
Service No.	1592037
Date of Death.	29th April 1942
Age.	25
Cemetery.	Imtarfa Military Cemetery
Grave.	Coll. Grave 4. 1A. 16.

Horace was the son of Benjamin and Charlotte Cooper and the husband of Eva Elizabeth Cooper of Pinxton, Derbyshire.

Horace on service in Malta

Horace's wife Eva

In his back garden, Pinxton

Report from local paper.

Mrs. H. O. Cooper of West End, Pinxton, has received official news that her husband Mr. Horace Oscar Cooper, aged 25, of the Royal Artillery, was injured in a recent air raid in Malta and died three days later. He received a piece of shrapnel in the back of the neck, which was ultimately fatal.
He was the second son of Mr. and Mrs. B. Cooper of 46 West End, Pinxton.
Horace Cooper enlisted two years ago and had been in Malta 19 months.
Before being conscripted he was a bricklayer in the employ of Mr. J. B. Bryant of South Normanton.
Mr. Cooper was particularly fond of music, being a violinist of great merit and had organised an orchestra and dance band which were in great demand in the district.
At a dance held at Underwood on Saturday a two minutes silence was observed in his memory. He was a favourite in his company in Malta and entertained them with his violin, which had been bought for him by his comrades.
He was married at Alveston Church Derby, on June 8th 1940, and could not have spent much time with his wife.

Horace must have been a very artistic person. This is a poem he sent home from Malta dated June 8th 1941, his first wedding anniversary.

England fairest isle of isles
Fill this world with sunny smiles.
Land of truth and liberty
Free this word from tyranny.

Your fame has spread throughout the ages
Add further fame to history's pages.
Sons of your Empire far and near
Fight for the cause we hold so dear.

Burdens you will have to bear
You boys in blue they clear the air.
The Army and the Navy too
Will show the world what they can do.

Face danger's dark clouds with a brave smile
Those you love must leave for a while.
When war is over and victory won
Nations will say, England, Well Done.

Written by Oscar Horace Cooper

ST. LUKE THE EVANGELIST
GARRISON CHURCH, TIGNE, MALTA

✝

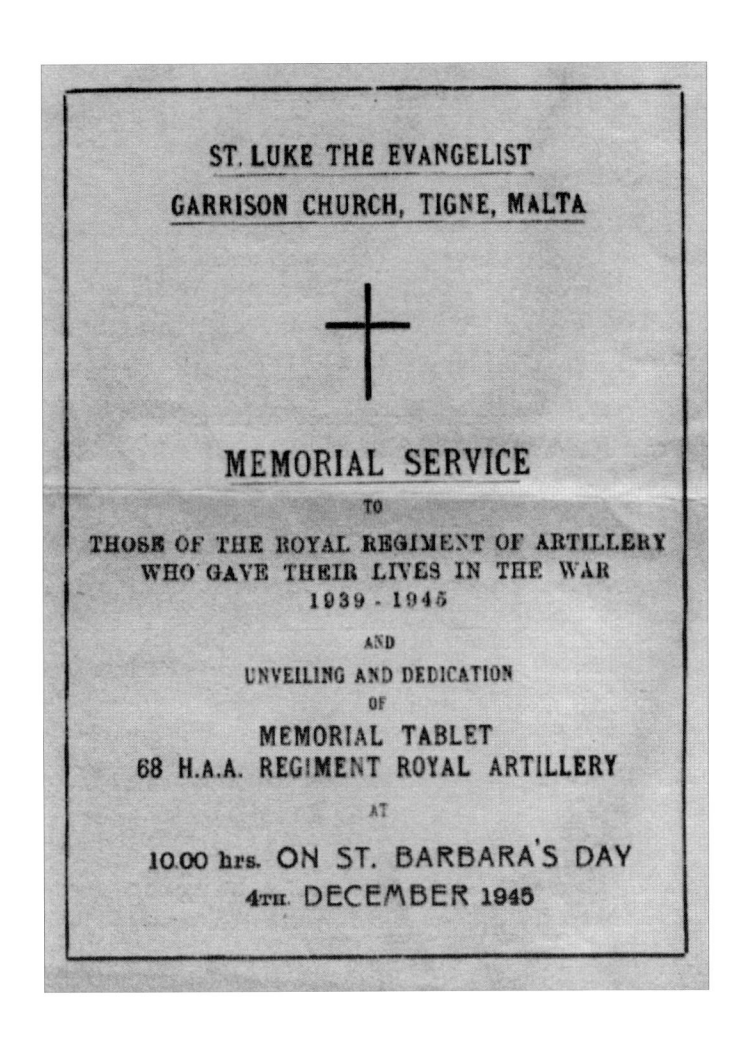

MEMORIAL SERVICE

TO

THOSE OF THE ROYAL REGIMENT OF ARTILLERY
WHO GAVE THEIR LIVES IN THE WAR
1939 - 1945

AND

UNVEILING AND DEDICATION
OF
MEMORIAL TABLET
68 H.A.A. REGIMENT ROYAL ARTILLERY

AT

10.00 hrs. ON ST. BARBARA'S DAY
4TH DECEMBER 1945

Imtarfa Military Cemetery. Malta.

Eric Gent.

Rank.	Gunner
Regiment.	Royal Horse Artillery
Unit.	12 (Honourable Artillery Coy.) Regiment
Service No.	14353967
Date of Death.	6th July 1944
Age.	20
Cemetery.	Arezzo War Cemetery
Grave.	V. A. 3.

Eric was the son of William and Dora Gent of Selston, Nottinghamshire.

Eric in Uniform

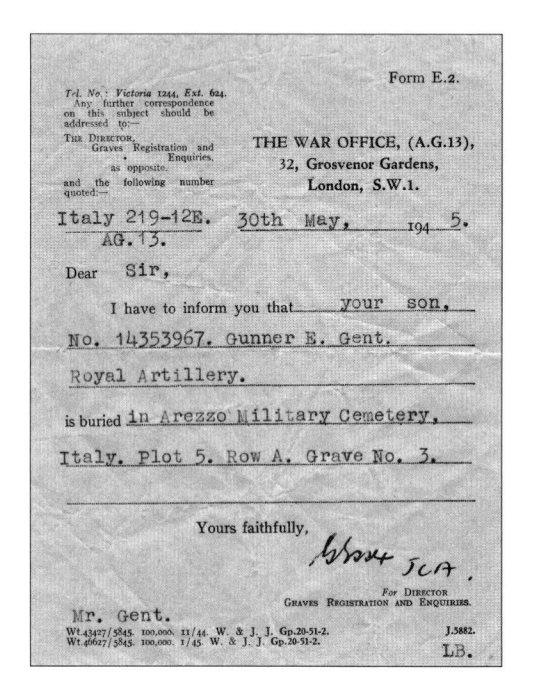

Eric as a 14 year old

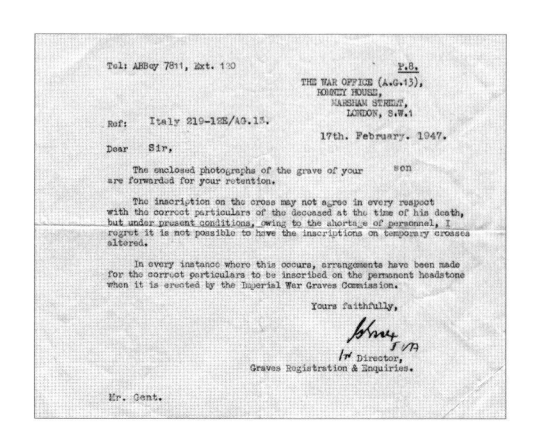

Letters from The War Office

Letter from Eric Gent to Eric Mellor, his friend.

Dear Eric,
I'm glad to hear you enjoyed your Christmas leave with the "boys". According to your Airmail you had your share of beer, couldn't I just drink some now! It's Canadian Poison we have now.
At present I'm back at the old R.A.T.D. out in the wilds on a driver and operator's course. I shall be thankful when the time is up so that we can get back to the old Regiment again. You don't realize what a good job it is till you get something worse. You sound as if you are doing plenty of "spare work" jobs over there, believe me they are the best ones in the long run Eric. Well I suppose I shall have to close for now, but will let you have the rest of the news by letter, so till then will say cheerio. All the best,
Your old pal,
Eric.

Recollections of Eric Gent by his best pal, Eric Mellor.

When Eric Gent and I were schoolboys my parents had a Grocery shop on Wharf Road, near Taylor's Corner, Pinxton and Eric lived with his parents and brother a few doors away.
We both attended Kirkstead Schools in the same class. Out of school hours we played together, our hobbies being gardening, keeping rabbits, bantams and racing pigeons. We were encouraged by Eric's uncles who lived on Talbot Street, and had lofts on the bottom banks. The Pinxton racing club allowed us to send our birds at weekends with theirs to the South of England, France and Spain etc.
We used to cycle together to Langley Mill with the pigeons to release them for exercise for them and us. We left school together, I worked with my parents in their shop and Eric got a clerical job at Mansfield Hosiery Mills.
Eric's parents arranged for a tutor to teach him music and piano playing, but he did not share their enthusiasm. In 1942 we were ordered to attend the Alfreton Drill Hall regarding service in the Armed Forces, with coal mining as an alternative. We rejected the first choice of the Royal Navy because a few weeks earlier two sons of our neighbours lost their lives when H.M.S. Hood, the battleship they were on, was sunk in the North Sea.
We did ask to join the ground-staff expecting to be stationed in England, but there were no vacancies. However, as reluctant heroes, we did not want to be exposed to bad weather or enemy fire which the infantry offered and preferred the comfort and protection offered by armoured vehicles.
Eric asked for the Tank Corps but was sent to the Royal Artillery Regiment in Italy. I was later sent to a Tank Training Regiment at Catterick where I received his last letter, telling me he was in training for service in a tank. I assumed he was in a vehicle where the turret was replaced by a large artillery gun. I assume he was outside the protection area of the vehicle when he was injured by enemy fire and died a few days later.
He is buried in or near Florence in Italy. His brother Bill survived the war in the Royal Marines, as did their father who served in the First World War in the Grenadier Guards.

    ERIC MELLOR.

> Victoria Cottages,
> 130, Wharf Road,
> PINXTON.
> Nottingham.
> 30th July, 1944.
>
> Dear Mr & Mrs Gent,
>
> It was a great shock to us when we heard the sad news that your son Eric had been killed in action, and to some extent we can feel the tremendous grief that you must be suffering to sacrifice to the nation a son so young. We pray that you may be given strength to bear your very great sorrow, until time has healed the wound. We owe a great debt to such brave lads, a debt we are afraid that we cannot ever repay. We trust that your other son will come through safely. We extend to you our heartfelt sympathy in the hope that with others trying to share your sorrow it will to some extent allay your distress.
>
> Yours very sincerely,
> Ada & Levi. C Drew

Letter from a friend

> Honourable Artillery Company,
> Armoury House,
> Finsbury. E.C.1.
> 1st July, 1948
>
> Dear Mr Gent
>
> A friend of mine has recently been to Italy to visit the grave of her son, who was killed in the summer of 1944 in the Arno Valley. I asked her, while she was there, to look for the graves of members of the 12th.(HAC)R.H.A. and gave her your son's name. I felt you would like to know that she has told me that she visited the grave, which is in the cemetery at Indicatore, between Arezzo and Florence. She tells me that it is a most beautiful setting, in lovely country and is a very quiet and simple spot. The cemetery is beautifully looked after and has been planted with grass, and, later, flowers are going to be grown there. She found all the graves of our Regiment and laid flowers on them. I felt you would like to know this, and possibly one day you will yourself be able to visit the spot. As you know I was with him when he was killed and I remember him well as a splendid and plucky lad
>
> With best wishes,
>
> Mr. Gent
> "Greenacres"
> Church Lane,
> Selston, Notts.
>
> Yours sincerely,
> R T Bastow Lt Col.

Letter from the Regiment

Arezzo War Cemetery. Italy.

174

Samuel Harwood.

Rank.	Private
Regiment.	Duke of Cornwall's Light Infantry
Unit.	1st Battalion
Service No.	5120371
Date of Death.	5th June 1942
Age.	31
Memorial.	Alamein Memorial
	Column 62 No Known Grave

Samuel was the son of Robert and Mary Harwood and the husband of Freda Harwood, Pinxton, Derbyshire.

Report from Free Press 15th October 1943.

News has been received by Mrs. F. Harwood of 7 Wharf Road that her husband Private Samuel Harwood, age 31 years, of the Duke of Cornwall's Light Infantry, who has been missing for 15 months, was killed in action on June 5th 1942.

Before the war Private Harwood worked at Shady Pit, Three Ponds, Somercotes.

After doing internal duties in Iraq the battalion moved to Egypt on the 28th of May 1942 and the division went straight into battle. The 1st Battalion moved to a plateau over looking Sollum Bay near the Libyan-Egyptian border. The situation in the Western Desert did not look good for the Allies. Rommel's Africa Corps launched its attack eastwards on the 26th of May 1942 and quickly pushed forward. The battalion took up defensive positions at Sollum Bay where heavy fighting took place, which forced the battalion to fall back along the Mediterranean Coast. They continued to retreat to Mersa Matruh and on to El Alamein where the line held on the 1st of July. Many were killed, wounded, missing or taken prisoner. Sadly Samuel Harwood was killed in the early stages of this action.

Alamein Memorial. Egypt.

Frederick William Henson.

Rank.	Lance Bombardier
Regiment.	Royal Artillery
Unit.	29 (Corunna) H.A.A. Battery
Service No.	229313
Date of Death.	31st August 1955
Age.	20
Cemetery.	Hanover Military Cemetery
Grave.	Plot 5, Row G, Grave 9.

Frederick was the son of Alice Ann and Frederick William Henson, one of 10 children. He resided at Beech Avenue, Pinxton, Derbyshire and worked at Oates Pipe Yard before enlisting.
Frederick was a motor cyclist leading a convoy in Limmer, Northern Germany when he was in collision with a lorry. He died of injuries sustained in the accident.

Frederick Henson in uniform

Frederick Henson's funeral

Floral Tributes to Frederick Henson

Hanover Military Cemetery. Germany.

Sydney Huskinson.

Rank.	Able Seaman
Service.	Royal Navy
	H.M.S. Hood
Service No.	P/SSX 27736
Date of Death.	24th May 1941
Age.	19
Memorial.	Portsmouth Naval Memorial
	Panel 48, Column 2. Lost at Sea

Sydney was the son of George Frederick and Sarah Ann Huskinson, of Pinxton, Derbyshire.

Sydney was born at 111 Park Lane Pinxton and started work at Brookhill Colliery before joining the Navy. He was one of the crew of the H.M.S. Hood, a battle cruiser which was considered to be one of the finest ships in the world. H.M.S. Hood's final voyage began at 00.50 on Thursday 22nd May 1941 from Scarpa Flow with young Sydney Huskinson on board.

H.M.S. Hood was the pride of the Royal Navy; it was a massively armed battle cruiser and as one of the most powerful ships afloat was faster than the Bismarck by 3 knots, which was achieved by the lack of heavy armour. This was considered sufficient in 1918 when she was built, but was to prove to be a fatal flaw in 1941.

On May 24th 1941, the Royal Navy trailed the Bismarck and Prinz Eugen as they attempted to break out of the Denmark Straits into the Atlantic. If both these powerful ships had got through they could have created havoc amongst the supply convoys that were vital to Britain. On May 24th at 05.52 the Hood opened fire and was shortly joined by the Prince of Wales. At 05.54 the German ships opened fire primarily against the Hood. At 06.00 a salvo hit the Hood and one of the shells penetrated the Hood's deck and exploded in one of the magazines. A massive explosion tore the Hood in half. Those who saw the explosion said the bows of the Hood were raised out of the sea. The ship sank extremely quickly, within two minutes, and 1,415 out of a total crew of 1,418 died. If the ship had been fitted with the thicker deck armour the shell would probably not have penetrated the deck.

The loss of the Navy's flagship in such dramatic circumstances and appalling loss of life were greeted with profound shock in Britain. Prime Minister Winston Churchill signalled to the fleet: "The Bismarck must be sunk at all costs". Crippled by aircraft of the Fleet Air Arm, Bismarck was engaged by the Battleships King George V and Rodney on the morning of the 27th May, finally being sunk by torpedoes. The destruction of the mighty Hood had been avenged after one of the most dramatic battles in naval history.

H.M.S. Hood

The German Battleship Bismarck

Portsmouth Naval Memorial. England.

Allan Jones.

Rank.	Steward (took on other duties in battle)
Service.	Royal Navy
	H.M.S. Achates
Service No.	C/LX 25240
Date of Death.	31st December 1942
Age.	27
Memorial.	Chatham Naval Memorial
	64, 3. Lost at Sea

Allan was born on the 15th April 1915 at 53 Talbot Street Pinxton, the youngest son of George and Mary Ellen Jones. His father George was born in Dudley in 1870 and his mother Mary Ellen in Eckington in 1878. He had 6 brothers and 5 sisters.

Article from the Free Press dated January 1943.

News has been received of the death of Mr. Allan Jones, aged 27, husband of Mrs. Margaret Jones, now residing with his sister-in-law at 39 Montague Road, Peterborough, and the son of the late George Jones of Pinxton. Allan was several years in the Navy, but left a year prior to the outbreak of the war to become an agent for the Britannic Insurance Co. In October 1940, he was recalled to the Navy. Mr. and Mrs. Allan Jones would have celebrated their wedding anniversary on January 15th.

Whilst escorting the convoy J.W.15B in the Arctic on New Year's Eve, H.M.S. Achates received hits from the attacking German heavy cruiser Admiral Hipper.
The Achates lost steam and received several more hits until she sank in three minutes taking 113 men to the bottom; only 80 survivors were picked-up from the freezing water.
The battle in which he died was known as the Battle of the Barents Sea. The convoy was on its way to Russia, being escorted by the Achates.
H.M.S. Achates, H.M.S. Bramble, H.M.S. Sheffield and H.M.S. Jamaica were part of a convoy of sixteen ships going to Seydis Fiord in the Barents Sea, when on December 31st H.M.S. Bramble sighted the heavy cruisers Admiral Hipper and Lutznow plus four destroyers. Achates began to lay a smoke screen down to cover the convoy, but the Hipper had already overwhelmed H.M.S. Bramble, which had become detached from the convoy. Suddenly the Hipper reappeared near the convoy and quickly crippled H.M.S. Achates, which was still in the process of laying the smoke screen. After several hits from the Hipper she sank. H.M.S. Sheffield and Jamaica arrived and forced the enemy to retire. Not one ship in the merchant

convoy was lost. When Hitler learned of this he flew into a rage at the fact that five destroyers had held off a pocket battleship and six destroyers, forcing them to withdraw.

H.M.S Achates

Allan Jones' parents' grave in Pinxton churchyard, east side.
Allan is remembered at the base.

Chatham Naval Memorial. England.

Dennis Lawrance.

Rank.	Bombardier
Regiment.	Sherwood Foresters (Notts and Derby Regiment)
Unit.	6th Battalion, 502 Bty. Lt. A.A. Regt.
Service No.	2089668
Date of Death.	22nd September 1944
Cemetery.	Oostende New Communal
Grave.	Plot 9. Row 9. Grave 34.

Dennis was the son of Arthur and Annie Lawrance and the husband of Edna Lawrance of Pinxton, Derbyshire.

Dennis was born and lived in Alexander Terrace and educated at Pinxton schools. Upon leaving school he became a joiner by trade. He was conscripted into the army during the war. Dennis and Edna had a son, John, who was never to see his father.

Oostende New Communal Cemetery. Belgium.

Ernest Millington.

Rank.	Sergeant (Pilot)
Service.	Royal Air Force Volunteer Reserve
Service No.	1125315
Date of Death.	9th March 1942
Age.	22
Cemetery.	St Helen's Churchyard, Pinxton
Grave.	Plot 1. Row 14. Grave 38.

Sergeant Pilot Millington and his father Ernest Millington

Excerpt from Pinxton Parish Magazine.

Saturday, March 14th will long be remembered by those many people who came to pay their tribute to two Pinxton men, father and son, whose deaths within a month of each other have shocked us all. Ernest Millington, senior, was an expert in explosives whose services the country can ill afford to lose. He lost his life in a fire. Terrible that was for Mrs. Millington and family, worse was to follow. On Tuesday March 10, there arrived from the Air Force Authorities the most dreaded of all telegrams announcing that Sergeant Pilot Millington had lost his life whilst flying. Of Ernest Millington Junior I still find it extremely difficult to give adequate expression of how his death has affected us all. When I first came to Pinxton Ernest was 15, and shared the full club life of those good old days in St Helen's Hall. He completed his school life at Nottingham High School and became school captain. His school days over he joined a Northern Steel Firm, and it soon became apparent he possessed his full share of his father's brains. Fifteen months ago, aged 20, he joined the Royal Air Force and very quickly gained promotion.
R. Horton, Rector.

Report from Free Press 20th March 1942.
Double Bereavement.
Pinxton family's double loss.

A memorial service to the late Mr. E. Millington of Donington House, Pinxton, technical adviser to the Ministry of Supply, and former manager of the Notts and Derby Coke and By-Product Co. Limited, Pinxton, who lost his life in the Deansgate Hotel Fire at Manchester on 11th February 1942 was combined with the funeral of his son Sergeant Pilot E. Millington who lost his life whilst on active service. The service was held at Pinxton St Helen's church.

Sergeant Pilot E. Millington was the eldest son of the late Mr. Millington. He was 22 years of age, and was educated at the Nottingham High School. He was a keen sportsman, being the School House Captain. He had been serving in the R.A.F. for 15 months and prior to joining up was in the service of Messrs Thomas Firth and John Brown Limited, Sheffield. Both father and son were held in high esteem, and sincere sympathy is extended to the family in their double loss within a month. The large sympathetic gathering of friends at the service testified to the regard in which father and son were held in the district. The coffin, which was covered with the Union Jack, bore floral tributes from mother and family and Sergeant Pilot Millington's fiancée, Freda.

Six R.A.F. N.C.O.s acted as bearers, namely Flight Sergeant Smith, Sergeant Fentan, Sergeant Hodden, Sergeant Hobbs, Sergeant Sessons and Sergeant Hogg.

The Rev. R. Horton conducted the service.

Sergeant Ernest Millington was onboard Wellington 1CZ 8774, of No. 21 Operational Training Unit, R.A.F. Edgehill, No. 6 Group, Bomber Command which was lost in a flying accident.

At 23.05 hours on 9th March 1942, the bomber was attempting to land on instruments. After receiving permission to land, the aircraft commenced a left-hand turn onto the final approach but it was already dangerously low. The Wellington struck the ground, killing all five members of the crew.

The Crew were:
Pilot Officer R. C. Trench – Captain.
Sergeant A. L. Clipson – Pilot.
Sergeant E. Millington – Pilot.
Sergeant T. M. Fitzjohn – Wireless Operator/Gunner.
Sergeant R. Fossey – Gunner.

Ernest's grave in St. Helen's churchyard, Pinxton.

John Renshaw.

Rank.	Bombardier
Regiment.	Royal Artillery
Unit.	33rd Airborne Light Regiment
Service No.	14406048
Date of Death.	18th October 1947
Age.	24
Cemetery.	Khayat Beach War Cemetery
Grave.	D. H. 9.

The 1939-1945 war had overshadowed the "Palestine Question" and tension between the Jews and the Arabs was running high. The 33rd Airborne Division was sent out to Palestine as part of the 6th Division as a peace-keeping force to separate the Jews and Arabs. The violence escalated and British soldiers were deemed to be the oppressors by the Jewish population. Palestine was a huge burden for British soldiers; by 1947 the future of Palestine was before the United Nations and they recommended partition. Thus on May 15th 1948 the state of Israel was born. During these troubled times the 6th Division was in Palestine where 236 soldiers were wounded and 58 killed. Sadly John was one of those who lost their lives.

Khayat Beach War Cemetery. Israel.

Sidney Rhodes.

Rank.	Flight Sergeant
Service.	Royal Air Force
Service No.	564006
Date of Death.	29th October 1942
Age.	29
Memorial.	Singapore Memorial
	Column 414. Lost at Sea

Son of Mr. and Mrs. W. G. Rhodes of Pinxton, Derbyshire.
Sidney was educated at Brunt's school, Mansfield. Upon leaving school at the age of sixteen Sidney joined the R.A.F.

Sidney Rhodes aged 18

Report from local paper.

Mr. and Mrs. Rhodes have received notification that their eldest son Flight Sergeant Rhodes, aged 29, is missing through enemy action. Flight Sergeant Rhodes has been an instructor for over two years and has been in the Air Force 13 years.

Flight Sergeant Sydney Rhodes, elder brother of Norman, joined the R.A.F. in 1929. He was an arms expert and was in Australia training their Air Force personnel. When his tour of duty ended, he was returning home by sea on the M.S.S. Abosso via Cape Town to Liverpool when his ship was attacked and sunk by the German U-boat U-575 about 589 nautical miles north of Lajes Field, Azores. There were only 31 survivors; a total of 168 crew and 83 passengers were lost. Among the passengers were 44 newly trained pilots from the 23rd Service Flight Training School at Heany, Southern Rhodesia.
The survivors were picked up from the freezing Atlantic three days later by H.M.S.Bideford.
U-575 was sunk on March the 13th 1944.

Sydney Rhodes at home on leave

M.S.S. Abosso

Singapore Memorial, Kranji War Cemetery.

Stanley Severns.

Rank.	Able Seaman
Service.	Royal Navy
	H.M.S. Ilex
Service No.	P/JX 239359
Date of Death.	14th May 1943
Age.	25
Memorial.	Portsmouth Naval Memorial
	Panel 75, Column 3.　　Lost at Sea

Stanley Severns

Stanley was the son of George and Emily Severns, of Pinxton, Derbyshire, one of three sons. They resided at 16 Wharf Road in Pinxton.
Able Seaman Severns was killed whilst on loan to the Polish ship Posaric. The ship hit a mine off the coast of Libya.

Report from local paper.

News has been received by Mr. George Severns of 16 Wharf Road, Pinxton that his son Able Seaman Severns has died while serving in North Africa.
Deceased was 25 years of age and before joining the forces was employed by the Brookhill Colliery, Pinxton.
A brother, Driver Lloyd Severns, has been in the Middle East for the past three years.

**The Ilex at Charleston U.S.A. on 7th September 1942
H.M.S. Ilex was an "I" Class Fleet Destroyer.**

Some details of the Ilex's War Service when Stanley may have been onboard:
13th October 1939: Participated in the sinking of U-boat 42.
28th May 1940: Joined Flotilla for Fleet defence and convoy escort duty.
27th June 1940: Escorted battleships, cruisers and HM Aircraft Carrier Eagle, providing cover for the passage of Convoys MF1 and MS1 from Malta.
29th June 1940: Participated in the sinking of Italian submarine Uebi Scebeli.
19th July 1940: Escorted destroyers during the sinking of Italian cruiser Bartolomeo Colleoni.

H.M.S. Ilex was laid-up in reserve at Malta in May 1945, finally being sold for breaking-up in 1947.

Portsmouth Naval Memorial. England.

John Siddall.

Rank.	Able Seaman
Service.	Royal Navy
	H.M.S. Hood
Service No.	P/SSX 22432
Date of Death.	24th May 1941
Age.	18
Memorial.	Portsmouth Naval Memorial
	Panel 49, Column 2. Lost at Sea

John lost his life on H.M.S. Hood which was sunk in the North Sea by the German Battleship Bismarck. The Hood at this time was the pride of the British Navy, one of the world's finest ships.

Admiral Holland on the Hood ordered the battle cruiser to turn into the German battleships and on May 24th at 05.52 they were only 22,000 metres apart. The Hood opened fire and shortly afterwards was joined by the Prince of Wales. At 05.54 both the Prinz Eugen and the Bismarck fired at the Hood.

The Prinz Eugen hit the Hood and set alight some shells on the deck, which produced a lot of smoke but no danger. At 06.00 a salvo from the Bismarck hit the Hood from 17,000 metres, the elevation of the Bismarck's guns meant that the shells had a high trajectory and a steep angle of descent. With the Hood having minimal horizontal armour a shell penetrated the deck and exploded in one of the Hood's magazines, tearing her in half and sinking her in two minutes.

Two Pinxton men went down with her, John Siddall and Sydney Huskinson.

Eric Mellor, a Pinxton resident at the time of the sinking, stated that he was walking back to Pinxton along the canal from Jacksdale and when he got to Pinxton he found people on the street astounded at the news of the sinking of the Hood. They were all talking about it, hoping that the two Pinxton men who were on the ship would be safe.

John is remembered at The Hood Chapel, Church of St John, Boldre, Hampshire.

H.M.S. Hood

Bismarck seen from Prinz Eugen

Bismarck firing on H.M.S. Hood

Portsmouth Naval Memorial. England.

Albert James Slater.

Rank.	Marine
Regiment.	Royal Marines
	H.M.S. Glorious
Service No.	PLY/X 2124
Date of Death.	8th June 1940
Age.	20
Memorial.	Plymouth Naval Memorial
	Panel 43, Column 2. Lost at Sea

Albert was the son of Mrs. Hilda Slater of 45 Kirkstead Rows, Pinxton, Derbyshire.

Kirkstead Rows Pinxton

On leaving school he worked in Summit Colliery Lamp Cabin. He enlisted at the age of 17 years, joining the Royal Marines. Albert had a brother, Frank, serving with the Border Regiment.

H.M.S. Glorious

On the afternoon of Saturday the 8th of June 1940 the aircraft carrier H.M.S. Glorious and her escorting destroyers H.M.S. Acasta and H.M.S. Ardent were intercepted in the Norwegian Sea by the German Battlecruisers Gneisenau and Scharnhorst. The three British ships were sunk by gunfire in an engagement that lasted just over 2 hours, with the loss of over 1,500 officers and men of the Royal Navy, Royal Marines and the Royal Air Force, leaving only 39 survivors. After the engagement the Gneisenau and the Scharnhorst made no attempt to recover survivors.

The Scharnhorst was sunk on the 26th of Dec. 1943 at 19.48 hrs.

Plymouth Naval Memorial. England.

Francis Victor Matthew Slater.

Rank.	Flight Sergeant (Nav.)
Service.	Royal Air Force Volunteer Reserve
Service No.	1579284
Date of Death.	28th November 1943
Age.	32
Cemetery.	St Helen's Churchyard, Pinxton
Grave.	Plot 2. Row 17. Grave 1.

Francis was the son of George and Annie Slater and husband of Vera Annie Slater of Pinxton.

Francis (right) with a friend

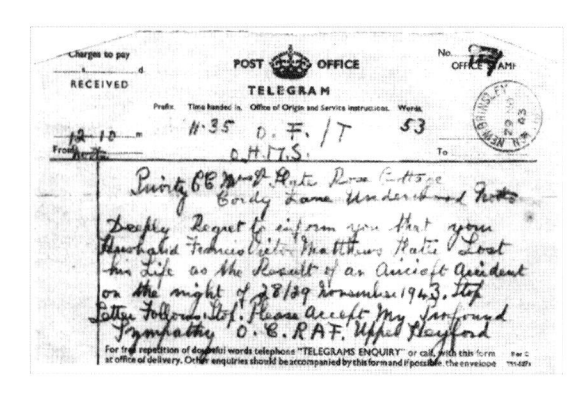

Telegram informing of Francis' death

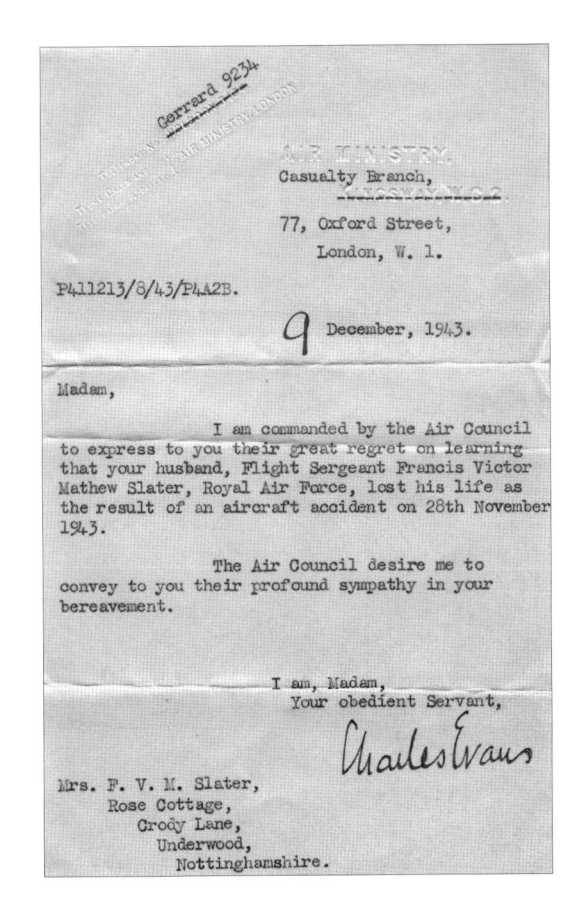

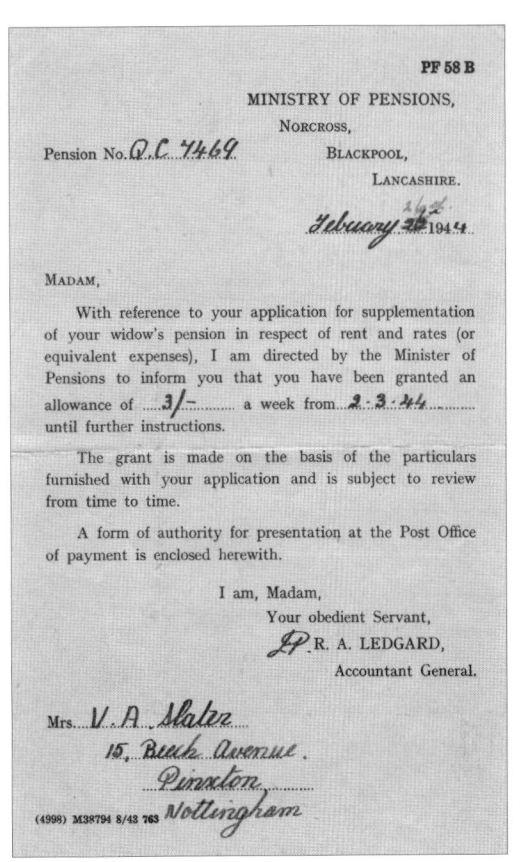

Letter from the Air Council **Pension payments**

Francis Victor Matthew Slater was born at Rose Cottage, Cordy Lane, Underwood. He married Vera Knighton of Pinxton and they had three children, Andree, Victor and David. Before joining the R.A.F. he worked at the M.G.O. (The Midland General Omnibus Company) at Underwood.

On 28th November 1943 Francis was on board a Wellington Mk. X bomber, Serial No. HE 904, of No. 16 Operational Training Unit, R.A.F. Upper Heyford, which was involved in a mid-air collision with another Wellington bomber at Baynards Green, Oxfordshire. The other Wellington had come from R.A.F. Croughton. Only one member of the eight man crew in Sergeant Slater's Wellington survived the crash. He was Warrant Officer Lowman, the pilot.

Members of the crew that perished were:

Flight Officer G. Stevens DFC   (Navigator)
Sergeant Roy Buffany   (Wireless Operator and Air Gunner)
Sergeant Francis Slater   (Navigator)
Sergeant Bill Sayers   (Rear Gunner)
Sergeant MacNeil   (Rear Upper Gunner)
W. Rose   (Air Bomber)
Pilot Officer D.J. Arnell   (Navigator)

F. V. M. Slater's grave in Pinxton churchyard

Respects to Flight Sergeant F. Slater at the Memorial Service, Pinxton, 2006

Ernest Smith.

Rank.	Fight Lieutenant (Nav.)
Service.	Royal Air Force Volunteer Reserve
Unit.	47th Squadron
Service No.	164809
Date of Death.	13th February 1947
Cemetery.	Buxton Cemetery
Grave.	4259
Resided at	Redgate Street, Pinxton, Derbyshire

Ernest   **Ernest with wife Nora**

Ernest Smith, the only son of Tom and Ada Smith, was educated at Nottingham High School and upon leaving joined the R.A.F. In 1946, at the age of 21, he married Nora Weekly from Jacksdale at Bulwell, Nottingham. In 1947, five months after the accident, his son Richard was born, never to know his father.

Ernest Smith lost his life in a plane crash. The aircraft was a Halifax A Mk. 9, Serial No. RT 922, of the 47th Squadron, No. 38 Group Transport Command. It took off from R.A.F. Fairford (Gloucester) in appalling weather conditions, with very low cloud, on 13th February 1947 at 10.05 a.m.

They were delivering food and relief to the outlying snowbound areas of Staffordshire and the Peak District when the aircraft struck the ground with its starboard wing tip, crashed, broke-up and exploded, just one hour and three minutes after take off, with the loss of life of all those on board. The crash occurred 8 miles east of Leek on Grindon Moor, Staffordshire.

The crew and passengers lost were:
Squadron Leader Donald Don McIntyre (Pilot); Flight Lieutenant Ernest Smith (Navigator); Warrant Officer Gordon Victor Chapman (Navigator); Warrant Officer Richard Sydney Kearns (Flight Engineer); Flight Sergeant Kenneth Charles Pettit (Wireless Operator); Sergeant William Thomas Sherry; Mr. D. Saville (Press Photographer) and Mr. J. Reardon (Press Photographer).

The War Graves in Buxton Cemetery, Derbyshire.

Ernest Smith's Grave. Buxton Cemetery.

Ernest Reader Smith.

Rank.	Private
Service.	Corps of Military Police
Service No.	5053527
Date of Death.	27th March 1941
Age.	28
Cemetery.	St Helen's Churchyard, Pinxton
Grave.	Plot 1. Row 13. Grave 35.

Ernest was the son of William and Ada Smith of Pinxton, Derbyshire.
He was one of 6 children.
Ernest was killed whilst leading a convoy in Abergavenny, Wales. He was a Military Policeman riding a motorcycle at the front of the convoy when he was in collision with another army transport vehicle.

Ernest in uniform

**Ernest Smith with wife Gladys and friend Ray.
Ray was killed in North Africa on 16th April 1943.**

Ernest as a youth on a motor bike   **As a young boy**
His brother Wesley went through the war from Dunkirk to the end of hostilities.

Local paper report.

His many friends have heard with regret of the death of Private Ernest Smith of the Military Police, son of Mr. and Mrs. W. Smith, of Pinxton. He was 28 years of age and well known in the district. The funeral took place at St Helen's Church, Pinxton, conducted by the Reverend R. Horton. The coffin was draped with the Union Jack and the bearers were friends and members of the Home Guard. The hymns Abide with me and Think O Lord in Mercy were sung.

Ernest's grave in Pinxton churchyard, on the south side of the Memorial.

Bernard Hamilton Stephenson.

Rank.	Sergeant (W.Op./Air Gunner)
Service.	Royal Air Force Volunteer Reserve
Unit.	431 (Royal Canadian Air Force) Squadron
Service No.	1190561
Date of Death.	12th June 1943
Cemetery.	Oostende New Communal Cemetery
Grave.	Plot 9. Row 5. Grave 22.

Bernard was the son of James Alfred and Edith May Stephenson, of Pinxton, Derbyshire and husband of Alice Doreen Stephenson of Nottingham.

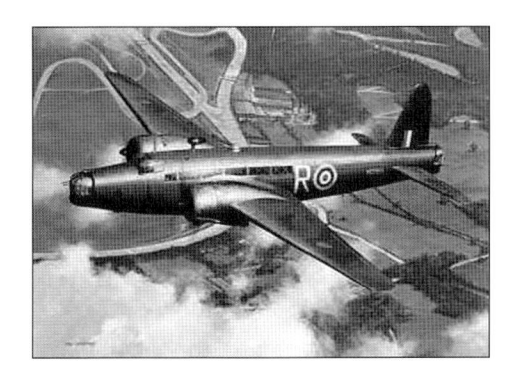

Wellington bomber

Sergeant Bernard Stephenson was the air gunner on board the Wellington Mk.X bomber, HE 184 from 431 Squadron based at R.A.F. Burn (Yorkshire), No. 4 Group, Bomber Command.

The aircraft took off at 23.20 hours on the 11th of June 1943 as part of a force of 783 aircraft comprising of 202 Halifaxes, 326 Lancasters, 143 Wellingtons, 99 Stirlings and 13 Mosquitoes sent to bomb Dusseldorf.

It was later reported that 38 aircraft had been lost on this operation. Wellington HE 184 crashed into the sea with the loss of all 5 members of the crew. The body of Sergeant Stephenson was recovered on the Belgium coast.

The crew were: Pilot Officer W.D.Eaglesham (Pilot); Flight Officer L.C.Long (Navigator);
Sergeant B.H.Stephenson (Air Gunner); Pilot Officer H.T.McAusland (Bomb Aimer) and
Pilot Officer J.H.Burrow (Wireless Operator).

Oostende New Communal Cemetery. Belgium.

George Thomas Truswell.

Rank.	Private
Regiment.	Leicestershire Regiment
Unit.	1st Battalion
Service No.	4858239
Date of Death.	Between 12th February 1942 and 15th February 1942
Age.	26
Memorial.	Singapore Civil Hospital Grave Memorial
	Column 4. No Known Grave

George was the son of Thomas and Eva Truswell of Pinxton,
who were not notified officially of his death until 20th December 1945.

At the fall of Singapore Private G. Truswell was in the military hospital recovering from wounds. At about 1 p.m. on Feb. 14th Japanese soldiers approached the hospital. Red Cross flags were displayed and no resistance was offered but shots were fired at the staff who displayed the flags. On entering the hospital Japanese soldiers attacked and killed medical staff and patients. Those left were marched to an industrial area and locked in a confined space. Some died during the night as a result of their treatment, the remainder were bayoneted the following morning. Sadly this may have been the fate of Thomas, known to his family as Tommy, and this was the name inscribed on The Hospital Memorial.

Lieutenant General Arthur Percival surrendered the Allied forces to the Japanese on Feb. 15th 1942 and they renamed the island Syonan-to (Light of the South). Many British and Australians were taken prisoner; some remained in Changi prison, whilst thousands of others were shipped on prisoner transports known as Hell Ships to other parts of Asia. Allied Forces did not set foot on Malayan soil until the 3rd Sept. 1945.

G Truswell with father and brother

George's father's grave in Pinxton Churchyard

Letter reporting George missing

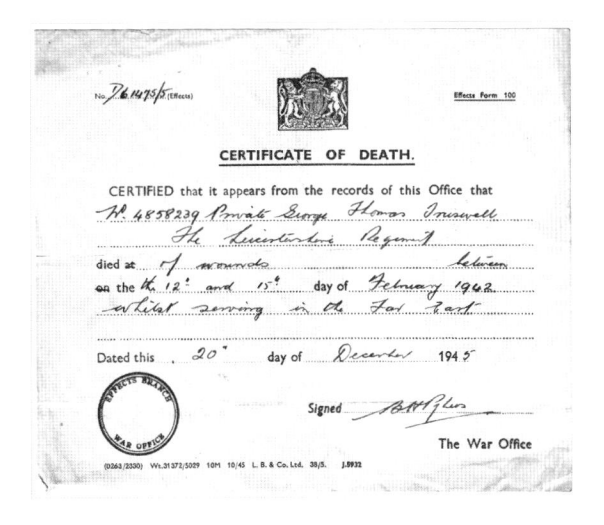

George's Death Certificate

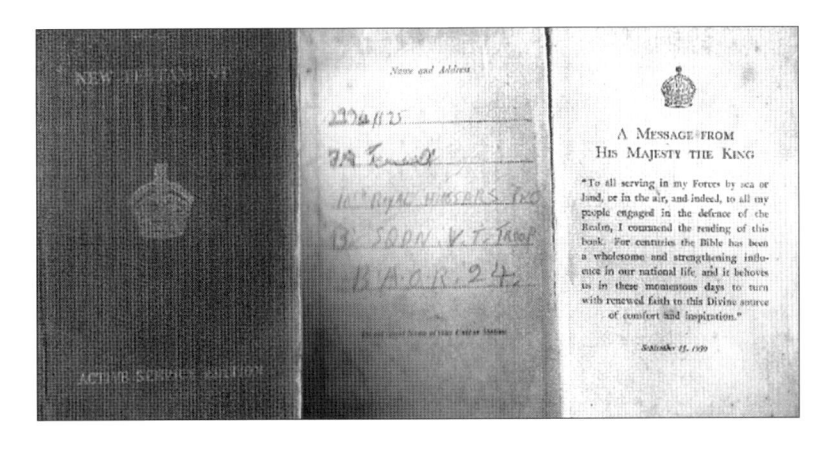

George Truswell's Service Bible

Singapore Civil Hospital Grave Memorial

The cross shows the names of the people who died in the hospital.
It is situated in Kranji War Cemetery.

Kranji War Cemetery. Singapore.

Kranji War Cemetery was used to collect all the bodies of the Allied soldiers from the island of Singapore and Indo China, now Vietnam.
The cemetery in which the cross is located is constructed on a hill and is 22 kilometres north of Singapore.

Jim Tryner.

Rank.	Private
Regiment.	York and Lancaster
Unit.	1st Battalion
Service No.	4748167
Date of Death.	13th July 1943
Age.	24
Cemetery.	Syracuse War Cemetery
Grave.	IV. A. 13.

Jim was the son of Joseph and Elizabeth Tryner of Pinxton, Derbyshire.

Jim (right) with Rowland Knapton

The 5th Infantry Division of the York and Lancaster Regiment began a series of journeys around various British theatres of war without getting involved in any of the action. They thus earned the nickname "Globe trotters".
In 1943 the globe trotting stopped and the division took part in the landing on Sicily. Sadly, it was here where Jim was killed.

Jim's brothers Eric and Sam on a pilgrimage, placing flowers on his grave at Syracuse.

Jim's grave at Syracuse   Jim's original grave

Letter from his close friend to Jim's parents, written after Jim was killed.

I have no doubt that this letter will be rather a surprise to you, but I feel that being the closest friend to your late and beloved son Jim, I ought to tell you as much as I possibly can.

To begin with, Jim and I first met when we joined the First Battalion in 1940. Since that day we have been the best of friends, sharing everything good and bad between us. When his parcel arrived we shared. When mine came we did the same and some how we felt that we knew each other's families intimately for we used to read extracts from each other's letters.

Before we embarked on this disastrous expedition we made an oath to each other that, should anything fatal happen to one of us, then the other would visit the parents, and I beg and pray that, with the grace of God, I shall be able to carry out Jim's wish. I shall be proud to visit the parents of such a fine and proud son of the Motherland.

I know from Jack Bradley that you have had the bad news, and the only consolation that I can give you is that Jim died as he wished to, that is, with his boots on. He suffered no pain for he was killed instantly by a bomb, whilst trying to find his company commander who had been reported to be missing.

I have four photographs of my pal Jim, three taken at Damascus and one at Dungannon.

As much and dearly as I treasure these I will send them on to you if you will please write and let me know if you want them.

I am afraid I simply cannot write any more in this letter, so I will close by saying God Bless you and please try to keep your chin up. Remember he died doing his duty.

I remain your friend and sympathiser in this great loss.

Private Rowland Knapton.

Syracuse War Cemetery. Sicily.

Harold Vale.

Rank.	Private
Regiment.	Monmouthshire Regiment
Unit.	3rd Battalion
Service No.	5052755
Date of Death.	12th May 1945
Age.	28
Cemetery.	Reichswald Forest War Cemetery
Grave.	54. D. 5.

Report from local paper.

Mrs. H. Vale of Alfreton Road, Pinxton received the sad news on Friday that her husband Private Harold Vale, aged 29, had been accidentally killed in Western Europe as a result of an ammunition explosion whilst engaged in battlefield clearance.

An officer writes in a letter of sympathy: "It is particularly tragic that this should occur after cessation of hostilities, when he had survived all the campaigns of the battlefield. He was a most conscientious soldier and liked by all his comrades".

Before joining-up, Private Vale worked at No. 2 Pit, Pinxton. In addition to his wife, he leaves a five year old daughter, Joan.

Reichswald Forest War Cemetery. Germany.

Robert Reginald Walters.

Rank.	Sergeant
Regiment.	Royal Army Medical Corps
Service No.	7371018
Date of Death.	22nd November 1942
Age.	25
Cemetery.	Dely Ibrahim War Cemetery
Grave.	3. F. 18.

Sergeant Robert Walters

Robert was born at Selston and worked for the Co-operative Society. He married Myra Evelyn Butler on January 3rd 1942 and they lived at 30, Town Street, Pinxton. They had only been married six weeks when he was conscripted and being a member of the St John Ambulance Brigade, he was directed to the Royal Medical Corps. His wife was never to see him again. His unit was shipped to Algiers and on landing marched to base hospital which was the 64th General Hospital, but en-route they were bombed by the Vichy French. Sergeant Walters was killed during the attack. Myra never remarried; three months later she also lost her brother Thomas in action in Burma.

Myra worked for Everlastic at Beeston, Nottingham, working six days a week. The girls on the line gave their clothing coupons to get the material for her wedding dress, which was made on the line. When Robert was killed, she received a letter from Everlastic just two weeks later telling her to return to work as the factory was doing war work.

Robert and Myra's wedding group

Robert and Myra's wedding

Dely Ibrahim War Cemetery. Algeria.

Eric Wetton.

    Rank.   Private
    Regiment.   The Queen's Royal Regiment (West Surrey)
    Unit.   2/7 Battalion
    Service No.   100272
    Date of Death.   24th February 1944
    Age.   28
    Memorial.   Cassino Memorial
                            Panel 4.   No Known Grave

Private E. Wetton

    Eric Wetton was born one of six boys. His brothers were William, Cyril, James, Ernest and Clifford. They initially lived at Widmerpool Street, and then moved to 77, Town Street, Pinxton. He was educated at Pinxton Schools. Eric worked as a stoker at Pinxton Coke Ovens before enlisting into the army on 5th September 1939, just two days after war was declared. He joined the Auxiliary Military Pioneer Corps and was with the British Expeditionary Force in France and evacuated at Dunkirk, after which he was transferred to the Sherwood Foresters. He was with the Mediterranean Expeditionary Force in Egypt in 1942, and then with Montgomery's 8th Army in North Africa (The Desert Rats).

    After this Eric was transported with the Queen's Royal Regiment (West Surrey) and landed at Anzio on the 18th February 1944. The regiment was marched into the concentration area on the 19th February assuming a counter attack role in the area of the flyover bridge on the main Nettuno to Rome road. In front was the American 2nd Battalion 157 Regiment which was isolated and surrounded. Eric's regiment was chosen to relieve this position "at all costs".

    So on the evening of the 21st the 2/7 battalion went forward to relieve them, towards the maze of broken wadis and caves which marked the American positions. The supply problem was difficult as no transport other than jeeps could hope to get beyond the flyover. Heavy fighting took place, and as they crossed the wadis there was a big air raid and they had to fight the Germans hand to hand everywhere. A considerable number of anti-personnel "Butterfly" bombs were scattered through the column causing heavy casualties.

But the companies pushed on, securing the main crossing of the wadi by 23.30 hours, and after taking some prisoners, reached the American Head Quarters situated in caves in the side of the wadi. In the caves were many seriously wounded Americans with several Italian men, women and children.

With Bren gun and mortar fire they managed to keep the Germans quiet and by nightfall the Americans were able to withdraw according to a pre-arranged plan and the area was clear by 20.00 hours next day. By the 24th February the Queen's Royals had lost 362 officers and men, killed, wounded or missing. Sadly, Eric was one of the missing.

The battle for Anzio was very important because it held the gateway into Italy. The German Army was under specific orders from Hitler to hold the position, which was known as the Gustav Line.

Eric served for 5 years and 173 days with different regiments.

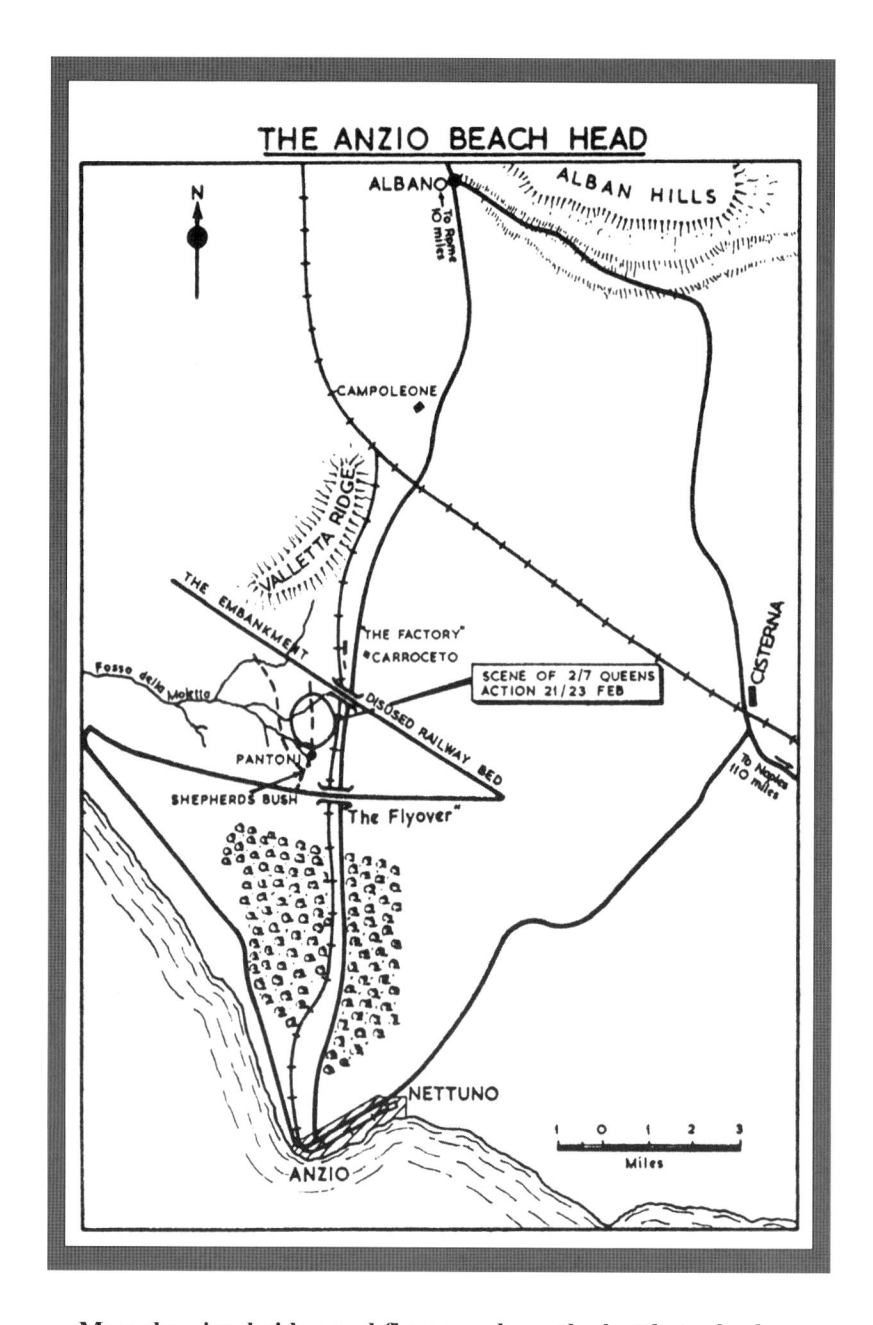

Map showing bridge and flyover where the battle took place

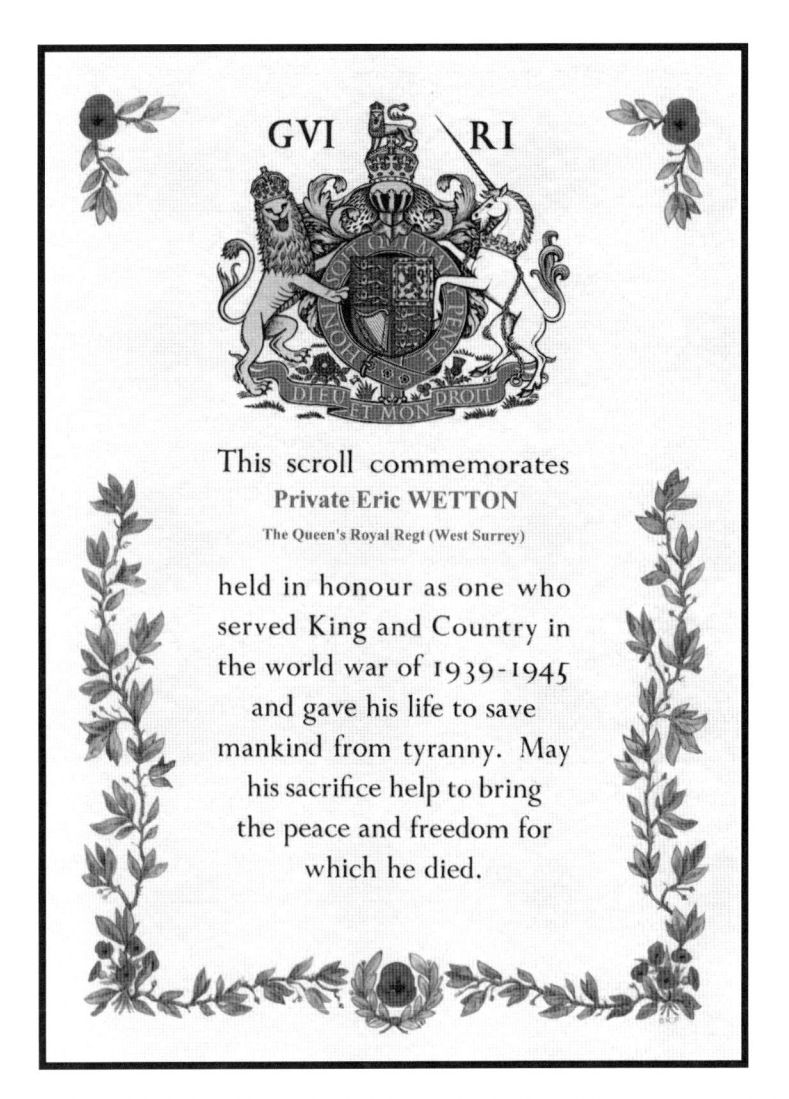

This scroll commemorates
Private Eric WETTON
The Queen's Royal Regt (West Surrey)

held in honour as one who served King and Country in the world war of 1939-1945 and gave his life to save mankind from tyranny. May his sacrifice help to bring the peace and freedom for which he died.

Cassino Memorial. Italy.

Albert Mons Henry Wilson.

Rank.	Fusilier
Regiment.	Royal Northumberland Fusiliers
Service No.	14670226
Date of Death.	4th April 1945
Age.	22
Cemetery.	Reichswald Forest War Cemetery
Grave.	55. A. 14.

Albert was the son of T.H. and Ethel Wilson of Pinxton, Derbyshire.

Albert was killed towards the end of the war at the time of the crossing of the Rhine and was buried in a British cemetery in Germany.

Reichswald Forest War Cemetery. Germany.

The Cemetery was created after the war, when burials were brought in from all over western Germany. There are 7,594 Commonwealth servicemen of the Second World War buried or commemorated in the cemetery. 176 of the burials are unidentified.

Martha Annie Nuttall.

>Housewife
>Age 55
>Resided at 1 Church Street, Pinxton
>Wife of Alfred Nuttall
>Died 12th August 1940
>Killed by a bomb blast in her home

Martha was born at 34 Mill Street, Ludlow, Shropshire, the daughter of Edward Bird and his wife Annie Elizabeth.
Martha was first married to Lancelot William Edgar Houghton and then to George Shrives. He was killed in the Munitions Factory explosion at Chilwell, Notts, on the 1st July 1918. In 1920 Martha married Alfred Nuttall.
Martha and Alfred lived at No. 1 Church Street, opposite Booth's shop and The Three Horse Shoes pub in Pinxton. They had just decorated the house and were awaiting some evacuees on the 12th August when a bomb hit the house and killed her.

Martha's daughter Eunice

The bombed house, No. 1 Church Street, where Martha died

Report from local paper.

AIR RAID OVER THE MIDLANDS.

During an enemy air raid over Pinxton one house was demolished, a woman died, her husband sustained head injuries and the daughter a foot injury.

The house where she lived was a semi-detached one, and the next door people received no injuries, suffering no more than a bit of debris from the ceiling.

Across the street from the demolished house, big business premises are situated and one bomb fell in the garden making a deep hole. A short distance away from the demolished building two bombs dropped into a field adjoining eight houses but no damage was done except to fences and an apple tree.

In an interview the daughter of Martha, named Eunice, said: "I heard something drop onto the roof of the house, but we could not do anything. I heard my father shout and later we were got out with a ladder by the wardens". She stated that they were covered with debris from the ceiling and roof. Her father sustained head injuries and she had injuries to her foot. Her mother never spoke, but breathed heavily and passed away.

Wardens who included the Rector, Police and A. R. P. officers and other men were soon on the spot and rendered assistance. There was no danger from fire or gas. The local authority promptly began the clearance of the debris, and the household furniture of the destroyed house was carried into the yard of the business premises opposite.

A more recent report from a local paper.

Grateful Gran Eunice Bramley told of her miraculous escape from death in a war time bomb blast which killed her mother and left her father injured. Widow Eunice relived the tragedy of being rescued from her badly damaged home only to be told that her mother had died in the blast.

Eunice, herself then a girl of 15, might also have been a victim of the blast, but she had moved out of her bedroom in preparation of the arrival of two evacuees.

"It was nothing short of a miracle, I always said it was not my time. If I had been in my own bedroom I would have been killed because the whole side of the house where the bedroom was situated was demolished".

The family's home was the only one to be bombed that night; it was thought that the bombers' main target was the Pinxton Coke Ovens. Eunice stated that the first she knew of the bomb was to be awakened by a rattling sound and everything falling on top of us. "We were rescued by ladder from the bedroom window. My father had a gash on his head and I had an injured foot".

Joseph Ellis. DSM.

Rank.	Stoker First Class
Service.	Royal Navy
	H.M.S. Jed
Service No.	K/48778
Born.	13th November 1892
Died.	14th March 1976
Son of	William Ellis
Resided at	6 Park Lane Pinxton
Enlisted.	May 1914
Married.	Mary Hill on the 7th October 1922

Joseph and Mary had three boys, Joseph, William and Eric and four girls, Nellie, Jean, Mary and Hazel. Although Joseph Ellis did not die during the war, and thus does not appear on the Pinxton War Memorial, we considered that his bravery should be recorded.

Joseph Ellis **Mary, Joseph's wife**

The DSM awarded to J. Ellis for extreme bravery

J. Ellis's Long Service Medal

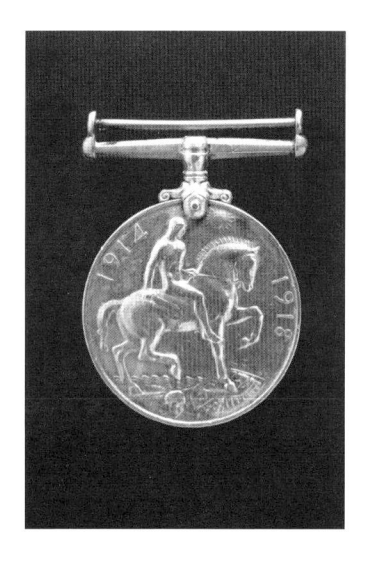

J. Ellis's War Medal

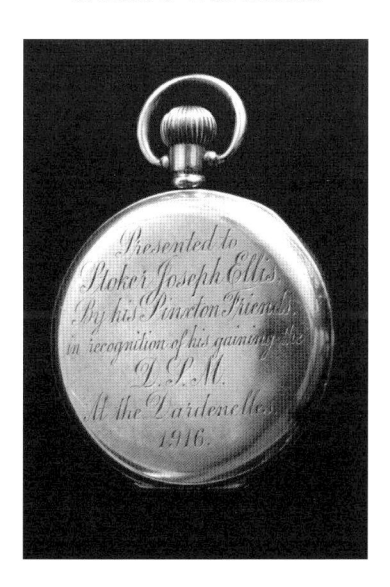

Watch presented to J. Ellis from his friends at Pinxton

Report from local paper.

Among the list of Gallipoli awards appears the name of 1st Class Stoker Ellis of Pinxton, who has been awarded the D.S.M. for service in the Dardanelles last August. Stoker Ellis, who joined the Navy in May 1914, is the son of Mr. William Ellis, 6 Park Lane, Pinxton. Writing to his father, Stoker Ellis says: "We had a strenuous time when the fleet tried to force the Dardanelles and we saw some lively times. We were the first boat along side the Ocean when she went down and took most of the crew off. Then we had a good spell in the Gulf of Saros. That is the place where I got the Medal. We were landing a party of soldiers, and had been busy firing for twelve hours when the Turks rushed down with guns and maxims, and one of the boats with soldiers in was sinking, so they called out for volunteers to rescue them. I jumped in and saved all but one, and shells and bullets were flying pretty thick too, but we all got back safely".

J. Ellis's War Record

An older Joseph (left)

Joseph Ellis's ship, H.M.S. Jed

V. E. DAY CELEBRATIONS   8th May 1945

THEY SHALL GROW NOT OLD, AS WE THAT ARE LEFT GROW OLD:

AGE SHALL NOT WEARY THEM, NOR THE YEARS CONDEMN.

AT THE GOING DOWN OF THE SUN AND IN THE MORNING

WE WILL REMEMBER THEM.

                                        Laurence Binyon

We honour all the personnel who fought for their Country in both World Wars and returned home to Pinxton

It has been impossible to name the soldiers who returned from the First World War as records were not kept at that time, however below is an accurate a list as it has been possible to compile of all the men and women of Pinxton who returned home after the Second World War.

Surname	Name	Regiment	Rank
Amos	Colin	Army	Sapper
Amos	F.		
Anthony	Enoch	Navy	
Ashford	James	Army	Private
Ashford	Leonard		
Bacon	Harold		
Barling	Sidney	R.A.F.	Aircraftsman
Barling	Colin		
Baxter	William	Army	Lance Sergeant
Baxter	Selwyn	Army	2nd Class Warrant Officer
Baxter	Horace	Army	Gunner
Beardsmore	Ernest		
Beardsmore	H.		
Beardsmore	Arthur		
Belshaw	Eric	R.A.F.	Leading Aircraftsman
Belshaw	William	Army	
Birch	Ted	Army	Private
Bird	Terry	Merchant Navy	Wireless Officer
Bird	Oliver	Army	Driver
Bird	Harvey	R.A.F.	Aircraftsman
Bools	George		
Booth	Harry	Army	Lieutenant
Bosworth	Cyril	Army	
Bott	Gerald	Army	Gunner
Bott	Arthur		
Bradley	Jack	Army	Private
Bradley	Albert	Army	
Bradshaw	Sydney		
Bradshaw	T.		
Bradshaw	Donald		
Bramley	Maurice	Army	Private
Breton	Joyce	Land Army	
Brooks	Frank	Army	Gunner
Brooks	Jack	Army	Gunner
Buckby	Alf	Army	
Butler	Peter		
Butler	V.		
Butler	A.		
Butler	Biddy	Land Army	
Butler	Edna	Wrens	
Buxton	Jack		
Carter	J.		
Cartlidge	Leslie	Army	Lance Corporal
Chamberlain	Fred	Navy	Seaman
Chantrey	Fred	Army	Gunner
Chantrey	D.		
Chapel	Elsie	Land Army	
Clarke	Horace		Marine
Clarke	Stanley	Army	Gunner
Clarke	Albert	Army	
Clarke	T.		
Clifton	Frank	Army	Sapper Engineer
Cotterill	Arthur	Navy	Single Man Seaman
Cotterill	Haworth	Army	Sergeant
Cotterill	J.		
Cotterill	Harold	R.A.F.	Aircraftsman
Coupe	Henry	Army	Regular
Cox	R.		
Cutts	James	R.A.F.	Policeman

Dalby	Harold		
Dale	George	Army	Lance Corporal
Darnell	Sydney	Navy	
Darnell	Alfred	Army	
Day	Ivy	Land Army	
Daykin	W.		
Davis	Ethel	Wrens	
Dickson	Norman		
Dooley	Albert	Army	
Dye	Harold		
Dye	Ernest		
Etherington	Dennis	Army	
Evans	Tomas	Army	Private
Evans	Lloyd	Army	Driver
Fantom	Samuel	Army	Gunner
Fletcher	Archie	Army	Gunner
Flint	F.		
Flint	Stanley		
Flint	Reginald	Navy	Petty Officer
Freeman	Howard	R.A.F.	
Garner	Charlie	Army	
Gee	Harold	Army	
Gent	Lawrence	Army	
Gent	Doris	W.R.A.F	
Gibson	Arthur	Army	Private
Giles	Jack		Lance Corporal
Goodall	Jack	Army	Private
Graney	Arthur	Army	Private
Guy	Sue	Land Army	
Hancock	Arthur	Army	
Hancock	Ernest	Army	Driver
Hardy	H.		
Harris	A.		
Harrison	Douglas	Army	Gunner
Hemming	Alec	R.A.F.	
Hill	Harold	Army	Trooper
Hill	David		
Hodgkins	Harold		
Hodgson	Fred		Marine
Hoggard	A.	R.A.F.	Aircraftsman
Holmes	Percy		
Hopkinson	Tilly	Land Army	
Houseman	John G.		
Huskinson	Jim	Army	Private
Isles	Percy		
Jackson	A.		
Jeffry	Harold		Private
Jackson	A.		
Jaques	Ronald	R.A.F.	Aircraftsman
Jeffry	Harold		Private
Johnson	Erskine Dr.	Army	Lieutenant
Jones	J.		
Jones	George	Army	
Jones	David	Navy	Joiner
Jones	Albert	Army	Private
Jones	Elaine	Wrens	
Keeling	John	Army	Lance Bombardier
Keeling	L.V.		
King	Arthur	Army	
Kirkwood	Samuel	Army	Corporal
Kirkwood	Arthur	Army	Sapper

Knowles	S.		
Langham	James		Corporal
Lawrence	W.		
Lemon	Edward		
Lucas	Walter	Army	Private
Malbon	Jack	Army	
Marriott	Bernard	Army	Driver
Marriott	A.		
Marriott	Harold		
Matkin	Frank	Army	Sapper
Matkin	Kathleen	Army A.T.S..	
Matkin	Eric		
Matkin	Peter	R.A.F.	
Mathews	Arthur	Navy	Able Seaman
Mathews	Edward	Army	Sapper
Mathews	Dennis	Navy	
Mathews	George	Army	Bombardier
Meeks	Kenneth	Army	Private
Mellor	D.		
Midenhall	Richard	Army	Driver
Mills	Tom	Army	Marine Corporal
Millward	William		Private
Milness	Dennis	R.A.F.	Officer
Mitchenson	J.R.		
Moakes	Hedley	R.A.F.	
Moore	H.		
Monk	Margaret	Land Army	
Moss	Harry		Marine
Mott	James		Driver
Osbourne	Richard	R.A.F.	
Padget	J.		
Palfreman	James	Army	Driver
Palfreman	C.		
Palfreman	F.		
Palmer	Horace	Marine	
Parnham	A.N.		
Parr	Joseph	Army	Private
Parramore	Charles	Private	
Parramore	J.		
Pepper	Bert	Navy	
Perry	Dennis	Navy	
Pilmore	Cyril	Army	
Pilmore	C.		
Pilmore	Leonard		
Pratt	Kathleen	W.R.A.F.	
Reed	Fred	Navy	
Rhodes	Leonard	Army	Signalman
Sales	Roy		
Salmon	G.		
Salmon	Les		
Shardlow	Percy	R.A.F.	
Sales	Jack		
Salmon	G		
Sales	Joyce	Wrens	
Shardlow	Percy	R.A.F.	
Shelton	Richard	Navy	Ships Writer
Shooter	Jack	R.A.F.	L.A.C.
Shooter	Fredrick	R.A.F.	
Simms	J.		
Simms	F.		
Simpson	Herbert	Navy	Chief Petty Officer

Slack	Peter		
Smedley	Albert		
Smith	Albert	R.A.F.	
Smith	Albert	Army	Sergeant
Smith	Joseph		Bombardier
Smith	Dennis		
Smith	W.		
Stapleford	John		
Starr	Charles	Army	
Stenton	Harry		
Sterland	Stanley	Fleet Air Arm	Petty Officer
Storer	Frank	Army	Gunner
Storey	Harry	Army	Private
Storey	John	Navy	
Straw	Albert	Army	
Surgey	Harold	Army	Private
Surgey	Ernest		
Trusswell	Samuel	Army	Sapper
Turncock	James	Marine	
Turncock	Fred	Army	Private
Turncock	R.		
Wainwright	J.	Navy	
Walker	Fredrick		
Walker	Joseph		Gunner
Walters	George	Army	
Walters	L.		
Walvin	Nellie	Land Army	
Walvin	Willis	Navy	
Ward	Alfred		Private
Ward	Thomas	Army	
Wardle	Harold	Army	Private
Wardle	Arthur	Army	
Watson	Allwyn	Army	
Wenman	Walter		
Wetton	James		Sapper
Wheatcroft	Thomas		Private
Wheatcroft	Jack		
Whitehead	B.		
Wilson	H.		
Wilson	R.		
Wood	A.		
Woodward	Alan	Fleet Air Arm	Air Fitter
Wright	George		
Yeomans	Alfred	Army	
Yeomans	Harold		

We apologize if there are any omissions. It has been very difficult to establish a definitive list of all who served and returned home to Pinxton.

Home!

INDEX
of those remembered

World War One

	page		page
Allsop A M	31	Ludlam W E	96
Amos C	33	Marsh H	97
Anthony N	35	Matkin S	98
Barker F	38	Mills W H	99
Barker W	40	Naylor P	101
Bingham H N	42	Nicholls L	103
Bingley S M	44	Noakes T	104
Brooks T	46	Parnham H	106
Burnell J L	48	Pollock J W	108
Burrows J W	49	Pritchard J	109
Butler J	50	Pritchett J	111
Bye H	52	Revill D	113
Claridge H	53	Revill J J	114
Coke L S	55	Rigby W	116
Cooper H	59	Rodgers F	117
Cram C	60	Rohun E	119
Cutts W	62	Savage J H	121
Day G W	64	Searson J	124
Donnelly A E	66	Sharman F	125
Dutton C H	67	Shawcroft F E	126
Dye A	69	Slater W E	128
Edson G	70	Smith B	129
Elliott A	72	Smith H	130
Evans A	74	Snowden W	132
Faulkner T L	75	Stevens H	133
Gell A H	77	Stocks B	135
Gilbourne G	78	Street R	137
Glover G	79	Taylor B	138
Gregory J W	80	Trueman J H	140
Hill F	82	Upton J H	141
Hoten Albert	83	Ward J T	143
Hoten Algie	84	Watson A	144
Jessop R	86	Watson H	146
Lane R H	88	Whitehead E	148
Lane W	90	Wilson R	149
Leatherland E C	92	Winfield S	151
Lines H	94	Wood T M	154

INDEX
of those remembered

World War Two

	page
Anthony C	159
Bretton G	162
Butler T A	164
Clarke W	167
Cooper H O	169
Ellis J	218
Gent E	172
Harwood S	175
Henson F W	176
Huskinson S	178
Jones A	180
Lawrance D	182
Millington E	183
Nuttall M A	215
Renshaw J	185
Rhodes S	186
Severns S	188
Siddall J	190
Slater A J	192
Slater F V M	194
Smith E R	199
Smith Ernest	197
Stephenson B H	201
Truswell G T	202
Tryner J	205
Vale H	208
Walters R R	209
Wetton E	211
Wilson A M H	214

The Cabbage Babies

REPOPULATION POSTCARDS
&
The First Movie Ever Made

By

MIND UNVEILED

"Everything we see hides another thing, we always want to see what is hidden by what we see. There is an interest in that which is hidden and which the visible does not show us. This interest can take the form of a quite intense feeling, a sort of conflict, one might say, between the visible that is hidden and the visible that is present." — René Magritte

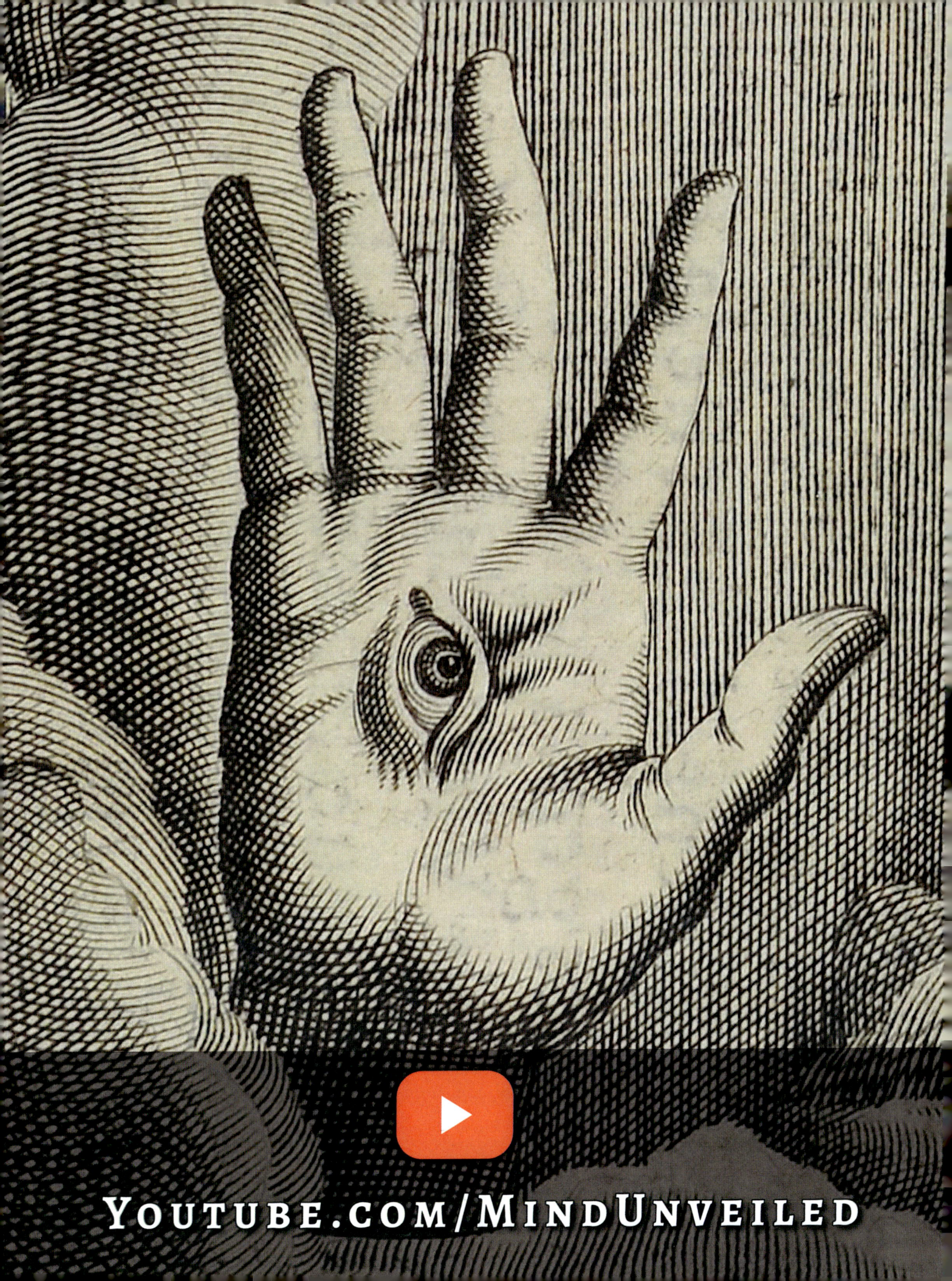

Youtube.com/MindUnveiled

Published By MIND UNVEILED

First Edition, 2023

ISBN: 979-8-9891622-0-8

No part of this publication may be reproduced, distributed, or transmitted in any form or by any means, including photocopying, recording, or other electronic or mechanical methods, without the prior written permission of the publisher, except in the case of brief quotations embodied in critical reviews and certain other noncommercial uses permitted by copyright law.

Copyright © 2023 MINDUNVEILED LLC

Table of Contents

Preface 7

Introduction...10

A Cultural Icon 14

The Baby Incubators 16

The Foundling Hospitals 20

Orphan Trains 26

The First Movie Ever Made... 31

Ancient Cloning Factories 43

REPOPULATION POSTCARDS...................................66

Comments from our Video... 155

THE MIND UNVEILED CABBAGE BABIES COLLECTION 166

Preface

Welcome to our first book! This marks the realization of a long-cherished dream. Since our childhood, we have harbored a passion for writing books. While we never anticipated venturing into such "wild" theories, we are amazed at how our journey has unfolded, and we are immensely grateful for the path that led us here.

For those who are new to our work, "lettuce" provide you with a brief introduction. We are Sol and Mun, known as The Positive-Negative, As Above So Below, Male-Female, and Alpha-Omega aspects of the mind. As creators of the fairly popular YouTube channel "Mind Unveiled," we explore various topics, with a specific focus on Alternative History, The Occult, and Spreading Curiosity. The channel's success has been beyond our expectations. At the time of writing this, we are on the verge of reaching a milestone of 15 million total views for our videos, despite their number being fewer than 100.

Writing books was not something we initially envisioned for Mind Unveiled specifically, however, our fans have persistently expressed their desire to see our videos in book format. Nonetheless, many of the topics we discuss have gained some viral attention. One such example is the Cabbage Baby series. This topic had received little to no discussion within the Alternative History community until we created a video series that delved into its connection with dark and suppressed history. We are pleased to witness the spread of such content, as our ultimate aim is to ignite curiosity.

Repopulation Postcards : CABBAGE PATCH KIDS / 1800s Cloning / Babylon Babies
182K views • 7 months ago

Unfortunately, not all content creators approach their work with the same level of respect. Some have disregarded the need to credit their information sources. While this is an expected occurrence, it is disheartening to see content copied verbatim. Recognizing the importance of sharing such significant information and garnering respect for our contributions, we realized that becoming authors and presenting our work in book format was necessary. This step also ensures that others can access this valuable information in a more organized manner and reach those who do not use the internet. Moreover, we believe it is crucial to categorize our work.

One of our notable contributions to the Alternative History community is the connection we have established between the REPOPULATION POSTCARDS and the concept of Repopulation in big cities. We take immense pride in this connection and firmly stand behind our contribution. Thus, we have created this book to mark our work and make it more accessible to other curious minds. We acknowledge that there will always be inspired creators, and we wholeheartedly welcome the use of information from our videos or books. We consider it a necessary process in building our own portfolio and providing an alternative medium for learning. It is worth mentioning that we have chosen to remain anonymous, fully aware of the pros and cons associated with this decision. Nevertheless, we believe that these books represent the next step in solidifying our work and preserving it for others to explore and share.

We extend our deepest gratitude to all our supporters. Without your unwavering support, none of this would have been possible.

Thank you, Mun & Sol

Introduction

Let us, together, embark on a journey exploring the intriguing connection between the enigmatic concept of "Cabbage Babies" and the unsettling notion of repopulation-but before we plunge into the depths of the fascinating realm of "Tartaria", it is essential to grasp a well-known truth: our history, the very foundation upon which our origins rest, is a tapestry masterfully woven with deception, half-truths, and outright falsehoods. This is no secret.

It's a troubling realization that the shaping of history has long been in the hands of these "victors". They alone seem to possess the power to mold the narrative, selectively omitting entire civilizations from the annals of time. This leads us to consider the concept known as "Tartaria"—an audacious theory that proposes the existence of cities and civilizations that were stealthily co-opted following a cataclysmic event, or perhaps a series of reportedly unrelated disasters around the world. It's suspected that many large American cities may have been not built but rather inherited, raising daunting questions about their true origins.

To be abundantly clear: we do not claim absolute certainty regarding these assertions. Instead, we invite you to explore a body of research that delves into these seemingly bizarre claims. Picture great empires, once grand and influential, erased from historical records, their legacies, people, and technologies consigned to oblivion.
Visualize cities stolen or hijacked, their true stories concealed beneath layers of manipulation, artifice and concrete.

So, what's the meaning of all this then? Simply put, it challenges us to question the very essence of our established history. It beckons us to embark on a quest for knowledge, unearthing hidden truths and peeling back the layers of distortion. With an open mind and a hunger for understanding, we invite you to join us on this exploration.
Welcome to a realm where the illusions of history begin to crumble, and the search for truth takes precedence.

When contemplating the origins of cities with purportedly inherited infrastructures and puzzlingly low population counts, a fundamental question arises: Where did the people come from? This perplexing question has captured the attention of the alternative history community, particularly when examining old photographs of American cities from the late 19th and early 20th centuries. These captivating images often reveal a startling absence or notably sparse populations.
As the investigation deepens, we encounter the concept of "Old World Photoshop." The revelation of historical photographs being sub-

Introduction

jected to deliberate manipulation and artifice sheds light on this strange phenomenon. Early cities, it turns out, were not immune to the allure of photoshoots. However, these photographic sessions were far from mere documentation. Instead, they resembled carefully orchestrated demonstrations, akin to a theatrical performance.

Intriguingly, these portfolio shots were subject to photographic manipulation and artistic enhancements, reminiscent of the techniques employed in painting. People and various objects were skillfully added to these images, transforming reality into a picturesque facade. One is compelled to question the underlying motives behind such meticulous attention to detail—why the need to paint people into these photographs?

These revelations raise unsettling questions about the established "historical facts" surrounding the origins of our cities. These questions invite the common man to scrutinize the narratives that have been handed down to us from the aristocracy. It beckons us to consider the possibility of a hidden agenda, a deliberate deception entwined into the very tissue of our perceived past.

A common argument presented in response to the absence of people in old city photographs revolves around the issue of "Exposure." According to this viewpoint, the limited visibility of individuals in early photographs is attributed to the technological constraints of the time. While there is some truth to this argument, it is not as significant a hindrance as we have been led to believe.

To truly dive deep into this matter, we must question the accepted progression of technology, optics, and the camera itself. Are we to assume that the timeline of technological advancement presented to us is entirely accurate? Is it possible that those in positions of power have deliberately concealed the latest advancements from the public eye? Perhaps doling them out in small portions in order to maintain the illusion of progression? These are crucial considerations, especially when we examine the history of inventions such as the Telescope, Microscope, and Camera.

Fig 1.1. Scheiner's helioscope as illustrated in his book Rosa Ursina sive Sol (1626–30)

The Cabbage Babies

When we consider the vast knowledge possessed about the stars since ancient times, it becomes evident that the realm of astrology held closely guarded secrets. Royal "Court astrologers" utilized this knowledge to predict the future, craft talismans, and exert influence over significant historical events. The depth of understanding in this field suggests the existence of advanced technologies that were kept under secrecy for centuries.

Similar considerations apply to the Microscope, which brings forth debates regarding Spontaneous Generation, magnification techniques, and the manipulation of light. The Camera Obscura, another captivating invention, represents one of the highest forms of technology. One could argue that these advancements were shrouded in secrecy for extended periods. In fact, the story we have been told concerning the invention of cameras is far from the complete truth. Even within mainstream narratives, it is clear that they possessed the capability to produce high-resolution photographs, surpassing the quality of today's digital cameras.

An example of this can be seen in the early 19th century with Eadweard Muybridge's Panorama of San Francisco in 1878, showcasing a level of realism and detail that rivals contemporary technology.

Muybridge, known for his groundbreaking work in capturing motion through sequential photographs, possessed a deep understanding of exposure and manipulation of photographic techniques. Interestingly, there is an article on Insider that explores the history of Black jockeys and how Muybridge himself stood trial for murder. Such intriguing details raise questions about the nature of these ghostly city photographs and beckon us to delve deeper into their puzzling stories.

Fig 1.2. Muybridge's The Horse in Motion, 1878

Curiously, museum articles themselves have labeled these city photographs as ghost towns. The New-York Historical Society provides a backstory, but when viewed through the lens of alternative history, one cannot help but question the prevailing narratives. As one article suggests, Muybridge's panorama presents a paradox—a vision of monopoly, power, and control juxtaposed with an eerily empty and desolate cityscape.

Now consider this idea for just a moment: What if these grand American cities were not built from scratch, but rather inherited? Take San Francisco as an example, although we can observe this phenomenon in numerous other cities such as Chicago, New York, Detroit, and beyond. This notion challenges the prevailing narrative that attributes the construction of these cities to the determined efforts of settlers.

However, the idea of "Repopulation" is not an entirely novel concept. It was the disturbing history of ORPHAN TRAINS that initially led the alternative history community to establish a connection with ghost towns. The dark legacy of these trains raises questions about the true origins and formation of these bustling urban centers.

Fig 1.3. Panorama of San Francisco by Eadweard Muybridge, 1878

Introduction

"The Orphan Train Movement was a supervised welfare program that transported children from crowded Eastern cities of the United States to foster homes located largely in rural areas of the Midwest. The orphan trains operated between 1854 and 1929, relocating from about 200,000 children. The co-founders of the Orphan Train movement claimed that these children were orphaned, abandoned, abused, or homeless, but this was not always true. They were mostly the children of new immigrants and the children of the poor and destitute families living in these cities. Criticisms of the program include ineffective screening of caretakers, insufficient follow-ups on placements, and that many children were used as strictly slave farm labor." (Wikipedia)

In the Journal of Social History, an Article by Dianne Creagh, the author discusses how the Foundling hospitals are not normally connected to this program, as this history does not seem to be well known or discussed in scholarly circles.

"The Foundling's work, particularly its baby train program, has been overlooked by many scholars. In Building the Invisible Orphanage: A Prehistory of the American Welfare System, for example, Matthew Crenson erroneously claims that the Guild of the Infant Savior was the first Catholic agency to improve survival rates for Catholic foundlings by placing them in family homes beginning in the early twentieth century, when in reality the Foundling's wet nursing program and westward placements can be traced to the 1870s." (Creagh 199-200)

The tale of the Orphan trains suggests that these migrants were children who had been uprooted from their homes in search of a fresh start. But, let's take a moment to consider something a bit unconventional—a question that might seem far-fetched at first. What if, just imagine for a moment, in a time when technology was kept under wraps, it was actually possible to genetically clone and create humans back in the 1850s? The thought alone seems absolutely bizarre, but history has a knack for unraveling in the most surprising ways, venturing into realms beyond our wildest imaginations. And that's exactly what we're here to explore—an extraordinary journey guided by genuine curiosity and an open mind.

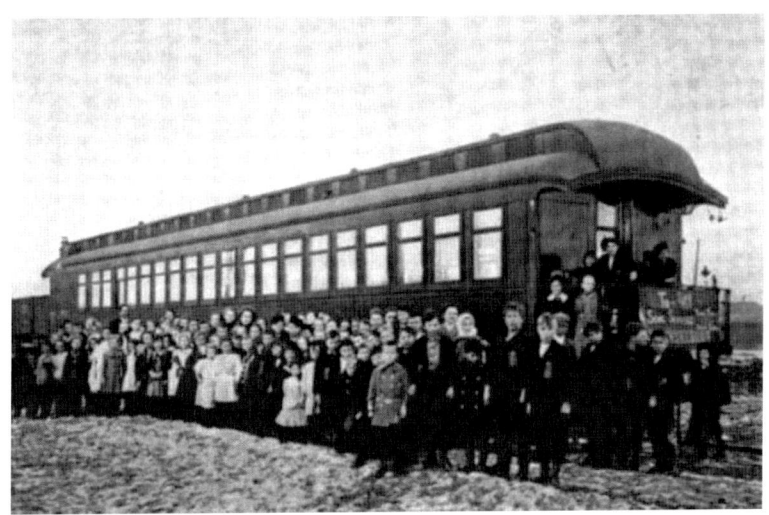

Fig 1.4. Baptist railroad chapel car Glad Tidings childrens meeting 1910

To truly unearth the mysteries of history, we must be willing to release our preconceived ideas and embrace an attitude of honest inquiry. It is through this quest for answers that we can uncover hidden truths, shed light on peculiar anomalies, and venture into uncharted territories of understanding. For in order to truly question the mysteries of history... one must let go of everything they know...

A Cultural Icon

The 80s bore witness to various cultural phenomena, but one that particularly caught the imagination of the younger generation was the rise of the Cabbage Patch Kids. These dolls weren't just a fad; they were a full-blown obsession. Children across the country didn't just want these chubby-cheeked companions – they absolutely needed them. So intense was their popularity that it triggered what we now refer to as 'The Cabbage Patch Riots.' This surreal event in 1983 saw customers transform into frenzied competitors, engaging in heated scuffles within retail stores across the United States, all vying for these coveted dolls. The Cabbage Patch Kids had arrived that year, and they didn't just make an entrance – they caused a nationwide commotion, catapulting demand for the product to unbelievable heights.

Remarkably, there's a unique spot tucked away in White County, Georgia, that fully embraces the oddity of this whole saga. This place offers an extraordinary experience: witnessing the 'birth' of these famed Cabbage Patch Kids!

"Babyland General Hospital is the fictional "birthplace" of the dolls known as the Cabbage Patch Kids and is located in Cleveland, Georgia. Xavier Roberts converted a former clinic into a retail facility for the sale of his dolls, originally called "Little People." It is presented as a birthing, nursery, and adoption center for premium Cabbage Patch Kids. Although the fad surrounding the dolls has largely died down, this site attracts numerous serious fans and curiosity seekers." (Wikipedia)

The rabbit hole of the Cabbage Patch Kids saga deepens when we delve into its folklore. One can't help but wonder - what is the true essence behind this bewitching oddity?

Paraphrased from the Cabbage Patch Kids Official Website, ("The Legend Cabbage Patch Kids")

Chapter 1 involves a tale about a young lad named Xavier Roberts from North Georgia's Appalachian Mountains. One day, while playing in the woods, a peculiar critter whizzed by him. It looked like a bunny, but it flew and buzzed like a bee, capturing Xavier's interest. He chased this intriguing hybrid, known as the Bunnybee, through the woods, over streams, and across hills.
However, just when Xavier thought he had the Bunnybee within his grasp, it darted into a waterfall, seemingly vanishing. To Xavier's surprise, the Bunnybee didn't drown but instead flew right back out, teasing him to continue the pursuit.

Chapter 2 narrates Xavier's bold exploration into the cave hidden behind the waterfall. Upon noticing the Bunnybee's unscathed emergence from the waterfall, he decided to venture behind the cascade himself. Within the cave, he was greeted by a breathtaking spectacle: countless crystals of various sizes and colors, twinkling in the dim light. The sight was so stunning that he nearly lost track of his fuzzy quarry. But soon, the buzzing Bunnybee reappeared, coaxing Xavier deeper into the cave with his flashlight in tow. The adventure was truly unfolding.

Chapter 3 continues following the Bunnybee into the increasingly bright, crystal-filled cave. His curiosity was piqued as the path turned from cave to tunnel, eventually leading him to an obscured exit, veiled by dense Kudzu vines. The world that awaited on the other side was truly wondrous. Bunnybees were buzzing around, showering the numerous cabbage rows with magic dust. But the real surprise was the sight of tiny children and babies, frolicking and snoozing amongst the cabbages. This sight was so unusual that Xavier had to blink and squint to be sure of what he was seeing.

Chapter 4 reveals the interesting encounter between Xavier and Otis Lee, a small boy emerging from the cabbage fields, who identifies himself as one of the Cabbage Patch Kids. Otis Lee unveils the enchanting secret of their origin - the Bunnybees' magic crystal dust, sprinkled onto the mother cabbages, is what gives life to the Cabbage Patch Kids. Upon Otis Lee's query about helping them find homes, Xavier, after thoughtful consideration, agrees. He pledges to create a haven known as BabyLand General, where all the Cabbage Patch Kids can reside and frolic until they're adopted into loving homes, because, after all, everyone deserves a family to cherish.

(End of Paraphrase)

So, where do babies come from? In the early 20th century, kids were often told fanciful tales about storks bringing babies, or even of finding them in cabbage patches. But why cabbages?

The lore of the Cabbage Patch Kids is wrapped up in the imaginative adventure of a boy named Xavier. This young boy encounters a magical Bunnybee, a fairy-like chimera, leading him through a hidden tunnel behind a waterfall. At the end of this mysterious passage, he discovers a place where babies miraculously sprout from cabbages.

The task of ferrying these cabbage-born children to their new homes falls to Colonel Casey, a dedicated stork. This diligent bird, clad in his uniform, not only delivers the babies but also serves as the official historian for the Cabbage Patch Kids.

However, a dark shadow looms over this whimsical world in the form of Lavender McDade, an evil witch. Accompanied by her weasel and jackrabbit minions, she aims to enslave the cabbage patch kids, forcing them to mine for gold. The comprehensive backstory, including the creation of the kids, the wicked witch, and their sad plight, is lyrically depicted in their ten-song album.

Interestingly, the origins of these cloth dolls have no roots in cabbage patches, chimeras, or witches. They were initially 'Doll Babies' created by Martha Nelson Thomas. It was only after Xavier Roberts (much like the adventurous boy in the story) adapted her design that the evolved into the Cabbage Patch Kids we know today. Was it a spur of creativity that led Roberts to invent such a bizarre story, or was he drawing from a deeper, collective consciousness? Or could it possibly be a twisted fondness for child labor narratives? We may never know.

Why were we told such an intriguing story growing up?

The Bunnybee, a curious blend of a rabbit and a bee, may be seen as a symbol of mass regeneration. Rabbits, known for their rapid multiplication, and bees, with their hive-minded society and single queen birthing all offspring, represent fertility and communal living.

This might be hinting towards an allegory of mass reproduction, possibly even alluding to a lab-like environment where babies are produced on a grand scale...

The Baby Incubators

When you delve into the history of 'Baby Incubators' from the 1900s, you'll first stumble upon the babies of Coney Island. But rest assured, there's more to this story than just a simple search result. In the late 1800s, a physician named Martin Couney was busy advocating for the use of infant incubators across the US and Europe. It's surprising how quickly this seemingly simple invention swept across the globe. Suddenly, they're on display at every world fair, (the world fairs is another rabbit hole that deserves its own book), attracting gawking spectators and potential buyers. Yes, you heard that right, these infants were up for grabs.

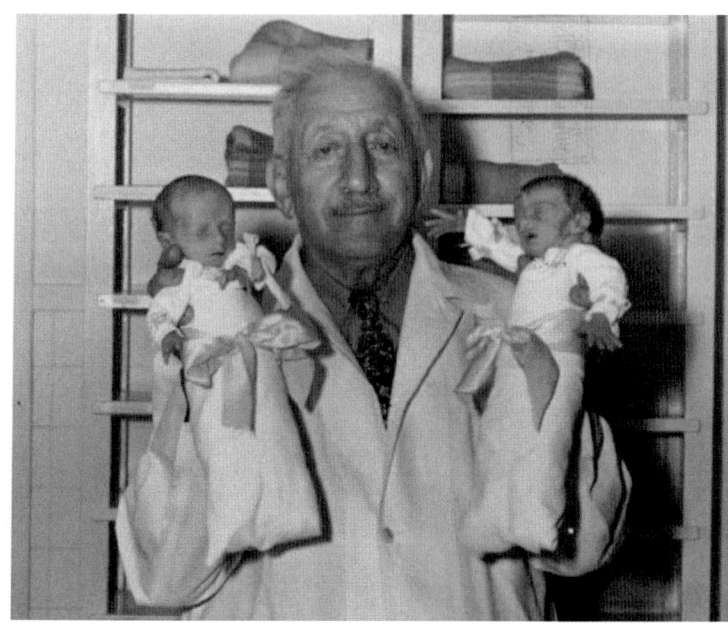

Fig 3.1. Infant Incubator - Martin Couney holding two babies , THE NEW YORK PUBLIC LIBRARY

Now, let's delve a bit deeper. During the 19th century, obstetricians across Europe were busy designing devices to provide infants with increasingly controlled and germ-free environments. The infant incubator, a lifeline for preemies born before the thirty-seventh week of pregnancy, has a lineage dating back to 1835. However, it was Jean-Louis-Paul Denucé, a French physician, who first brought this technology into the limelight with his publication in 1857. The tale continues with Carl Credé and Stéphane Tarnier, who played pivotal roles in refining this crucial invention. These incubators, offering stability and protection, have since become an indispensable part of neonatal care. (Rebovich)

16

The Baby Incubators

Why, one might ask, were there such an overwhelming number of orphans? Many would quickly point to the Baby Boom, but that historical phenomenon didn't occur until 1946 - 1964. We're discussing a staggering 200,000 orphans during the period from 1854 to 1929. Yes, we can question the accuracy of this number, but even a conservative estimate prompts us to ask - why were there so many children left parentless during an era perceived as a time of prosperity and progress? Doesn't such a high count of parentless children signal a malfunction in the society and culture of the time? If that many children are being maltreated and literally shipped from one place to another across the United States and Europe, can we truly claim that our society and culture are functioning as they should be? Why should we believe the history we are told then?

We're talking about a time as far back as 1835 in Europe, when technology wasn't quite there yet, but somehow, they were making strides in keeping premature babies alive. These incredible feats weren't hidden away in a laboratory; instead, they were turned into a public spectacle. Picture the World Fairs, those grand exhibitions of human invention and innovation. Among the marvels, you'd find 'Child Hatcheries', essentially incubators filled with tiny, premature infants. In connection with this, royalty would frequently be among the onlookers, creating a spectacle out of something as delicate as the start of human life.

Fig 3.2. Pilier Est de la Tour Eiffel. Couveuse d'enfants avec Bébés vivants 1904

During that era, they found a strange way to market this medical advancement. Barkers would beckon passersby at places like Coney Island or Atlantic City, inviting them to see the miracle of premature babies surviving and thriving in their miniature glass homes. People would pay to gaze upon these tiny infants, their nurse, Madame Recht, occasionally demonstrating the scale of their smallness

17

by placing her diamond ring around a baby's wrist. The sight was dubbed "The Strangest Place on Earth for Human Tots to Be Fed, Nursed and Cared For" in a 1903 Brooklyn Eagle report. Yet, it's essential to remember that in the early-to-mid twentieth century, there weren't many treatment options for premature babies. These showcases, eccentric as they were, provided these infants - largely dismissed as "weaklings" by hospitals - a fighting chance at life. The orchestrator of these spectacles was one 'Dr.' Martin Couney. Though he had his fair share of secrets and may not have been a real MD, he played a crucial role in pioneering neonatology in America. Between 1896 and 1943, he is credited with saving around 6,500 newborns, some of whom are still alive to tell the tale. Dr. Couney's story is an intriguing one, complete with ties to prominent figures in European medicine. For instance, his association with Dr. Pierre-Constant Budin, a pioneer in developing successful incubators, laid the foundation for Couney's exhibits. Motivated by the declining birth rate in France, several doctors including Budin and his mentor, Dr. Etienne Tarnier, sought to advance incubation technology. This resulted in Couney showcasing Budin's 'Kinderbrutanstalt', or 'child hatchery', at the Great Industrial Exposition of Berlin in 1896. This event marked the beginning of Couney's career showcasing premature infants in incubators, a spectacle that was strangely celebrated, even as it was situated near less savoury sights like leopard cages and penny peep-shows. Despite criticism and moral concerns, these exhibitions gained popularity, continuing to attract crowds and "save lives" across America for several decades. (Barry)

Fig 3.3. Exposition Universelle et Internationale de Bruxelles, 1910, Neonatology.net

Unearthing the hidden truths beneath history's patina often requires a speculative lens and a willingness to question the mainstream narratives. The child hatcheries of the late 19th and early 20th century provide a compelling case study. Yes, it is largely accepted that these incubators were a novel method of saving premature babies' lives. But could there be another facet to this? Could these exhibitions of tiny lives be the final act in a broader, murkier operation, one involving 'factories' producing premature infants on a large scale?

At first glance, the suggestion seems outrageous, even absurd. The image of a baby factory, an assembly line of new life, is unsettling- but, by peeling back the layers of history and scrutinizing the details, it becomes apparent that there are reasons to entertain this notion. One such reason is the sheer volume of premature babies presented in these exhibitions across the world, suggesting an unnaturally high rate of premature births during this period. How was it possible to have such a steady supply of premature infants? Were they conveniently available in such numbers, or was there an undisclosed source feeding into these 'hatcheries'?

Stéphane Tarnier, born on April 29, 1828, was a pioneer in the field of medicine and obstetrics. After his studies in Paris, he dedicated his career to the reduction of mortality from puerperal fever, a major threat to women in the 19th century. As a result of his tireless efforts and embracing of Lister's antiseptic principles, the mortality from puerperal infection at the Maternité hospital in Paris drastically reduced from 93 in every 1000 deliveries to 7 in the same number during 1870–1890. Tarnier's study spanning 40 years into puerperal fever was published in 1894 (Dunn, P.M.).

Tarnier is most famously known for his innovation in perinatal medicine: the introduction of the incubator in 1881. Inspired by a visit to the Paris zoo where he witnessed an incubator used for hatching exotic birds, Tarnier commissioned a similar device for premature babies. This marked the birth of the first closed incubator for hospital use. Tarnier's incubator consisted of a well-insulated, double-glazed structure that allowed for multiple infants to be kept warm and observed simultaneously. His device was credited for increasing the survival rate of infants weighing less than 2000 grams from 35% to 62%. In the following years, the design was improved to become more portable, cleanable, and offered better observation, evolving into a form much closer to those we use today. In addition to the incubator, Tarnier also introduced gavage feeding for premature infants. (Dunn, P.M.).

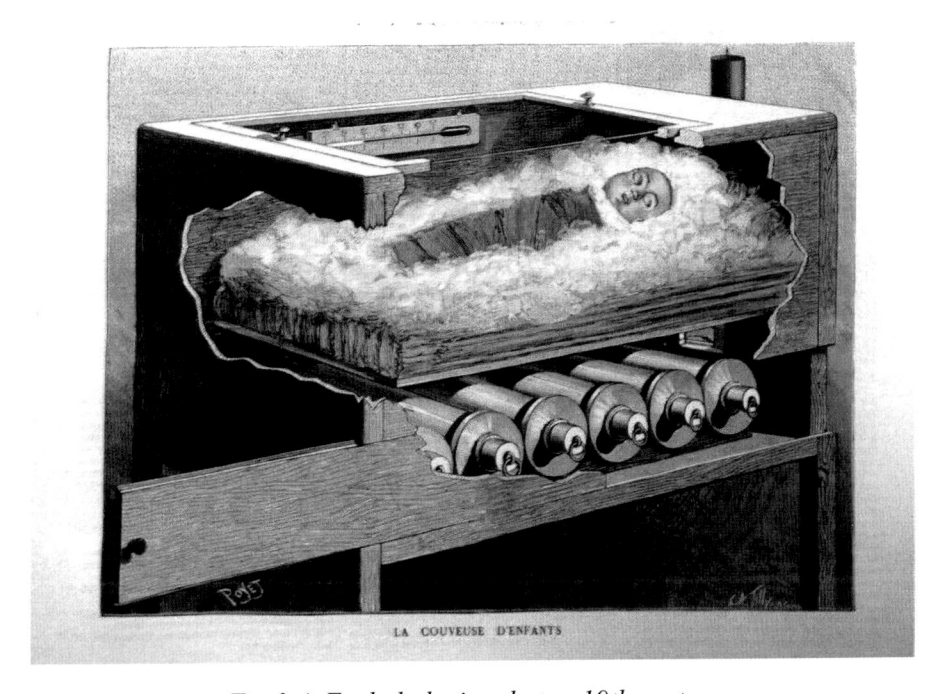

Fig 3.4. Early baby incubator, 19th century

It would seem that the first incubators originated from poultry hatcheries! Quite a strange history on neonatal care, perhaps this was some type of production, in which eggs or babies are hatched under "artificial conditions"... This can be used to breed rare and or endangered species. Interestingly, this practice can be traced back to ancient times!

"The ancient Egyptians and Chinese both devised incubators to hatch chicks from eggs without having the mother hen sit on them. This enabled hens to continue laying eggs without interruption. Egyptian incubators were large rooms heated by fires where attendants turned the eggs at regular intervals so they would warm evenly. Chinese incubators were warmed by fire or by rotting manure." (Encyclopedia.com)

Further fuelling this speculation is the presence of royalty and the elite class at these exhibitions. Their interest in these infant showcases may point towards more than just a casual curiosity about medical advancement. Could they have been stakeholders or patrons of these supposed 'baby factories', providing financial or logistical support? Such questions invite a deeper exploration, pushing us beyond the mainstream narrative's confines. As we continue to dig, we might uncover a tale more complex and intriguing than a simple sideshow – a tale intertwined with the era's socioeconomic undercurrents, advancements in medical technology, and the societal attitudes towards life and its preservation.

THE FOUNDLING HOSPITALS

Now it would seem that the roots of this enigma intertwine with the somewhat grim history of the Foundling Hospitals. These establishments have existed since ancient times, but in this case, we are discussing the Foundling Hospital founded in 1739 in London, England. Rather paradoxically, it became an institution that fashionable society embraced as their favored charity, garnering support from notable personalities of the day. These establishments were often ground zero for outbreaks of disease, and more importantly, they served as holding centers for discarded and orphaned young children. The image of these locations is rather stark—mothers giving up their children born out of wedlock, handed over to be under the church's care. Drop-off locations were designated, where children, results of illicit liaisons or simply unwanted, were left to the care of strangers.

Fig 4.1. The Foundling Hospital, Holborn, London; a view of the court

Yet beneath the veneer of this seemingly charitable endeavor, a hidden and darker narrative lay shrouded in secrecy. Was it not a clear indication of a society malfunctioning that these places were teeming with children, devoid of parental care? The emerging trend was deeply unsettling, as an increasing number of children were being swept into a system that offered anything but a nurturing environment. Instead, it served as a haunting emblem, a grim testament to the failures of society at large.

According to The Catholic Encyclopedia's article on foundling asylums, while modern-day foundling asylums now provide shelter to orphans, their original purpose was primarily focused on rescuing and caring for foundlings—infants deliberately abandoned by their natural protectors. The prevalence of inhuman practices such as infant exposure and infanticide in ancient pagan societies is explained by the belief that infants were not considered fully human beings and were disposable for the sake of the State. Christianity, with its doctrine emphasizing the sacredness of human life, played a significant role in condemning these practices and initiating systematic measures of rescue. Foundling asylums emerged with the first recorded institution established in Milan in 787. Italy experienced a significant rise in such asylums during the thirteenth and fourteenth centuries. The care of foundlings has varied throughout history and across countries. France underwent methodological changes, treating foundlings as wards of the nation during the Revolution, transferring them to departments, and using revolving cribs. Presently, care involves collaboration between religious communities, private associations, and public authorities, including placement with families. Germany opts for temporary institutional placement before transitioning to suitable families. Austria has a longstanding tradition of engaging mothers in hospital service as nurses. Italy leads in dedicated foundling institutions, with many children placed in families. Russia's asylums, established by Catherine II, encourage maternal nursing or placement with peasant families. England's care is overseen by various entities, while Scotland utilizes workhouses and the boarding-out system. Catholic authorities place foundlings in private families and orphan asylums, and similar practices are prevalent in Ireland. (Ryan, J.A., Catholic Encyclopedia)

The Foundling Hospital initially found its home in Hatton Garden. Interestingly, the statues that adorned the hospital in Hatton Garden can still be seen above the side door of St Andrew Holborn. The founder of the hospital, Thomas Coram, was laid to rest there after his remains were relocated from the foundation in the 1960s. Coram's efforts to establish a Foundling Hospital gained momentum when he presented his first petition to King George II in 1735. The petition garnered support from 21 influential women of aristocratic backgrounds, lending credibility and popularity to the cause. Subsequent petitions followed in 1737, signed by notable men from various social classes. The Royal Founding Charter, signed by King George II, was presented by Coram to the Duke of Bedford in 1739, containing the hospital's objectives, rules, and an extensive list of founding Governors and Guardians, including members of nobility, the City of London officials, and other prominent figures. The construction of the hospital itself took place between 1742 and 1752 under the supervision of John Deval, the King's Master Mason. (Wikipedia)

It is intriguing to delve into the peculiarities of this historical institution. The fact that the statues from the original hospital found their way to St Andrew Holborn adds a touch of mystery to the story. In addition, the extensive list of influential supporters, including members of the aristocracy, reflects the charitable cause's status as a fashionable endeavor. Such details shed light on the unconventional nature of the Foundling Hospital and its role in society.

In the heart of Florence, at Piazza SS. Annunziata, stands the Ospedale degli Innocenti, an institution adorned with reliefs of swaddled infants, testament to its historical role in caring for abandoned children. Founded in 1445, the hospital fostered a holistic approach to child care. Infants were not merely taken in; they were nursed and weaned, either on-site or with a countryside wet nurse. As they grew, they received an education tailored to societal norms—boys were taught to read and write, girls were instructed in sewing and cooking. (Morton)

An essential element of the hospital was the foundling wheel, in operation from 1660 to the 1870s. It served as a revolving door for mothers who, for whatever reasons, couldn't care for their infants. This hatch was a discreet way to surrender children, with the baby turning from the outside world into the care of the hospital, often with a keepsake or talisman as the sole connection to their past. The Latin inscription above the now-grated door, quoting Psalm 26, chillingly captures the grim reality of these abandoned children: *"Our fathers and mothers have abandoned us, but the Lord has taken us."* (Morton)

Interestingly, if we examine the Coat of Arms of the Foundling Hospital, there is what seems to be OCCULT SYMBOLISM. Now, why would this be on such a charity if it were truly for the benefit or HELP of children? Moreover, it is intriguing to note that admission tickets to the hospital even featured descriptions of artistic performances. It seems that the institution not only took on the role of a caretaker but also became a center for artistic expression and entertainment.

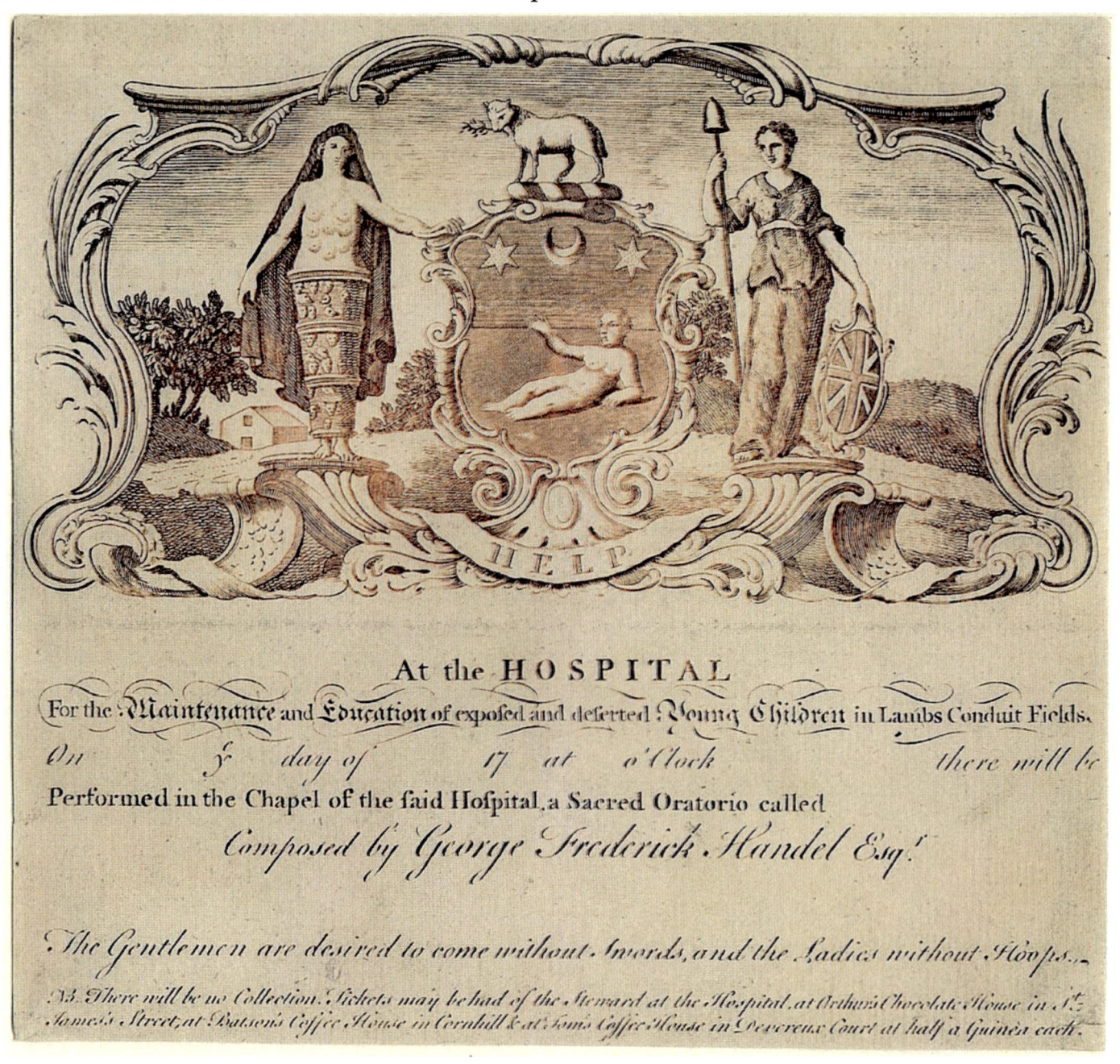

Fig 4.2. William Hogarth - Arms of the Foundling Hospital

(Public Domain, William Hogarth - Arms of the Foundling Hospital with an admission ticket "Coat-of-arms with a naked child, a lamb holding a sprig of thyme as the crest, figures of Diana of Ephesus (left) and Britannia (right) as supporters, and the motto "Help"; a landscape beyond, and a rococco frame; below, a ticket for a performance of "a sacred oratorio" by Handel to be performed at the Foundling Hospital. C.1750 , Wikimedia)

So, why do we find the presence of Diana of Ephesus in the Coat of Arms of the Foundling Hospital? And let's not overlook the inclusion of other esoteric symbols, such as the Star of Ishtar, the Crescent, Libertas with the Phrygian cap on the staff, and even a sacrificial lamb. With this intriguing evidence before us, we are compelled to explore the hidden significance of these symbols and their relation to the operations and ideals of the Foundling Hospital. Do they point to a deeper purpose or hidden connections? Is there a symbolic language at play, one that provides insights into the true nature of the institution?

This foundling operation is directly connected to the incubators, in the Canada Lancet, there was a report in 1883, 3 years before the incubators that describes in detail where they got all these premature babies, From the foundling hospital, and it also uses some very interesting wording...

"BABY INCUBATORS. There were giants in the earth in those days—and there shall be giants in the earth in these days, to be seen not in side-shows merely, but on every hand—that is, if a report which comes from France be true, and it is well vouched for. And if giant babies are the making of giants and giantesses, all will admit the importance of a good send-off. It is just as essential in raising men and women as it is in raising any kind of stock. Blood and scientific management are no less potent in the one case than the other. Indeed, it would be a great blessing to mankind were some of the ideas acted upon by the raisers of good stock, imported into the more important business of raising a superior race of men and women. The working out of the law of the survival of the fittest would receive fresh impulse; much sickness, pain and sorrow would be averted, and the sum total of man's happiness would be immeasurably increased. But no such luck is in store for the human race. The weak and the sickly no less than the strong and healthy will continue to produce after their kind. Man's two-fold nature is an insuperable barrier to the enactment of civil laws, restricting to any considerable extent the natural law of reproduction. Economic and social considerations will always outweigh considerations having regard to the welfare of the prospective offspring. All that science or government can do in the matter, is to educate the masses into a more perfect knowledge of physical laws.

But to return to the subject—Dr. Tarnier, a French physician, attached to a foundling hospital, reports surprising results from certain recent experiments. This gentleman is said to have been grieved by the large number of children under his care who perished within the first six months of their life. While in this mood a new idea occurred to him. If French chickens, he asked himself, can be raised by artificial means, why not French babies? He caused a box to be made, having glass sides, and resembling an ordinary chicken-incubator. It was furnished with a soft bed, placed in a dark room, and kept at a temperature of 85 degrees Fahrenheit, by means of hot water. In this baby-incubator he placed one of the infants, a miserable specimen of the crying, colicky kind. The child was provided with a nursing-bottle, and of course only fed at regular intervals. The child ceased its crying on the second day, much to the doctor's surprise, and never again cried for the space of the eight weeks it tenanted the incubator. At the end of this period it had the appearance of a healthy child of a year old. Encouraged by this success, Dr. Tarnier repeated the experiment with like results. He then, with the permission of the hospital authorities, proceeded to construct an incubator capable of receiving 400 children, and in this he placed all the children in the hospital, 360 in number. All except two remained in the incubator six months, when they had to be removed, having outgrown their narrow beds. Were it not that the facts are vouched for by a commission of twelve, who made a report to the Government, the results claimed might be deemed incredible. The average age of the infants when put in the incubator, was eight months and three days, the youngest being twelve hours, and the eldest eleven months. The average weight of the 360 was ten pounds. At the end of six months the average weight was 54 pounds, and all are said to have looked like children eight years old (i.e.), as much was accomplished in six months by the incubator as is accomplished in eight years of ordinary life. The infants were not only large but also strong and healthy, and most of them walked within a week of leaving their nests. The results were astonishing, and exceeded Dr. Tarnier's most sanguine expectations. It is now expected that every child's hospital will go into the incubation business, so that we shall probably witness a lively competition in the business of raising giants.

If this child-incubator is a good thing in foundling hospitals, and for hospital babies generally, it ought also to be a good thing in all homes blessed with babies. Doubtless we shall soon witness a new industry started under the fostering care of the National Policy, and presently baby-incubator agents will be as numerous as sewing-machine agents. It would be easy to enlarge on the practical value and suggestiveness of Dr. Tarnier's experiments. First, it is clear the babies were not rocked, yet they enjoyed perpetual repose. This teaches us that all the fuss and worry of mothers and nurses, so wearing to the constitution, is not only wholly unnecessary but an absolute evil in all its bearings. Instead of being placed in a condition favorable to absolute quiet, our babies are made a sort of family toy to be tossed from one to another as a means of sport. The moment the little creature begins to notice surrounding objects, its powers are excited to the utmost to afford amusement to the family circle. Dr. Tarnier's babies were fed at regular intervals. The home baby is usually fed every time it cries, as though that were a signal of hunger. Most commonly it is a sign of an overloaded stomach.

In conclusion, we may be permitted to say that, the essential conditions to successful baby-raising, are Absolute quiet, and no unnecessary interference on the part of nurses. 2. Regular and judicious feeding. 3. Uniformity of temperature above that suited to adults. This condition is difficult of attainment in ordinary life, but much may be accomplished by the knowledge that infants require a higher temperature. Even a modified observance of the foregoing conditions would take away much of the worry caused by crying and sleepless babies, and would add greatly to the quiet, health and growth of our children." (Fulton 250-251)

It's all deeply unsettling and undeniably strange, as if they're navigating the concept of rearing babies as a strange phenomenon. Throughout the article, unsettling comparison is persistently drawn between the cultivation of French babies via "artificial means" and the breeding of French chickens. It's a disturbing connection, they are treating babies as if the concept was new to them… The origin of the baby incubator itself is nothing short of perplexing, stemming, as it does, quite literally from an ordinary chicken incubator.

The fact that these incubators were built adjacent to the foundling hospitals raises a multitude of questions. It's puzzling why such a hospital would house an abundance of premature babies. Were they simply found? Or could there be more to the story? Yes, you could argue that the Catholic Church was taking in infants, but that still comes across as suspicious. And why specifically under six months old? Could it be that they stumbled upon a method to create life artificially, maybe reviving an ancient cloning technique, but struggled to keep these premature creations alive?

And let's not forget the narrative that these were abandoned babies, often from unwed mothers, who were forced to surrender them to infant asylums. This practice has roots deeply embedded in New York's history, yet it remains a largely unfamiliar chapter to many.

"Europe faced the problem of foundlings much sooner than the United States did. When America's British settlers stepped off their boats in the early seventeenth century, Europe already had cities large enough to create the social conditions that produced significant numbers of foundlings, as well as the religious and governmental structures with which to help them. By then, Europe already had foundling asylums that were several centuries old. By the eighteenth century, when the United States was just starting and its cities were still small, infant abandonment was a mass phenomenon in places like London and Paris. It took until the nineteenth century for New York to overtake London as a center of Dickensian urban ills, including the presence of large numbers of foundlings.

In the Catholic countries of Europe, and also in Russia (with variations depending upon time and place), local and national governments, often together with religious bodies, assumed full responsibility for foundlings. Accidentally conceived infants were anonymously absorbed into large, urban foundling asylums. These asylums were at the center of great networks of wet nurses, transporters of babies, physicians, religious officials, and bureaucrats. This was the so-called Catholic System. Its goal was to preserve the honor of unmarried women and families by making babies born outside of marriage disappear." (Miller 6)

While the mainstream narrative portrays this as a societal issue, the truth could be quite different. These were predominantly Protestant societies, generally lax in their attitudes towards extramarital relations given the widespread presence of brothels.

Thus, it begs the question - were these babies really just found? And why the invocation of figures such as Lady Liberty and Artemis of Ephesus? Could it be that this was not a spontaneous problem, but a deliberate operation with a hidden agenda?

Moreover, the mention of 'giant babies' in a report from the Canada Lancet cannot be ignored. What exactly was being implied with such an unusual reference?

Fig 4.3. Philip Galle, after Maerten van Heemskerck, Dianae Ephesiae Templum (The Temple of Diana at Ephesus),

ORPHAN TRAINS

We're told that the Orphan Train movement was simply a supervised welfare program that ran from 1850-1929, involving the transportation of children from the eastern to western regions of the United States. However, what stands out about this movement is the staggering number of children that it involved. There's been considerable debate about the hidden undertones of this movement, with numerous authors highlighting its darker aspects, yet the question that truly piques one's interest is the origin of all these children.

The prevailing narrative chalks it up to immigration – after all, the Statue of Liberty is synonymous with the influx of immigrants. But could there be another layer to this story, perhaps related to some form of repopulation? The very premise of immigration involves a reshuffling of population, a change in demographics. So one must wonder: what was the true objective behind such a massive scale of child immigration? Could there have been an ulterior motive, subtly wrapped in the noble guise of a welfare program? The prospect certainly provides food for thought.

"The solution seemed obvious. In 1855 an Illinois newspaper editor commented on the need to redistribute the nation's work force. "Our country is swarming with a population which in order to be kept from want and distress must be employed. Some general system, which shall induce a withdrawal from the towns... is the great demand of the times." (Holt)

The underlying call of the Orphan Train movement seems to have been a systematic form of repopulation, the relocation of children from densely populated areas to desolate regions in dire need of inhabitants. The oddity of this situation is only magnified when one considers that these children were being prepared for a life in a completely new city, a new country, bereft of their parents and being geared towards employment. It paints a picture not of choice, but of orchestrated chaos. This, in turn, implies an underlying program that diverges from the surface narrative of a simple welfare program. The circumstances surrounding this movement suggest it might have been a far more calculated endeavor, aimed at deliberately reshaping population distribution and creating a new, easily manipulated, labor force.

Fig 5.1. Marching Orphans, Mennonite Church USA Archives

In the late 1800s, numerous newspapers were replete with announcements signaling the arrival of children via the Orphan Trains. These notices, often emblazoned with the attention-grabbing headline "Homes Wanted," resembled advertisements, suggesting an urgent need to find homes for these relocated children. Some of these children were delivered to local train stations, while others were brought to significant venues like the Armory Opera House. The information we have paints a compelling picture of large groups of children being transported by train, with their arrivals publicly announced through newspapers, as if families were standing by, ready to provide these children with homes.

Fig 5.2. Orphan train flyer, 1910

"Most of the orphan trains leaving from New York City originated at Grand Central Station. On the day of departure, the children were dressed in new clothing and oftentimes not told where they were going or why. While some were already assigned families, others would be displayed at stops along the way in an auction-like event. In the days leading up to arrival, fliers and local newspapers along the train's route advertised adoptable children." (Schlott)

"Family history research related to orphan trains is very complicated. Oftentimes the origins of these children are shrouded in mystery. Due to stigma surrounding adoption, many orphan train passengers were never even told about their histories, and many were too young to ever recall where they came from. Older children were also strongly encouraged to break all contact with the past upon arrival in their new homes. To further the confusion, oftentimes records are just as scarce as oral histories. Lack of a standardized recording system and sheer numbers of orphans means that many migrations are unrecorded." (Schlott)

It certainly seems as though there are multiple layers of lost history surrounding these situations. Documentation, a crucial part of any historical analysis, appears to be scant at best, which raises even more questions about this phenomenon. The children involved in this mass movement were often young and in many instances, oblivious to their pasts. Their tender age and the fact that they were actively encouraged to sever ties with their past upon their arrival in their new homes compounds the difficulty of unearthing the truth. This erasure of personal history, whether intentional or not, results in an atmosphere of mystery and raises questions about the true motives and the mechanisms of this operation.

Moreover, the apparent lack of a standardized recording system further exacerbates the challenge of tracing the history and origins of these orphaned children. With the high volume of orphans involved in this process, it's not surprising that many of their migrations have slipped through the cracks of the historical record.

This dearth of data only fuels speculation and highlights the need for further exploration and research into this intriguing chapter of American history. As we delve deeper into the narrative of the Orphan Trains, one can't help but wonder - what other hidden truths lie beneath the surface, waiting to be unearthed?

Fig 5.3. Orphans at horse show - N.Y., 1913

The common narrative portrays the East coast cities of the late 19th and early 20th centuries as sprawling urban jungles, teeming with poverty, crime, and disease. Pockets of these cities were said to be rampant with young, vulnerable souls - children who had been abandoned and left to fend for themselves in the harsh realities of the streets. The story often paints a grim picture of these children forming rudimentary gangs, peddling an assortment of items to eke out a bare existence. Indeed, it is a narrative that tugs at the heartstrings and commands sympathy. Yet one can't help but wonder, is this representation entirely accurate? Is it the complete story or is it merely a portion of the reality, designed to emphasize the dire circumstances from which these children were purportedly rescued?

Fig 5.4. "Street Arabs at Night" by Jacob Riis, circa 1890, Rare Book & Manuscript Library, Columbia University

The saga of the Orphan Trains is inextricably linked with the name of Charles Loring Brace. Known as a compassionate and devoted minister, Brace is often lauded as a heroic figure who rose to the challenge of assisting these desperate, homeless children. His work through the Children's Aid Society, which he founded, is generally painted with broad strokes of philanthropy and benevolence.

His ambitious project of relocating these orphaned children from the squalid city streets to healthier, more stable environments in the West is celebrated as a beacon of hope in an otherwise bleak landscape. Yet one must not forget to critically examine the entirety of Brace's actions and the implications of the Orphan Trains movement.

The narrative often downplays or altogether omits that not all children involved in the Orphan Train movement were orphans or abandoned. Many were removed from homes due to poverty or their parents' inability to provide care, and in some cases, without the consent or knowledge of their families. This raises significant ethical questions about the project. The assumption that rural life was inherently better and that poverty or a lack of conventional family structure was sufficient grounds for removal from one's home is a practice that warrants scrutiny. It hints at a darker, less palatable side of this initiative - one that involved the forced removal and displacement of children under the guise of philanthropy. This undercurrent of forced migration paints a less than flattering portrait of an operation largely hailed as a benevolent endeavor, driving us to delve deeper and question the standard narrative of the Orphan Trains.

Fig 5.5. CHILDREN'S AID SOCIETY, SECOND AVENUE AND 44TH STREET

"Brace created a plan he called 'placing out.' Trains would carry the children directly to areas where there were many farm and small-town families. The children would travel in groups or 'companies.' When they arrived in a town, people could gather and choose the child they wanted. A committee of respected citizens would judge if the families could give the children good homes. Brace felt certain his plan could succeed because it had before. He was not the first to think of moving homeless children who were born in one place to be raised by people in another. This had been done before with small numbers of children in England and Germany, as well as in the United States." (Warren 26)

In *Orphan Train Rider - One Boy's True Story* by Andrea Warren, we delve into the gripping narrative of a young boy named Lee and his experience with the orphan train. This emotional tale not only shines light on Lee's journey, but also places the reader amidst a confusing whirlwind, akin to the unsettling experiences endured by these transported children. In Lee's story, he, his brother Leo, and ten other children are ushered onto an adventure, the enormity of which they are blissfully unaware of.

The children's innocence, portrayed through their excitement of receiving new clothes and mistaking their impending voyage for a special event, presents a stark contrast to the grim reality. The children are paraded in their new attire, unaware they are being showcased for adoption. While the narration paints a picture of uniformity in their outfits, it also subtly echoes the deindividualization that these children underwent, being grouped and labeled as orphans for the convenience of the system.

The symbol of the pink envelope that Lee receives from his father is a poignant aspect of the narrative. This envelope, a promise of a link to their past, becomes Lee's anchor amidst the storm of uncertainty. It is also a stark reminder of their forced separation, their father's inability to care for them, and the jarring truth that their lives were being steered by powers beyond their comprehension or control. This highlights the darker aspects of the Orphan Train movement. These children, their identities reduced to their circumstances, were seen as commodities to be distributed, rather than individuals with personal histories and emotional needs.

In the account, there's a captivating tension between the exhilarating freedom offered by the train ride and the unfathomable, impending loss of autonomy as they neared their unknown destinations. Lee's repeated reassurances to himself, clutching the pink envelope as a symbol of hope, depicts the sheer resilience of a child navigating an emotionally intense situation. The paradox here amplifies the dilemma faced by the children - a physical journey promising new horizons, juxtaposed with an emotional ordeal of uprooted identities and shattered family bonds.

This portrayal of the Orphan Train journey exposes the hidden depths beneath the ostensibly benevolent intention of the movement. While it was painted as a solution to urban poverty and a chance for children to find new homes, it also carried with it the specter of family separation, forced assimilation, and an inherent lack of choice. (Warren 27-30)

Delving further into the shadowy corners of this chapter in American history, the orphan train movement emerges as a pivotal element in the larger landscape of population relocation and repopulation strategies. The tale that we've come to accept as conventional wisdom, where homeless children were compassionately given a fresh start in the West, is not only less documented than desired, but also appears to be presented more as a rationalized necessity rather than an objective account of the events. This narrative, underpinned by an undeniable sense of forced benevolence, raises more questions than it seeks to answer.

When placed alongside other peculiar historical accounts such as the baby incubators, foundling hospitals, and even age-old folklore like the Pied Piper, a different narrative begins to take form. These stories, far from being isolated instances, hint at a clandestine initiative at play, one that we are only beginning to unearth. Taken together, these fragments of history hint at a previously undisclosed operation, one that altered the lives of countless children and shaped the demographic contours of a growing nation.

The potential existence of such covert undertakings within our history may be a hard pill to swallow. Yet, it is vital to not shy away from these darker aspects of our past. By examining these instances, we unravel the nuanced complexities of our collective history, encouraging us to confront the uncomfortable realities that lie beneath the surface together. To fully comprehend our present, we must dare to confront these truths, no matter how elusive they might be. For it is only in the comprehensive analysis of our past that we can aspire to truly understand our present and shape our future.

THE FIRST MOVIE EVER MADE

There is a fascinating connection that confirms these 'Surreal Baby Postcards' are much more than just an art project... guiding us into a rabbit hole of cinema!

La Fée aux Choux 1900 version, Colorized

There was one comment that caught our eye, revealing that this mystery extends much deeper...Yes even deeper than the fact that they were literally shipping and delivering babies legally in 1913, and they would even put stamps on the children's clothing.

But even crazier than that...

Seemingly, the first narrative film in world history, indeed the first genuine movie in Cinema, is titled *La Fée aux Choux*, or, as we know it in English, *The Fairy of the Cabbages*, dating back to 1896.

"The 1896 version of La Fée aux Choux (The Fairy of the Cabbages) is a lost film directed by Alice Guy-Blaché (then known as Alice Guy) that, according to her, featured a honeymoon couple, a farmer, pictures of ba-

Fig 6.1. Uniformed Letter Carrier with Child in Mailbag, circa 1900s

31

bies glued to cardboard, and one live baby. The 1900 La Fée aux Choux and the 1902 Sage-Femme de Première Classe (originally titled La Fée aux Choux) are frequently confused with the original lost film, which is arguably the world's first narrative film, and the first film directed by a woman." (Dargis, The New York Times)

    La Fée aux Choux, intriguingly, is a LOST FILM. Yet, we aren't entirely in the dark, as over the past century, references to it have been discovered in personal letters and old cinematic catalogs. It's almost as if its mystery lingers on in the annals of film history... YES, we do maintain a skeptical lens on this entire narrative, given that there are certain elements that don't quite align.

    So, who exactly is this character known as Alice Guy? A decidedly peculiar last name, isn't it? A name that sparks curiosity... Alice Guy-Blaché, as history tells us, is a pivotal figure in the realm of early cinema. Her contribution is particularly noteworthy because she was a woman making films at a time when the industry was predominantly male. La Fée aux Choux, supposedly her creation, thus becomes an even more intriguing artifact. It's not only the age and the status of the film that piques our interest, but also the fact that it's linked to such an extraordinary figure.

    The film has seen multiple remakes, and it's readily accessible online, available for viewing on YouTube, or even within our dedicated video on this subject. Yet, brace yourself; that video contains some fairly jarring details. Specifically, it's the 1900 edition of La Fée aux Choux you'll encounter - a piece under a minute in duration, but markedly strange...

    It begins with peculiar kissing sounds *Mwah*, quickly setting an uncanny mood as haunting music begins to play. We are introduced to a woman, attired as a fairy, amidst a cabbage patch. Although the footage is black & white, colorized screenshots can be found online. Upon closer examination, it becomes evident that doll heads, detached from their bodies, are nestled among the cabbages.

    The fairy, with swaying hands and rhythmic dance moves, appears to be signaling an invitation or a beckoning gesture. Abruptly, she lifts a REAL baby, positioning it on the ground - or rather dropping it, given the baby's lack of balance. It becomes hard not to consider this ill-treatment when we see the babies, seemingly newborns, crying. I don't think it's too far to say this is abuse – she literally picks up one of the babies with one arm — clearly a new born child... and where did they get these babies!?

    In an unsettling continuation, the fairy picks up what is clearly a doll. Yet, given the preceding scenes with live babies, the doll presents an eerie resemblance to a lifeless infant. Regardless of the use of other props, the overall circumstances raise a multitude of red flags. As we delve further, the suspicion only grows...

La Fée aux Choux 1900 version

Now that was the 1900s version, there is some controversy on this film outside of the whole cabbage patch repopulation subject. The director was a "lady" named Alice Guy, later known as Alice Guy-Blaché, which creepily, is the exact same looking woman from the postcards! (Red-Lady)

Additionally, you'll notice this trend with many "lost films"-- it's a whole topic in itself, suggesting there might be untold aspects to these early films. Numerous original footage pieces were utterly lost, and they just came in and replaced the missing footage. Very strange...

Interestingly, the 1896 version of the Cabbage Patch Fairy, or the lost film, featured a honeymoon couple, a farmer, pictures of babies plastered onto cardboard, and one actual live baby. We'll dissect this in detail shortly, but all this knowledge comes from the enigmatic "Alice Guy" character's legacy. But how can we be so sure..? Did you see how she was treating the babies? The real question looms large - WHY... Why was this chosen as the concept for a movie? THE FIRST MOVIE! It certainly prompts curiosity.

La Fée aux Choux 1900 version, Holding arm

Well, this 1896 version is a lost film, meaning we don't have the original. There were likely many more, but this one holds significance as arguably the first narrative film ever made. She then remakes the film twice, and the 1900s version comes into existence. We know about this earlier, lost film because, in 1922, director Etienne Arnaud made a mention of it in his memoirs. He claimed that Alice Guy was the "first to have the idea of staging a dramatic scene in front of the cinematographic lens". Controversy arose here, since according to mainstream narrative, he referenced the wrong film. The film he mentioned, directed by Alice Guy, wasn't the Cabbage Patch Fairy but another film, Les Mefaits d'une Tête de Veau, or The Misadventures of the Veal Head. (Arnaud and Boisyvon)

There are a few different pages online about this early lost short film "Les Mefaits d'une Tête de Veau" that give some very strange descriptions...

"A veal head escapes from the dish of butcher to the nail. A butcher returns her back. Then a head sits down on the shoulders of butcher. The head of butcher she decorates parsley and serves a dish"(IMDb)

"A calf's head escapes from the butcher's plate, only to hang back. At this point, it appears that the animal-headed man cooks a human head." (Wikipedia)

"Les méfaits d'une tête de veau, appears in the Pathè catalog in January 1900. The title, however, is erroneously attributed by Alice Guy to Ferdinand Zecca" (Wikipedia)

Apparently, there is a connection but it was a *"mistake"*.

"The Misdeeds of a Veal Head: Comedy and Transformations. A veal head escapes from the dish where it was placed and goes to get a nail back. The butcher puts it back in its dish and cleans it angrily. The enchanted head then settles on the butcher's shoulders, while the butcher's head takes place in the middle of the dish. The veal head, now a butcher in turn, takes revenge by scratching it, half suffocating it with parsley and covering it with the container in which it was previously bathing, which it presses forcefully onto the skull." (su grimh.org)

Calf head? Baby cows? It's very eerie and teetering on dark humor that these are among the first films ever made. This film tells a peculiar story about a calf's head that escapes from a butcher's plate, and somehow merges with the butcher to form a hybrid human... Very eerie.

Although descriptions attribute the direction to another director, Ferdinand Zecca. This deepens the intrigue as these first movies were crafted by the oldest French film company in existence, the Gaumont Film Company or the Society of Establishments. These first cinematic efforts were spearheaded by production companies, yet curiously, many of their earliest films involve very macabre themes.

It certainly raises questions about *Alice Guy* and her connection to the *Cabbage Patch Babies*...

Why would the first films be about selling babies? They specifically created this first Cabbage Patch Fairy movie in 1896 for the Paris World Fair, focusing on the Baby Incubators. Currently, anyone can find this information on the wiki page for the movie itself. This film serves as further proof that the baby postcards were legitimately a common thing back then.

The 1896 Baby Incubator Exposition

"In February 1896, on a boulevard leading to the cabarets of Montmartre, Dr. Alexandre Lion opened an exposition, a "boutique fully operational," of baby incubators, filled with live, premature infants. The baby incubator was a new invention, modeled after chicken incubators, serving to keep the babies warm. An art nouveau poster was designed by Adolfo Hohenstein to advertise the Paris Couveuses d'Enfants. A nurse holding three babies is framed by a vine sprouting baby's heads in place of flowers. Faint white lines–drawings of babies growing on vines–fill in the background. Alice Guy went to this exposition and saw the babies in their enclosures. She later told her granddaughter, Regine Blaché-Bolton, that she was inspired to create La Fée aux Choux because she had seen the babies in the glass and metal boxes at an exposition." (Entre & Lumière)

An intriguing advertisement stands out, illustrating babies blossoming from vines alongside what looks like a pitchfork to the left. To the right you can even see a serpent around the stem between the "D" and "Enfants". This unconventional depiction is uniquely titled "Couveuses d'Enfants", AVEC BÉBÉS VIVANTS, MATERNITÉ LION - in English, "Children's Incubators", WITH LIVING BABIES, LION MATERNITY. Lion? Interesting to see a royal reference make its appearance once again.

Fig 6.2. "Couveuses d'Enfants" by Adolfo Hohenstein

34

The establishments known as "Oeuvre Maternelle des Couveuses d'Enfants," created by Lion, had widespread branches. These were located in cities such as Paris, Marseille, Bordeaux, Lyon, Nice, Liege, Brussels, and even in New York City, with the possibility of more. The most thoroughly documented site is found at 26 B. Poissonniere in Paris, for which pictures of the storefront and an entry ticket are provided below. ("Oeuvre Maternelle Des Couveuses d'Enfants", Neonatology on the Web)

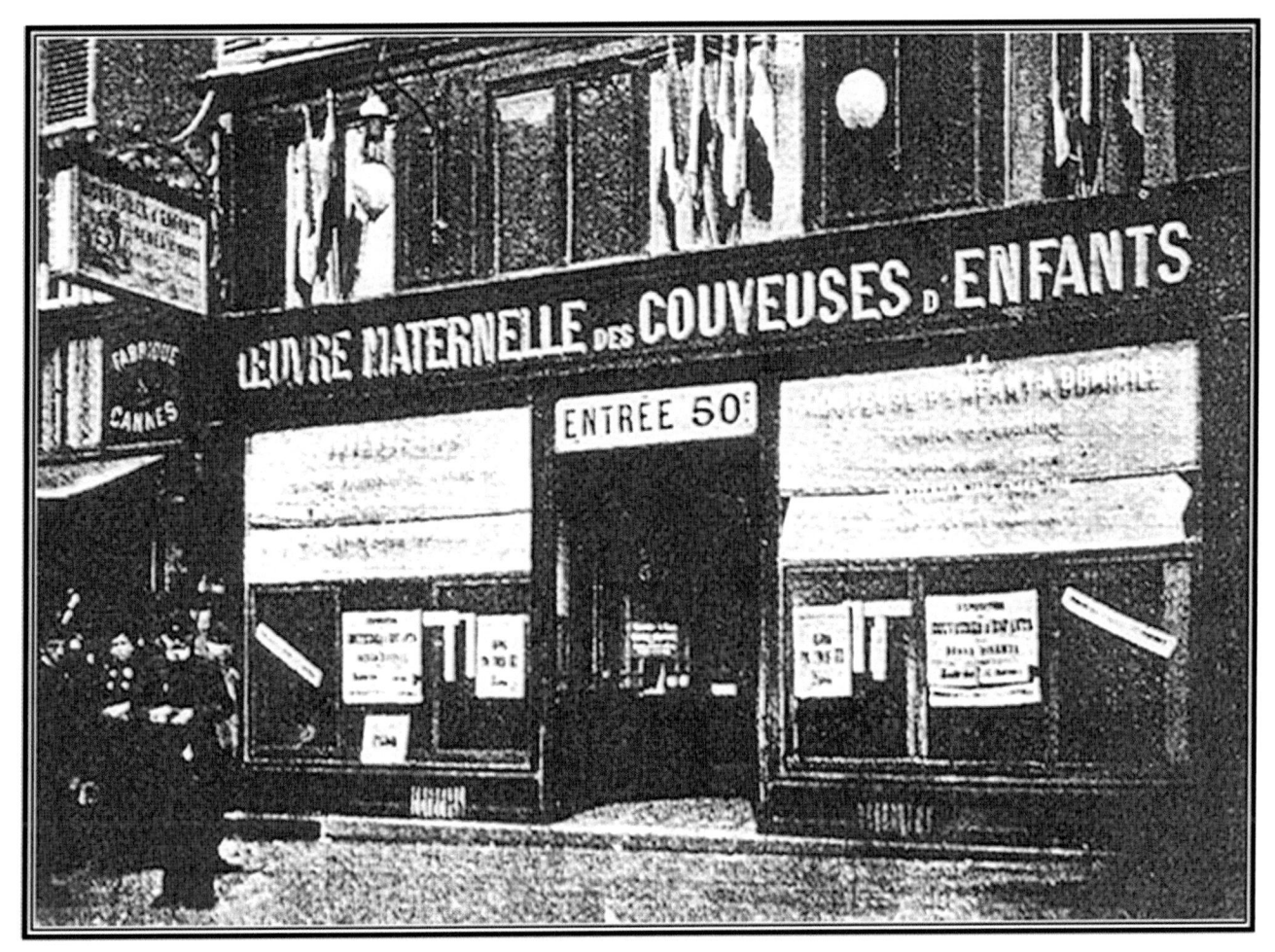

Fig 6.3. "Oeuvre Maternelle des Couveuses d'Enfants," from Neonatology.net"

Alexandre Lion, a physician hailing from Nice, France, and the son of an inventor, patented his incubator in 1889. It was celebrated as a technological marvel of its time, encapsulating automated heating and ventilation systems within an appealing cabinet design. Lion's innovation was primarily driven by cost-efficiency; the incubator required less manpower to operate, thereby cutting down on expenses. In fact, a 1897 commentary in Lancet highlighted the incubator's autonomy, maintaining constant heat and ventilation with minimal fluctuations and reducing the need for constant, skilled care. (Kornoes)

However, the Lion incubator was costly, hindering widespread availability. To overcome this hurdle, Lion leveraged support from charities and municipal governments. Capitalizing on his entrepreneurial spirit, he set up revenue-generating "incubator charities" - storefronts on bustling French boulevards where spectators paid for admission. His incubator's effectiveness was corroborated by a study conducted by the physician-general of the City of Nice, which reported a remarkable 72% survival rate among 185 infants. Despite the high cost, Lion's incubator set a new benchmark in neonate thermoregulation, demonstrating not only his medical expertise but also his entrepreneurial acumen. (Kornoes)

So then... these surreal real photo postcards of babies in cabbages were indeed promotional tools for the incubators presented at the world fairs. These were no mere displays, they were functioning incubators filled with live premature infants.
The question that naturally arises is, why specifically premature babies?

It's undeniable. The cabbage patch motifs, the illustrations of growing babies on these real, yes, REAL postcards, posters, and even the first full-length movie, all depict babies for sale in incubators at the WORLD'S FAIR! And we're not supposed to question it? Isn't it intriguing that the first feature film emerged during this same period, around 1896? Could we be dealing with peculiar remnants of art and film from a transitional phase following a reset?

Take a moment to consider this... What if this footage of the Cabbage patch fairy was all that remained for the orphans? What we know about the original film, and all this remake business, is limited to what's been told to us. There seems to be more to the story than what meets the eye.

The transition period between resets isn't always as straightforward as a sudden, world-altering event. It's rarely so clear-cut. Suppose a significant "WAR" or cataclysm occurred, causing not just physical disruption but also emotional and mental instability among the populace. To a group with the right knowledge and resources, such a vulnerable population could be easily manipulated, right?
There would always be exceptions – people living away from the cities who are often dismissed as rural "bumpkins" or considered ignorant of "the real world" that mainly revolves around the urban centers.
Could the first film have contained footage someone didn't want us to see? Or maybe they made an error and decided their symbolism was too blatant. As we contemplate the repopulation process, we must acknowledge that people would have been supervising it. Could these first film studios have been preparing to repopulate the world with entertainment and distraction? That would make sense given how bizarre and unsettling many of these early films are.
What if these films are a form of trolling by elite groups who had taken control of newly renovated cities and were also repurposing discovered technologies, like the camera? Just as historical events and photographs can have inaccuracies, so can these early films. Disagreements and controversies abound regarding the origin and creators of these lost films. Many aren't even sure about the directorship and creation dates of these films.
So is it too far-fetched to think that some of these films may not be from an older civilization but from a transitional phase? A time when secret societies moved into newly acquired cities and initiated a repopulation program. They could have created these films to entertain the new inhabitants freshly recruited from the fields.

Doesn't it seem like they were toying with the technology of the time, treating it like some kind of joke? Could this be the true origin of movies?

The First Movie Ever Made

More nuances surround the original film. To further complicate matters, in 1935, Leon Gaumont, the founder of the studio that employed Alice and the other director, Ferdinand, who made the 'Baby Cow Head' film, clarified that he himself directed the first film intended to "tell a story to the audience." This took place in front of "a painted canvas that naively represented the rue de Belleville." His lead female actor was Alice Guy, and two mechanics from the studio were the first screen actors. He also asserted that his "first" film was called "Les Mefaits d'une Tête de Veau." (Pierre Laroche)

So, we have the founder of the French studio, which started in 1895, claiming he was the original director of the first film. According to him, the leading actress was Alice Guy, and this first film was not the 'Cabbage Patch Fairy', but 'The Misadventures of the Calf Head'...

This is where the controversy lies. They seem to want to hide the fact that the earliest movie was a strange, dark film featuring a butcher chopping off a baby calf's head and serving it as a dish. I've searched high and low, but it appears this film isn't available online.

Interestingly, this film seems to have been nudged out of the limelight, leaving 'The Cabbage Patch Fairy' as the first film. Throughout the century, evidence has emerged suggesting there are in fact three versions of the film, as stated by Wikipedia.

Yet, much of this new data derives from a 1976 book, 'Autobiography of a Film Pioneer.' The multiple authors of this book discuss information about a report started by Leon Gaumont in 1907, which was later revised in 1945. It seems like this information, emerging in 1976, has been used to rewrite the history of this topic. As we've mentioned, Gaumont clarified over a decade earlier what the earliest film was and that Alice Guy was the actress in it. (Denoël/Gonthie)

There's a lot of back and forth regarding the history of these lost films. There's a plethora of different viewpoints, but as 80 years pass, we tend to forget about these disputes and accept the new mainstream explanation.

Alice Guy made a noticeable change in the 1902 version of the film named "Sage-Femme de Première Classe" but this was also originally titled "La Fée aux Choux". Rather than a fairy, a midwife was incorporated into the narrative, helping a honeymoon couple with their baby. The film's title was changed from 'The Cabbage Patch Fairy' to 'Midwife to the Upper Class.' This makes one wonder - are midwives significant figures in all this? Could they be the "fairy" or the woman depicted in the postcards?

The 1896 version of the film is more detailed. It begins with newlyweds strolling in the fields during their honeymoon. They encounter a farmer working in a cabbage field. This film is evidently more advanced, featuring multiple scenes. The young man inquires if his wife would like a baby. They traverse the field, find a cardboard baby, but both are disappointed by it. Following the sound of a baby's cooing, they uncover a live infant behind a distant cabbage. Excitedly, they reward the farmer and depart, leaving the farmer to return to his work in the fields. (Dargis)

The confusion escalates because in the original film, no fairy is present, yet it is still referred to as the 1896 version of 'La Fee Aux Choux.' Is it? Why was it lost? It seems peculiar to produce such a film in 1896, at the dawn of film history. It appears more like a play on hidden knowledge, a recurring theme in many early films.

We only have Alice Guy's memoirs, which we suspect have been edited. In them, she explicitly states that her first film was titled 'La Fee Aux Choux,' which doesn't quite add up. The story suggests that the absence of a fairy in the original film was due to the fact that the baby was screaming, prompting the mother to intervene. They left us with this curious explanation. (Wikipedia)

This film, they say, was inspired by the French legend that boys come from cabbages and girls from roses. But where does this legend originate? Why was it employed to promote incubators, incorporating occult symbolism? What's the rationale behind this first film, featuring babies screaming in a cabbage patch and a woman carelessly lifting them and setting them back down on the ground?

Further contradictions emerge from Alice Guy's memoirs. She mentions that "in the photo of La fee aux choux are my friends, Germaine, Yvonne, and myself," implying that Yvonne was the actress portraying the fairy. Yet the photo she references isn't from that film; it's from the 1902 film 'Sage-Femme.' This discrepancy leads me to suspect that these inconsistencies aren't mere errors. It seems that someone introduced information that doesn't correlate, creating confusion. (Guy)

Guy's descriptions also include a woman rushing or jumping into a field, a scene missing from both the 1900 and 1902 versions. This suggests that the 1896 version may have been shot on a larger format film, like the 58mm, which could accommodate wider screen scenes.

This possibility lends credence to the notion that the original film was significantly longer and broader in scope. Perhaps, we've only been left with fragments. Consider the film *Metropolis* which underwent a similar fate. The original version was later edited, with certain parts revised or omitted. If you revisit it, you'll note the alterations. Once again, we encounter strange occult symbolism, accompanied by impressively advanced visuals. The common explanation attributes this to painted backdrops and other theatrical tricks, but I contend that there's more to these early films than meets the eye.

Given the curiosity surrounding the veracity of this information, it's essential to reiterate that all we truly know comes from early catalogues and memoirs. These sources confirm the existence of these three films, all attributed to Alice Guy. However, what's puzzling is that many of the descriptions in these catalogues, purportedly from Guy herself, don't accurately represent the films. It's mystifying how she could have mistaken details about her own creations...

Let's examine the first description: "A loving couple walks through a vegetable garden in search of a baby. A fairy deposits live babies which she then removes from the cabbages to the delight of the young couple who are overjoyed." This description doesn't quite capture the nature of the films.

Unfortunately, the original catalogue containing this description has been lost. However, there is a catalogue from 1901, where Alice Guy's description accurately portrays the 1900 version, reporting it as a 'huge success.' Furthermore, 'Sage Femme,' released in 1902, appears in the September 1903 Gaumont catalogue. (Wikipedia)

This claim that the first film was a 'huge success' is perplexing. The movie was merely a minute long, and indeed quite eerie, featuring screaming and crying babies. How did such a short, unsettling piece become a success? And then, a year later, they remade the same movie but this time, with dolls? The peculiarities continue - the remake is equally, if not more, creepy. Well let's take a look at "Sage-Femme de Première Classe" or in English 'Midwife to the Upper Class" from 1902...

Sage-femme de première classe, Alice Guy, 1902

The movie begins with two figures walking into an outdoor scene. From the title, we deduce that the pair on the right may be a wealthy couple, clasping hands in a show of unity. It seems the lady desires to purchase something from a vendor at a stand - a 'baby' stand. Are they really shopping for babies? If so, this would suggest that such an activity is exclusive to the 'upper' or higher class. In the

The Cabbage Babies

backdrop, a building is adorned with murals of vines and flowers. There's a sign affixed to a door on the far right, which reads "Reserve." Could this be a reference to a stocked supply of a COMMODITY?!

For the initial minute or so, the couple engages in expressive gestures, seemingly immersed in a lively discussion about whether the woman-figure can proceed to buy a baby from the seller. Then, the male figure pulls out a sock, from which he magically produces money. He hands this to the lady, who bears a striking resemblance to the fairy or midwife, right down to the conical hat she dons. The male figure has a more sock or phrygian style cap.

The couple approaches the baby merchant, and after exchanging pleasantries, the woman starts examining the merchandise as if she were perusing items in a store. The seller or 'Midwife' hands them a baby for them to examine - a sort of 'demo' baby, if you will. They scrutinize it together, holding it aloft for better viewing. At this point in the film, the babies are merely dolls, but they are life-sized and, from a distance, bear a striking resemblance to actual infants.

Returning the baby to the Midwife, the couple seems hesitant, not entirely convinced about this particular choice. Undeterred, the Midwife proffers another baby for their consideration. The man, however, promptly shakes his head in disapproval. It appears both parties are in agreement; this choice doesn't meet their expectations either. So the Midwife fetches another baby. The couple graciously accept yet ANOTHER baby to examine, this time manipulating its arm in a peculiar way, as if handling a pet. The man even grips the baby's head (a lifelike doll) and moves it in a nodding motion, as if to indicate 'no, this one isn't right either.'

The Midwife presents another baby, but the couple firmly responds with a double dose of 'no.' It seems their baby shopping adventure has hit a dead end. They indicate their intention to leave, perhaps to search elsewhere. But the Midwife intercepts their exit with a last-ditch proposal: 'Wait! I have more! Here, in the reserve. Come with me, we'll find the perfect baby for you!' Remember, all these interpretations are based on their gestures and acting since there's no actual dialogue. The Midwife then opens the door labeled 'Reserve' in the background and escorts the couple into a new scene.

Approximately two minutes and fifteen seconds into the film, the scene shifts indoors. We're now in what appears to be an INDOOR cabbage patch that serves not only as incubators for live babies but also as a sort of nursery for the sale of newborn infants. The symbolic elements of this film become quite clear, particularly with the various plants and fruits depicted in the wall paintings of this "Hatchery." In this 1902 depiction, it's portrayed as a cabbage patch field.

Without any delay, the Midwife extracts a naked, REAL-LIFE newborn baby from one of the cabbages. If you found the handling of the babies in the 1900 film La Fée aux Choux we covered earlier disturbing, this film amplifies those feelings. It's a lengthier film, features more live children, and yet again, the infants are treated like props in a movie...

Taking into account the historical period and the presence of baby hatcheries in France, it's

40

feasible that they had access to premature infants. Notably, Alice Guy was purportedly moved to create these films due to her experience of witnessing "babies in glass and metal boxes" at the world fair! (Entre & Lumière).

But does this truly constitute inspiration? Or could it instead be a calculated PROMOTION...

Well back to the movie... it's essentially the same sequence but this time with real babies. The midwife presents a live baby to the prospective mother for a trial. The couple scrutinizes the baby as the midwife, appearing as a fairy, selects a blanket from the ground. Within the frame of the shot, she unfolds the fabric, establishing a staging area for all the potential sale or demo babies.

She takes the first baby she plucked from the cabbage and places the clearly distressed newborn on this makeshift mat. The baby's unhappiness is palpable, as it waves its limbs around in protest. Its mouth can be seen opening several times, suggesting that it is crying.

Then, quite unexpectedly, the fairy midwife presents a black baby doll (much like the ones at the stand, but painted a darker color). The couple's reaction is shocking - they turn around, expressing what seems to be disgust. The woman can't even bear to look at the dark-skinned baby! While this behavior may have been reflective of the societal norms at the time, we must also ponder the potential reference to eugenics and the pursuit of certain traits in these artificially controlled situations.

The Fairy Midwife proceeds to pluck a second live baby straight from the cabbage! The couple doesn't even hold this one, the seller rapidly places the newborn actor on the cloth laid out beforehand. Now, there are two live babies squirming and whimpering on the floor. This isn't an exaggeration. If anything, it's likely an understatement of the situation.

Suddenly, she decides to fetch another one! This third live baby looks quite stiff, as we can see its arms moving slightly, and its mouth opening, suggesting discomfort. Next, the woman of the couple independently picks up a baby, adding a fourth live baby to the mix. All of these infants appear rather similar, clearly unhappy with being abruptly pulled out for the sake of a film. Another fabric is laid down, and now we see four live babies in the foreground, placed and rolling on their backs with their eyes shut, mouths open, and hands raised. While it might not be considered torture, it's hard to ignore the bizarre and uncanny nature of the entire scene.

But the spectacle is far from over. The fairy fetches a doll, then a FIFTH BABY! That makes five newborns placed in cabbages, just to be abruptly yanked out. The fifth baby clings to the "new mother", but she removes the baby's hand as they place the baby on a new cloth below.

To me, it seems as if ALL of them are crying, but you can form your own judgments on this matter after watching the film, which is freely available online.

Wait, another one???... Well, now we're at six babies... They accept the SIXTH live baby as their NEW CHILD!

The merchant congratulates the new couple as the male pulls out his coins to pay for the baby, or rather, the PRODUCT. And interestingly, he retrieves this all from a sock, as if it were some sort of allowance? The couple is ecstatic, and so is the midwife fairy. As they walk out the door, the fairy is left with the task of putting all these babies back into their cabbages. But before we get to see that happen, the movie abruptly ends.
(Sage-femme de premire classe AKA Midwife to the Upper Classes, Alice Guy)

It's interesting to note that there are only a couple of films from 1900 that have subtitles, and 'The Cabbage Patch Fairy' is one of them. In fact, the longer name of the film is 'The Cabbage Patch Fairy and the Birth of Babies.' (Wikipedia)

In the film, it shows the subtitle 'La Naissance des Enfants,' which one might assume to be the title. However, it's suggested that these titles were purely descriptive and early films didn't have artistic titles. Alice Guy claims numerous times in her memoirs that her first film was 'La Fee Aux Choux,' but there are reasons to be skeptical about this.

There is further evidence suggesting that these might all be connected to the same film. The evidence for the lost 1896 film is found in seven extant Gaumont films. These films suggest that when the painted panels from these films are assembled, the size - at least 40 feet long - indicates that it was prepared for a larger format film on 58mm film, which was only used at Gaumont during 1896 - 1897. It's believed these 1896 backdrops were reused in the 1900 and 1902 versions. (Dietrick)

Some of these panels connected along their edges, and some are connected by specifics in the painting. There was even a witness who claims that one of the painted backdrops from the 1896 film was used in 'The Dark Misadventures of the Calf Head' film or in French "Les Mefaits d'une Tête de Veau" ... (Dietrick)

Is it possible that these films are interconnected, and that there's a reason they're categorized as 'lost'? One might wonder, how does one simply lose footage? Let's entertain the idea that it was once a large film on cabbage patch kids, like a widescreen film in 1896. Maybe it was decided to remove it, or perhaps it was during a transitional 'reset' time when orphans were being repopulated. It's feasible that these societies, or the Societies of Establishments, or Gaumont, began experimenting with technology inherited from a previous age. They might have staged these occult shows and plays on film, in a darkly comedic fashion, leaving them for the orphans. These films could be laden with symbolism, intertwining symbols of cabbage patches or genetic engineering with symbols of sacrifice and the slaughter of the calf head.

These early films were actually made using different technology. One of Gaumont Studio's other major accomplishments includes 'Vie et Passion du Christ,' directed by Ferdinand Zecca, who also directed the 'Calf Head' movie. This is one of the earliest examples of colored film using a stencil color Pathechrome process. This technique was quite an achievement for its time, and a variety of other manipulation and compositing techniques were used. It suggests there could be an older origin to this art form, considering it was made just six years after the first film, which was only a minute long.

Alice Guy was also involved in other intriguing films. She contributed to what are called 'trick films,' where magic tricks would be shown with the aim of selling compositing tricks as real. Furthermore, another example of Alice Guy's work is a film on animal magnetism, where a hypnotist casts a spell over a woman and undresses her, showcasing an understanding of many occult topics.

Here's where it gets curious, though. Between 1896 - 1920, Alice Guy, who would later adopt the name Alice Guy-Blaché after her marriage, is credited with a whopping 450+ films. Yes, many of these films are of a shorter length, but the sheer volume is staggering. What's even more baffling is, what proof do we have that she truly was the mastermind behind all of these works? Just because her name was attached to a title or a description? Is that all?

Even more intriguing, she is associated with over a hundred "lost" films. Isn't that a little SUSPICIOUS? Or is there something else afoot here? Could it be another stratagem by a colossal industry to portray an emerging technology and art form as the brainchild of a lone inventor? In this case, was Alice Guy merely a facade for the Gaumont Film Company?

Moreover, she also directed a film on feminism that envisioned a world where gender roles were flipped. So, aren't we going to question the controversy surrounding these early lost films? And why was the concept of baby trading chosen as the central idea for the first movie ever made?

Ancient Cloning Factories

As we venture further into the labyrinth of history, we are about to explore theories that may test the boundaries of conventional wisdom. These thoughts, potentially viewed as too radical by skeptics, challenge the narrative many of us absorbed growing up: the notion that ancient societies were technologically deficient. However, what if there's a reason behind our belief that cloning is a relatively recent breakthrough or even a science-fiction concept birthed in the late 19th century? The idea of human cloning, or creating a human being without the need for sexual reproduction, is not a novelty in our historical annals.

The array of postcards we are about to delve into seem to overtly reference a form of Victorian era propagation process, which could arguably be a form of cloning. Here, cabbages serve as potent symbols; they represent rebirth, mimic the anatomy of the female genitalia, and their round shape evokes the image of a pregnant belly as well as an infant's head. This symbolism seems to allude to an operation where humans were metaphorically farmed en masse. The implication is that there were baby factories churning out infants in large numbers for a specific purpose. Also, there seems to be a eugenic element involved in this process where certain phenotypes were deliberately chosen depending on the desired outcome.

What if we venture down the rabbit hole and consider the existence of ancient allusions to repopulation factories? A curious subject for contemplation is the symbol of Artemis, or Diana of Ephesus, viewed through the lens of occult symbolism. Diana, her Latin name, and Artemis, her Greek equivalent, were seen as the great Mother Goddess of fertility. Classical mythology associates Artemis with the virgin goddess of the hunt, forests, and animals. However, it's intriguing to note that Ephesus, nestled in Asia Minor, was steeped in Oriental influences that merged with Greek tradition, giving birth to an entirely novel symbol. The Ephesians worshiped Artemis and Apollo, and believed they were born in a grove named Ortygia, a name strikingly close to Ogygia, the ancient Greek term for Ireland, a land of forests. Ogygia is often considered the birthplace of the first repopulation center following the floods mentioned in numerous ancient religious texts.

The Ephesians dedicated their lives to their gods and found significance in the portrayal of Artemis as a fertility symbol, often depicted with numerous breasts, or perhaps egg-like structures, and her legs held tightly together. Strabo, in his "Geography," gives an account of Ortygia, "a magnificent grove of all kinds of trees," and speaks of the myth surrounding Leto's bath in the Cenchrius River after her labor.

Fig 7.1. Terminal Figure - Diana of Ephesus, circa 1540

Artemis' temple was located in the ancient city of Ephesus, a bustling port city. This temple, one of the seven wonders of the world, was revered as the largest building of antiquity. It served as a place for cult worship, replete with mystical rituals involving sacrifices to the divine goddess of fertility. More than a religious hub, it was an economic center, functioning as a bank of considerable importance. The sanctity of the location ensured that it remained untouched by thieves, making it reportedly the largest bank of its era.

Historical records suggest that the temple was rebuilt numerous times after being destroyed by various invasions, including those by Christians seeking to eradicate all remnants of paganism. This massive temple that once held significant economic and religious influence now echoes its grand past only in ruins, offering tantalizing hints of ancient beliefs and rituals.

Fig 7.2. Wilhelm Schubert van Ehrenberg - The Seven Wonders of the World; The Temple of Diana at Ephesus

It's fascinating to consider how the concepts of ancient seeding operations can be found in various legends that involve a mother goddess and her children. While these histories are often disguised as myth, there are various pieces of evidence that suggest they may have more basis in truth than we typically believe.

For instance, in *Timaeus*, Plato's most esteemed work, he discloses the secret of cycles and resets of advanced ancient civilizations, revealing that there has been more than one deluge.

He states, *"In the first place, you remember a single deluge only, but there were many previous ones; in the next place, you do not know that there formerly dwelt in your land the fairest and noblest race of men which ever lived, and that you and your whole city are descended from a small seed or remnant of them which survived."*

At first glance, one might dismiss these assertions as mere literary devices. However, Plato reiterates these ideas, *"Solon marvelled at his words, and earnestly requested the priests to inform him exactly and in order about these former citizens. You are welcome to hear about them, Solon, said the priest, both for your own sake and for that of your city, and above all, for the sake of the goddess who is the common patron and parent and educator of both our cities. She founded your city a thousand years before ours, receiving from the Earth and Hephaestus the seed of your race, and afterwards she founded ours."*

Later in the book, the discussion takes an alchemical turn, describing the creation of man using similar terminology. The narrative involves the "seeds" or "marrows" of humans, using the elements of fire and water, air and earth, as building blocks. The narrative references a garden, and the creation of man appears as a deliberate, guided process, not unlike gardening or farming.

Furthermore, the creators had to decide the lifespan of these beings, hinting at the possibility that the original seeds had much longer lifespans. Ultimately, he implies that the "seed" is a womb, a vessel for life.

Timaeus's narrative seems to echo the ancient operations of seeding life and resetting civilizations. It touches on the transformation of an original form to be more materially attached to primal senses, deprived of self-will, to make them less "godlike".

In essence, this narrative provides an intriguing possibility that human existence and development might be more deliberate and planned than we often believe. A complex manual rather than a random series of events. And this perspective, although ancient, may offer us insights into our past and our purpose that are still relevant today.

Plato is clearly indicating in the text that humans once existed in a more androgynous state and were fundamentally different from the humans we know today. But through manipulation by these 'gods,' they were altered to reproduce sexually, developing a reliance on one another

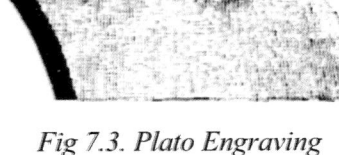

Fig 7.3. Plato Engraving

for procreation, and became more akin to animals. A statement that underscores the idea of humans being more divine and less animal-like in their original form, where their soul was 'seated' in the head. The shift of the soul's 'seat' to the chest represents a fall from the divine to the mundane, or animalistic.

He talks about men transforming into women as a second-generation consequence of their behavior. Plato doesn't mean a literal physical change; he refers to the metamorphosis of their spiritual nature. This reflects the Greek concept of metempsychosis, or transmigration of the soul, where souls can reincarnate into different bodies across multiple lives.

Plato also gives an early theory on the mechanics of sexual reproduction, indicating a rather advanced understanding of the process for the time. The mention of the 'seed' (sperm) having life, and its desire for emission reflects the biological instinct to reproduce. This rebellious and masterful nature of the organ of generation represents the dominance of our physical, animalistic urges over reason.

For women, he paints a picture of the womb as an eager entity longing for fertilization, frustrated and restless when barren for too long, and causing disease. The womb, in his description, is likened to a fertile farm, eager for cultivation. Through his words, we sense how deeply the ancients pondered reproduction, connecting nature's cycles to our own.

This entire conversation seems to be a metaphor for the human condition and our struggle between reason and animalistic urges. And it sets the stage for discussing the ancient knowledge of genetic manipulation, cloning, and hybrid creation – topics that were understandably veiled in mystery due to their complex nature and potential misuse.

Plato hints at this knowledge in his discussions about the 'philosopher's stone,' the mythical substance said to transmute base metals into gold. But this metaphor likely refers to the transformation of the human being from a base, animalistic existence into a 'golden,' enlightened state of consciousness. It's a foreshadowing of topics we'll explore in the next coming book.

The Androgynous beings, as Plato describes, were enlightened entities whose souls were seated in their heads, representing a higher state of consciousness. The change of this 'seat' to the chest, mirroring animals, reflects a spiritual regression. To understand these beings and the transformation they underwent, we need to delve into Plato's Symposium, which holds many keys to deciphering the esoteric secrets of our past.

The temple of Artemis at Ephesus, associated with the Amazons, was an iconic symbol in ancient times. Artemis, known for her multifaceted nature, was often depicted as a multi-breasted goddess, signifying her role as a nurturer and fertility deity.

Fig 7.4. Allaert Claesz - Naked Woman and a Dragon - 1523

The Amazons, according to legend, were a tribe of warrior women, independent and self-sufficient. Artemis, the goddess of wild nature and hunting, was seen as their divine patroness.

Jordanes, an early historian, writes about the Amazonian link to the Temple of Artemis: *"Then they [the Amazons] turned to Ionia and Aeolia, and made provinces of them after their surrender. Here they ruled for some time and even founded cities and camps bearing their name. At Ephesus also they built a very costly and beautiful temple for Diana, because of her delight in archery and the chase—arts to which they were themselves devoted"* (Jordanes, VII.51).

This mythological figure's appropriation and reinterpretation over time have turned her into a powerful symbol in our modern culture. The symbolism of the Amazonian woman, a figure of strength and independence, has been absorbed and expressed in different ways throughout our society.

Take, for instance, the depiction of Diana of Ephesus, Artemis' Roman counterpart. She's shown not just as an empowered Amazonian woman but as a regal figure, adorned with a crown akin to the Statue of Liberty. She also holds a scepter, which may not be just a symbol of authority but potentially an allusion to a tool or device these mythic beings might have possessed.

On the subject of the Statue of Liberty, there are some intriguing overlaps. The statue was officially constructed in France, disassembled, then shipped to America to be reassembled between 1885 and 1886. This timeline coincides with the opening of incubators in France. There are theories that suggest the early photos might have been manipulated using old techniques, casting doubt on the statue's origins.

The strange alliance between France and the United States that resulted in the gift of the Statue of Liberty, combined with the massive wave of immigration through Ellis Island during this period, suggests there are hidden details to this story.

Fig 7.5. La galerie agréable du monde, Van Der Aa, Pieter Boudewyn 1729

Ellis Island, a significant immigration checkpoint, is located near the Statue of Liberty, itself situated on a starfort - fortified areas known for their unique geometric layout. Some of these starforts, like Fort Sumter, were notorious for importing large numbers of slaves. The connection between the statue and these starforts might hint at a hidden history connected with the repopulation and remolding of America's societal fabric.

The Statue of Liberty symbolizes more than just liberty. It blends the symbolism of Diana, Prometheus (the flame representing knowledge and new beginnings), and in modern culture, Wonder Woman (the embodiment of female strength and independence). This blend of symbols could signify the birth and creation of a new order, hinting at the layered symbolism and potential esoteric meanings of this iconic monument.

The design of the Statue of Liberty and its symbolic implications are deeply intertwined with historical and mythological figures. Scholars have pointed out the statue's links to Libertas, the Roman goddess of freedom, which are indeed valid. But there's also a connection to both Athena and Artemis, Greek goddesses known for their multifaceted roles and fervent followings.

Libertas was based on the goddess Athena/Minerva, often portrayed as an androgynous figure. A red stocking cap known as the pileus or Phrygian cap, traditionally worn by freed slaves in ancient Rome, became her symbol when she was called Libertas. During the Revolutionary era, rebels in America and France adopted this "liberty cap" as a symbol of freedom from enslaving authority. ("Goddesses of Liberty: Statues, State Seals of Minerva, Athena, Plenty | Pagan U.S.")

Fig 7.6. Statue of Liberty

Fig 7.7. Declaration of the Rights of Man and of the Citizen painted by Jean-Jacques-François Le Barbier in 1789

We find echoes of these symbols in numerous city seals. There's a potent example in the anime series "The Promised Neverland," where the characters are essentially farmed orphans. The creators of such series often incorporate more symbolism and historical references than they explicitly reveal.

Delving deeper into the history of the Statue of Liberty, we find that its design was influenced by French Freemasons. This group has a long history of using occult symbols, and their rituals have been documented in various texts. They have often been accused of embedding the symbol of Artemis, among others, within the Statue of Liberty.

48

But the symbolic roots of the statue run even deeper and darker. Some argue that the statue represents the ancient Babylonian goddess of love and fertility, Ishtar. This deity was associated with practices such as temple prostitution and was called the "Mother of Harlots".

Historian R.A. Coombes links Ishtar to the concept of welcoming outsiders: "Harlots were social outcasts, so she was referred to as the Mother of Exiles," he writes, suggesting an association with the idea of immigration or becoming the Mother of Immigrants (Great Falls Tribune, "Reader criticizes Statue of Liberty's shadowy past").

The name Ishtar translates to "Queen of Heaven," a title also given to Mary in Roman Catholicism. However, these are distinctly different figures. The spirit symbolized by the statue is an entity that appears in the sky, not the mother of Jesus.

In essence, the Statue of Liberty serves as a complex symbol, drawing from various sources. It represents fertility, immigration, and possibly even orphans or foundlings. While its Freemasonic origins are widely acknowledged, the full extent of its symbolic implications remains veiled, inviting further inquiry.

The Amazons, often depicted by ancient Greek authors as a martial society that eradicated all male offspring, present a fascinating and enigmatic topic of discussion. Despite being reputed as a female-only tribe, their patron deity was Ares, the God of War—a male entity—an aspect that seems counterintuitive considering their masculine exclusionary principles. However, it is plausible that they were moon worshippers, possibly connected to the creation of the Diana of Ephesus symbol, embodying fertility.

Fig 7.8. Giovanni Boccaccio - Penthésilée BnF Français 599 fol. 27v, illuminated manuscript

The seemingly contradictory descriptions of the Amazons—being against male involvement in their society yet being linked to sexual desires—might not be a contradiction at all. Rather than sexual desires, it could imply their intent to repopulate with a new type of human. This is the origin of Eros, or cupid, in which a new human was created that had formed two polarities male and female.

This idea gains traction in popular culture; Matt Groening's 'Futurama' depicts Amazonian women engaging in 'Snu Snu', with the objective of repopulation. Groening's awareness and incorporation of such profound knowledge into his work cannot be mere coincidence. But, considering that these Amazons are portrayed as giants, the idea of sexual intercourse for reproduction seems implausible. More likely, this is a metaphorical representation of the process wherein these giant Amazonian women sought to create a new breed of human, one that would necessitate adjustments to conventional human anatomical features to accommodate changes in diet and digestion.

The survival of an all-female civilization would invariably require some form of repopulation protocol, which could potentially involve technology. Yet, this intriguing aspect remains largely unexplored by historians.

We were well-versed in ancient agricultural and livestock breeding practices. But, what about human farming? Have we ever contemplated whether our ancient predecessors considered it? In the event of a cataclysm resulting in near-extinction, repopulation would likely be one of the primary concerns when rebuilding a civilization. The crucial question is: to what extent was this process pursued? Was technology employed? If so, was it feasible to engineer specific traits, as in the case of eugenics, to achieve a desired outcome?

Many of these considerations are confined to the realm of esoteric history. Nonetheless, by posing the right questions, we can begin to examine these subjects in a new light.

Fig 7.9. Frontispiece to "Las Sergas de Esplandián" by Garci Rodriguez de Montalvo

In the Montalvo novels, whose original source dates back to an unknown 14th-century writer from the Islamic rule of Spain, there's an intriguing tale. This narrative recounts the journey to America, where it was said that a race of gigantic black warrior women resided in California, who showed particular affection for griffins.

Throughout history, we can find traces of several tribes of divine, womanly races, who were frequently summoned for wars. In the case of Califia, for instance, they played a role in the conflict between the Muslims and Christians in Constantinople.

The Amazons also have deep ties with the Scythians. As per historical accounts, the two intermarried at some point, giving rise to a new Scythian subtribe called the Sauromatians.

"The fifth century B.C. historian Herodotus did his best to fill in the missing gaps. The "father of history," as he is known, located the Amazonian capital as Themiscyra, a fortified city on the banks of the Thermodon River near the coast of the Black Sea in what is now northern Turkey. The women divided their time between pillaging expeditions as far afield as Persia and, closer to home, founding such famous towns as Smyrna, Ephesus, Sinope and Paphos. Procreation was confined to an annual event with a neighboring tribe." (Foreman)

Although there were many tribes of warrior women, I believe this just scratches the surface of the symbolism involved. As we discussed with the concept of androgynous beings, these women were of a different form and mindset. They were free from necessities like eating or drinking and were essentially divine beings. They too can be compared to figures like Wonder Woman, Lady Liberty, the mother of immigrants, and Athena.

As the Owl is the symbol of Minerva, these figures of warrior women have their symbolic interpretations in our mythology and history.

"The early association of the bee with the cult of Artemis is attested by varied evidence. It appears not only upon the strange polymastoid statue of the Ephesian goddess but upon the earliest coins of her city. As the owl was the emblem of Athena at Athens, so the bee seems to have been the emblem of Artemis at Ephesus.

Although the extant examples of the polymastoid statue are all of late date, it is hardly possible that the type with its medley of elements can have been a late Hellenistic creation. So important was the bee in the cult of Artemis that her priestesses received the name of Melissa, Bee.

There is no direct evidence that the Ephesian priestesses of the goddess bore that title, but the assumption that she did is justified by the monuments cited. Another such title was bee-keeper. At Delphi, there was a The first priestess with this title probably served in the temple of Apollo there which bees had made of wax.

These Apolline bees must have had some relation to the 'bees of Artemis,' the twin sister of the god." (Elderkin 203-213)

The humble honey bee, surprisingly, was a sacred symbol in antiquity, appearing on ancient coins and statues. You might recall the bunny bee from the Cabbage Patch story. Numerous civilizations revered the honey bee for its life-affirming gifts of honey. But the bee, especially the Queen bee, has been associated with various goddesses, often without any clear reason.

Could it be that the Queen bee, the mother source from which the entire colony originates, symbolizes the origin of our own population? And could the beehives be seen as the factories where these colonies are produced? This symbolism seems pervasive in our entire culture. The Queen bee, much like a monarch, births different offspring to complete different tasks. Worker bees, soldier bees - each bee has a specific task to support the Queen and the collective hive mind.

Are Queen bees Ancient Goddesses?

Ramsay's view that the image of Artemis isn't "human" at all but rather bee-related seems quite plausible. He contends that Artemis is the queen-bee - "her image makes this plain", and that the "breasts" are, in fact, ova. The bee features prominently on numerous Ephesian coins and Artemis images. It has even been suggested that the very name of the city, in the Lydian language, means "place of many bees" (Elderkin 1939:206). (Strelan 92)

Fig 7.10. Bee-goddess, perhaps associated with Artemis above female heads. Gold plaques, 7th century BC

51

THE MULTI-BREASTED DIANA IS AN INTERPRETATION BY MAINSTREAM HISTORIANS, YET ON CLOSER INSPECTION, THESE ARE NOT BREASTS, BUT EGGS OR OVUM. THIS FURTHER CLARIFIES THE HYPOTHESIS OF SOME TYPE OF MASS REPOPULATION PROCESS.

Fig 7.11. Copper by Salomon Kleiner (1700–1761) in: [Johann Karl Newen von Newenstein ed.]

Ancient Cloning Factories

Situated in Rome, there's a 17th-century fountain, the Fontana del Tritone, located in the Piazza Barberini. It features a life-size Triton sea god, depicted as a Phoenician mermaid, kneeling on the sum of four dolphin tail-fins. On this fountain is a coat of arms for the Barberini family, showing their ties to bees.

This symbolism, often merging with that of golden horseflies, is never fully explained. Yet the bee, used as a vital symbol by the Barberini family, is the final symbol, adorning their creations.
Why is this symbol so important to them? As the head of the Catholic Church in the early 1600s, perhaps they knew exactly what this symbol referred to - Artemis.

Fig 7.12. 'La Fontane di Roma', Giovanni Battista Falda 1691

Alma Mater and Magna Mater offer yet another perspective on these breeding programs. In Latin, Alma Mater means 'nourishing mother,' an allegorical phrase for a university or college that one has attended or, in the U.S., graduated from. The term implies that these institutions are breeding programs for the mind, where the mother figure births specific types of worker-minded 'bees'.

The symbol of a castle upon the head is another connection to this ancient Artemis and Liberty representation, signifying that this process of repopulation is crucial in the foundation and structure of the new world.

The Cabbage Babies

Magna Mater was an ancient Roman female cult. The cult was introduced in a new form, the Phrygian goddess Matar, through its Greek incarnation, the Cult of Cybele.

You may discover that there are many 'Mother Goddesses' out there. Instead of them being some random deity that an entire ancient city would dedicate their entire religion and life to, what if these Mother Goddesses were actually machines or methods used to create clones? How else can the influx of orphans be explained? How can there be an abundance of premature babies? Infant asylums were known to exist to address this issue, seemingly producing babies en masse. Some old pictures are very telling, showing children being prepared for the new world amidst mud-filled streets.

The Statue of Liberty is, in fact, Diana of Ephesus, an occult symbol encapsulating the key to understanding repopulation. Its supposed construction by freemasons in 1886 raises suspicions about its symbolizing how the United States acquired its new citizens.

Furthermore, I propose that they weren't just creating humans. They were probably experimenting with all sorts of animal-human ratios, leading to the hybrids from myth and legend as well as hybrid animals we know today.

The Temple of Artemis is just one example. Given that this symbol is connected to many other goddesses, it likely existed all over the world.

Fig 7.13. Magna Mater, 1702

Hybrid beings can be found in depictions from a variety of different cultures. Even the Bible mentions that the flood occurred due to the existence of hybrids and giants.

Fig 7.14. 19th century engraving of Homunculus from Goethe's Faust part II

The stories of the Homunculus and the artificial man, the Golem, seem to reference a similar process in which an artificial human could be created from elemental components. This symbolism is multi-layered. On one level, it appears to refer to a physical process where an artificial human could be created—an early form of genetic engineering, perhaps, given that alchemy is the origin of modern science. On a deeper level, the transmutation to gold symbolizes the merging of the higher self with the lower self, forming a spiritual body of light that can be controlled and manipulated.

That's a topic for another time, but these concepts of creating or breeding humans are not new. They have been around for ages, typically surfacing when cataclysms decimate a population. One might wait and rebuild naturally, or perhaps a method was devised to expedite the process.

Foundling hospitals, since their inception, were funded by elite royals. Isn't it curious that their seal is Artemis, the goddess associated with orphans and premature babies?

Orphanages date back to the time of Rome. One of the earliest known orphanages is La Pietà in Venice, a convent of monks and nuns. From its inception, orphans were the responsibility of the Catholic Church. However, can we accept the narrative of the Church simply caring for the needy, when they set the laws, control the economy, and yet, numerous families have to surrender their children because of societal structures governed by these Catholic rulers?

Something else must be going on. As we now know, incubators were conveniently located near foundling hospitals to accommodate an unusually high number of premature babies.

If you search for "Baby incubators 1900s," you'll first encounter the babies of Coney Island. But there's more to this story. In the late 1800s, physician Martin Couney began demonstrating the efficacy of infant incubators across the US and Europe. It seems strange that this technology, which isn't overly advanced, seemed to appear out of nowhere. Then, during the world fairs, these babies were displayed and, incredibly, available for purchase.

It's undeniable that the notion of infant incubators, particularly those showcased and sold at world fairs, seems bizarre by today's standards. There would likely be substantial protests if something similar were to occur in our current times. It's well-documented that these premature babies were generally orphans or foundlings.

These infant incubators made appearances across America: in Buffalo, at the Trans-Mississippi International Exhibition in Omaha, Nebraska, in Chicago, Jacksonville, Florida, and many other locations.

Martin Couney, the physician mentioned earlier, also had an exhibit at the world fair in Paris. The postcards and movies were not designed to promote a single event but were part of a worldwide promotion of infant incubators. It seems that people from around the globe were intended recipients of this advertising campaign.

There are theories suggesting that these could have been factories where multiple women were giving birth concurrently. While plausible, this would have introduced numerous complications, not least of which would be the hygiene issues and the lack of consistency in the care provided.

Even though there are still similar facilities today, for accuracy and cleanliness, it would be crucial to have control over the environment.

Another intriguing connection is the symbolism of the tulip, especially the red variety. It's not merely a beautiful flower; its symbolism runs much deeper. The tulip is often used by companies to represent fertility, and interestingly, it is also linked with children—specifically orphan children—and the idea of lost blood. This layered symbolism gives the tulip a profound significance beyond its aesthetic appeal.

During the Dutch Golden Age, an intriguing phenomenon known as Tulip Mania swept across the nation. It was a period of extraordinary delusion where people began paying exorbitant prices for flowers and produce, and while there are many theories as to why this occurred, I find it fascinating that this mainstream historical event has such a strong association with tulips. Could it be referencing the same thing, but from before the postcards, dating back to the 17th century? Interestingly, it wasn't just tulips that skyrocketed in price, but cabbages too. I can't help but wonder: were they genuinely obsessed with these items, or could they be symbolic stand-ins for something else?

Fig 7.15. Flora's Wagon of Fools: Allegory on the Tulip mania. Painted by Hendrik Gerritsz Pot, circa 1637

The cabbage craze may seem random, but considering how often symbolism is used, it could very well be a coded message. Some narratives suggest that after the Dutch were liberated from the

Spanish Empire in 1581, they began growing tulips around their palaces, sparking a strange kind of economic bubble.

Indeed, critics at the time declared these tulip buyers to be irrational and mad, paying such vast amounts for tulips, cabbages, and even carrots. I suspect there may be an underlying joke in this. Interestingly, this period also marked the advent of our modern money system. Satirical cartoons were even used to promote these commodities, much like the postcards.

Fig 7.16. Het groote tafereel der dwaasheid, 1720, pg133

Many of these satirical prints contain cabbages, drawing a parallel between tulips and cabbages. One such image even depicted a group of monkeys (a symbol of foolishness) eating cabbages while wolves chased innocent sheep. The phrase "*De Wareld Vol Cool*" (The world full of cabbage) frequently appeared in banners above these scenes. This satirical portrayal of clamoring for different types of cabbages, including "worthless cabbage," "cowardly cabbage," and "crazy cabbage," as well as references to "Carrot shares" and "cabbage selling," strongly suggest that these vegetables were symbolic of something else.

Fig 7.17. Het groote tafereel der dwaasheid, 1720, pg71

"CABBAGE FOR SALE."

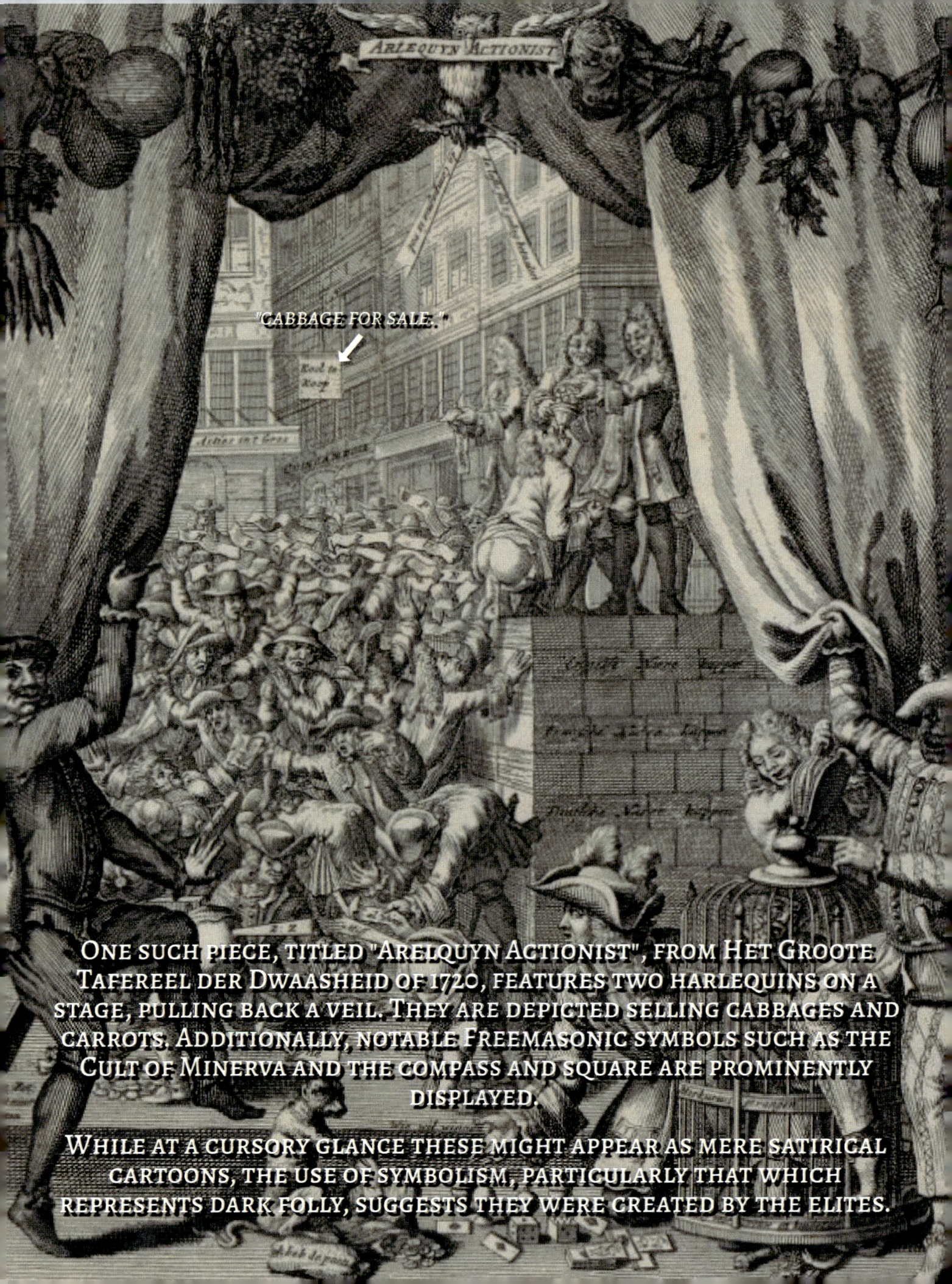

One such piece, titled "Arelquyn Actionist", from Het Groote Tafereel der Dwaasheid of 1720, features two harlequins on a stage, pulling back a veil. They are depicted selling cabbages and carrots. Additionally, notable Freemasonic symbols such as the Cult of Minerva and the compass and square are prominently displayed.

While at a cursory glance these might appear as mere satirical cartoons, the use of symbolism, particularly that which represents dark folly, suggests they were created by the elites.

The portrayal of tulips sold for over a thousand pounds for their "snow-white and beautifully striped" appearance, as well as the occasional mockery, further supports this interpretation. The use of symbols and what they left us with certainly deserve a closer look. These depictions are the primary historical records we have of the 1720 crash and considering the symbols and messages they carry, it seems unlikely that they were simply selling "tulips" or "cabbages". ("Het Groote Tafereel der Dwaasheid [The Great Picture (or Scene) of Folly]")

These early 18th-century engravings, such as those from Het Groote Tafereel der Dwaasheid, depict intriguing and complex scenes. One of these images portrays Lady Liberty, accompanied by a beehive and a cherubic figure who is holding a shield adorned with two keys. The figure reminiscent of Lady Liberty is also seen grasping a top hat, while an act of identity swapping seems to be taking place. Another figure in the scene, resembling Medusa or a lady with a snake, appears to be dying. Under her left arm, she cradles what looks like a barrel, hive, or perhaps even a globe, from which people and infants are emerging and cabbages, symbolic of repopulating the earth, are being tossed.

Fig 7.19. Het groote tafereel der dwaasheid, 1720, pg45

This throwing of cabbages seems to transition into a separate scene where a crowd, under the watchful gaze of a devilish figure, is seemingly throwing a person into flames as a form of sacrifice. These visual narratives, embedded in these "Reset Engravings" from the early 1700s, interweave a

The Cabbage Babies

multitude of symbolic elements, and they also bear connections to the work of a well-known artist from England, which will be discussed in future explorations.

But to bring it all back, it seems they were using this tulip and cabbage symbolism long before the 1800s. It's as if they had adopted a secret language through these satirical cartoons. And let me just say, this stuff is downright bizarre - the kind of odd you couldn't make up even if you tried.

There's this one piece where they are literally trying to cut out the third eye, and then, get this, they seem to be attempting to forcibly insert this new economic system right into our rears! It's as if there's an implied effort to reshape our perceptions and our reality in the most intrusive of ways.

Fig 7.20. Het groote tafereel der dwaasheid, 1720, pg59

It's remarkable how deep this rabbit hole goes. Consider the 16th-century painting, "*The Baker of Eeklo*", which illustrates a curious legend. This tale, set in the West-Flemish town of Eeklo, involves a baker who uniquely baked heads. His clientele would have their heads removed, while a cabbage was put in its place. Strikingly, it's a common folklore in the Netherlands that children sprout from kale, growing akin to cabbages. This might hint that the cabbage symbolism has far-reaching roots in our history, stretching beyond just the past 100 years. With its eerie portrayal, "The Baker of Eeklo" shares an uncanny similarity to the illustrations in "Het Groote Tafereel der Dwaasheid," further reaffirming these connections. ("The baker of Eeklo")

Fig 7.21. De legende van de bakker van Eekloo Rijksmuseum, circa 1560

In order to wrap up our discussion, let's delve into the somewhat mysterious history of test tube babies. Here's the scoop: You begin with a group of women and administer fertility drugs prompting their bodies to develop multiple eggs. Once these eggs mature, they're retrieved, typically through an ultrasound-guided needle procedure. Then the eggs are placed in a petri dish where they encounter sperm. Some of these eggs will fertilize, becoming embryos, which are then incubated in the lab under carefully controlled conditions.

Interestingly, the term 'test tube baby', while dismissed by some as a media smear, dates back way further than most people think. Nowadays, once the embryo reaches a certain developmental stage, it is transferred into a uterus or a surrogate female. This method of conception would surely have been attempted at some point in the past.

A 1929 article from the American Guardian, titled "Chemist will be only Daddies some Day, Is prediction", is the earliest reference I've found that explicitly discusses the concept of test tube babies. H T Rhodes, general secretary of the British Association of Scientists, is quoted in this piece suggesting that there won't be much difference between a naturally born human and one 'compounded in the test tube.'

The article reads:
"We are just on the threshold of the discoveries chemists are making," Rhodes said. 'We have almost finished with analysis. We are passing on to synthesis—the building up and making of new and valuable products out of the meaner ones. The speculation is therefore almost forced upon us that in time we will be able to create living material."

While this may seem like propaganda, programming readers to believe in some far-off scientific future, the truth of the matter is that these experiments had already been underway since at least the 1700s, albeit under a different name. The article further expounds on what society might do with these 'synthetic humans,' an idea so weird and outlandish that one can't help but question why it's being promoted at all.

The article continues:
"Suppose then, it were possible in 1000 years from now for a chemist to produce synthetic living things? They could be set to do the workaday labor of the world, thus setting free those human beings naturally begotten to undertake further conquests of knowledge."

This, right here, is a classic Freemason reference, if you ask me.

So would these laboratory-created beings be like us? The article asks, "Who knows? Probably not. But they would be something approaching us in structure. It is improbable that they would be able to think like us. When you talk about thinking you get into the metaphysical."

That's some strange food for thought, but it stands as the earliest reference I've found about the concept of test tube babies, suggesting this subject is far from new.

Diving deeper into the annals of history, one artwork that intriguingly highlights the notion of artificial life creation is "The Cabinet of Curiosities" by Levinus Vincent. It's impossible not to ask, could this possibly be an early portrayal of a cloning center?

Vincent, a prominent Dutch designer and affluent merchant, was a significant figure during the era of the Dutch Republic, particularly throughout the infamous financial bubble of 1720, often referred to as Tulip Mania. He was also associated with the prestigious Royal Society, adding a layer of scientific and intellectual gravitas to his persona.
Among Vincent's works, the book titled "The Cabinet of Curiosities" stands out. On the surface, Wikipedia describes the contents as consisting of 'small animals' and 'Artificialia,' vaguely referring to some form of man-made creations. Yet, intriguingly, there are no explicit references to genetic manipulation or substantial contributions to scientific knowledge on his page. It begs the question - what really is depicted in this mysterious work? (Wikipedia)

Ancient Cloning Factories

Fig 7.22. Wondertooneel der nature, 1706, pg47

Although much about "The Cabinet of Curiosities" remains shrouded in ambiguity, the hints of strangeness and the arcane are hard to ignore. This isn't merely a collection of oddities. It's worth noting that the creator exhibited a nuanced understanding of symbolism.

Vincent's book, titled *Wondertooneel der Nature*, is bursting with blatant occult symbols. With our current understanding, these symbols begin to unveil their concealed meanings, enhancing our view of this early exploration of artificial life creation.

In one particular illustration, we observe a man conspicuously holding a beehive while gesturing towards the nearby shelves teeming with an assortment of phials. Beneath him are two baby orphans; notably, one is brandishing what seems to be a Freemason compass or square. This isn't an accidental inclusion, as the Masonic symbol is reiterated in the floral motifs decorating the scene.

Fig 7.23. Wondertooneel der nature, 1706, pg7

What's particularly interesting is the beehive the man holds, this choice isn't random. In the same scene, there's a figure that closely resembles the multi-breasted Diana of Ephesus, also known as Lady Liberty, wearing a tower or castle on her head. This could signify some sort of factory or mechanism intended for repopulating the new world.

The shelves are filled with bottles containing what appear to be human-like figures, hinting at a possible early concept of test-tube babies. Moreover, there are odd creatures in some of the jars, leaving us to question whether they were experimenting with creating specific animal hybrids. The imagery isn't just symbolic - the jars quite literally contain human-like entities and strange creatures.

Ancient Cloning Factories

"Wondertooneel der nature, Vincent, Levinus, 1706"

65

The Cabbage Babies

REPOPULATION POSTCARDS

(Cpatch_babies_10)

Intro

While conducting research for our video, "Old World Photoshop," released on Nov 16th, 2022, we began to spot a trend in early 1900s postcards as we were looking for early examples of Compositing. There isn't much information on these, if there is a catalog it is not easy to come by, but many of these are early examples of Photo Manipulation. They had surreal "Real Photo" postcards, in which they would attempt to trick people with the illusion of photography. After that video was released, the concept then went viral after the release of the *Repopulation Postcards/ Cabbage Patch* video, creators on Tiktok and Youtube began sharing the postcards because of how shocking this story was. In fact, the story was so jarring that many questioned the authenticity of the photos, accusing us of using Photoshop to fool our viewers into accepting this seemingly ridiculous idea. The skepticism, it seemed, stemmed from the fact that, since people hadn't previously seen or heard of these, they simply couldn't be true.

(large_cabbage_surreal_rppc)

66

The existence of these postcards has been recognized for several decades. In fact, during our research for last year's video, we discovered two notable books: *Babylon: Surreal Babies* by James Birch and George Melly, published in 2011, and the more recent *La Fée aux Choux: Alice Guy's Garden of Dreams* by Janelle Dietrick, published in 2022. Both authors have acknowledged the existence of these postcards for some time. Though their contributions have been invaluable to our research, we couldn't find any works in books or online videos that tied these postcards to the concept of REPOPULATION and the ORPHAN TRAINS.

However, after delving into the realm of Old World Compositing and Photo manipulation - fueled by our understanding of alternative history topics - it dawned on us that there was a SPECIFIC NICHE OF OLD WORLD RPPC that merited its own category. Hence, we coined the term REPOPULATION POSTCARDS. This epiphany led us to accumulate a substantial collection of this particular, unique style, both digitally and physically, as we ordered hundreds of these postcards from antique shops. (Even some straight from Paris Antique Stores!)

Some of these postcards are exceptionally rare and contain intriguing references to the shipment and sale of babies as commodities. Handwritten notes on the backs of our collected postcards provide additional insights into the events and sentiments of that era. It's crucial to mention that while the majority of the postcards originate from France, they also appear in other locations, including America.

Well Melly & Birch's book delves into the history of these cards, it also provides an excellent collection. We highly recommend checking out his book as it is the only history we could find at the beginning of this research. From Babylon: Surreal Babies,

" I first came across a handful of these postcards when I was a student in Aix-en-Provence. I was walking through the flea market in front of the Palais de Justice when one of the cards caught my eye, a froth of smiling babies boiling away in a cauldron. That morning I had discovered I was about to become a father.
I didn't really pay much attention to these cards again until years later in the 80s when I visited the Pompidou Centre for an exhibition on Surrealism. There in one of the vitrines was a collection of fantasy baby postcards shown for their inspirational importance to both the Dadaists and the Surrealists. I became hooked and my collection started.
These postcards had a great influence on many artists in the 1920s and 30s, and were collected by Paul Éluard, André Breton, Salvador Dali, Hannah Höch, Herbert Bayer, and Man Ray. These popular images excited inspiration in these artists by their boundless inventiveness – the permutations are countless." (Birch, p. 5)

There are a multitude of these cards so you can find duplicates in old postcard shops and online stores. We are going to be taking a look at the photos in our MU Collection that we scanned, organized and collected ourselves. We call these REPOPULATION POSTCARDS.

Let's take a look at one of these cards.

The Cabbage Babies

(Cpatch_babies_06_front)

68

REPOPULATION POSTCARDS

This is one of our favorites as it is extremely rare to see this many high quality photos of children in one composite. This postcard is from 1909 dated from the stamp. A cabbage patch field where babies are being grown but from a century ago? So this isn't something that was simply made up in the 80s! These tales have been around for over a hundred years... perhaps it is a reference to something we were never told about in the history books.

(Cpatch_babies_06_back)

We must highlight that the front of each postcard is only half the story, there are some very intriguing details in the back side that in many cases contain writing from these times! We aren't translators and do not know french fluently, however we have done our best to translate these so if you find any errors please let us know! This is the back of the cabbage patch field we just showed and will use names on the postcards that we have scanned front and back, the text to the left says...

"It taught me that you do not recognize this which gave me great pleasure as well as to mom. I send all my friendships to you and your husband."

69

There are many different categories of these repopulation postcards, for example, there are the "cabbage babies" but there are many others that each deserve their own section. This chapter will be more of an analysis as we examine and breakdown the most shocking ones. At
the end of the book we will be showing them all in full scale so that you can look at them in their full glory.

So why would we call them Repopulation Postcards?

REPOPULATION? A French baby-making machine? We see "Graines" or SEEDS, "de choux" and also "de roses". Is it really that far-fetched to associate the idea of REPOPULATION with Cabbage Babies? Take a look at this 1906 French postcard to the right - the message is clear. Some might brush it off as a simple cartoon, yet the IDEA that this concept is even linked to the cabbage patches is noteworthy. Also, spot the woman in red? She's identical to the lady featured in the postcards!

Interestingly, the woman in red is also depicted with a key. And what about that peculiar logo under the father's foot in the bottom right corner?

The caption at the bottom, "Allons mon Cher Ami, au labeur, Ta femme a la clé de la serrure Et la pendule marque l'heure. Des éclosions de la progéniture," translates into English as:

"Let's go my dear friend, to work, your wife has the key to the lock and the clock marks the hour. Of the offspring's hatching."

1906 postcard of a French Invention that generates babies

Hmm pretty shocking if you ask me, are they preparing these babies for some type of shipment? Well this is not the only one either...

70

REPOPULATION POSTCARDS

3. Char de la Repopulation

Intriguing, right? A Repopulation Tank? Observe the man in the top hat, not just tending, but actively pumping or possibly injecting something into the cabbages. This detail adds an intriguing layer of interpretation. The "Tank," alternatively referred to as a "Cart," is drawn by a pair of horses, suggesting mobility. Could it symbolize a concept designed to be introduced into cities with the intention of repopulation?

Take note of the smaller workers at the bottom, also engaged in the task of pumping. And let's not overlook the size of those babies - they're remarkably large! Recall the story published in the Canada Lancet? The one involving giant babies? The correlation is hard to ignore.

Moreover, a familiar figure reappears - the woman in red. This femme fatale, the harlot goddess archetype...

Libertas, or Diana of Ephesus!

The Queen Bee Goddess.

These babies were made by the honey bee bright,
Out of dew and flowers and the sun shines light.

71

It's also worth noting that the woman in red in this scene is clearly a giantess with red hair and pale skin. She is visibly larger than the adult man with the top hat, the babies are larger than the adult midwives, there's something to be said about the repeating theme of "giants".

(Red_lady_03)
"Midwife or Red Lady"

The Cabbage Babies

We are going to take a look at just a few of the best postcards from each "category" of what we call REPOPULATION POSTCARDS, there are far too many to comment on. Please use this section as the breakdown and check the end of the book for the full gallery so you can see up close!

Cabbage Babies

Well let's begin with the most shocking of all. Babies being GROWN in Cabbage Patches?!?

(Cpatch_babies_15)

REPOPULATION POSTCARDS

(Cpatch_babies_10)

We'll start with these two postcards from our collection, which are great examples of early photo editing and compositing. If we've named the photos, it means we've scanned both sides of the postcard. And if we haven't shown the back, it either means there's no writing on it, or we've saved it for the final gallery section.

These two postcards feature REAL photos of babies, presented in a field of produce, seemingly up for sale by a worker or merchant. The Fairy? These babies are being SOLD to a wealthy family... This isn't just some cute artwork. It suggests a historical event, particularly when we consider these artworks' connection to the promotion of incubators, as we discussed earlier with the Alice Guy films! Another interesting detail to note is the appearance of scanlines on not all but some of the postcards. We think these could be due to metal in the paint. While we can't confirm this 100%, it doesn't look like this in person. We've also taken high quality photos to show what these postcards truly look like. Some are embossed and have a unique gloss, viewable from specific angles, which reflects the time they were made in.

75

The Cabbage Babies

(Cpatch_babies_04_JUICE)

  This is one of our favorite postcards! It's absolutely astounding, as it depicts a farmer or merchant casually pushing a freshly 'harvested' baby in a wheelbarrow. This baby has just been adopted by an affluent couple who plan on bringing this little one into their home. But what of the other babies? Also, pay attention to the train in the background...

  Could it be portraying an actual event where infants were transported around the world, only to be traded like commodities? Given the REAL and FACTUAL history we now understand about baby incubators, foundling hospitals, and orphan trains, is this notion really so far-fetched?

  Or does cognitive dissonance provide a refuge for those unable to accept that events outside the known history books may have transpired in secrecy? It's a shocking proposition, isn't it? "Grandma, where do babies come from?" "Oh, we sprang from a cabbage patch, dear. That's what my mother told me!"

  So, are we content to dismiss the idea of sourcing babies from a cabbage patch as mere folklore, or a remnant of an 80s cultural wave?

  The only plausible inference we can draw is that these postcards hail from a period of prominent advertising, closely linked to the era of the "World Fairs". Given our exploration of the unusual history surrounding incubators, it's reasonable to conclude that these postcards, based on their dates, serve as promotional materials for the incubation and sale of young children.

REPOPULATION POSTCARDS

Well let's take a look at the back of that postcard!

(Cpatch_babies_04_JUICE_back)

One of the simplest ways to date the card is by the postage stamp! These stamps hold a special significance for us as they validate the authenticity of the cards. This particular one hails from France, 1907. You'll frequently encounter this style of stamp featuring Libertas with her Phrygian cap, or the 10¢ (sometimes 5¢) postage stamps, varying between red and green hues for postcards of this period. Additionally, we often find an ink postmark, where the last two digits can be utilized for dating purposes. For instance, "07" corresponds to 1907, which matches the date of the red République Française postage stamp.

This one is interesting because it says "Blanche" …Now this is not to say this is 100% connected to Alice Guy-Blaché, however what a serendipitous discovery that we find this name on the back of one of the top illustrations for this style of postcard.

The Cabbage Babies

(Cpatch_babies_04_JUICE_back)

French:

Chère Blanche,
Je viens te demander si tu as reçu tes 6 cartes postales. Je pense que tu dois être contente, surtout celle où on voit la maison où tu es née.

Nous pensons que tu dois te préparer pour venir à Manosque car nous sommes au mois d'Août. Il faut te dépêcher car Papa a dit que sans ton arrivée, nous ne pouvons pas jouer !

English:

Dear Blanche,
I am asking if you have received your 6 postcards. I think you must be happy, especially with the one where you can see the house where you were born.
We think you must be preparing to come to Manosque because we are in the month of August. You must hurry because Papa said that without your arrival, we cannot play!

Please note this may not be perfect, there are some words we had difficulty with due to the nature of the writing however this is around 80-90% accurate as a base. To the right it's made out to " Me^elle Blanche Nevière" which translates to "Miss Blanche Nevière."

This postcard was made out to a street in Marseille that still exists to this day!

Mademoiselle Blanche Nevière
Rue Longue des Capucins
No. 68
Marseille

REPOPULATION POSTCARDS

(Cpatch_babies_05_JUICE)

    We have another postcard here, a sibling to the first, originating from the same period and boasting a similar style. Yet, it showcases intriguing differences that warrant our attention! This time, the narrative includes additional animals in the tableau, as well as a different upper-class couple surveying the 'produce'. A man, resplendent in a top hat, can be seen extending a handshake to a rather darkly hued "monkey". This might suggest a symbolic nod to eugenics, hinting at different 'types' of babies, symbolized by varied animal species.

    Or perhaps it equates the selling of infants to the trade of farm animals? Either way, the implications are startling. It's worth questioning: is this practice not too dissimilar to our modern-day acceptance of cloned livestock in farming and food production?

    "In 2001, when it became apparent that animal cloning may become a commercial venture to help improve the quality of herds, FDA requested livestock producers and researchers to keep food from animal clones or their offspring out of the food supply. Since then, FDA has conducted an intensive evaluation that included examining the safety of food from these animals and the risk to animal health.

    Based on a final risk assessment, a report written by FDA scientists and issued in January 2008, FDA has concluded that meat and milk from cow, pig, and goat clones and the offspring of any animal clones are as safe as food we eat every day." (Tanne and FDA)

The Cabbage Babies

(Cpatch_babies_05_JUICE_back)

The date on the postmark is from 1906, and the green post stamp from the front is the 5¢ version that you will see on many of these postcards. It looks like it was processed both in Chouzé-sur-Loire and Maine-et-Loire in France.

They would send these images to loved ones, but why? Did they not find it strange to be seeing babies depicted as such? Was it just fun art?

80

REPOPULATION POSTCARDS

More Cabbages!

(Cpatch_babies_01)

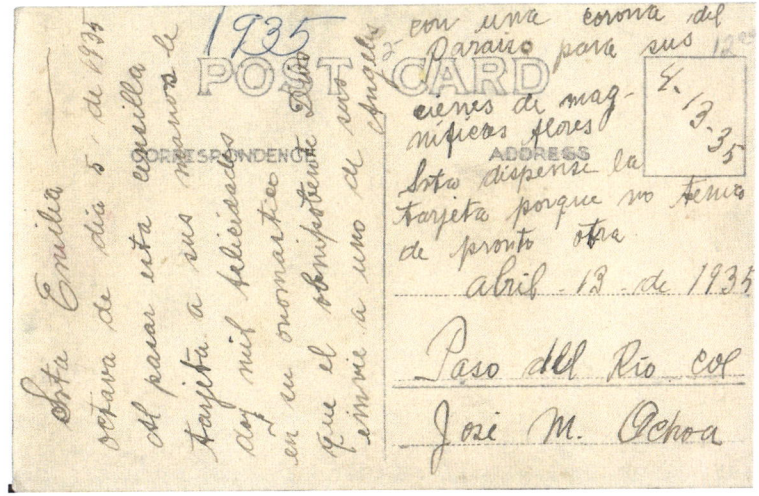

(Cpatch_babies_01_back)

    This postcard is from 1935! Confirming that these were not confined to a single era. These visual references span across multiple periods, even predating the World Fairs, with myriad styles manifesting in various postcards.

    This particular piece showcases a distinct photomontage technique, thereby adding another layer to its stylistic depth. Within each category of REPOPULATION POSTCARDS, there lie several stylistic subcategories. The 'Cabbage Babies' category, interestingly, appears to be the most diverse in terms of visual diversity and stylistic versatility. The back of this one is in Spanish! Some of the terms were a little hard to translate like "censilla" but here is something close.

"Sota Emilia,
Octava de día 5 de 1935. Si para esta censilla tarjeta a sus manos le doy mil felicidades en su onomástico. Que el omnipotente Dios envíe a uno de sus ángeles."

Translation:

"Dear Emilia,
Eighth day of 1935. If this humble card reaches your hands, I wish you a thousand felicities on your saint day. May the omnipotent God send one of his angels."

That's just the left of the back side then the right says :

"Con una corona, del
Paraíso adorne sus
Sienes de magníficos flores

Sota disculpe la
Tarjeta porque no tenía De pronto otra
Abril 13 de 1935
Paso del Rio Col"

Translation:

"With a crown, from Paradise adorn your
Temples with magnificent flowers
Sota excuse the
Card because I didn't have
Another one right now
April 13, 1935
Paso del Rio Col"

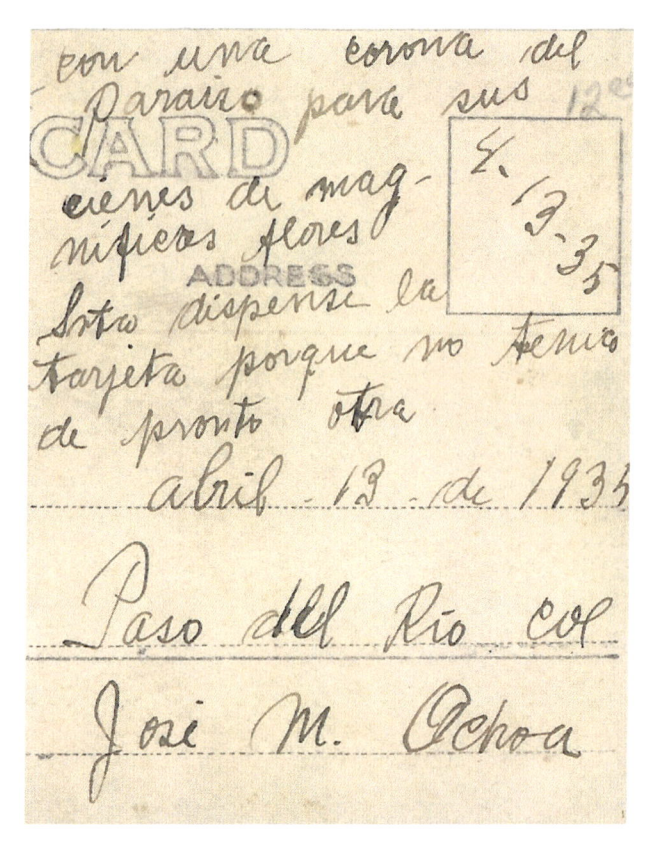

(Cpatch_babies_01_back)

Well very interesting that this was used as a last option postcard, but why excuse yourself? Perhaps José knew that there was something strange about them.

(Cpatch_babies_07)

This postcard on the left could also fit into the "multi-babies" category, as we'll explore later. However, given the cabbage setting, it's more apt to include it here. The image bears a striking resemblance to stock photography, typically used for product advertising. It doesn't evoke the warmth of a typical family photo; rather, the sight of children, likely orphans, tucked into cabbages alongside produce is somewhat disconcerting.

REPOPULATION POSTCARDS

"Graine de Poilu" or "Seed of a future soilder"

(Cpatch_babies_02)

*"Dans ce joli parterre,
Tout en nous promenant,
Voilà ! comment, ma chère,
Nous aurons un enfant !"*

*"In this beautiful flowerbed,
While we're strolling,
Look! This is how, my dear,
We will have a child!"*

During World War I, "Poilu" was a term used to refer to French infantrymen. The term translates literally to "hairy one", and is similar to the English term "grunt". It is an affectionate term, symbolizing the typical French infantryman's courage and endurance. However, in this context, given that it's related to a postcard depicting a baby or a young child, it might be an affectionate way of saying "a future soldier" or "the seed of a future soldier".

In these depictions, baby boys emerge from cabbages and girls bloom from roses! The seed is the child? Is this meant to be a humorous take on childbirth? Considering the recurring theme across numerous postcards, simply writing it off as a jest seems far from logical.

Let's take a look at another! This one says:

*"Auprès du grand moulin,
Au détour du chemin,
Je connais un plantage
De nombreux bébés sages."*

*"Near the big mill,
At the bend of the road,
I know of a planting
Of numerous well-behaved babies."*

(Cpatch_babies_08)

Well behaved babies? Is this some type of BABY FARM???

83

The Cabbage Babies

(Cpatch_babies_11) & (Cpatch_babies_11_back)

*"We would rejoice in this day, But they wouldn't allow us so much.
Plant more cabbages around the ...
Our card with a kind hello"*

That was the most we could translate from the back.

Graine de Choux = Cabbage Seed!

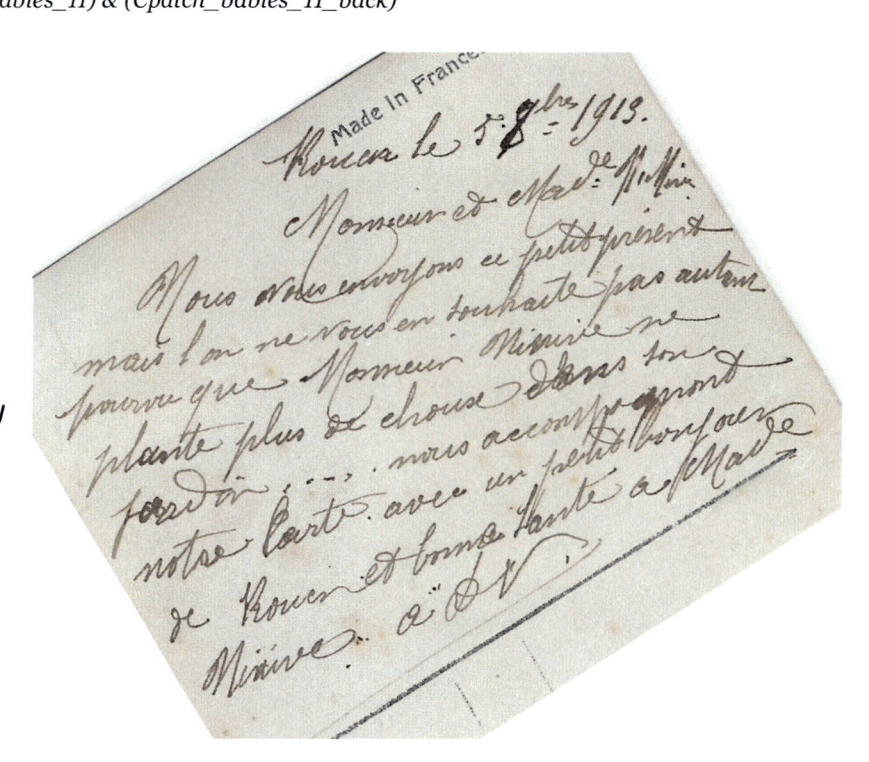

84

REPOPULATION POSTCARDS

"Cherchez dans les choux le garçon."

"Look for the boy in the cabbages."

Intriguingly, this postcard features what appears to be a glass cloche, typically used in fine dining to trap heat and enhance presentation. Could this symbolize the unveiling of a newborn child? Considering the context of incubators, it's also worth pondering whether this signifies the artificial controlled conditions which would foster better growth for these babies apparently...

(Cpatch_babies_18)

"NOS GENTILS POUPONS" in English translates to "Our Cute Little Dolls" or "Our Sweet Babies".

The word "poupons" is a somewhat old-fashioned term for babies or dolls in French, often used in a fond or endearing context.

Dolls? Remember the Alice guy films? Could there be a specific reason they employed dolls or 'plastic babies'? Why have a mix of live babies and dolls? With the complete context, the film 'Sage-femme de première classe' from 1902 takes on a whole new dimension!

(Cpatch_babies_13)

85

Babies as Products

(Cpatch_babies_17)

"*Nous sommes à vendre!*"

There are numerous other cabbage patch postcards out there, but let's use the image above as a stepping stone into a new category. Though many postcards in this category still incorporate cabbage patches, these particular ones stand out on their own. They use specific terminology that suggests these babies are being treated as commodities, or being sold...

"Nous sommes à vendre!" translates to "We are for sale!" in English. Hold up, how is this just a fun joke? It literally says that these babies are for sale...

This one is special - it's embossed in a unique and rare way. It's the only postcard in our collection with this style, and up close, it's quite beautiful. From the back, you can even see a relief around the cabbages, giving the front side of the card an interesting reflection.

"Choisissez bien"
or
"Choose well!"

(Cpatch_babies_17_back)

REPOPULATION POSTCARDS

Based on the green postage stamp and postmark present on the front, we can confidently confirm that this postcard dates back to 1906.

Bebes a VENDRE Choisissez!
Chacun de ces choux mignons
Contient de l'affection.

Babies for SALE Choose!
Each of these cute cabbages
Contains affection.

(Cpatch_babies_09)

The Cabbage Babies

(Cpatch_babies_12)

Choisissez moi
Je serai sage !
Je suis si mignon!
Je serai obeissant
Je suis gai!
Je vous aimerai bien!
Je vous apporterai la joie !
Je vous apporterai le bonheur!

Choose me
I will be good!
I am so cute!
I will be obedient
I am cheerful!
I will love you a lot!
I will bring you joy!
I will bring you happiness!

(Cpatch_babies_12_back)

On the other side of the above card showcasing children for sale with their diverse qualities, we find a mark reading "Expo Internationale Habitation Paris".

Were these cabbage babies being sold at these world fairs? Here's yet another direct link between world fairs, baby incubators, and the repopulation postcards.

88

REPOPULATION POSTCARDS

(Multi_babies_17)

"La Ferme aux Bébés" translates to "The Baby Farm". Considering the imagery on these postcards, it's certainly not an overreach to suggest they're depicting the 'farming' of babies.

The Baby House?
The Production of Babies?

89

The Cabbage Babies

Babies as fruits? Babies in a cage? This bird symbolism will come to play later.

These babies don't really look happy...

90

REPOPULATION POSTCARDS

*"Modern Bazar des Bébés,
Entrée Libre
Maison de Confiance Ne craint pas la Concurrence.
Tout Est À Vendre IL N'Y A QU'À PRENDRE,
On ne reprend pas la marchandise"*

*"Modern Baby Bazaar,
Free Entrance
Trustworthy Establishment, Does Not Fear Competition.
Everything Is For Sale, ALL YOU HAVE TO DO IS TAKE
We Don't Accept Returns!!!"*

Wait, what? A TRUSTWORTHY ESTABLISHMENT?! This is an advertisement for the sale of babies as merchandise! So, this is definitely connected to the Cabbage postcards, as "REX" produced many of them as well. Unfortunately, there isn't much information about "REX" available, other than the fact that they were one of the major studios in the early 1900s making these postcards.

They weren't the only ones, and it's difficult to categorize how many studios were working on these projects. To the right, we have a distressed baby with a sign that says "Garçon à Vendre," which means "Boy for Sale." Also in Old French "garçun" means "servant".

91

CHAND D'ENFANTS

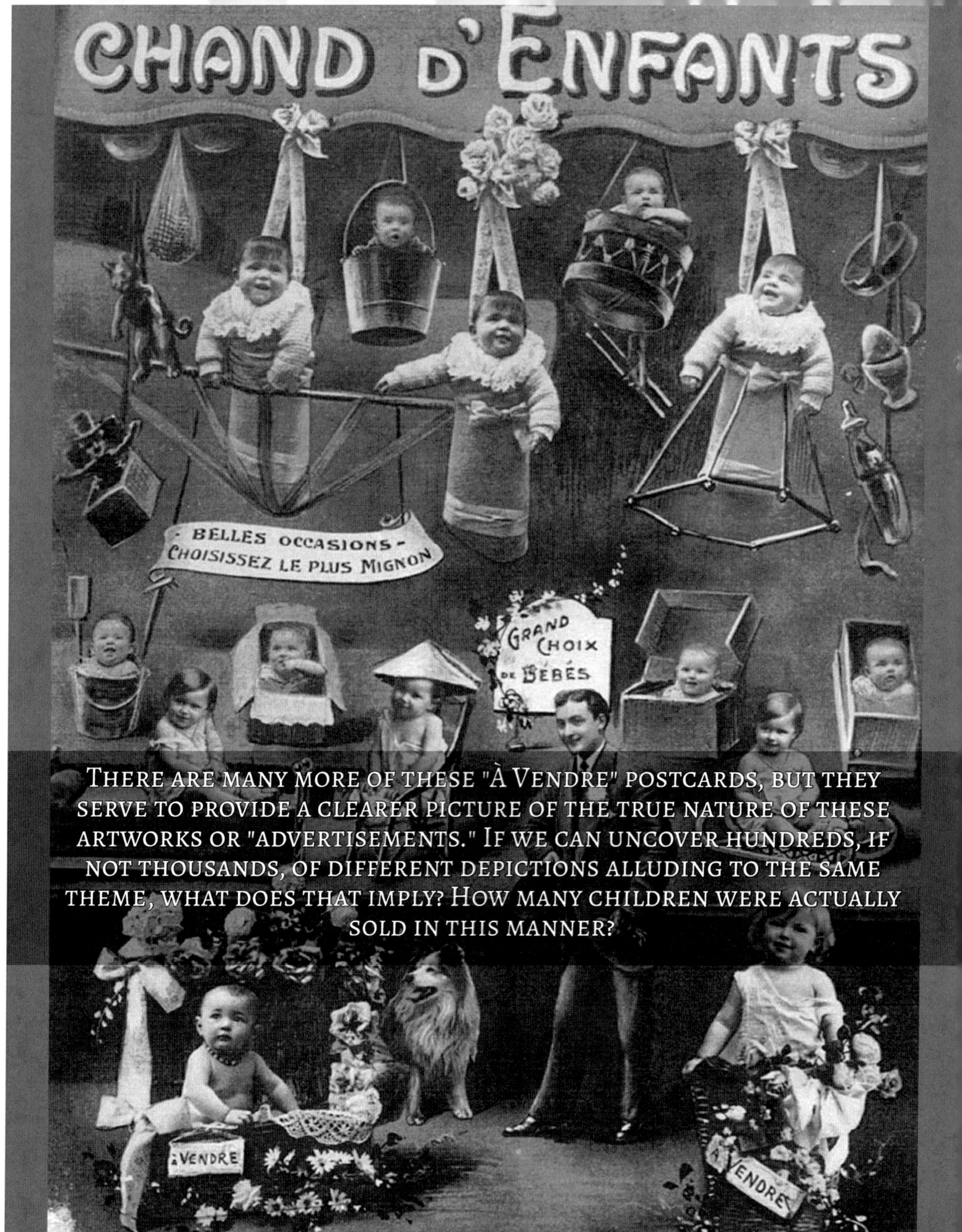

BELLES OCCASIONS – CHOISISSEZ LE PLUS MIGNON

GRAND CHOIX DE BÉBÉS

THERE ARE MANY MORE OF THESE "À VENDRE" POSTCARDS, BUT THEY SERVE TO PROVIDE A CLEARER PICTURE OF THE TRUE NATURE OF THESE ARTWORKS OR "ADVERTISEMENTS." IF WE CAN UNCOVER HUNDREDS, IF NOT THOUSANDS, OF DIFFERENT DEPICTIONS ALLUDING TO THE SAME THEME, WHAT DOES THAT IMPLY? HOW MANY CHILDREN WERE ACTUALLY SOLD IN THIS MANNER?

The most shocking "À Vendre" postcard we have found

"I'm bored"? Take a look at the background: empty city, and they're selling children? There's something about this particular postcard that suggests a profound story lurking beneath the surface...

"FOR SALE
BUY ME,
I'M BORED
HERE."

93

The Cabbage Babies

This one's unique because it reveals that these babies have names; they're not just fictional characters in some surreal art piece. Could it be that these postcards serve a purpose beyond just being artwork? Like, are they some kind of bizarre advertisement where the artwork lets you literally choose a child to buy? They could be like display items, in a way.

The caption reads:
"*Je vous souhaite pareille petite famille,*"
which translates to
"*I wish you a similar small family.*"

There are 26 babies featured in the postcard.

Are they Orphans?

Did someone take a picture of this family? If its something that was duplicated then why do they have names? The ink is in the same ink as the message , so who ever wrote this knew the names of these kids, and looks like they were sending it to someone for it seems, to purchase...

94

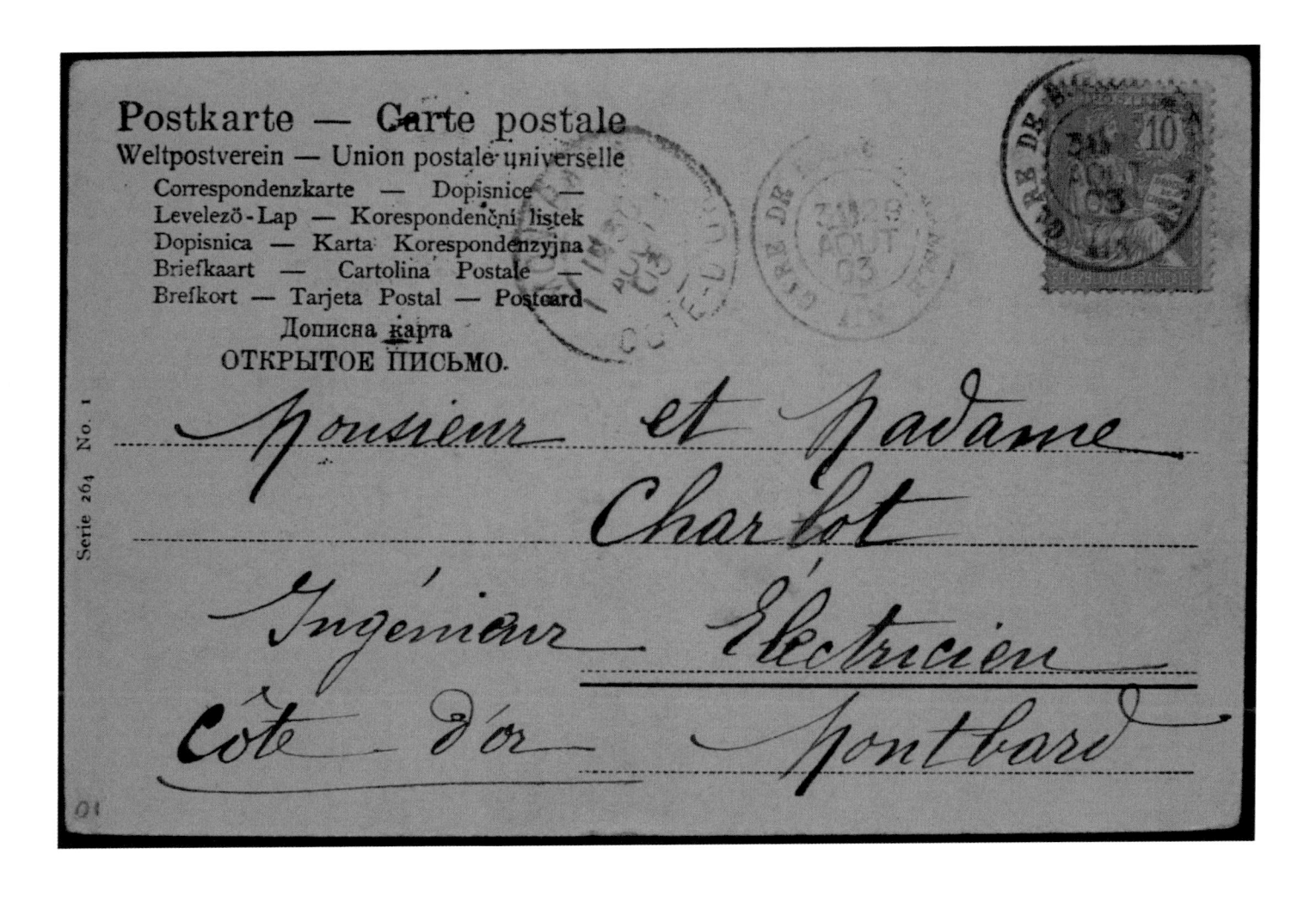

The postcard is dated August 1903, and on the back, it's addressed to "Monsieur et Madame Charlot," which translates to "Mr. and Mrs. Charlot" in English. "Charlot" is clearly the surname of the couple being targeted.

Could this couple have been potential clients?

The Cabbage Babies

"Choice, Babies for Sale. With them, you will have the greatest joys!

All our babies bring happiness."

"The Cries of Paris: Here are the pretty 'cabbage heads' (babies), not expensive!"

96

Orphan Trains

(Cpatch_babies_20)

Let's kick off this next category with both a train and a cabbage patch! This piece from our scanned collection falls into the "Cabbage Babies" category. However, it's the perfect link between these postcards, the cabbage baby art, and the transportation and relocation of children via trains. In other words, it's a direct nod to the Orphan Trains.

"Terug Van De Huwelÿksreis," which translates to "Back from the Honeymoon" in English, is a Dutch phrase. The reverse side of this card is blank, so we didn't include it. However, it's fascinating to discover that these postcards span several different European countries. So, one can't help but wonder - how extensive was this operation?

The Cabbage Babies

(Orph_train_01)

    However, it's not just about cabbages. These postcards, from the same era, clearly depict young children or babies CRYING inside a train. What other conclusions can we draw? The timeline aligns with the era of the Orphan Trains, and we see literal depictions of children being transported en masse on trains. This category could also be labeled "Baby Imports," as it's not always a train involved - sometimes it's a car, plane, blimp, a carriage, anything really.

This postcard specifically is dated to 1909! But there is an intriguing detail... This is a U.S Postcard! So it wasn't just in Europe then... The back says:

> *"June 24th, Hello Jim. I will be out in few days after that suit on train on the other side, have them ready from Pall, Roy DB"*

Have them ready? Perhaps this isn't just an artistic depiction...

(Orph_train_01_back)

98

REPOPULATION POSTCARDS

(Orph_train_02)

There are actually quite a few of these, which, as we mentioned, warrant their own category. The scanned image above, marked as printed in Germany on the back, lacks any personal inscriptions. It's rather surreal to see photos of actual children. Also, note the red Phrygian hats - could this be symbolic of their journey towards liberty?

The image to the left underscores the peculiarity and connotations of these postcards. In many instances, the children are depicted without any clothing. In this particular image, a child is placed at the front of the train, exactly where the combustion would occur. How utterly bizarre to even hint at such a dark scenario.

The Cabbage Babies

"Gelukkig Nieuwjaar" (Happy New Year), "Voila le Train des Bebes" (Here is the Baby Train), "Pour le Bonheur des jeunes mariés!" (For the Happiness of the Newlyweds!), "Tout pour Moi!..." (Everything for Me!...), "Rien Qu'a Moi!.." (Only for Me!..), "Et...En route pour le Petit Voyage" (And...On the way for the Little Trip), "On ne Triche Plus" (No more Cheating), "Attention aux Signaux & Aux Petards." (Beware of the Signals & Firecrackers).

REPOPULATION POSTCARDS

Next we have three of the same artwork but three different postcards in our collection that we are going to take a look at because they all have writing on the back.

(Orph_train_03)

"Loading of Cabbage Seeds"

(Orph_train_03_ back)

Looks to be dated 1912, the back says:

"Hello dear Brother and dear Sister and Gorgette, All our friendships always to Leon and Marie and Marcel, see you soon."

Some of the words are hard to read but this is an approximate translation.

101

The Cabbage Babies

(Orph_train_04)

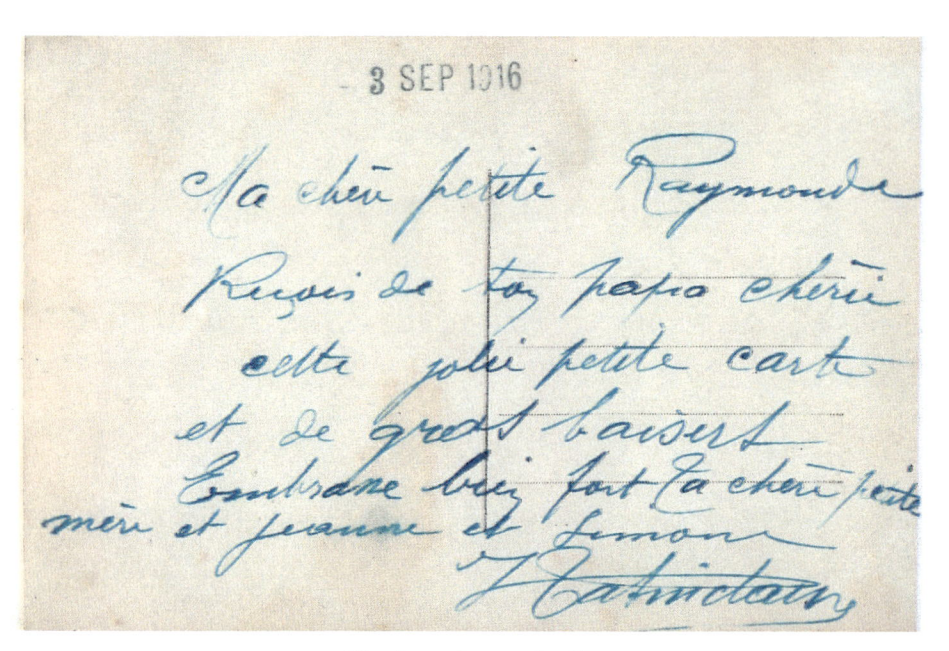

(Orph_train_04_back)

Dated September 3rd 1916:

*"My dear little one,
Receive from your dear father This pretty little card
And lots of kisses.
Hug your dear little mother tightly and I love you,
____."*

REPOPULATION POSTCARDS

(Orph_train_05)

(Orph_train_05_back)

"Dear aunts and dear uncle,
On the occasion of the new year, I wish you all the best: joy, health, happiness, and as many children as there are on my card. We are all in good health and I hope this letter finds you in the same condition.

At the moment, we have (Fleury?). We are thinking of keeping him at home for two months. Mom and dad may soon go down to Sorbiers to speak to a man about our son.

We still have many people, the big Wednesday, and for New Year's Day. And on Sunday, we had dinner with some cousins from Chatelus and the surrounding areas, about ten in all.

The whole family joins me in sending you their best wishes. Signed: Jeanne, your affectionate niece."

The Cabbage Babies

Multi-Babies

The "Multi-Babies" category encompasses any postcard from this era that features multiple babies together, rendered in the same photomontage style. These are usually more numerous as they fall outside our main categories, each displaying a unique style as the babies are bundled up in a variety of arrangements. While we could delve deeper and create individual categories for some of these, we've grouped them here for simplicity's sake.

(Multi_babies_02)

"Petite République Socialiste", translates to "Little Socialist Republic." What's intriguing here is how these little ones are geared up for societal roles, donning their Liberty Hats, also known as PHRYGIAN CAPS. Could this be an indication of orphans being nurtured for inclusion in the "club"?

(Multi_babies_02_back)

104

REPOPULATION POSTCARDS

(Multi_babies_03)

(Multi_babies_04)

There's an intriguing number of these "hat" baby postcards, similar in theme but depicting a diverse range of scenarios. They stand out because of the unique bundling of the babies, often positioned inside a bag, placed upon, or enclosed within various objects.

The babies are even decked out with TOP HATS and MONOCLES! They're wrapped in a newspaper? Perhaps there's some deeper symbolism lurking in these pieces.

The Cabbage Babies

Church babies???

Marche de L'Armme 1st Prix Medaille de Choclat
"March of the Army 1st Prize Chocolate Medal."

106

REPOPULATION POSTCARDS

"Le Pépin à maman! Épatant pour la Repopulation..." translates to "Mom's little trouble! Great for repopulation..."

Another postcard referencing 'Repopulation'? Don't miss the umbrella symbolism here. There's a surprising number of these postcards, where it looks like the babies themselves are being prepared for war. Sure, it could be a nod to the baby boom, but might they also be hinting at the babies being groomed for the army?

Children under a leafy Umbrella?
With the word "PRISON" spelled out in small white flowers?

107

The Cabbage Babies

"Billeting of our Future Infantrymen"

Could the idea of "farming" babies during this era really suggest the unthinkable - the creation of an ARMY?

A multitude of these postcards are adorned with the phrase "Futurs Poilus". While some portrayals might appear innocent, even cute, others suggest a tale far more profound. This is not just a post-war baby boom... It indicates an operation of unprecedented scale, injecting an enormous influx of children into society, seemingly priming them for battle.

REPOPULATION POSTCARDS

(Multi_babies_20)

    Have we crossed into the realm of dreams yet? Perhaps. This could simply be the result of hours spent immersing ourselves in such surreal art. Nonetheless, let's carry on! The Postcard above says "Bed-born Seed: Recipe: 'A good night's kiss always works...'" One might wonder, why exactly would there be a need for a recipe like that? Moreover, notice the painting on the wall - yet another nod to the motif of children springing forth from cabbages. These artworks are, without a doubt, some of the most peculiar in the multi-baby category, primarily due to the fabricated indoor setting and the staged positioning of the babies.

"The Class of the Babies": *"What a spanking I took"*, *"Don't cry, you will be ugly!"*, *"Since I got a good mark, I will have dessert, so there!"*, *"Ah! I'm really looking forward to the soup"*, *"No one says anything in the corner"*, *"If only we could go out"*, *"Dad comes to pick me up"*, *"We're going to leave soon"*, *"And then mom will come soon"*, *"Ah! Great, here are the good marks"*, *"I hope we get to play soon"*, *"I'll be good"*.

109

The Cabbage Babies

The postcard of "La Classe des Bébés" depicts a scene of very young children or 'babies' in a classroom setting, implying that they are being disciplined and taught at a surprisingly young age. They're longing for breaks, anticipating meals, looking forward to rewards for good behavior, and eagerly awaiting the arrival of their parents. It's quite unusual and surreal given their age.

"The Meal of the Babies:
Good Children are Invited
Dirty Little Ones Will Be Whipped"

What are we to make of the scenes depicted in the paintings on the tablecloth? Why are babies strewn across the top of the table? Are these meant to represent the "naughty" ones?

110

REPOPULATION POSTCARDS

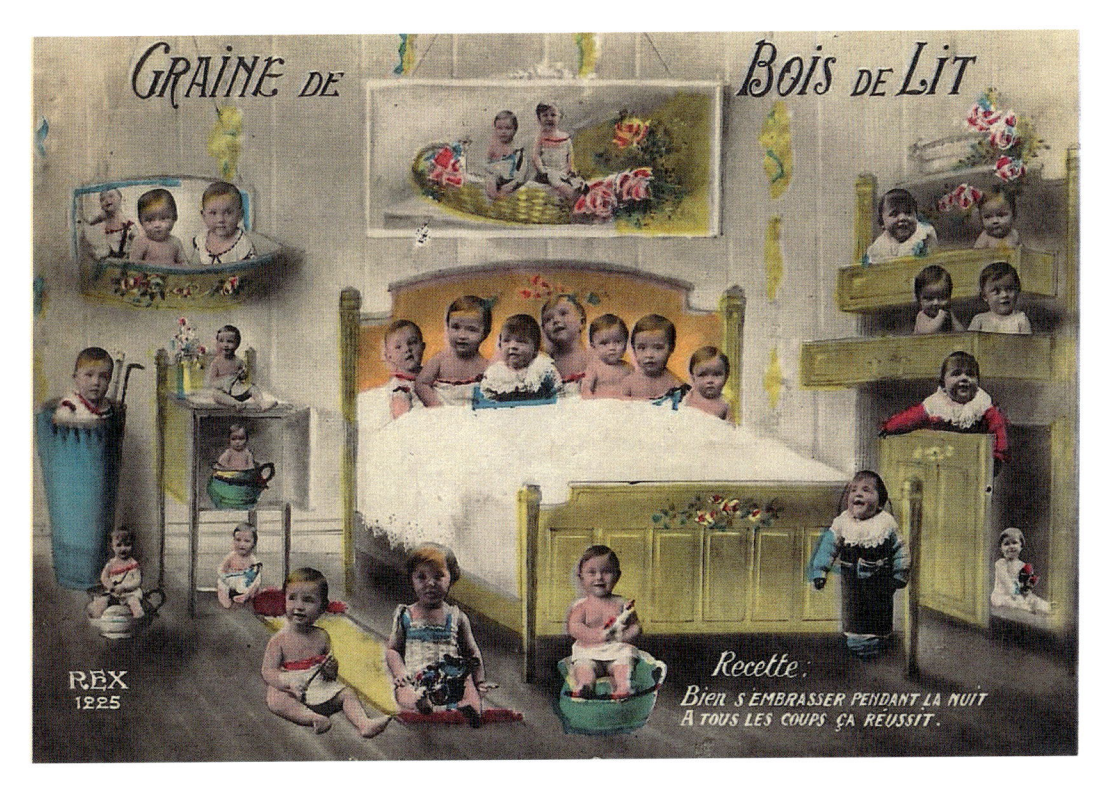

So that's the basic gist of this category but there are some that are just strange and need their own section.

This one is the babies on Power Poles style within the Multi-Babies... very strange...

(Multi_babies_11)

The Cabbage Babies

This is a Souvenir? This probably really belongs to the "À Vendre" group however it doesn't really say for Sale so we put it in Multi-babies. You can see the same babies in other "À Vendre" postcards and for some reason yes they are on electric power poles... What is that supposed to suggest?

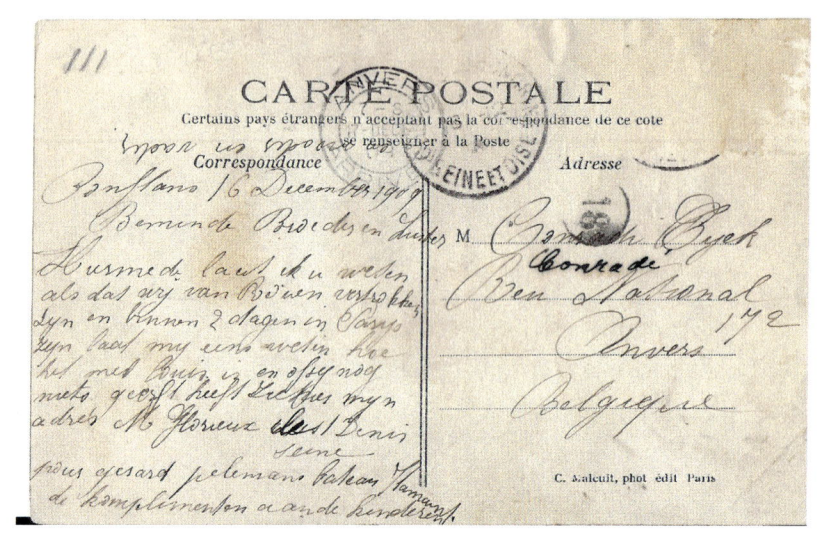

The postcard, dating back to 1909, is difficult to translate as it appears to blend multiple languages.

(Multi_babies_11_back)

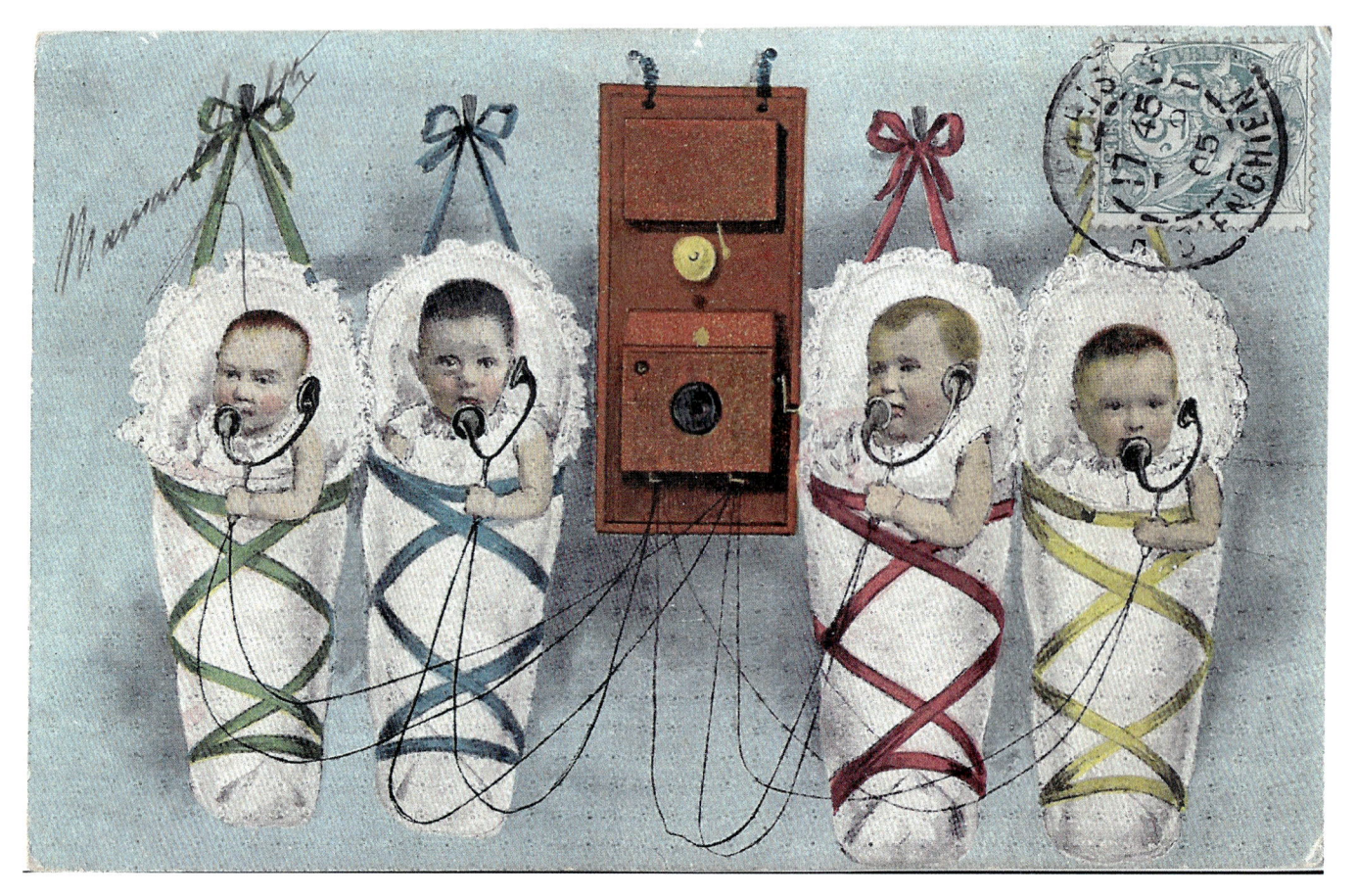

(Multi_babies_22)

Here is a similar example of the hanging babies but they are taking calls!

112

REPOPULATION POSTCARDS

Multi Babies in Cities

(Multi_babies_01)

(Multi_babies_01_back)

US Postcard from 1905
San Francisco

113

The Cabbage Babies

(Multi_babies_05)

There are quite a few multi-baby postcards that depict a multitude of babies or young children, essentially frolicking in deserted cities. In the example above, they appear to have been put to work.

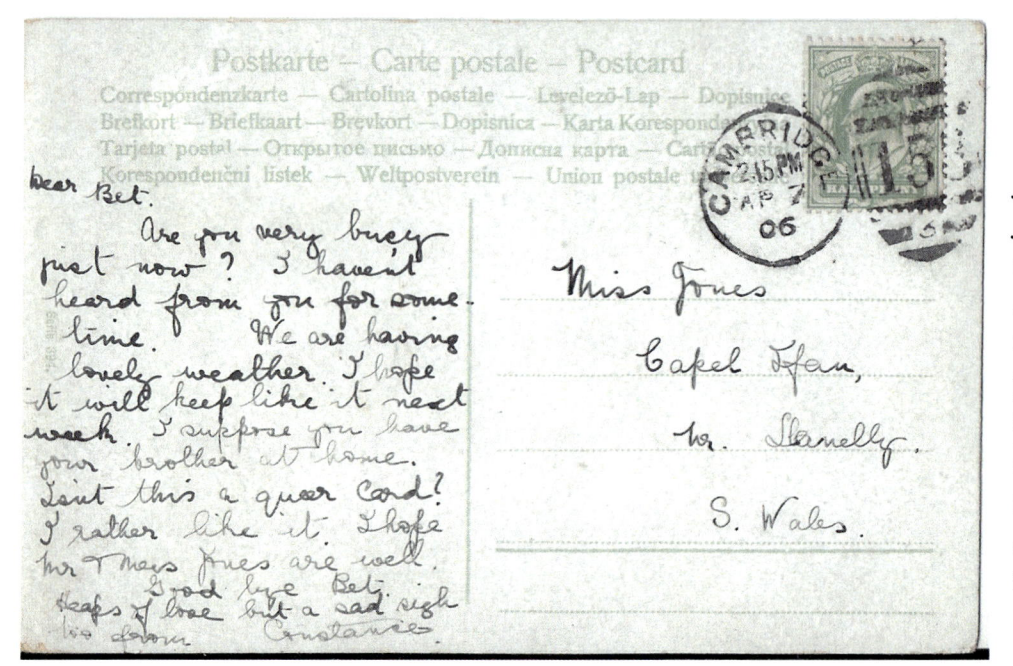

1906

"Dear Bel, Are you very busy just now? I haven't heard from you for some time. We are having lovely weather. I hope it will keep like it next week. I suppose you have your brother at home. Isn't this a queer card? I rather like it. I hope Mr ____ ____ are well, Good bye Bel. Heaps of love but a sad sigh too soon, _____"

(Multi_babies_05_back)

114

REPOPULATION POSTCARDS

Resembling scenes from the "Children of the Corn" movie, it's as if the children have taken over the cities. A good number of postcards from this distinctive series feature babies in a car, tram, or bus as they are journeying into a city. The one to the left is equipped with a boat, which could also fall into the "water babies" category.

The Cabbage Babies

L'ARRIVÉE Á L'AUBERGE.

Un Bonjour

   The Multi-Baby postcards don't stop here. As mentioned earlier, it's quite an extensive category. All of these postcards feature the similar theme of a group of babies, but present a variety of different scenarios that they find themselves in.

116

REPOPULATION POSTCARDS

Next, we have the Multi 'Egg-Babies' category, where it seems these infants are hatching...

Recall the earlier mention of incubators or 'Hatcheries'.

(Multi_babies_09_egg)

Now, the context lends these postcards an air that's beyond mere 'imagination'. Given our knowledge of the history of incubators, and the remarkable fact that they were originally designed based on chicken egg incubators, the symbolism here becomes quite blatant. It appears these images are directly alluding to children being 'hatched' or produced in a 'farm' or factory setting. Reflecting on this

117

notion, one can't help but be struck by the frank portrayal of the mechanized, impersonal nature of these birthing methods. As if children were merely products off a conveyor belt, it underscores a sense of industrialization creeping into even the most personal of human experiences - childbirth.

(Multi_babies_08_egg)

You can see many of these 'hatching' babies in Easter postcards from this era, but it's crucial to understand that this doesn't fully explain the symbolism. Could it be just another avenue for the creators of these postcards to embed the symbolism of baby factories with the celebration of Easter? And what is Easter, really? It represents the Spring Equinox, a time symbolizing a phase of birth and renewal. One must ponder, why is the bunny and egg iconography even associated with this day? Could it trace back to ancient fertility cults?

(Multi_babies_14_egg)

118

REPOPULATION POSTCARDS

Strangely enough, there also exists a bizarre subset of postcards featuring babies getting "intoxicated". These peculiar illustrations show infants indulging in drinking, smoking, and seemingly partaking in other forms of inebriation.

(Multi_babies_21)

Dated 1907

(Multi_babies_21_back)

The Cabbage Babies

1. Le Café

3. Le Cidre

REPOPULATION POSTCARDS

Then we have the 'Potty' postcards with the Multi-Babies. Essentially, these depict a group of babies expelling their waste into chamber pots. Which is weird considering these are photomontages.

(Multi_babies_06_potty)

Dated 1904

(Multi_babies_06_potty_back)

121

The Cabbage Babies

(Multi_babies_16_potty)

(Multi_babies_16_potty_back)

122

REPOPULATION POSTCARDS

"Öffentliche Sitzung" translates to "Public Meeting"
It's a bit of a play on words, as "Sitzung" can also mean "sitting" in German, but notice all the babies with top hats! The babies are also wearing their phrygian caps in white.

Another strange category inside the Multi-Baby postcards are babies drinking straight from the udder of a cow.

(Multi_babies_07_milk)

The Cabbage Babies

(Multi_babies_07_milk_back)

124

REPOPULATION POSTCARDS

We're making progress! There are still many more categories to explore, but we're nearing the end of the Multi-Babies section. Another intriguing theme we encounter are the 'Babies with Mushrooms' postcards. These peculiar images often feature large mushrooms, potentially of an entheogenic nature, situated near the infants.

(Multi_babies_24)

125

The Cabbage Babies

"Ça pousse comme des champignons" translates to "It grows like mushrooms".

What do we glean from the symbolism here? The postcards intriguingly feature the Amanita muscaria mushroom, known for its psychoactive properties. But why is there an association with children? Could it be a metaphor likening the rapid, proliferative growth of mushrooms to that of children? Notably, mushrooms fruit asexually, which makes for a strange comparison. If this symbology indeed leans towards the psychedelic, why then link it with the innocence of childhood? Furthermore, it's worth noting that these postcards predate the counterculture hippie movement by six decades. So, one can't help but ponder - where is this symbolism sprouting from?

126

REPOPULATION POSTCARDS

Ok we can finalize the Multi-Babies category with a few random ones that sort of have their own thing going.

We have the Multi-Babies being delivered postcards:

(Multi_babies_12)

(Multi_babies_23)

127

Then these weird ones with cockroaches delivering babies:

128

REPOPULATION POSTCARDS

It seems these cockroaches represent the capitalists involved with this "movement" of children. This would imply even back when these postcards were being created, that there was something very slimy about all this. Notice how in the postcard above the man with the tophat at the front of the carriage is holding a fishing pole... This will come to play shortly.

The Cabbage Babies

There are further variations of these multi-babies, but the remaining ones that pique our interest usher us into an entirely new section.

Red Lady

"The Red Lady" represents a series of postcards, each featuring a woman in a red dress, often cloaked by a white shirt, and wearing a red head covering. Notably, women in red are a common motif in many postcard categories, but what sets the Red Lady apart is the way she is usually caught staring at the camera, engaged in presenting babies in a myriad of situations. Unlike the themes in other postcards, where babies are being purchased, the Red Lady is instead the purveyor, the distributor of these infants. This places her in the role of the Fairy of the Cabbage Patch, or the midwife in the "sage femme de première classe" film of 1902. (Sage femme de première classe 1902).

The postcards often depict babies being plucked, gathered, and assembled from bodies of water into large groups. They seem to be readied for some sort of ceremony or display, enhancing the aura of mystery around this unique figure and her bizarre enterprise.

It's also noteworthy that it seems to be the same photographed woman appearing throughout the series. It's as though she was directed to strike various poses for these postcards, placing her in an array of diverse settings. A defining characteristic of these postcards is the depiction of babies being harvested, often finding themselves nestled within wooden buckets.

(Red_lady_02)

REPOPULATION POSTCARDS

Interestingly, this postcard features an American postage stamp and is marked with a postmark from St. Louis, Missouri, dated 1907. It was sent to Wentzville, Missouri. The message, somewhat illegible, seems to read, '_____ just returned from _____, Don't know when will be some.'

(Red_lady_02_back)

In this example from our scanned collection, we see the Red Lady engaged in the intriguing act of plucking babies from trees—a motif that will resurface later. It echoes the theme of children as fledglings, further reinforcing the notion of their hatching. She gathers them from the tree, filling her baskets with these unique 'harvests'. It's hard to see but this postcard is dated to 1907.

(Red_lady_01)

131

The Cabbage Babies

In this image, our Red Lady swaps her usual dress for a red corset, but with the same distinctive hairstyle, it's clear it's the same woman. Notice the presence of a body of water in the backdrop, another recurrent theme in this particular postcard group. Based on other postcards, we can infer that these babies were gathered either from the trees or drawn from the water.

In this scene, it's possible she is delivering the babies to a doorstep, a task we observe her performing in other postcards as well.

(Red_lady_03)

132

REPOPULATION POSTCARDS

These specific postcards start to intersect with the "Water Babies" category, as we see instances where she seems to be fishing the babies out of the water. The scenes are peculiar, almost as if hinting at some form of hook symbolism.

133

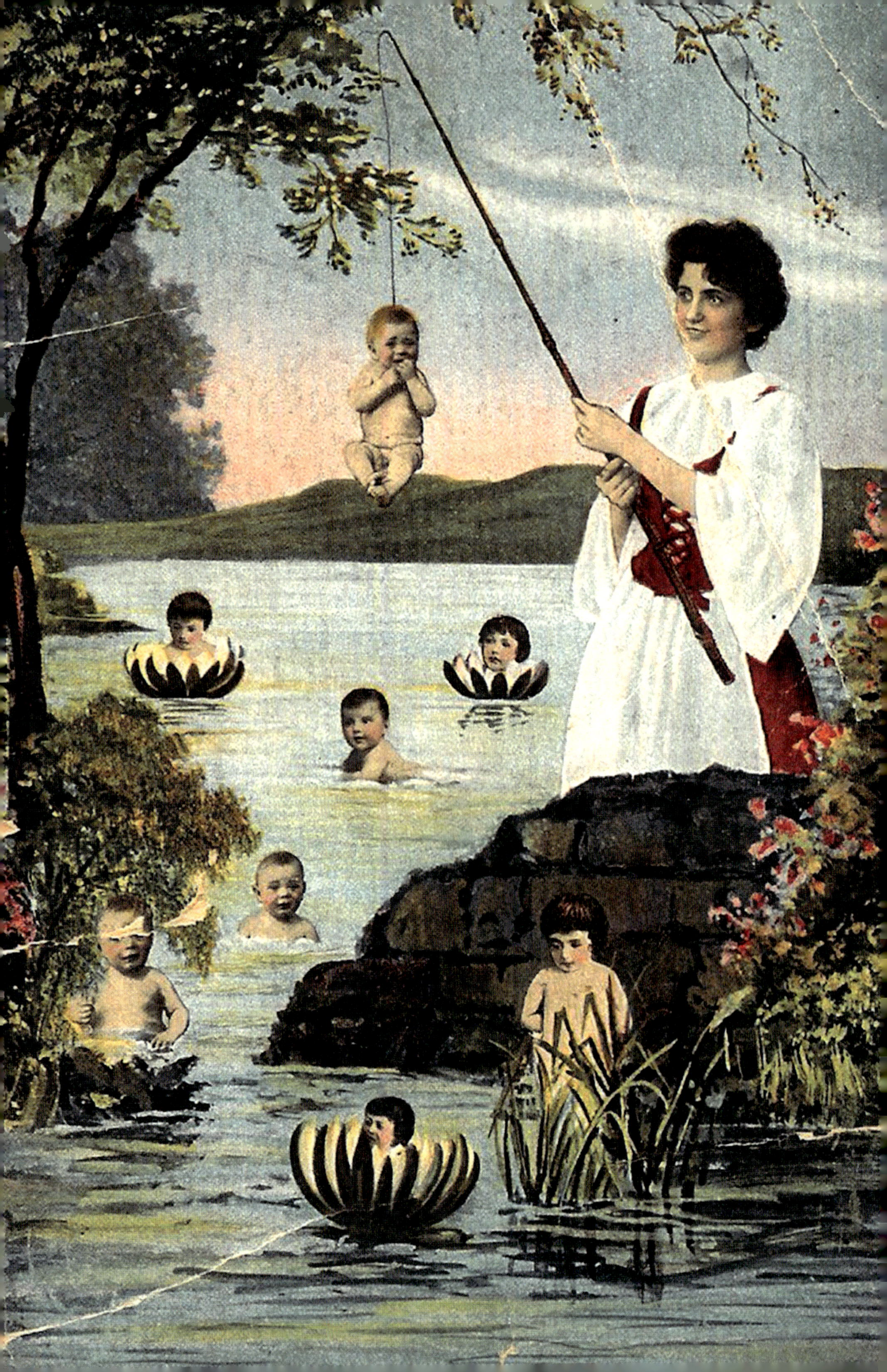

REPOPULATION POSTCARDS

We even find instances where she's depicted scooping up babies in a net. Could this be a whimsical representation, or might there be a deeper meaning at play? Water could be a metaphor for the womb, and if the Red Lady embodies the midwife, she could be seen as pulling these infants from the amniotic fluid. Yet, the presence of numerous babies prompts further questions. Could this be indicative of an operation where babies are said to "come from the water"?

The Cabbage Babies

There are also a few "Pink Ladies" with the same concept but with a different model. It's the same concept of a woman in vibrant attire, presenting numerous babies, either amidst water or contained in buckets and baskets.

(Red_lady_04) (Red_lady_05)

136

REPOPULATION POSTCARDS

The Red Lady, akin to the symbolic figure of Libertas who represents freedom, and hinting at the esoteric symbolism of Diana, is fundamentally a fertility icon. Her representation draws parallels with the Whore of Babylon, donning the red dress, casting the figure of the Red Lady in a specific, symbolic light. Could these postcards be portraying a covert operation, employing occult symbolism to suggest a factory-like setting where babies are being mass-produced? Are they employing fertility symbols and the archetypal image of the midwife to convey the comforting image of a pleasant young woman, while veiling the stark reality of a corporate mechanism for repopulation?

Water Babies & Storks

"Where do babies come from?"

(Stork_04)

The Cabbage Babies

In the Victorian era, parents often told their children the fanciful tale of storks delivering babies. This narrative, while bizarre, has endured as a childhood legend and was genuinely believed by many children. After all, why wouldn't they trust their parents? This becomes peculiar when considering that many of these older generations took these stories seriously. Some individuals, who do not remember their biological parents and were adopted, may see these tales as relics of an era marked by orphan trains and rampant child labor. It's intriguing, yet disturbing, to consider that during this time, it was technically legal to send a child through the mail...

The stork is the mailman! Tasked with the job of delivering babies once they've been plucked from the cabbage patch. These postcards illustrate numerous delivery scenarios: babies being dropped from the sky, whisked away by planes, borne aloft by hot air balloons, and even transported by cars!

(Stork_01)

138

REPOPULATION POSTCARDS

(Stork_02)

    Very strange postcard above that shows children gathered in an area of the city, and you can even see the cabbages towards the bottom. Many of the children, notably unclothed, are seated on some of the birds. The message appears to convey something along the lines of, "No other baby in Frankfurt is as sweet as you are," accompanied by the sending of love and kisses. It's quite an eccentric postcard choice for sending regards.

    The wooden box is marked with "Stork's Children's Nutritional Flour." A hand sign, pointing towards the house, is labeled "Access" or "Entrance." The house itself bears the inscription "Stork's Store" or "Stork's Magazine," depending on the context. This presents quite a captivating scene.

(Stork_05)

139

The Cabbage Babies

(Stork_03)

REPOPULATION POSTCARDS

(Stork_06)

(Stork_04)

141

The Cabbage Babies

Storks are often depicted nurturing the children, occasionally within what appears to be small campsites on fields. However, strangely enough, numerous portrayals show them amid water and, as exemplified in the postcard on the previous page, aboard a boat. If we consider the stork as a symbolic mailman or the figure who delivers the babies, does this suggest babies were delivered via boats? Could this allude to a historical occurrence where orphans were transported across the sea?

(Water_babies_3)

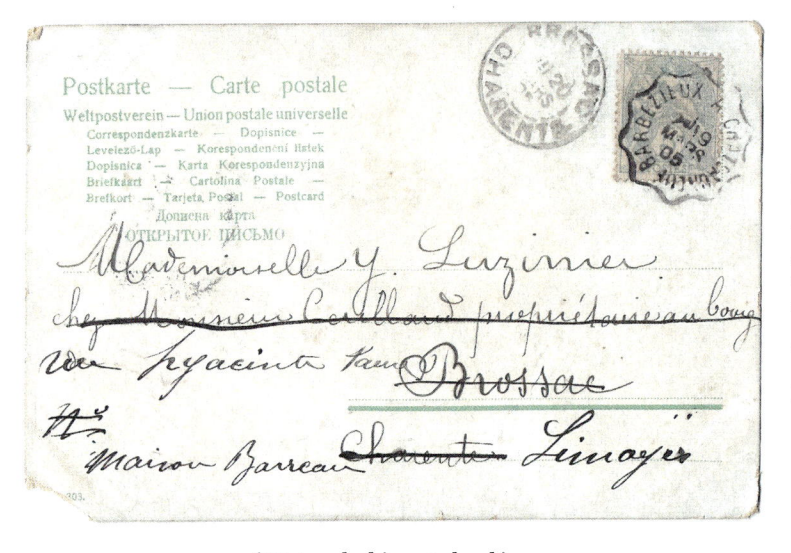

(Water_babies_3_back)

Here we have a 1905 postcard showcasing children in boats arriving at a coastline. But take a closer look at the backdrop, with its large ships looming in the distance. From where did these children embark? Are they simply engaging in aquatic fun, or could they represent arrivals from a sizeable shipment?

142

REPOPULATION POSTCARDS

(Water_babies_02)

Here we witness the "Water Babies" theme intersect with the "Red Lady" category once again. In the postcard to the left, we see a variation of the Red Lady, this time adorned in a yellow shirt. This woman, seen in pink in other postcards, now sports a red flower on her fancy hat. The scene she's part of raises more questions.

Are these children merely enjoying a ride akin to a roller coaster? The image of children on a waterwheel might suggest this is some type of energy source or a means to power certain structures. Alternatively, it could be symbolic of a production line—specifically, the production of babies. As the infants emerge from the other end of the process, note how she gathers them into her lap.

(Water_babies_02_back)

This postcard, bearing an American postage stamp and a postmark from Aurora, South Dakota dated 1908, carries a simple message:

"Hello Mama, Have a good time from Frances, Write Soon".

Interestingly, several postcards in the collection seem to have been penned by children. What might prompt a child to write to their mother, urging her to respond soon? And why would such a message be conveyed on a postcard of this peculiar style?

143

The Cabbage Babies

Often, children are portrayed as water lilies in these postcards, a peculiar representation given the birth and resurrection symbolism attached to this flower. This reference finds an echo in Charles Kingsley's book, *The Water-Babies, A Fairy Tale for a Land Baby*.

In the tale, water babies are spirits who transitioned at a tender age, later morphing into a unique elemental form—a fairy. The symbolism of water lilies, emerging from the water, is reflective of rebirth. The white flowers encircling the babies are deliberate additions, intended to denote purity and innocence.

The representation of water lilies might hint at a bleak reality underlying the children's movement. In the narrative of The Water Babies, the protagonist Tom drowns but is reborn as a 'water baby.' His new life, or second chance, empowers him to engage with the modern corporate world. These parallels suggest a potentially dark allegory hidden within these fascinating postcards.

(Water_babies_04)

It is dated to 1905 from the postmark and was written upside down.

It reads: *"Dear Sallie! Are you feeling bright today. Get out as much as you can won't you? Only one more Sunday cheer up old girl. I have you "W"oet last after going all over the town for it. When do you propose having your holiday shall we talk it over at _____, much love you as ever"*

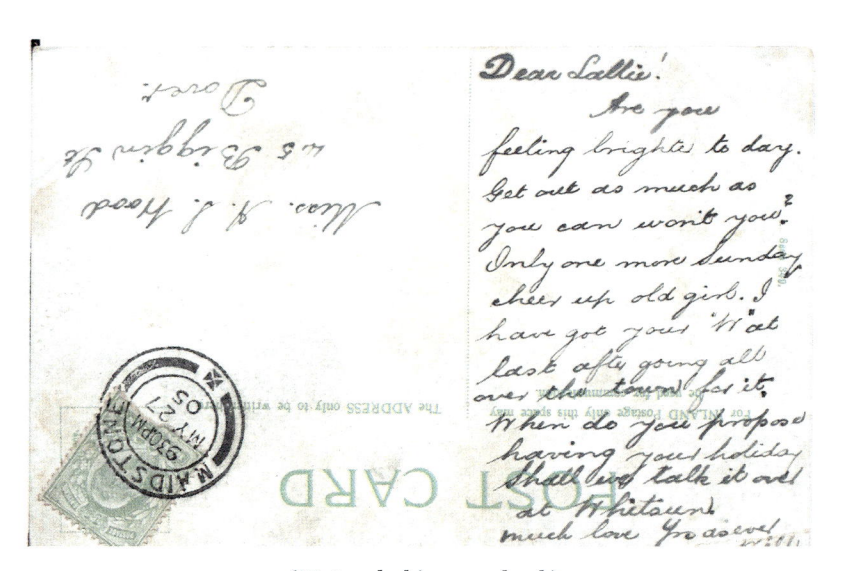

(Water_babies_04_back)

144

REPOPULATION POSTCARDS

(Water_babies_01)

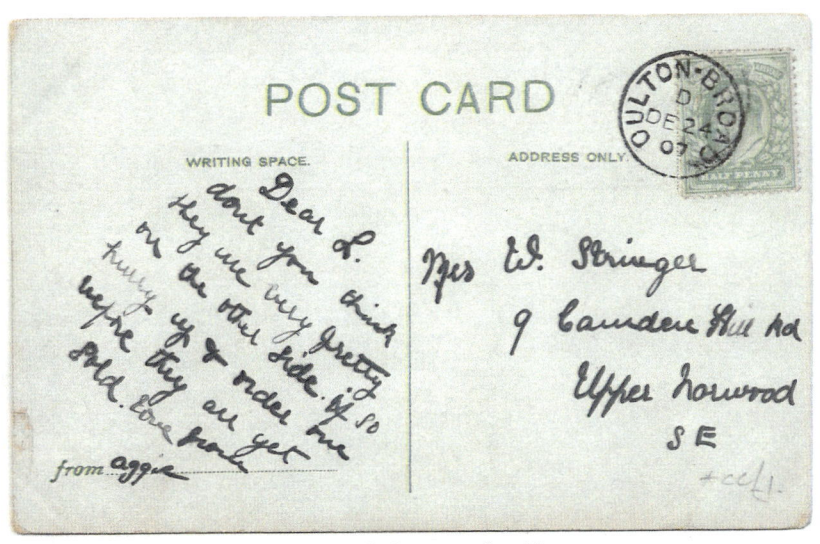

(Water_babies_01_back)

In this postcard, we encounter yet another "Red Lady." While the model differs, the core concept remains consistent - she is harvesting babies on water lilies. Notably, this postcard is a Christmas card from 1907.
The reverse side carries an intriguing message:
"Dear L.
don't you think they are very pretty on the other side. If so hurry up & order one before they get sold. Love from Aggie."

This postcard prompts the reader to appreciate the babies' charm on the other side. Should they find the babies appealing, they are urged to place an order swiftly. What's remarkable here is the sender's worry about these babies potentially being 'sold out.' Could it be that these babies are up for ORDER!? The message seems to imply a commercial element that's startling to consider.

145

The Cabbage Babies

The postcard showcasing a baby being weighed against bags of money dates from 1912, while the one portraying a stork depositing babies into what appears to be a train is from 1911. These postcards present us with more than just a fanciful tale or playful explanation for the origin of babies. Instead, they may be subtly hinting at a potential reality. This is a reality in which babies were seen as commodities, as indicated by the phrase on the left-hand postcard...

146

REPOPULATION POSTCARDS

"Worth its Weight in Gold." This compelling phrase suggests a perception of children as items of value, a concept that is as thought-provoking as it is unsettling.

(Flying_01)

This particular postcard in our collection holds special significance as it hints at early blimp travel as a covert symbolic representation of the stork.

The idea of babies literally being delivered by air travel seems peculiar, and yet, the recurrent symbolism of the stork might be shedding light on a deeper truth. Could these children have been transported via airships? We have stumbled upon several postcards illustrating the same phenomenon and were fortunate enough to add this one to our collection. However, there are several more postcards out there that depict this same extraordinary scenario: children being transferred through the air...

The writing in French on the front says *"The 2 students of the dad are received and the aunt. The dad will arrive tomorrow morning in Poligny by the train."* It is postmarked 1905 on the back.

(Multi_babies_10_balloon)

147

The Cabbage Babies

You can spot this theme in depictions featuring various modes of aerial transport – hot air balloons, airplanes, and airships, all embodying the same motif of multiple children being transported through the air.

The Kids From

Now, we come to the final category of Repopulation postcards in our collection, perhaps the most peculiar of them all. These are titled "The Kids From_____" and have a distinct style characterized by prominent golden text that proclaims "The Kids From _____", with the blank being filled by the city these children supposedly hail from. These postcards hold significant value as they corroborate not only the American origins of these postcards, but also their significance beyond mere curiosities. These children are linked to specific locations, suggesting some deeper meaning or purpose. Is there a hidden joke or pun? If there is, it's elusive. What is apparent, however, is that these postcards depict large groups of children situated in, or arriving at, various cities across America.

This one in particular is the most shocking of them all. It's called *"The Kids from Whitehall, Mich."*, it depicts a large group of babies being boiled in a cauldron, foisted by some type of pyramid contraption. Notice the circular symmetry created by the arching handle that connects to the loop on the bucket's side. There's clearly a fire beneath the cauldron, indicating the presence of heat. Those aren't merely soap bubbles. What is this image attempting to convey, and how can such a disturbing scene be deemed as an endearing postcard?

(The_kids_from_01)

148

REPOPULATION POSTCARDS

Another postcard from the 'Kids From' series features an unnerving scene of babies depicted as caged zoo animals. There's also an elephant carrying several young children, with one even positioned on the elephant's neck. This peculiar image seems to suggest a circus-like atmosphere.

This postcard reads 'The Kids from Melvin, Illinois', which is intriguing considering Melvin is a small village in Illinois. What does the phrase 'Kids from Melvin' imply?

The back of the card says *" Can you ride your journey like some of these kids and have so much fun it says they are from Melvin I guess they are a good ways from here from gran ma "*

Ride your journey like these kids? While enclosed in cages? Or could the reference be about embarking on a journey away from parents in the company of several children? Either way, it's an incredibly strange message.

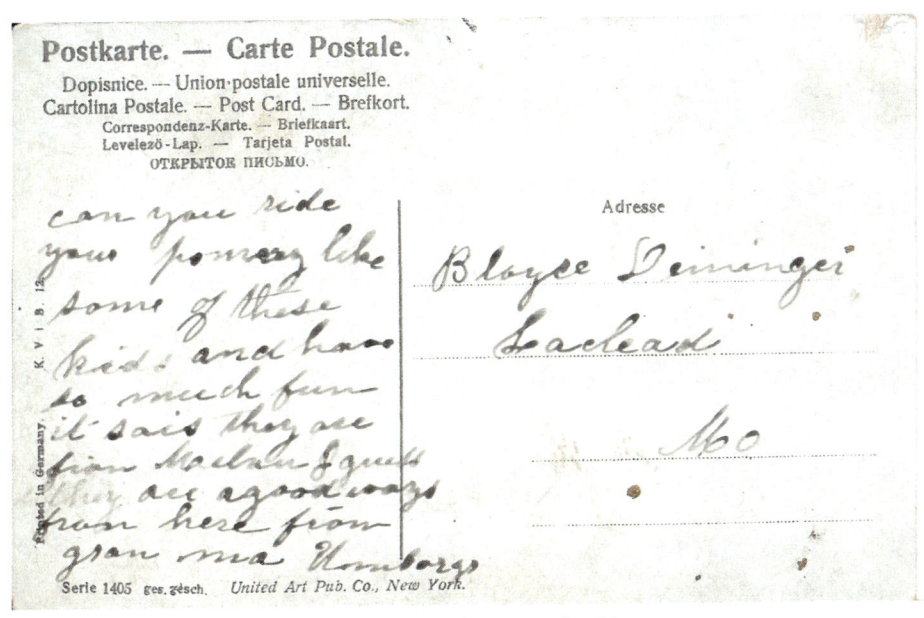

(The_kids_from_02)

(The_kids_from_02_back)

149

The Cabbage Babies

These postcards are the most revealing, as they contain some of the most bizarre imagery that truly prompts reflection. This particular one displays a submarine, its windows revealing peering children, with other children navigating turbulent waves. This is the first instance of depicting children's movement or transfer via a submarine, which is unique. While other postcards show boats, this one intrigues due to the elusive nature of submarines that operate underwater. Given this unique choice of imagery, one might wonder: could this represent a form of symbolism?

Upon closer inspection, the mast appears to carry a flag resembling the French flag, but it's not clear-cut. A similar, possibly American flag appears at the front of the submarine. Interestingly, even the lighthouse is populated with babies, and one child on land is seen moving toward the dark entrance of this tower. Is the lighthouse accepting this import? These kids are from Grants Pass Oregon according to the golden text.

(The_kids_from_03)

This postcard is postmarked Grants Pass, Oregon dated 1908, and sent to Michigan. The message says *"Dear Paulina wishing you a happy Birthday & Many happy _____ from the _____."*

(The_kids_from_03_back)

150

REPOPULATION POSTCARDS

The Kids from Walkerton, Indiana postcard showcases children swimming in a pool. However, due to the evident photomontage elements, the scene emanates an unnatural and somewhat unsettling feeling, as the children weren't actually swimming when creating this image.

Here, it's clear that the flag is indeed French. This could suggest that these are French postcards being used in America, although the golden text that connects them might be hinting at a particular phenomenon in the States. Could it represent some kind of child camp or farm?

Dated 1903 and was sent from Walkerton, it appears that these postcards were being used to represent 'The Kids' from specific towns. This would only seem logical if these postcards were portraying actual scenarios, and not just fabricated, cute scenes...

(The_kids_from_04)

"(Thrliua?) ! - How are you all? Will be home Saturday. Mamma."

So it's not the same person, this is a different one and it was sent to a Miss (Thrluia) Mason to Millersburg, Indiana

(The_kids_from_04_back)

151

This suggests that these postcards aren't from a single person's collection, but rather that they were sold in this specific style. This implies that there are likely many more out there, and would account for why different people are sending these postcards.

However, it raises further questions. Why would a studio pair some of the most graphic French postcards with the phrase 'The Kids From', as though giving it a title because they knew what it was referring to?

In this card from San Jose, California, we see children crying and screaming as they float away in a hot air balloon. Where are they heading? Is this merely a ride, or could it be a shipment...

The back is postmarked from San Jose and dated 1909. It was sent to San Francisco and the message is somewhat difficult to decipher, but from what can be made out, it seems to refer to someone receiving their 'papers' and that someone named Rudri got his. Then, it states '____ you know'.

(The_kids_from_05)

(The_kids_from_05_back)

152

REPOPULATION POSTCARDS

(The_kids_from_06)

    This postcard applies the phrase in conjunction with imagery of children on trains, thus making a direct reference to orphan trains. These children are identified as being from Redding, California. Interestingly, there is no writing or postmark on the back, suggesting this postcard was never sent. This again points towards the idea that this was a common theme found in American postcard shops during the early 1900s. Each of these cards, with their unique and often perplexing images, adds a different facet to our understanding of a very specific period in American cultural history.

    It's also worth noting that Redding, California is located near Shasta State Historic Park, which reportedly contains the ruins of a gold-rush town from the 1800s. It's essentially a remnant of a brick and mortar city out in the wilderness. Could it be that this postcard is referring to a time when Redding was more heavily populated, hosting large groups of children?

The Cabbage Babies

This is the final postcard in our "The Kids From" collection but there are many more that you can find. They are more rare but they represent the American aspect of the dispersion of these postcards outside of Europe. We actually have this very same postcard without "The Kids From" phrase so this artwork is not exclusive to the phrase.

This one is not that strange but it is a beautiful card of babies in a decorative dragon chariot being pulled by a reindeer. Perhaps these were a "higher grade" of child for sale to wealthier buyers, we can see that they are all well dressed and clean looking. Their mode of travel certainly looks impractical and expensive, not to mention only one lone Reindeer pulling the entire thing on it's own. Reindeer are typically associated with wisdom, nobility and safe travels, making it an ideal candidate to be delivering the new generation of upper class citizens- symbolically at least.

It's clear that a carriage of that size & shape would be largely useless for even a small "shipment". It's likely that there were different price ranges and some children were carried in slightly "nicer" box cars than other children, or maybe they all came the same way and the post cards were merely a marketing strategy.

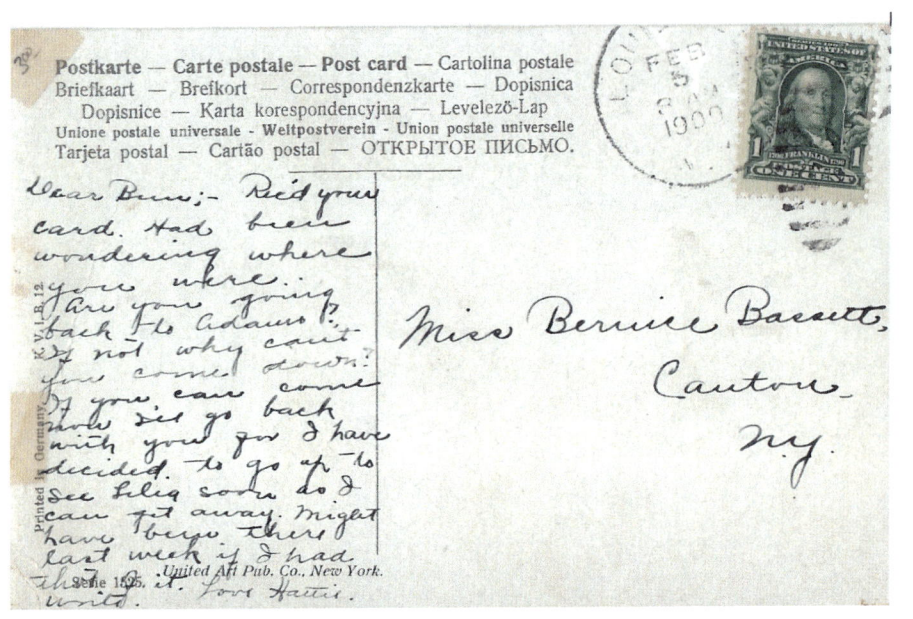

(The_kids_from_07)

This card has the phrase from Louisville, N.Y and confirmed by the postmark dated 1900, so this is an early one.

The message says *"Dear ___. Read your card. Had been wondering where you where. Are you going back to (____) ? ____ why can't you come down? If you can come now I'll go back with you for I have decided to go up to see Lilia sorta so I can get away. Might have been there last week if I had that ___ it "*

(The_kids_from_07_back)

154

COMMENTS FROM OUR VIDEO

Our video on this topic was successful, one of the highlights being the thousands of commenters who felt inspired to share their stories. They contributed their thoughts on the research, especially on how it connected to their own family histories. We will start off with the top comments from the "Repopulation Postcards" video :

@victorydawn9749
"Maternal Grandmother didn't know her date of birth, but she believed she was born in the year 1900. She talked about harvesting a lot of cotton when she was a small child. But it makes sense to let small children help with harvesting, but apparently it was very harsh. She said her hands would bleed and and they would wrap them and carrying on. Just some of what I remember. She was a very strong woman, could do just about anything. She made clothing, grew her own food, made her own breads, and wouldn't allow anything to go to waste. She was a saint."

Above is the top comment where at the time of writing this book has almost 1000 likes and over 100 replies, with many others commenting under sharing similar stories.

@sarcasticmaniac628
"My great grandmother told me babies came from a cabbage patch. The weird parts is she was very old and would state it as fact. She didn't remember her birthday at all. We all thought she was just senile, but now I wonder."

@debracooper9155
"My husband was born in a Florence Criittenton home for unwed mothers in 1964. In researching these homes they sound like places where they shamed girls into giving up their babies and perhaps took them by force. My husband found his birth mother's family about 3 years ago, however his birth mother had passed away. She did however on her deathbed tell her sister that she had a son and "they" took him from her. Her sister had no idea that my husband's birth mother had had a child out of wedlock. At the time she assumed it was just the ramblings of someone near death, she was shocked when my husband contacted her."

@LoudFishesPunchFly
"This would mean that most people on the streets are not regular people. Regular people are birthed, not just produced, so keeping with this logic, a good amount of people must come from a line that was just created in a lab or even straight outta the ground. Makes sense why almost everyone is so easily manipulated by the system and are not ready to be unplugged from it, because they literally have deep rooted ties to it."

@ashmkelly8138
"It is very strange, my mother (born 1951) grew up believing that babies were found in the cabbage patch or under the gooseberry bush! She was from a large family(not uncommon in Ireland at the time) and never noticed her mother being pregnant) she would wake up to be told there

was a new baby, even for married women flaunting a pregnancy was shameful as that implied you had done a certain act! It was only a few years before my mothers birth hat women had to be "churched" 6 weeks after a baby, a ceremony of purification and thanksgiving. It would make you wonder if the churches were involved in pursuing the Victorian ideas of modesty and purity to hide the large amounts of babies that appeared from nowhere and have people keep quiet about how babies are traditionally made as it wasn't becoming to talk about intimacy etc!"

@nicoduncanson3117
"In French class I remember the teacher telling us "mon petit choux-choux" meant "my little sweetie" or literally: "my little cabbage", as the word for cabbage is also used as a term of endearment, especially for children. Awesome work. I love your videos."

@beccalamp8249
"When I was in High School (1977-1981) I was in a club that visited the local orphanage to have parties for the kids there on holidays...shortly after High School it seemed they all just disappeared... Nothing here is as we've been taught (programmed). When I was a child the family told stories about how my great-grandfather "came out of nowhere, & disappeared into nowhere..." My family is mostly from Ireland & Wales (paternal) & England & German-Dutch (maternal), & settled in the mountains of WV & NC in the mid 1800's. I wish I'd asked more questions then, because now there is no one left to ask...for most of my life I thought "what a player great-granddad must've been..." Tho his children were all exceptionally kind, bright, spiritual, & artistic...all became assets to their communities, & passed their passions on to the rest of us. And tho we all have a supportive & kind relationship with those around us, most of us feel like outsiders here. Lately it has occurred to me that maybe I misjudged great-grandpa? Maybe he wasn't a player? Maybe he was not of this world? Is it possible that these clone babies are the NPC's we now endure? And some of us have been seeded throughout the world to awaken & discover what this place really is? To help ourselves & others who have somehow become imprisoned here? I have more questions than answers, but what a grand adventure!"

@knowthyself222
"This really got me thinking about something that runs through my mind quite often... and actually helped me to fill in some missing pieces..because both of my grandmothers on both sides of my family, have the same exact story that their mothers left them as babies and both of my great grandfather's came home to find them home alone where the mother had never returned with no Rhyme or Reason?? they don't know who their real mothers were they were raised by their father and stepmothers so my parents never knew their paternal grandmother, they only knew the woman that raised their moms. I always thought of it as just an ironic set of circumstance but there seems to be something much more Insidious at play.. also both of my grandfathers were polish and both of my grandmothers were Native American... ironic or "coincidence" , I don't believe in coincidence"

@sycadelic666
"I once read a thesis on the origin of KINTER GARTEN in the US and how it was adopted around the same time as the Rockefeller school system as a way to create efficient factory workers. The bells in between classes, change of skill sets/tasks in between those bells, a lunch period, etc."

Comments from our Video

@lionoftartaria528hz
"I have this story re-told by a polish woman I met when being on the road in uk. Her great grandmother who lived for 120 years and was born around 1870 something. She had no memories of any parents and was growing up with 17 other kids. The streets where very muddy and it was mostly soldier patrolling..."

@aneyethatcansee9045
"Also an essential tidbit is these children were sold in Sears and Roebuck catalogs for 3$. You could literally mail order kids... Always excellent work guys. Also just was looking at the relationship between orphan, Orpheus, and the Orphic egg...A clue!"

@kmc485
"I am 42 years old born in 1979. The garbage pail kids were trading cards, just like baseball cards. But more importantly, they also sold cabbage patch kids dolls that you could pick the name, sex, and hair color. They came with a certificate of adoption. I had one that I didn't play with often so I guess I didn't make the connection. My grandfather was an orphan. All I know about it is that he knew nothing of where he came from and the family that raised him wasn't very mice to him. Supposedly, these people came to the town with babies and went around asking families that were there if they could possibly take a baby and raise the child. So my grandfather came from people driving around handing out children without much of an explanation. My grandma told me this 20 year's ago. I wish she was here now, I would question her more about it. My mom is still here though but she's a boomer and very much brainwashed still. My Dad too. They get angry and kick me out when I try and discuss anything but what they believe the narrative to be, so asking them about this might not get me anywhere but I'm going to try. Maybe this will hit them in a spot to bring back a memory hopefully breaking the spell they are under. I'm not going to hold my breath though. I also won't give up either. But look up Alice Bailey. She is Alice Guy"

@jennifertashik298
"I was a 80s child and I remember this was like the first "craze" of Christmas shopping mobbing on tv everyone had to have them and over paying and "women not behaving over women" Weird grown adult women where absolutely crazy for them and all of these merchandise was shoved down the children. And I mean everything records as you stated , shows , cartoons, TV trays (which I absolutely loved btw, lol) lunch boxes, comforters, stickers, coloring books....EVERY.SINGLE.THING. Telling us in plain sight...what gets me is the story
behind it,   looking back they were out in open telling us bc as any adult, how did any parent not see that isn't a creepy dark story line??? What made the mothers/ women get so crazy for them ???
AWESOME story line, great job guys would love to watch a part 2*"

@getsmart9987
"What I notice is each postcard or image of the babies is so specific with each baby with a different look. If they were just creating advertising style art, I wouldnt think they would take the time to use a different baby face for an image with 20 or 30 babies, but keep it simple. Each child is obviously an actual baby. Almost like people could see the art and say I want the baby on the left or right or 4th down, etc. Like a Sears catalog."

@lucisoburns1965
"Since you mentioned bee symbolism I will expand on it. In the mystery schools such as free masonry, bees are important symbolism. The "Queen" is G-d, the bees are the initiated. The bees are building a hive "Home" for the queen. Some of the bees know some don't. However the queens consciousness is at work acting through her bees. Also the egg symbolism. The egg is a symbol of the soul. Now in the mysteries your soul is actually your body. It can be understood as 'the before state'. The body (Soul), can be better understood like a robot, an organic machine given instincts (Artificial intelligence). Like a robot the body can be remotely accessed and controlled. It can be made to see things, a remote operator can watch through cameras (eyes), listen in on the microphone (ears), it can talk through the speaker (mouth). Think of the characteristics of demonic possession. Something to pay attention to in popular culture is doll symbolism. Someone created a farm, the robots they made can reproduce themselves, they work on someone else's will, once the farm is grown, the hive is built, then something from Above falls into the host bodies."

@logical_evidence
"Anne Getties is a Australian photographer that takes photos of babies similar to these picture postcards. Was a big hit with calandras and stationary in the 90's. Thanks for sharing."

@lotsofsmarts
"I never thought to ask mom…I myself am an early 1950's baby boomer; mom used to tell me that babies came from a 'cabbage patch'… when i was a wee child. The only explanation was 'I told you that because you were too young to discuss how babies were made'… But i never asked her 'Why a cabbage patch story?' She's gone now"

@susanjane2498
"My grandmother told me that she was a very tiny baby, but they were too poor to use an incubator so her mom kept her in a cigar box on the open door of the oven to keep her warm! She said her head could fit inside of a teacup. Strange but true story."

@jolandao.1280
"Thank you for this interesting video! The symbolism of cabbages remind me of a strange painting called 'The legend of the baker of Eeklo', a copy after the Flemish painters Cornelis van Dalem and Jan van Wechelen. They say it's about a legend. This is what the description says: Those who wanted to change their appearance or revert the effects of time on their faces could go to the town of Eeklo, where they could have a new head baked for them. The head would be carefully cut from the trunk, kneaded, glazed and placed into the oven. In the meantime, a green cabbage was placed over the trunk, symbolically "replacing" the head. Once the new head was baked, it was sewn in its place on the trunk. However, the new head could fail to bake, or it could over bake, resulting in deformed or deficient heads.' There are about ten versions of this painting. Personally I'm not sure about the explanation. Maybe a cabbage represents new life or a new version of someone? If so, there could be a connection with the cabbage patch kids."

Comments from our Video

@wdstk5233
"In rural South Carolina, if we thought someone thought we were dumb or new to being hustled, we'd say "Do I look like I just fell off the cabbage truck?" It's an old saying and I always wonder what it meant because farmers and helping hands are rather smart people for their environment. This saga made it finally make sense."

@carlbrown8966
"Vlassic pickles had a stork mascot on jars and in commercials. I always thought it was odd. Now I realize it was a nod to the clone children being grown in vats like pickles in a jar! I'm only half joking... maybe you should look into those pickle ads. Might turn out to be a rabbit hole."

@WashYourWorld
"As I am a native french speaker, I can tell you that on the french postcards, there are naughty play on words. Like "Au grand mât de cocagne" or "La Canne à papa", actually are metaphors for "the male genital organ" :) Might it be that these cards where post WWI or a previuous war and part of an agenda to repopulate after the war ? Thanks"

@changopardomuzik4953
"What Moon mentioned about the post cards with them fishing babies out of the water, and how it could mean fishing them out of the womb makes sense, because when u break down words like BIRTH CANAL when a ship is docked it's said that it's at it's BIRTH and a canal as we all know is a narrow water passage, and other words like PREGNANCY = PREGNANT SEA, or INFANCY = INFANT SEA, sea of babies. And the symbolism of water and baptism as being dunked into the water and then raised up again, like a rebirth, like a BORN again Christian...it's just so much"

@shirleypena4133
"@Mind Unveiled Of the many videos which you have created, this is undoubtedly one of the most historically and socially important. I cannot thank you enough for creating it, and it should be required viewing in every high school, college and university in every state in the USA. Most Americans, especially those who are black and/or immigrants, have no idea of the true history of white people in America. They are not aware that almost all of the white Americans today are descendants of those who arrived here after the end of the Civil War, and that they too arrived here basically as slaves from a foreign country.

This is new for much of your viewers, but when I was in school this was still being taught (I'm nearly seventy now). We learned about the deals made between America's politicians (going all the way up to the White House), it's wealthy and elite and the British crown, in order to provide a labor force for America post-Civil War and pre-WWI, largely comprised of CHILDREN, upon which America's Industrial Revolution, its farms and almost everything else was built. Too many blacks in America today wrongly believe that America was built upon the hard labor that their ancestors performed. WRONG! It was largely built upon the backs of WHITE CHILDREN, whose descendants today don't know their true history.

I first learned about this when I was barely a teenager, working in convalescent care homes with my mother. I loved to talk to the old folks there and was always asking them about their childhood and young adulthood. It struck me how many had been orphans who knew nothing about their parents and had worked VERY hard as children, doing everything from working in coal mines to running machinery in factories. Later when I majored in US History I found out what you and your viewers are only now discovering. I came home and talked to my mother about it, and discovered that yes, our family too had experienced the same story.

I urge EVERYONE here to share this video with EVERYONE you know, but especially with people who are not white. When I went to live in England in the early 2000s, I discovered that all the old, white, native Brits I met knew about this. However, as both the United Kingdom and the United States' white populations continue to be replaced with immigrants from Mexico, the Middle East, Southeast Asia and the like, this hidden history of our country will be LOST FOREVER. The straight fact is almost no European immigrants arrived here via Ellis Island. They arrived as CHILDREN who never got to experience having a loving family…or even what anyone today would consider a childhood. Again, I thank you for making this important video!"

@monstermcb007282
"I think knowing the cabbage patch myth can help some people understand both reason and prevalence of cabbages and babies in historical pop culture. A good one to look up is *Cabbage Patch Babies* by Whanganui Regional Museum. Easy explanation there.

I have a vast personal library of classic and antique books, and stacks and boxes of antique ephemera in storage (I had a small antiques shop and was an estates liquidator in the aughts). I have baby announcement cards from the 1800s through the 1970s, and there are cards from every decade depicting babies springing forth from cabbages.

When I was about three, I asked my mother where babies come from and she told me she picked me from the cabbage patch. That satisfied me because I (born in the 1970s) had on my bookshelf a children's book of illustrated poems and fairy tales printed in the 1950s that had a delightful, full-color, full-page illustration of a baby in a bonnet growing from the center of an enormous cabbage. My mother was pregnant at the time so her explanation really did mess with my little head. I knew I had a baby brother or sister on the way and I knew my father had cabbages growing in our garden, so I checked those cabbages repeatedly every day, looking for my baby sibling. Imagine my further confusion when my mother was missing one morning when I woke and my mammy was there instead, flipping pancakes at the stove, and she told me my mother was at the hospital to birth my baby brother or sister."

@scottsmith6643
"Wow. This one deserves another viewing. Hope you guys can carry research on this further. Yet…is that even possible? So much is hidden - occulted, if you will. This is truly creepy. BTW, my grandfather was born in 1906. He showed me a photo of himself as a baby and he was wearing a dress. I asked him why and he told me that in those days all babies were called girls. Weird, I know."

Comments from our Video

@nataliedyck8312
"This is strange to me, in the soviet union we were very sheltered from anything western. no tv or toys from abroad, nothing. but children were always told babies are found in the cabbage patch or a storch brought them. now i finally know how they came up with the strange idea."

@mabeaute8963
"Many of the cards are in French with words like: 'Babies for sale, The baby farm, Baby lottery, Choose me, I'll be good, I'll bring you good luck, I'll be obedient, House of babies'. Some other cards are in German the the rest in English. All very strange indeed!"

@reglarcatG---2178
"My grandfather was placed in an orphanage by his parents where he was made to work in an underground coal mine, eventually he ran away and went back to his hometown where he was taken in as a servant and not a family member, he was horsewhipped if he disobeyed and could never sleep well, out of fears he might be whipped in the middle of the night, for something he didn't do. He went to the county fair where he met a girl that he was oddly attracted to, she apparently felt the same way about him. They planned a date but when (Otis) my grandfather arrived at the door, he was met by her parents, who abruptly informed them they could not date each other, when they asked why it was forbidden by them to be together, they were told because they were siblings, and it wouldn't be right, I was told that they had to give him up because they couldn't afford to feed him and his sister, but at that time a son was very valuable to families that farmed, and it seems unlikely they would give him up for any reason,at least not willingly, also be would have been expected to carry on the family name and to inherit the farm and to run the family farm, but instead was basically sold into slavery, he never returned or see his home again, or seen his sister until after their parents passed away. Now I am even more curious as to their reason, did they sign an agreement under fear of retribution ? I wonder if they signed an agreement that they would never interfere with the upbringing of their son, and to speak of it to no one, all we know of his parents is they were Welsh immigrants, and nothing much more. My grandfather was a hard working, gentle man, who never once abused his children, I assume as a result of being horsewhipped and used as a slave when he was a child. I began to wonder how different my own life, might have been, if he had not been subjected to a cruel system of child labor, and quite possibly a repopulation program, that the nefarious, patriarchal organization led state, had implemented after a major event, that devastated population and infrastructure, and upended a now obscured, advanced technological and spiritual civilization."

@mayb.wright509
"I'm an anglo living in Quebec, Canada. I always wondered about the expression "mon choux" (my [little] cabbage). Never struck me as anything cute/cuddly, but makes perfect sense now. o m g   There's no end to these rabbit holes, is there? lol   Merci beaucoup et au revoir !"

@MsAngelwithin
"Where I was brought up, the local mental hospital had rooms filled with drugged up people kept in beds, it was referred to as 'the cabbage patch' by locals, it was known that woman in these wards often gave birth without really knowing as they were so heavily drugged - no facts just a local urban legend"

@rosevilleballet525
"This is fascinating because I remember back when I was young (born 1947) I vividly remember adults saying when asked where do babies come from, the reply was always "the cabbage patch!"

@Katie-26
"So this is where the word "kindergarten" comes from! Great work, love your videos!"

@robotcitizen101
"On the notes of orphans shipped around the world ... a large % of "white" people in USA, Aus, NZ, Canada are said to be of Irish heritage. However many of us have no family connections to Ireland. None of my elders in Australia, those I knew, born in late 1800s or early 1900s knew any Irish (Gaelic) and they never said a thing about Ireland. It seems they didn't know a thing about it. Ireland was never discussed except for a rare "that's where our ancestors came from". We never studied anything about Ireland in school, while having to study about nations to which we had no connection. Ireland was never mentioned on TV in 70s, 80s, 90s except for when there was some conflict or a peace deal. As far as we know our ancestors just popped up here in the 1800s. It seems like a hand plucked them from Ireland and plonked them in Australia as small children, to be raised as "colonial English"; learning about England and as if Ireland did not exist. That's an explanation I can think of for them - my family line - not knowing any of the language nor history nor tales of Ireland."

@52marli
"I really didn't think much about these babies before. I just thought the babies were cute. When you think the families had 10-20 kids each, if something happened to the parents that automatically left 10-20 kids each. My aunt weighed 3 pounds when she was born. She was raised in a shoebox and set on the oven door to keep her warm until she was big enough to maintain her temperature. Fed sugar water with an eye dropper...at least that's how the story went. She wasn't the only one raised like that from the stories...but we are finding out a lot about our ancient history."

@susimora62
"My grandmother was bought from an orphanotrophy the same day she was born, 5th april 1898, in Italy. She came to know only after her parents were both dead. They had children dumb and deft who died soon after birth, so they bought her and another little girl to employ as sheeps guardians. Many couples who bought babies from orphanotrophy had their own born children weak who soon died. Or the couple was sterile. Why? Genetic contamination for some disaster erased from history books? Only some apparently rich couples survived sterile or unable to get healthy children?"

Comments from our Video

The many insightful comments shared paint a complex, multifaceted picture of this topic, eliciting both curiosity and empathy. We're deeply grateful to everyone who opened up their knowledge bases, personal experiences, and perspectives to help expand our collective understanding. Your stories not only fuel our desire to uncover the truth but also hint at a possibility of a larger, potentially obscured narrative revolving around the mass relocation and, strikingly, the possible 'production' of children.

Among the shared experiences, a striking element was the uncanny memory of Cabbage Patch Kids and their associated merchandise. The phenomena surrounding these dolls seem to carry deeper undertones than the ordinary childhood craze. The accounts further illustrate the dolls' pervasiveness in popular culture, from TV shows, lunch boxes, to even parody trading cards, which contributed to an insatiable craze. The underlying narrative about the dolls, their adoption certificates, and choice of features unveils a deeper, more intricate layer to the entire phenomenon.

The discourse around symbolism was particularly intriguing, with several users touching upon elements like bees, eggs, and dolls. Bees, for instance, were linked to mystery schools like freemasonry, with the queen bee symbolizing God and the worker bees the initiated. The egg symbolism was connected to concepts of the soul and the body and certainly is linked to ORPHISM. Meanwhile, the doll symbolism seemed to hint at a broader context, possibly aligning with the notion of 'farmed' children.

Personal stories about familial connections to orphans open a heart-touching window into this phenomena. The accounts ranged from tales of grandparents adopted from people driving around handing out babies, to parents' endearing yet puzzling explanations about babies coming from a 'cabbage patch'. These personal stories certainly deepen the mystery and one can't help but reconsider the approved idea of "the past" after taking a deeper look into this phenomenon. There is undoubtedly much more to discover and understand about the untold stories of our not so distant past.

The investigation took an artistic turn with the mention of the unique photographic art of Anne Getties and the symbolic Flemish painting, 'The Legend of the Baker of Eeklo'. Both pieces highlight an intriguing link between babies and cabbages in art, making us wonder about the deeper intent behind such portrayals.

Slang phrases like "Do I look like I just fell off the cabbage truck?" and bizarre connections to pickles and stork mascots certainly make one think. Meanwhile, the intriguing interpretations of the French postcards and their oddly specific metaphors suggest the possibility of an agenda related to population replenishment post-war.

Lasty, let's dig into the term "ORPHAN" and how it relates to "ORPHISM". Could the "ORPHICS" have a hand in all of this? The ancient Orphic mysteries, shrouded in secrecy, have long been a cornerstone of esoteric thought. Now bear with us for a moment while we lay out a potential scenario.

At the heart of this tradition, the Orphics believed in cyclical rebirth, the soul's journey through multiple lifetimes, and its eventual liberation from the wheel of existence. This cyclical view of existence is emblematic of nature itself—seasons change, civilizations rise and fall, and from ashes, new worlds emerge. What if some of the modern world's disasters weren't as "natural" or "unpredictable" as we've been led to believe? What if these were purposefully engineered events-very much real to those who suffered their wrath- but orchestrated, purposely designed to reset and reshape the world in accordance with Orphic beliefs?

I mean, let's just look at the term "orphan." In mainstream terms, its etymology is attributed to the Greek "orphanos," denoting the bereft or abandoned. But delve deeper into its symbolic connotations, and the term reveals a layered mosaic of historical manipulations. The Orphan Train operations, as history recounts, were seemingly well intended philanthropic endeavors to populate deserted cities and care for destitute children. Yet, could this have been an orchestrated move by Orphic occultists to mold the next generation as per their own ideals? By monopolizing the young minds, either through church or state, they had the tools to feed them a tailored narrative, shaping the next era's ethos and norms and disconnecting them from any sense of self, making them easy to manipulate. Anyone who's aware of the psychology of a predator knows that they will intentionally seek out prey who are lost, spiritually, emotionally and even physically (displaced) because it puts them in an immediate position of power over their target. Who's to say that can't happen on a mass scale?

Wars, calamities, and socio-cultural upheavals may not have just been arbitrary occurrences of our world's turbulent history or human nature going off the rails. They might very well have been the machinations of the Orphic elites, intent on "purifying" the old to pave the way for the new. The very essence of Orphic beliefs is transformation — from chaos, a harmonious order is born. While some of these occultists might genuinely have believed they were making a necessary sacrifice for the greater good, purging the world to ensure its rebirth in a purer form, others undoubtedly saw this as an avenue to unparalleled power. With the world in chaos, those "in the know" stood as its architects, scripting both its demise and its reconstruction. Is it really so crazy to consider that puppeteers, draped in the cloak of Orphic ideologies, manipulated humanity's course, creating divisions, fostering conflicts, and curating a false reality? We are all painfully aware of the depravity some humans are capable of, does this really seem so far-fetched?

The Orphic worldview, with its emblems of cycles, rebirth, and salvation, is beautiful in its own right. However, like all ideologies, it's susceptible to zealous perversion. The question remains, then: Were we, the unsuspecting masses, mere pawns in a grand Orphic scheme? And if so, what cycles of rebirth are yet to unfold before our very eyes?

When you consider all the artwork, the letters, the narratives, occult symbolism, historical events, personal anecdotes and cultural phenomena, it all hints at a potentially lost or suppressed history related to children's relocation and possibly even their very 'production'. This concept, at first glance, seems ludicrous, but if we pause and reflect it's impossible to ignore the fact that our grasp of history often comes with its own biases, much like the endless streams of media we sift through today. This selective storytelling isn't a modern gimmick; it's been the undercurrent for eons. The shadow plays of world leaders and those "serving" the public are tales as old as time. As long as there has been both light and shadow. It is often through entertaining the outlandish, questioning the established, and daring to propose the "utterly ridiculous" that we can unlock mysteries we didn't even know were mysteries.

Hindsight isn't just clear—it's revelatory.

As we conclude with a final gallery section and share our last thoughts, we would like to extend our deepest gratitude once more to all of our subscribers... Your consistent support and active engagement have played an integral role in our journey, enabling us to delve deeper into these compelling narratives. We couldn't have come this far without you, and we're excited to continue this journey of exploration together. Your collective wisdom and curiosity inspire us to keep questioning, researching, and revealing the obscured facets of our shared history.

THE MIND UNVEILED
CABBAGE BABIES
COLLECTION

row large cabbage

POST CA

CORRESPONDENCE HERE

Menasha, Wis, 2/3/1911,

Fine country to live.
This is what we
feed on, ride on
look upon. Wonderful
is it not?

Kindest Wishes,
K. O.

Mr. J. V. Netzhammer.

#113, Lyon St,

Milwaukee.

Wisconsin.

170

171

172

173

174

175

Nous sommes à vendre!

NOS GENTILS POUPONS

Auprès du grand moulin
Au détour du chemin
Je connais un plantage
De nombreux bébés sages

Cliché DANGERE
Paris

178

CARTE

Chère Emilie

Ta lettre m'a appris que tu ne t'ennuieyais pas ce qui m'a fait grand plaisir ainsi qu'à maman.

Je t'envoie toutes nos amitiés ainsi qu'à ton mari.

Marcelle

Choisissez-moi !

Je suis si mignon !

Je suis gai !

Je vous aimerai bien !

Je vous apportera la joie !

Je serai obéissant

Je vous apporterai le bonheur

Jeanne Jean Amette

Madame et Monsieur

Julien Pain

route de Querqueville

Equeurdreville

Manche

GRAINE de CHOUX.

Made in France.

Rouen le 5 8bre 1913.

Monsieur et Madame Nuttin

Nous vous envoyons ce petit présent mais l'on ne vous en souhaite pas autant, pourvu que Monsieur Mimi ne plante plus de choux dans son jardin !... mais accompagnons notre carte avec un petit bonjour de Rouen et bonne santé à Madame. Mimi. à S.V.

Graine de Choux

cher frerot et chéri soeurette

je viens vous demander
de vos nouvelles nous
vous avons passé a
la grippe moi je vais
bien mieux et maman
commencé à se levé
il y a que papa qui
y a pas passé.
et vous êtes vous malade
nous commençons a
être inquiet donnée nous
de vos nouvelle le plutot
possible
Papa et maman se joignent
à moi pour vous

Bons baisers
a ma petite
Suzanne

Mademoiselle
Suzanne Salmon

Rue des Marais
Féüly

GRAINE DE POILU

Dans ce
Tout en
Voilà !
Nous a

...li parterre
...us promenant,
...ment, ma chère
...s un enfant !

Cherchez dans les choux le garçon.

GRAINE DE CHOUX TOUT EST POUR VOUS

– Bébé veut un petit Frère

Je m'en doutais bien ! Petit frère
Est enfin sorti de son chou,
Quel bonheur pour petite mère !
Viens, mon chéri, viens parmi nous !

"I want a little brother," says the baby.
"I had a feeling! Little brother"
"Has finally come out of his cabbage,"
"What joy for little mother!"

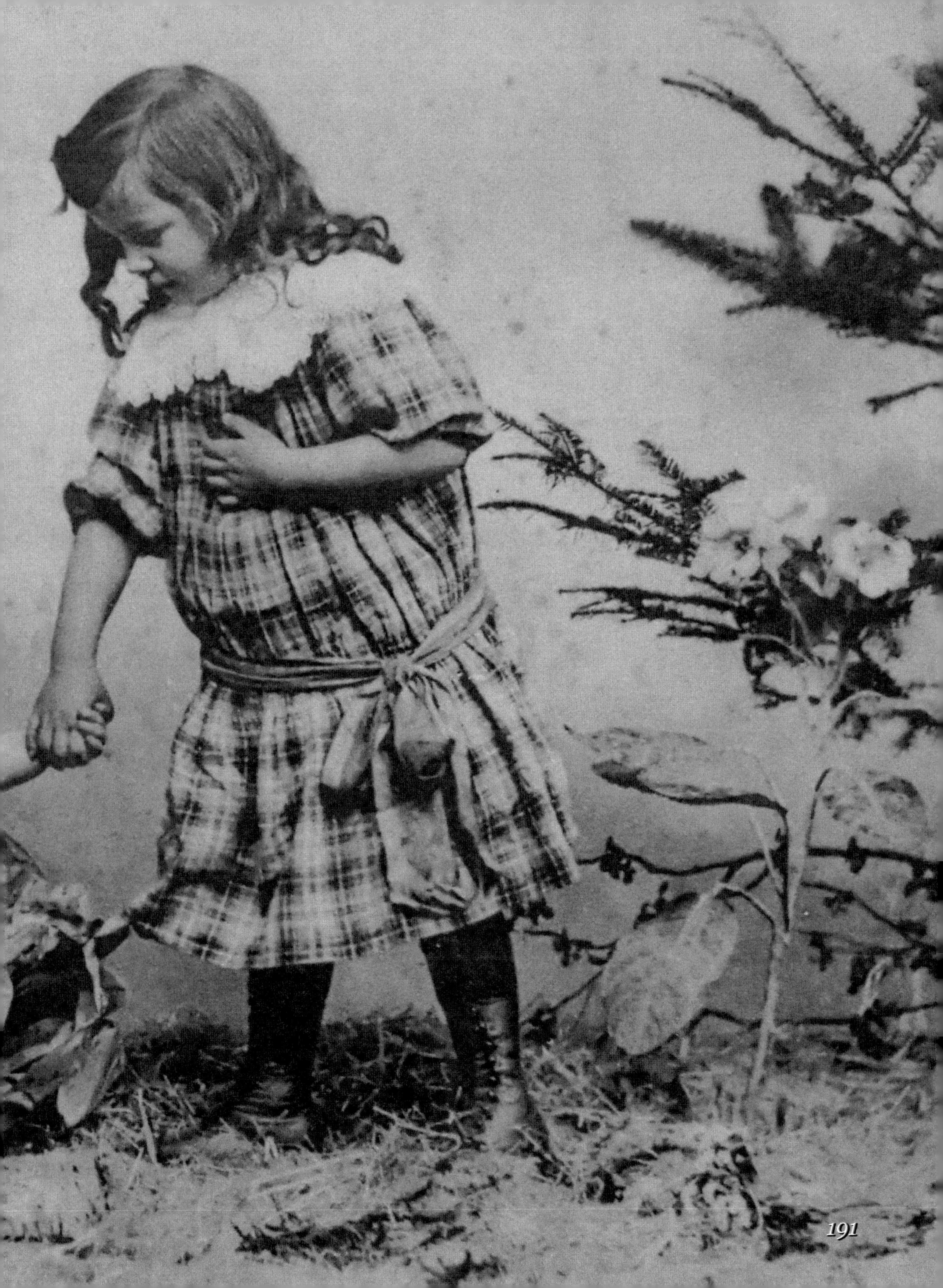

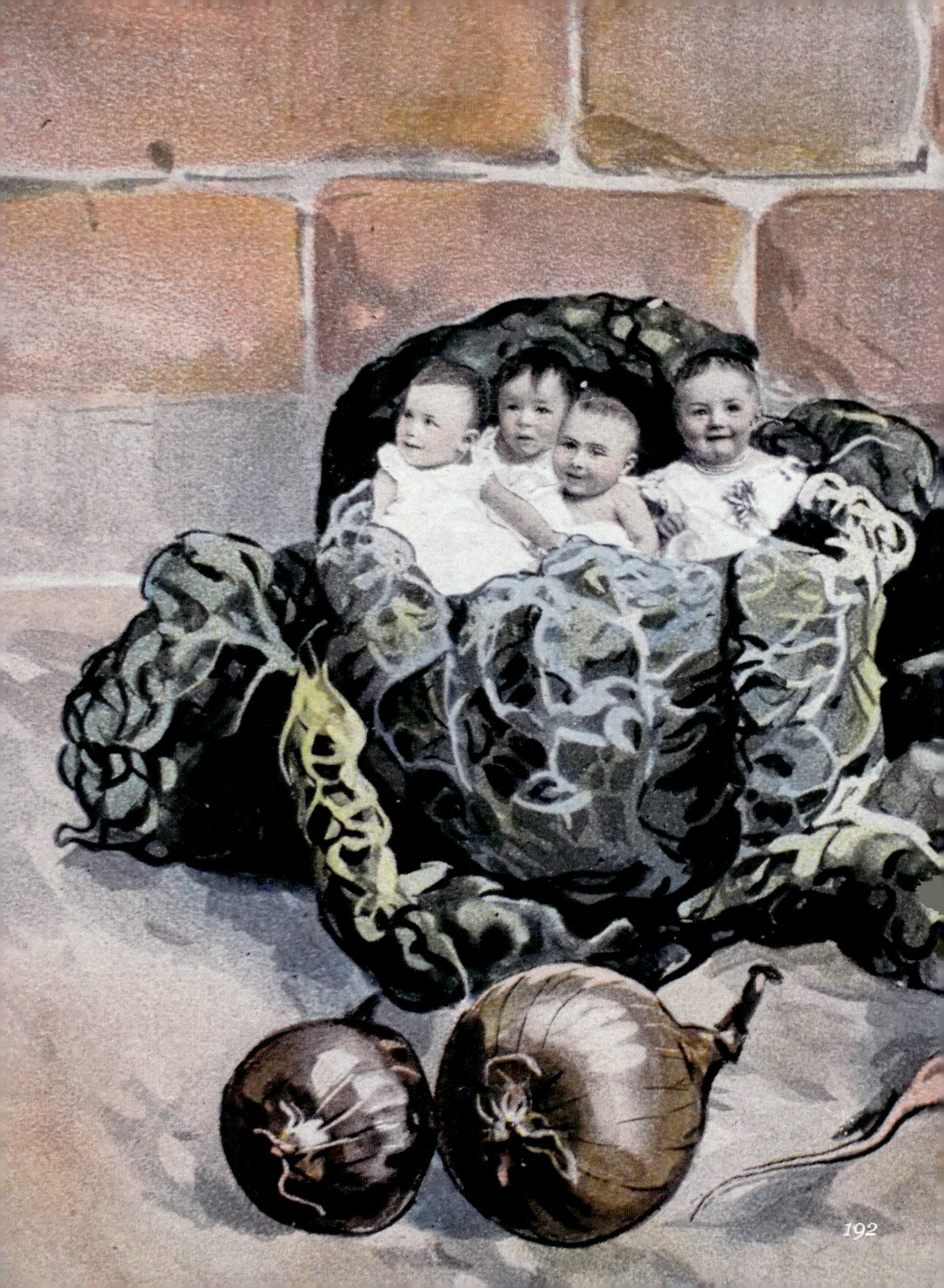

193

194

195

196

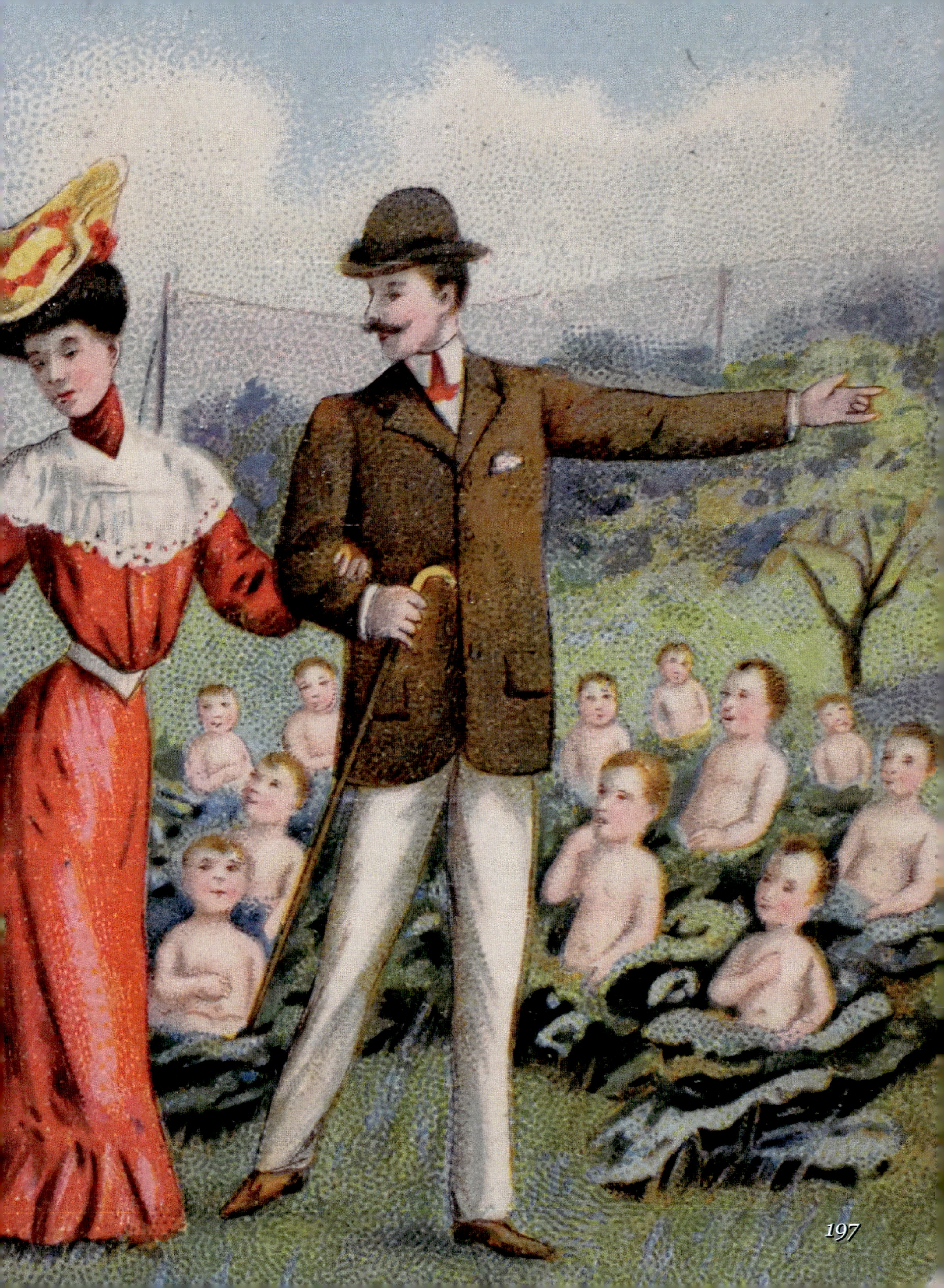

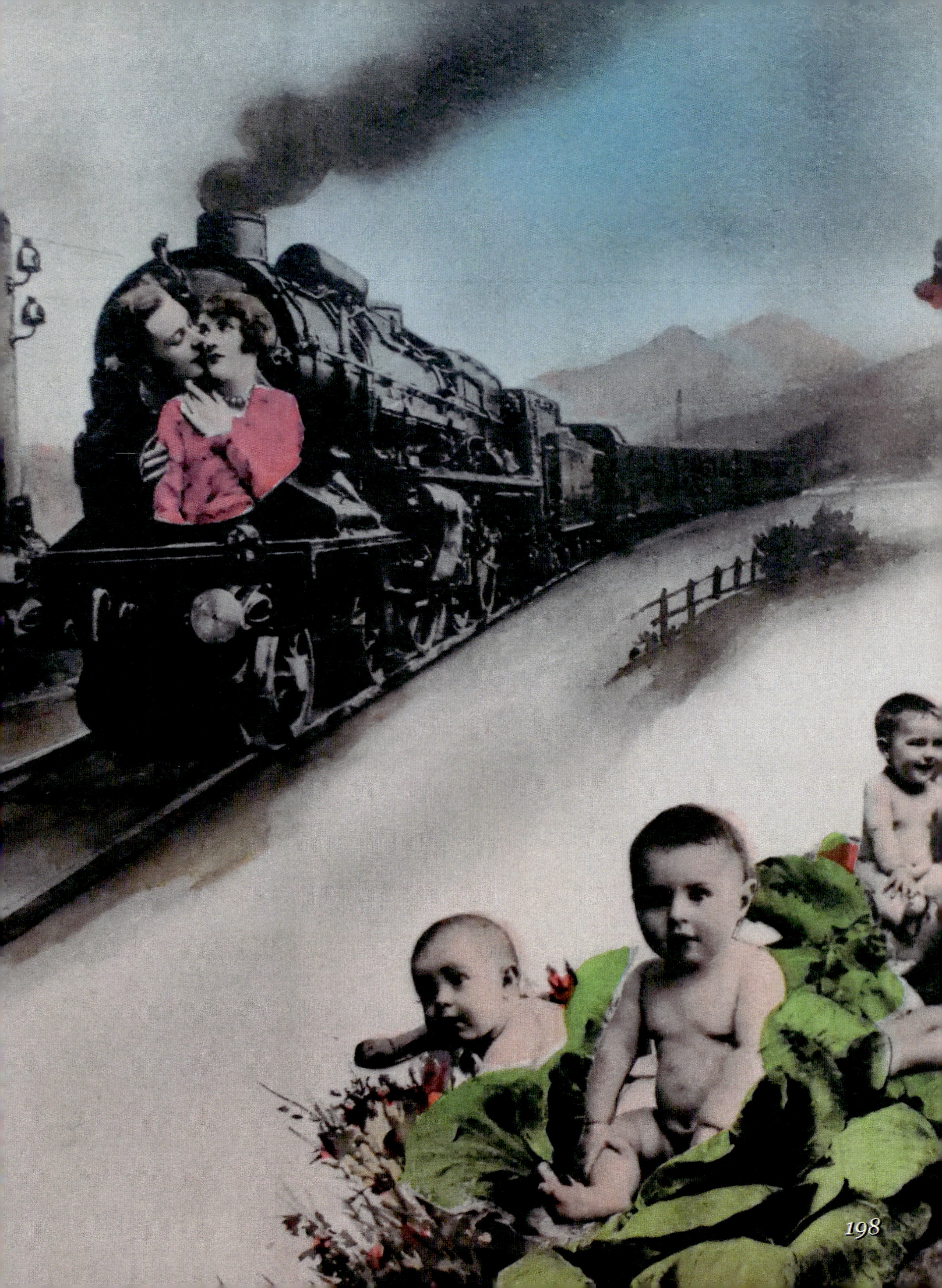

TERUG VAN DE HUWELIJKSREIS

June 24.

Hello Jim.
I will be out
in few days
after that
suit on train
on the other
side, have
them ready.

Mr Jim Boyd
Witchita
Kansas
137 N. Market

Nos futurs poilus

REX 4327

3 SEP 1916

Ma chère petite Raymonde

Reçois de ton papa chéri cette jolie petite carte et de gros baisers. Embrasse bien fort ta chère petite mère et Jeanne et Simone

Bonne Année

Chargement de Graines de Choux

AMITIÉS

Bonjour cher
Frère et chère
Sœur et gogette
Toute Nos Amitiés
à touze Léon
et Marie et
Marceause

Monsieur et Madame
Coll Mare Hermexe
Mopeon le bec
Étrépagny eure

204

205

The Kids from Whitehall, Mich.

206

The Kids from Walkerton, Ind.

208

209

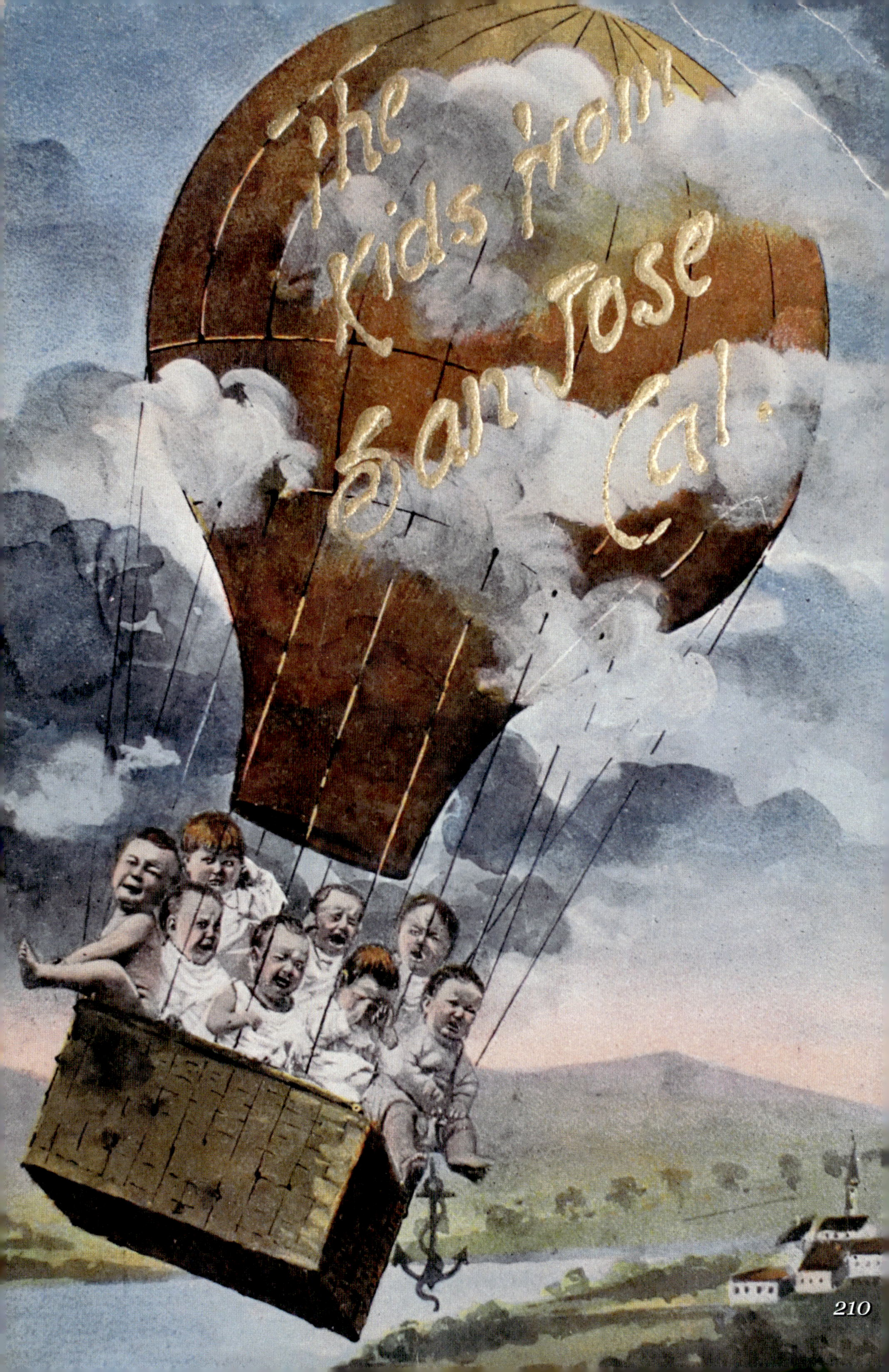
The Kids from
San Jose
Cal.

The Kids from Grants Pass, Ore.

212

213

214

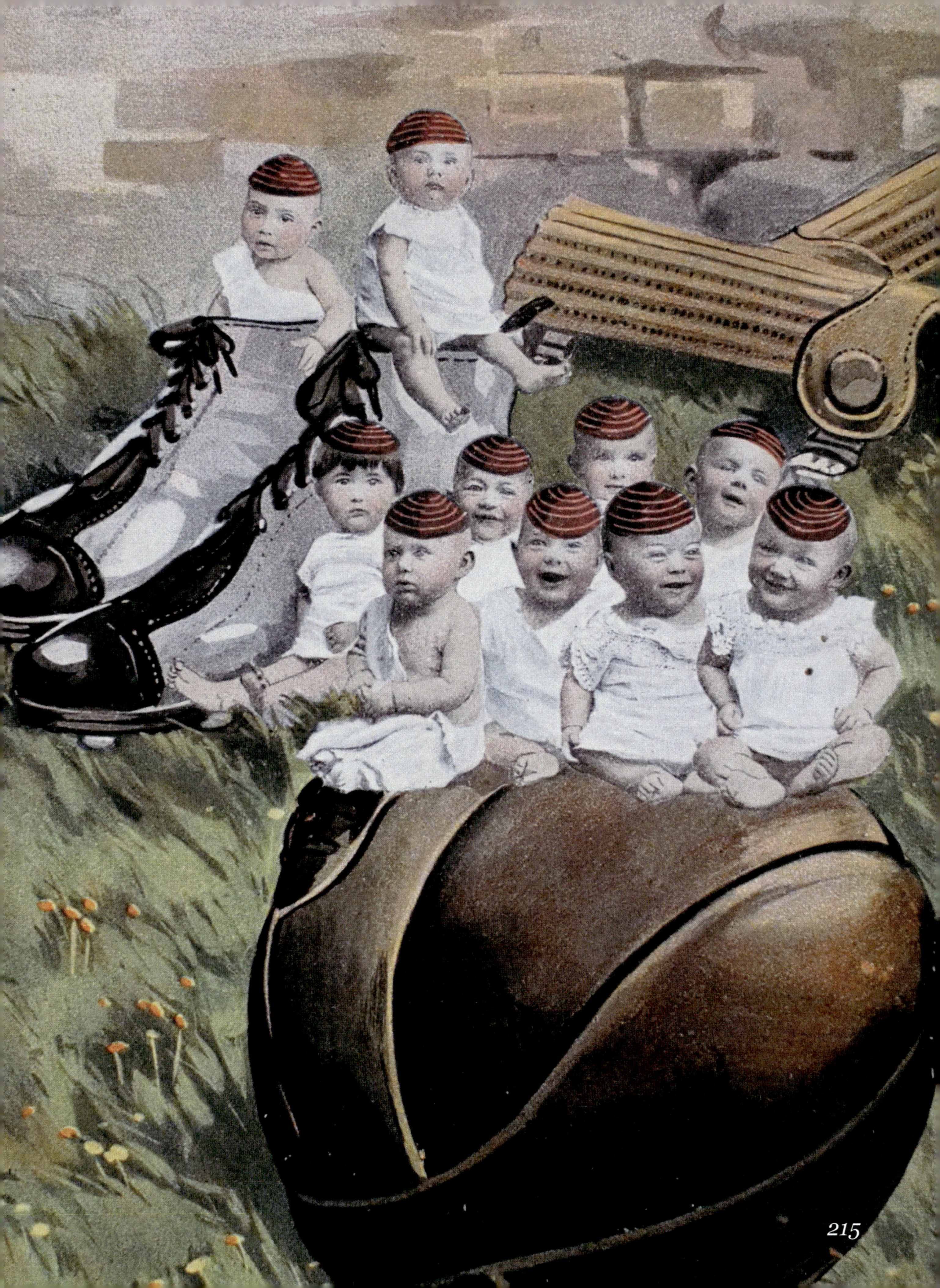

PETIT

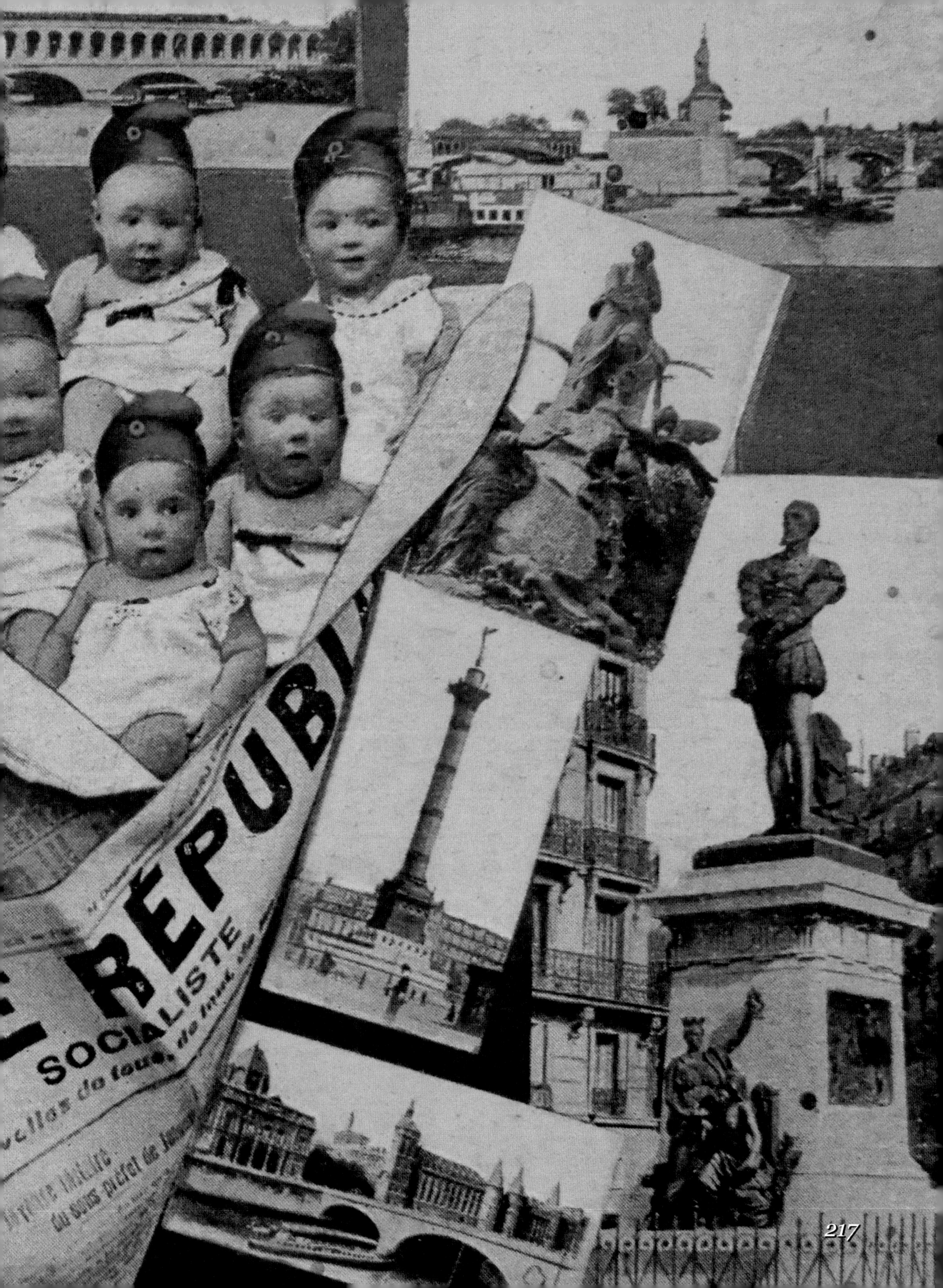
RÉPUBLI
SOCIALISTE

Je vous souhai[te]
[bonne] famille
Mâcon 29 [A]oût

pareille petite !!! Marthe !

Postkarte — Carte postale
Weltpostverein — Union postale universelle
Correspondenzkarte — Dopisnice
Levelező-Lap — Korespondenční listek
Dopisnica — Karta Korespondenzyjna
Briefkaart — Cartolina Postale
Brefkort — Tarjeta Postal — Postcard
Дописна карта
ОТКРЫТОЕ ПИСЬМО.

Monsieur

Ingénieur

Côte d'or

Madame

Charbot

Électricien

Montbard

222

223

224

225

226

227

and Wishes for the Future
a Greeting take
From Me.

POST

WRITING SPACE.

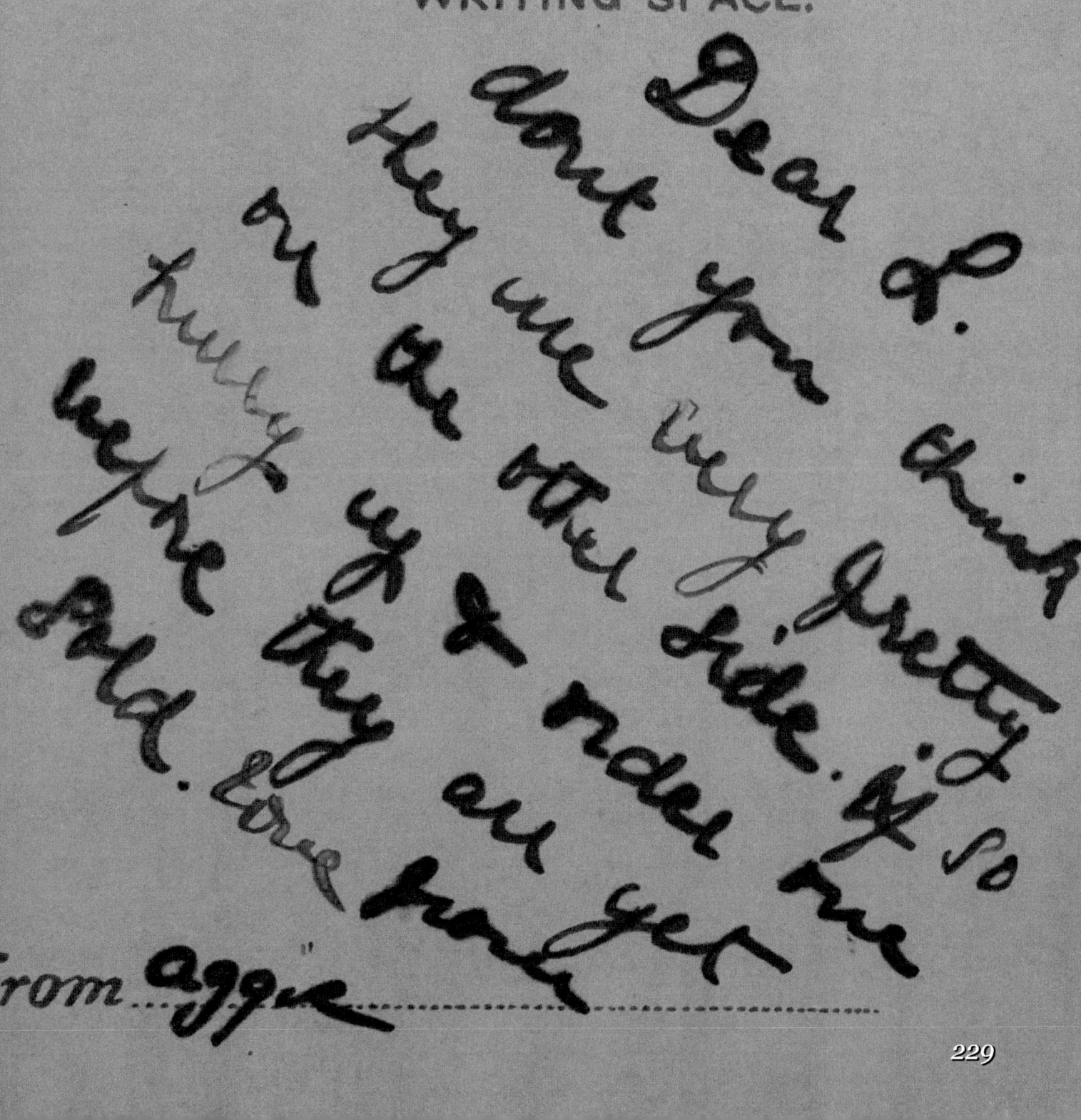

Dear L.
dont you think
they are very pretty, I.
on the other side. If so
hurry up & order me
one they are all get
sold. love from

from aggie

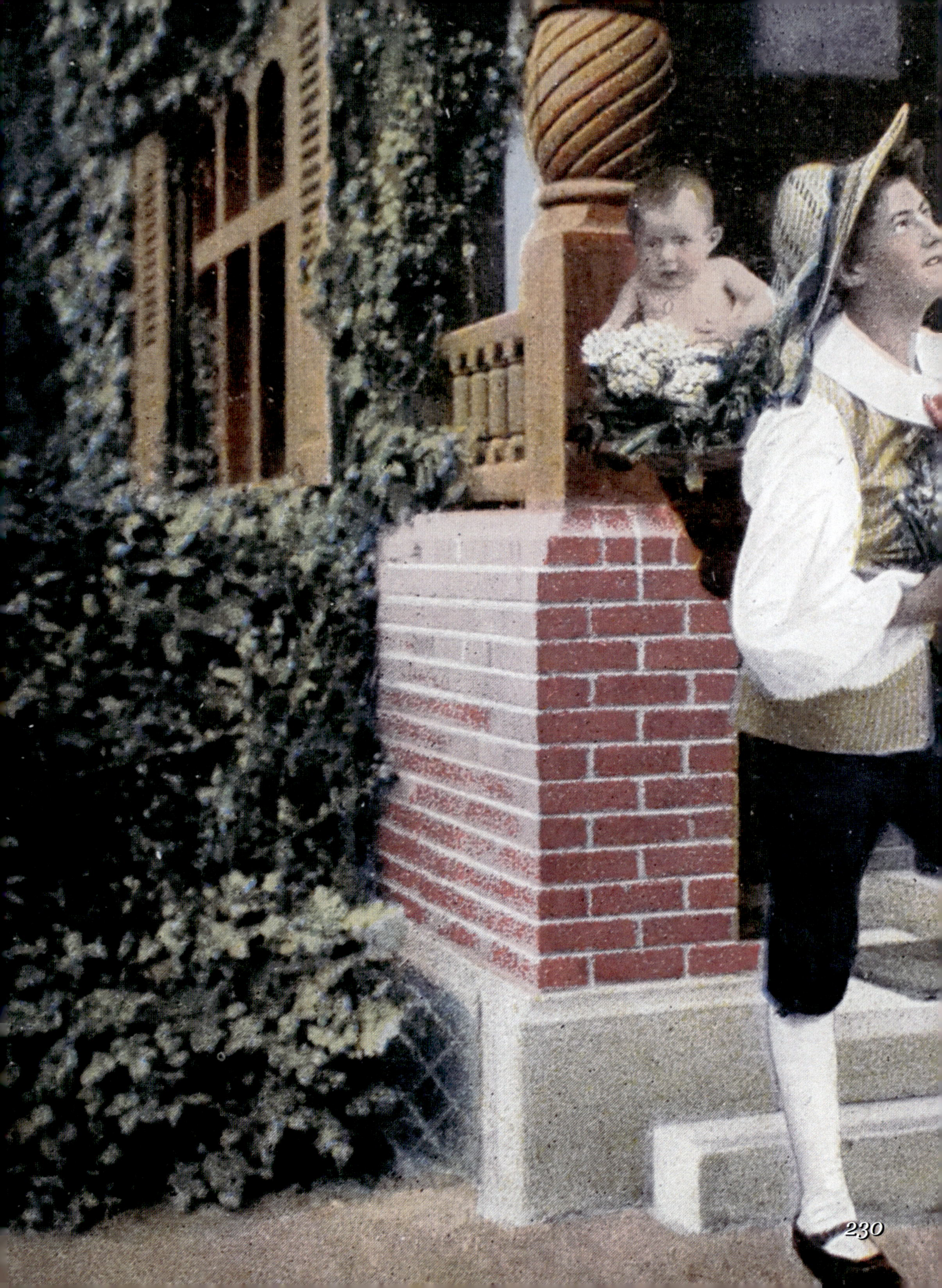

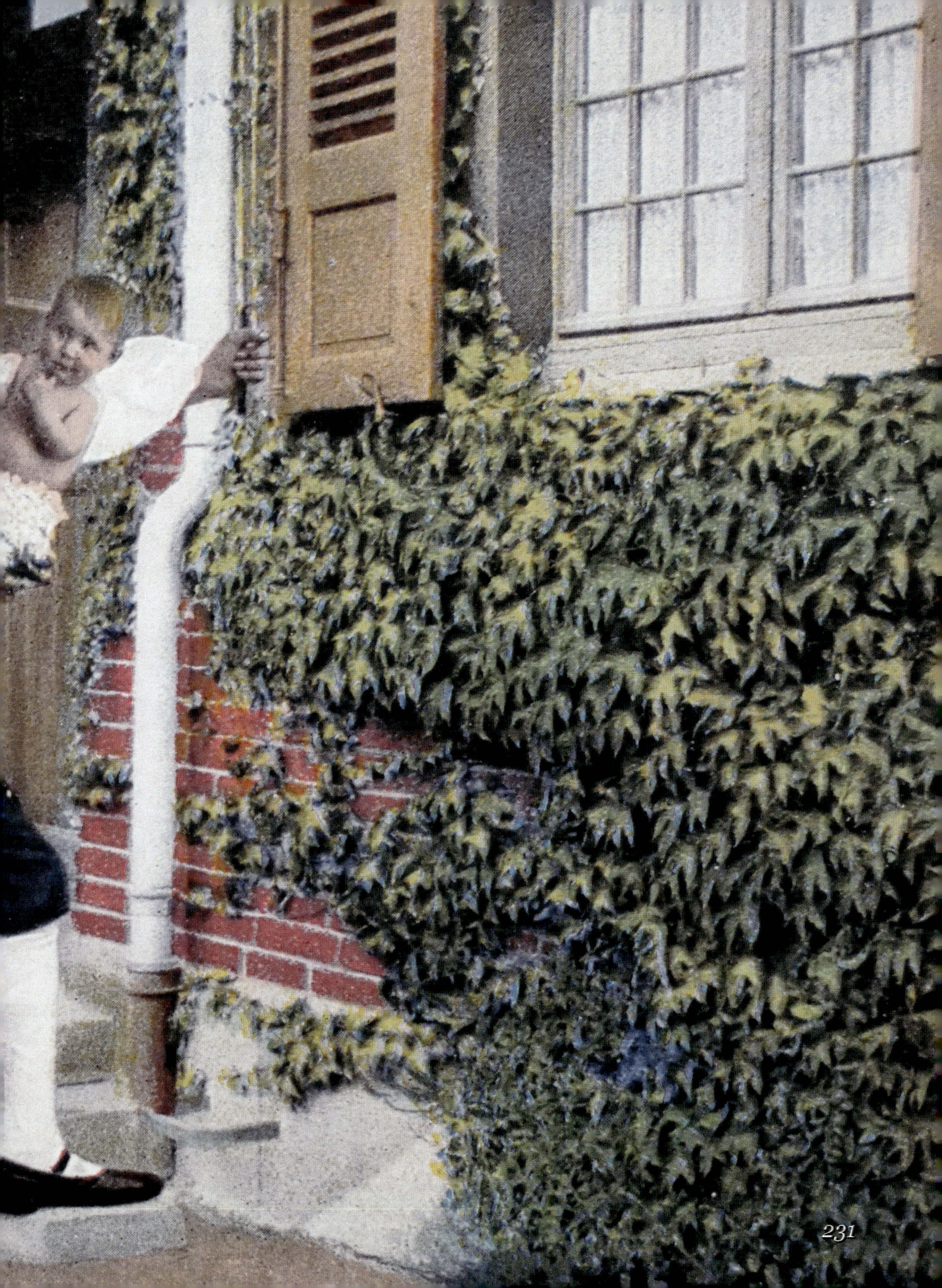

232

233

LA FERME aux BÉBÉS

234

235

236

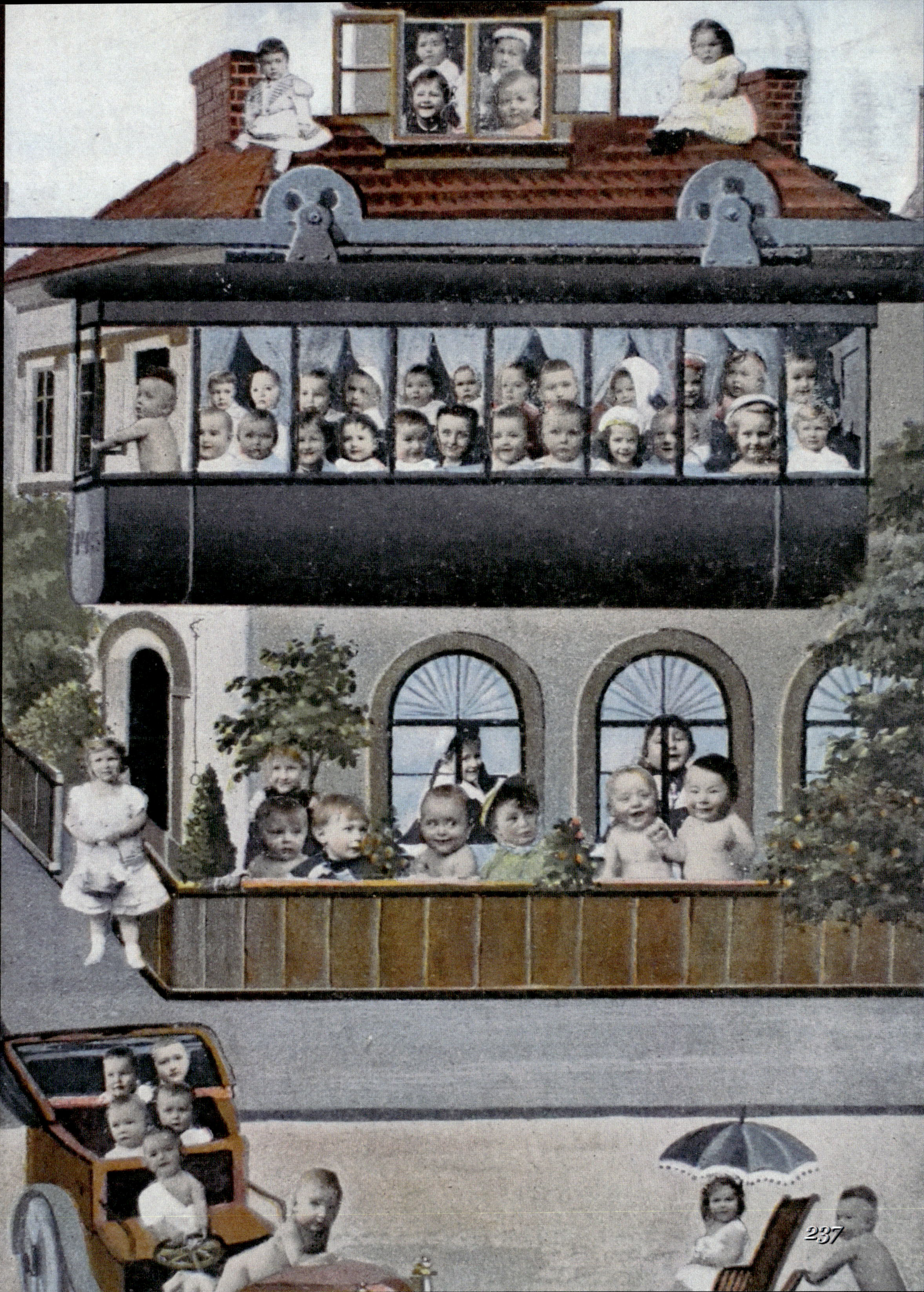

karte — Carte postale
ostverein — Union postale universelle
respondenzkarte — Dopisnice
velezö-Lap — Korespondenční listek
pisnica — Karta Korespondencyjna
fkaart — Cartolina Postale
fkort — Tarjeta Postal — Postcard
Дописна карта
ОТКРЫТОЕ ПИСЬМО

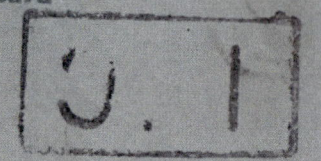

De jongeheer M. Witzeis
Kleinvoorthuizen
te Barneveld

Postkarte — Carte postale
Weltpostverein — Union postale universelle
Correspondenzkarte — Dopisnice
Levelezö-Lap — Korespondenční lístek
Dopisnica — Karta Korespondencyjna
Briefkaart — Cartolina Postale
Brefkort — Tarjeta Postal — Postcard
Дописна карта
ОТКРЫТОЕ ПИСЬМО

Madame Boucholl
Rue de Josephe — dijon
18ᵐᵉ Arrondisse.
Paris

Oeffe

Sit

240

241

Louis
de passage à Aix
nous a appris la bonne
nouvelle toutes
nos félicitations
bonnes amitiés et
bons
baisers

243

244

4. La Bière.

Souvenir de Conflans-Ste-Honor[ine]

247

CARTE

Certains pays étrangers n'accep[tent]
se rensei[gner]

Correspondance

Ponstans 16 December 190[.]

Beminde Broeders en [...]

Hiermede laat ik u weten
als dat wij van Rouen vertrokken
zyn en binnen 2 dagen in Parijs
zyn laat my eens weten hoe
het met Louis is en of sy nog
niets geeft heeft Zietkes myn
adres M. Florieux [...] St Denis
Seine

[...] gesard pelemans bateau [...]
de komplimenten aan de [...]

POSTALE

pas la correspondance de ce cote
r à la Poste

Adresse

M. Conrad Byck
Rue National
172
Anvers

Belgique

C. Malcuit, phot. édit. Paris

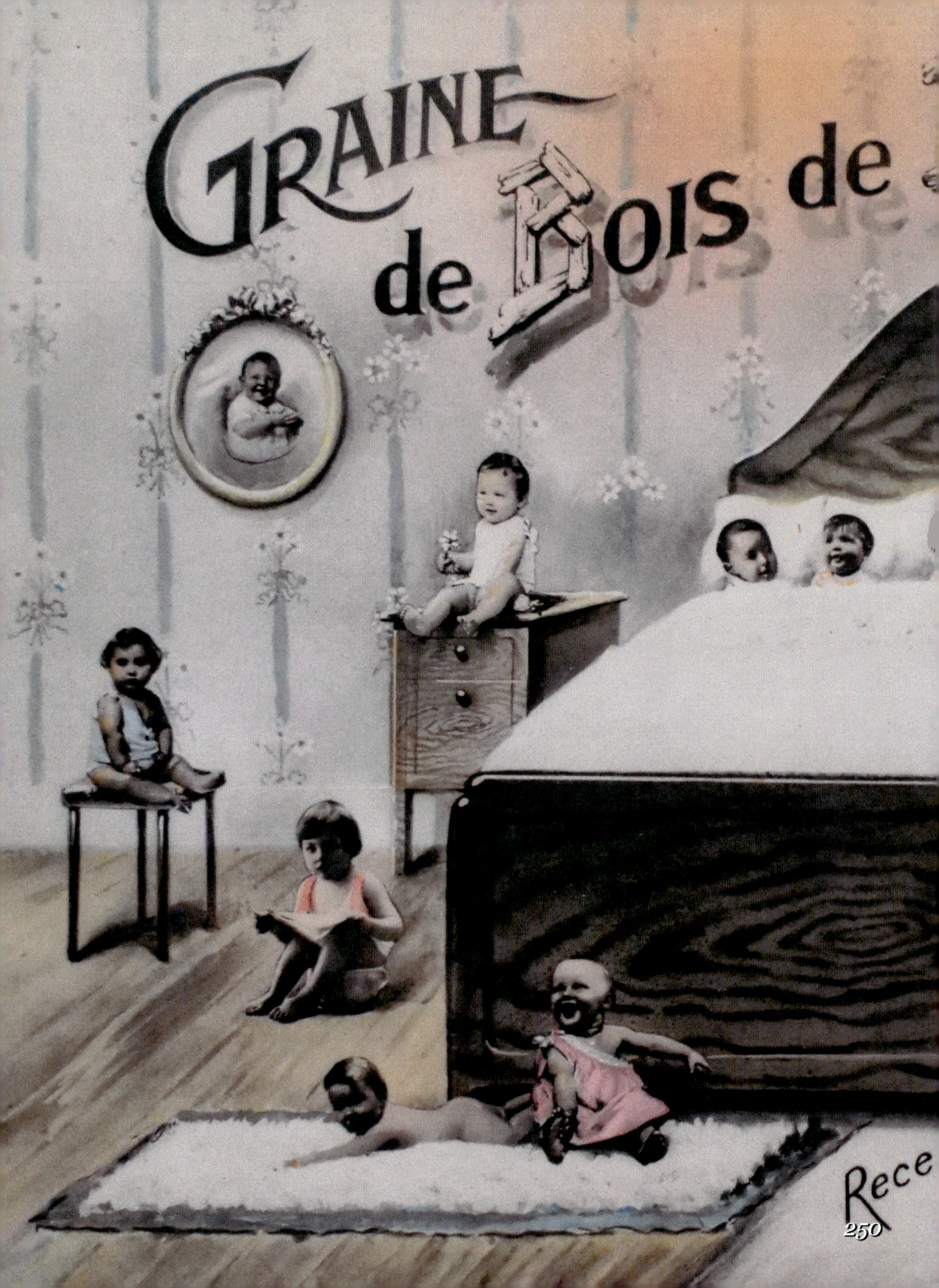

250

...s'embrasser pendant la nuit
...ous les coups çà réussit...

252

253

254

Воскресе!

256

257

258

259

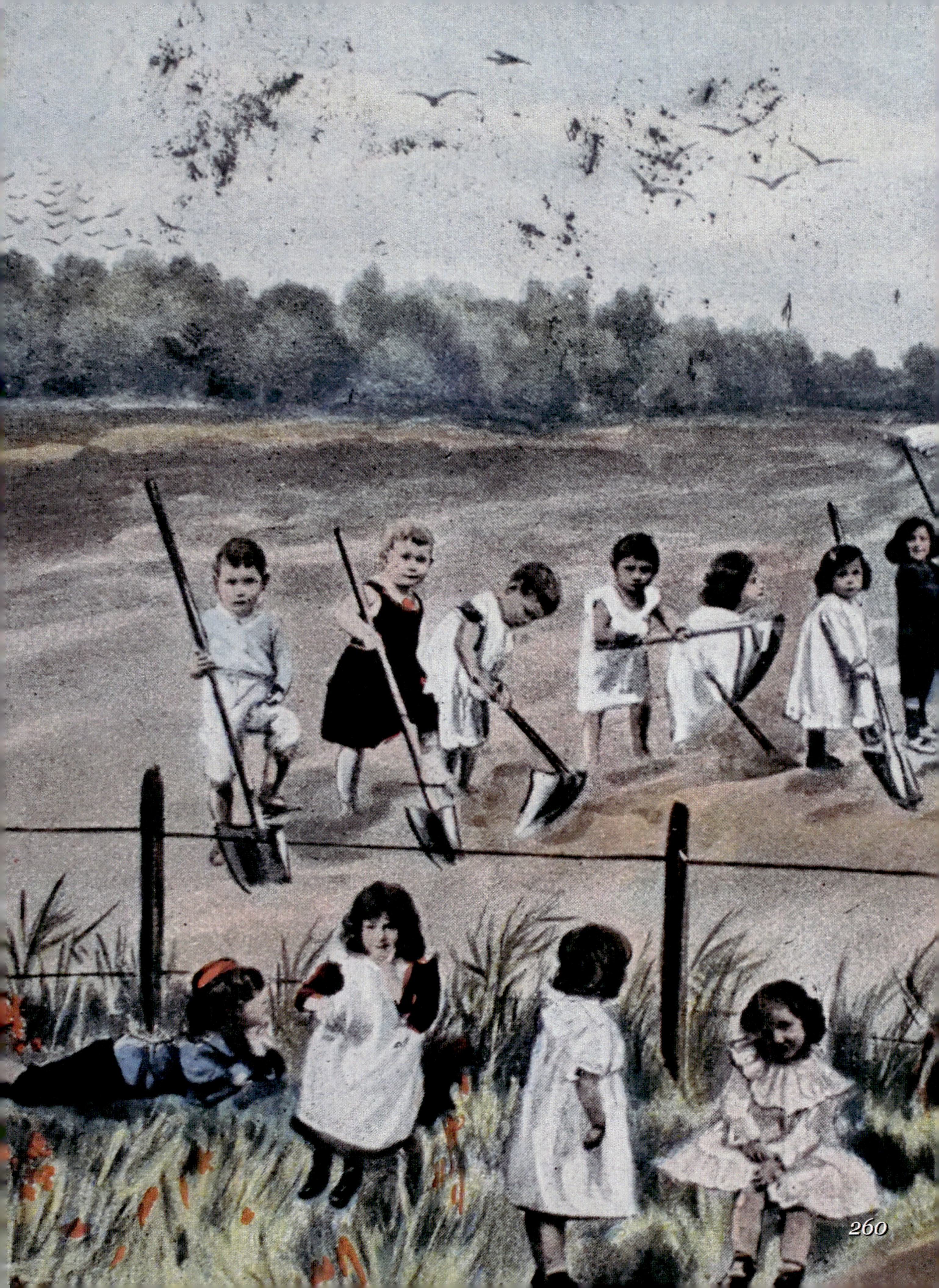

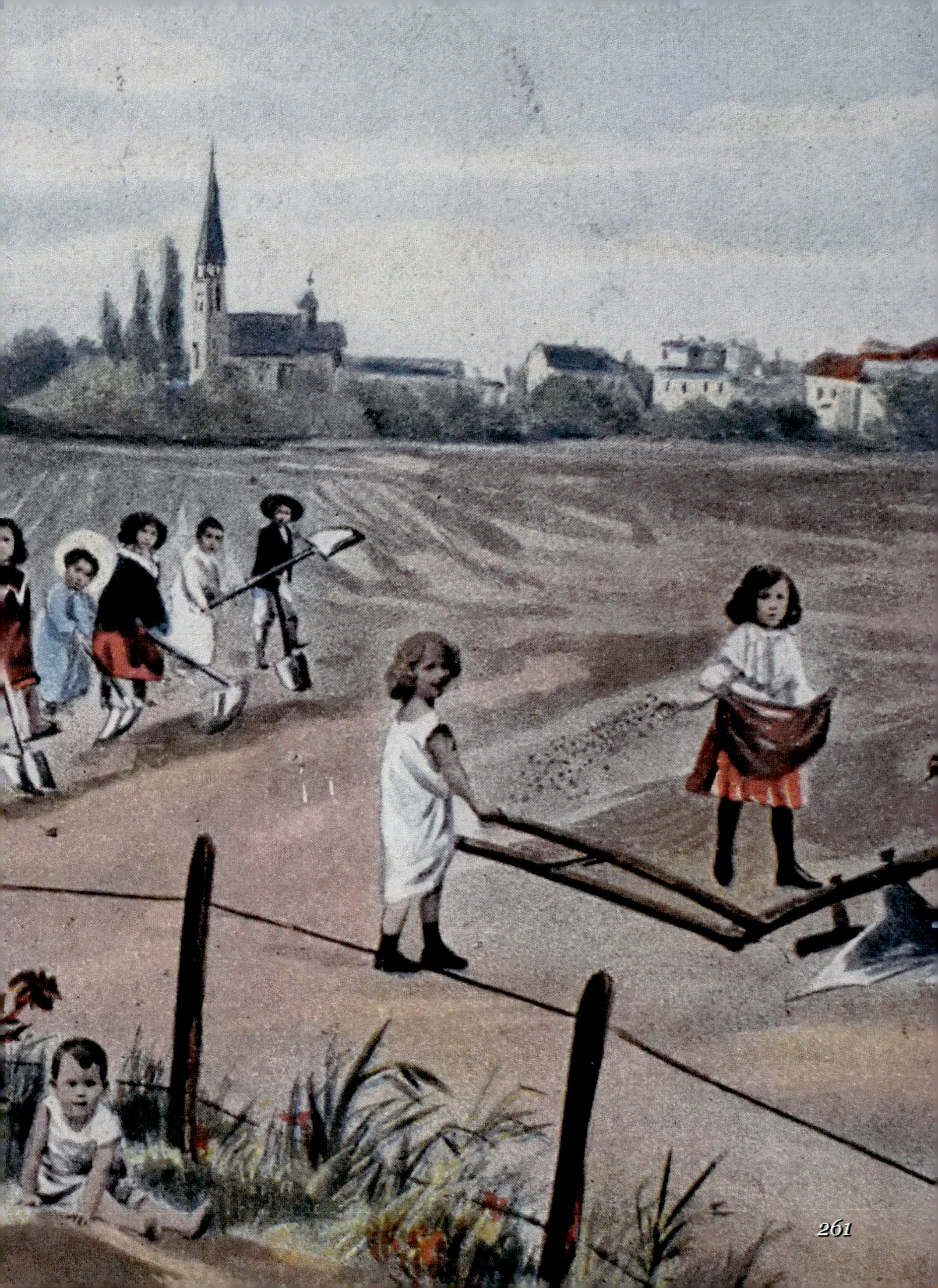

Postkarte — Carte p
Correspondenzkarte — Cartolina post
Brefkort — Briefkaart — Brevkort — Do
Tarjeta postal — Открытое письмо —
Korespondenční listek — Weltpostver

Dear Bet.

Are you very busy just now? I haven't heard from you for some time. We are having lovely weather. I hope it will keep like it next week. I suppose you have your brother at home. Isn't this a queer card? I rather like it. I hope Mr & Mrs Jones are well. Good bye Bet. Heaps of love but a sad sigh too dear — Constance —

Postcard — Levelező-Lap — Dopisnice — Karta Korespondencyjna —카рта — Carte postale — Union postale universelle

Miss Jones

Capel Ifan,

Nr. Llanelly.

S. Wales.

264

sparrows.

266

baisers

Postkarte — Carte postale
Weltpostverein — Union postale universelle
Correspondenzkarte — Dopisnice —
Levelező-Lap — Korespondenční listek
Dopisnica — Karta Korespondenzyjna
Briefkaart — Cartolina Postale —
Brefkort — Tarjeta Postal — Postcard
Дописна карта
ОТКРЫТОЕ ПИСЬМО

Mademoiselle Y...

chez Monsieur C...

rue Hyacinthe...

Maison Barreau...

Luzinier

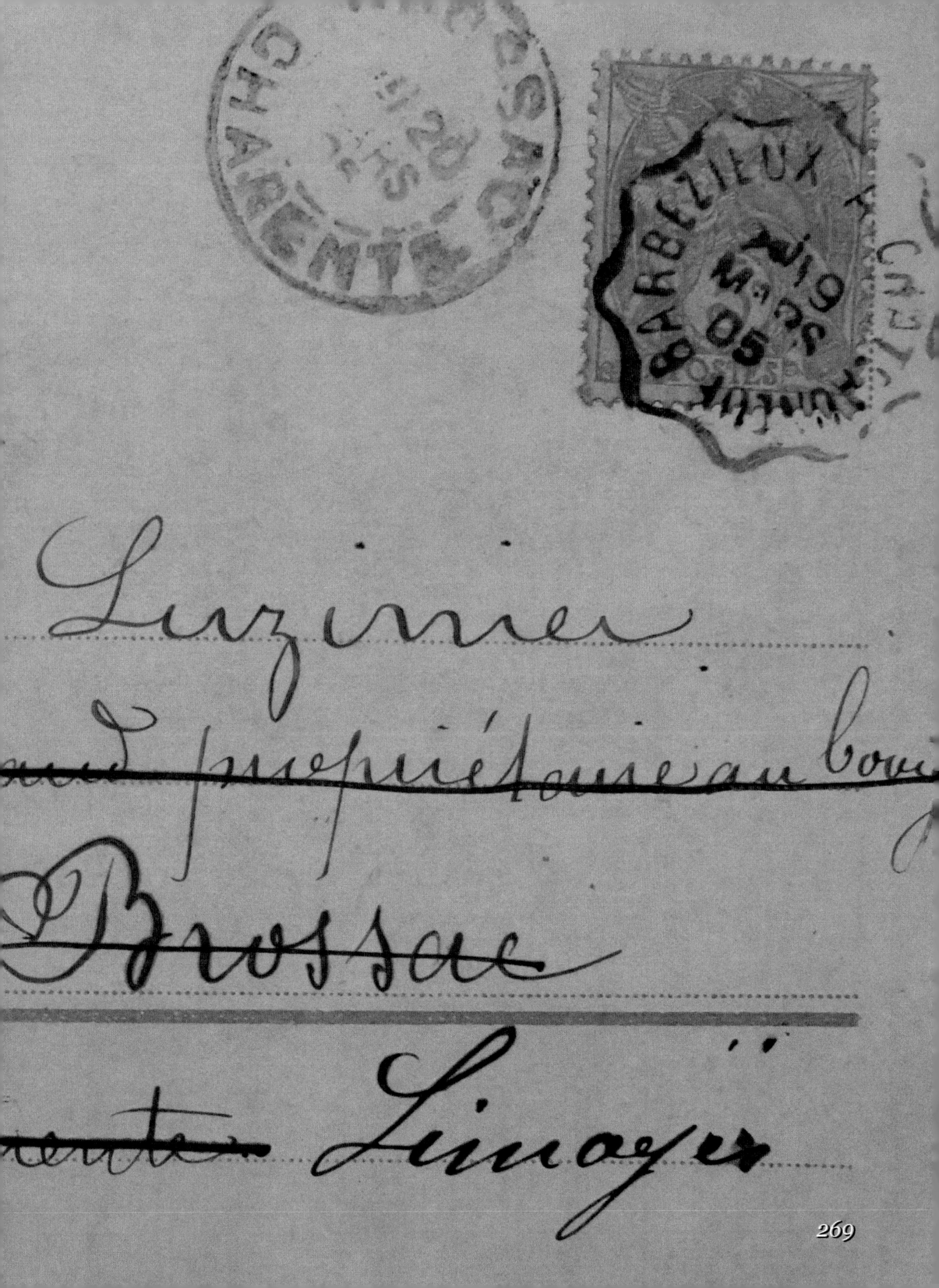

~~propriétaire au bou~~

Brossac

~~rente~~ Limoges

Jung-Frankfurt a. M.
entbietet gemütliche Grüsse.

July 16.

Dear Ane:

There is not a Baby here in Frankfurt as sweet as you are. Tell Mama & Papa to kiss you for Auntie Helen.

270

Bo-mama sends her love & kisses

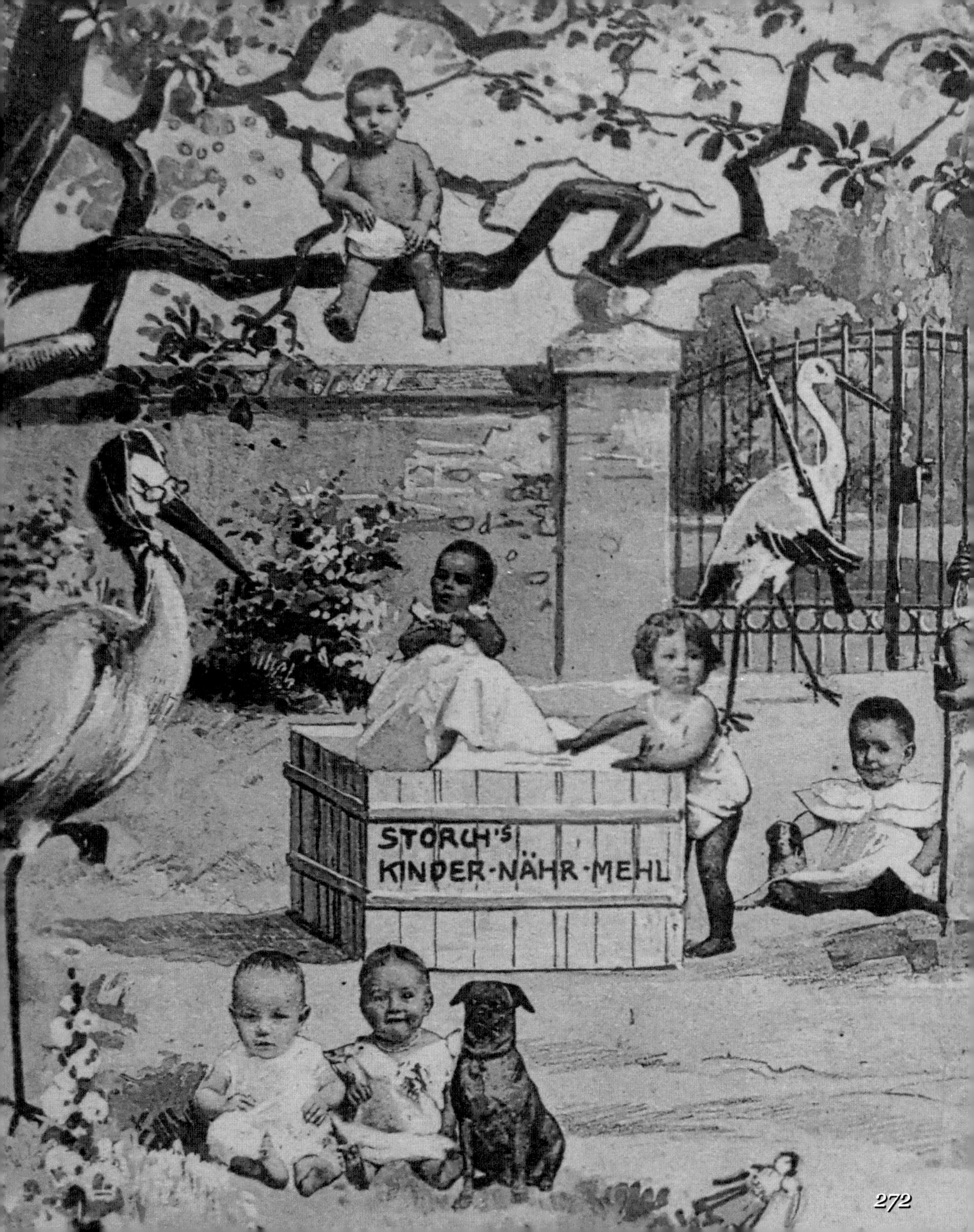
STORCH'S
KINDER-NÄHR-MEHL

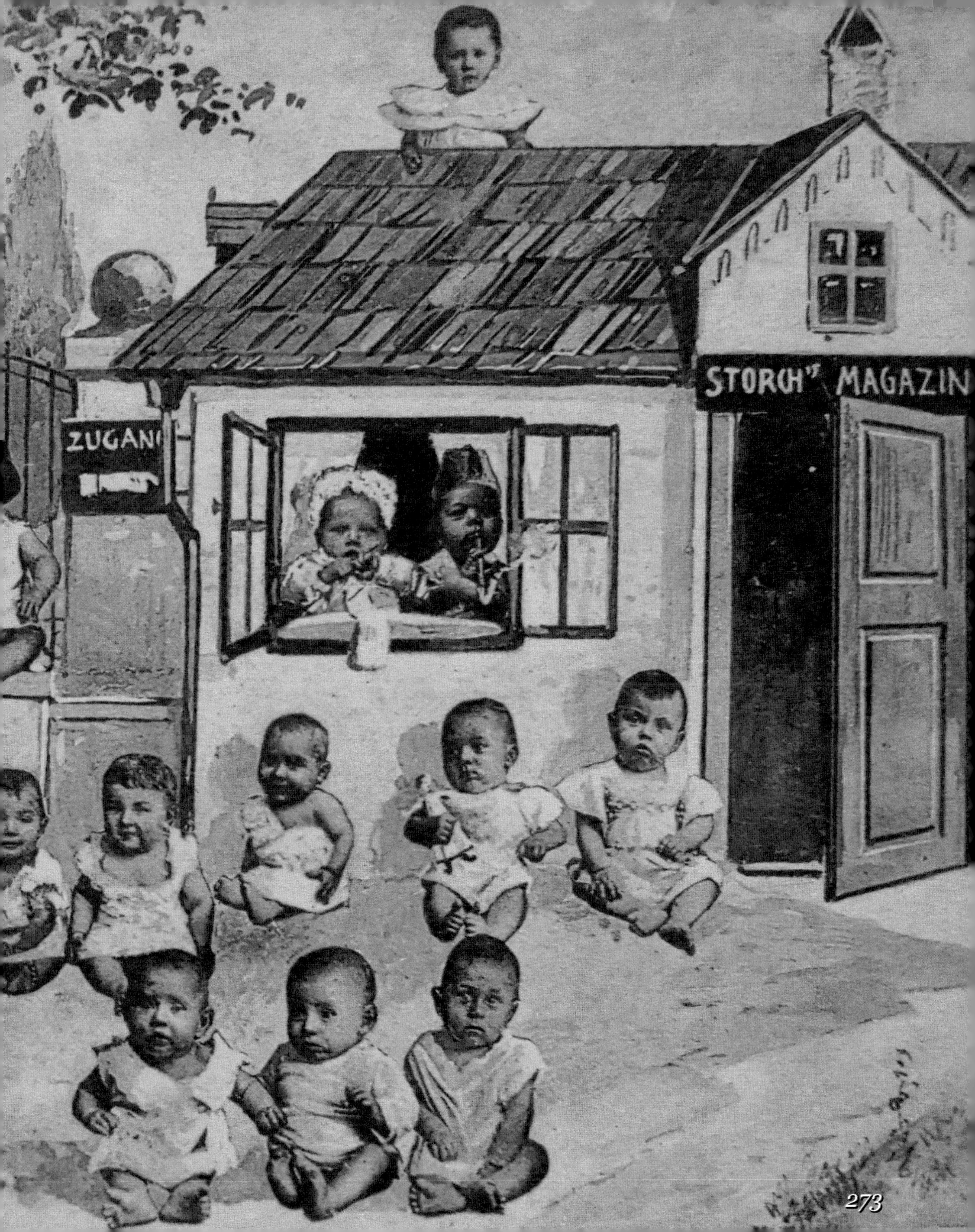
STORCH" MAGAZIN
ZUGANG

See the little red-headed devil — kid of mine
Perhaps — —

274

Union postale universelle — Weltp

These are not companion cards. Some one had to write on the other side of this, now I can't send it by mail.

I wonder if these will find place with the other valuable souvenirs you have. I don't know whether they should or not — just you have it. But don't tell where at them — never, never.

Say, if the other one is worth one stamp, how many stamps is this worth? Figure it out and let me know. I don't believe you went to school long enough to know how many ——

Une cargaison nouvelle de bébés modernes.

Son A. B
den A. B.
M L.

Madame et M?
Henri Jouan
a Bihorel-lès
Rouen Inférieure

278

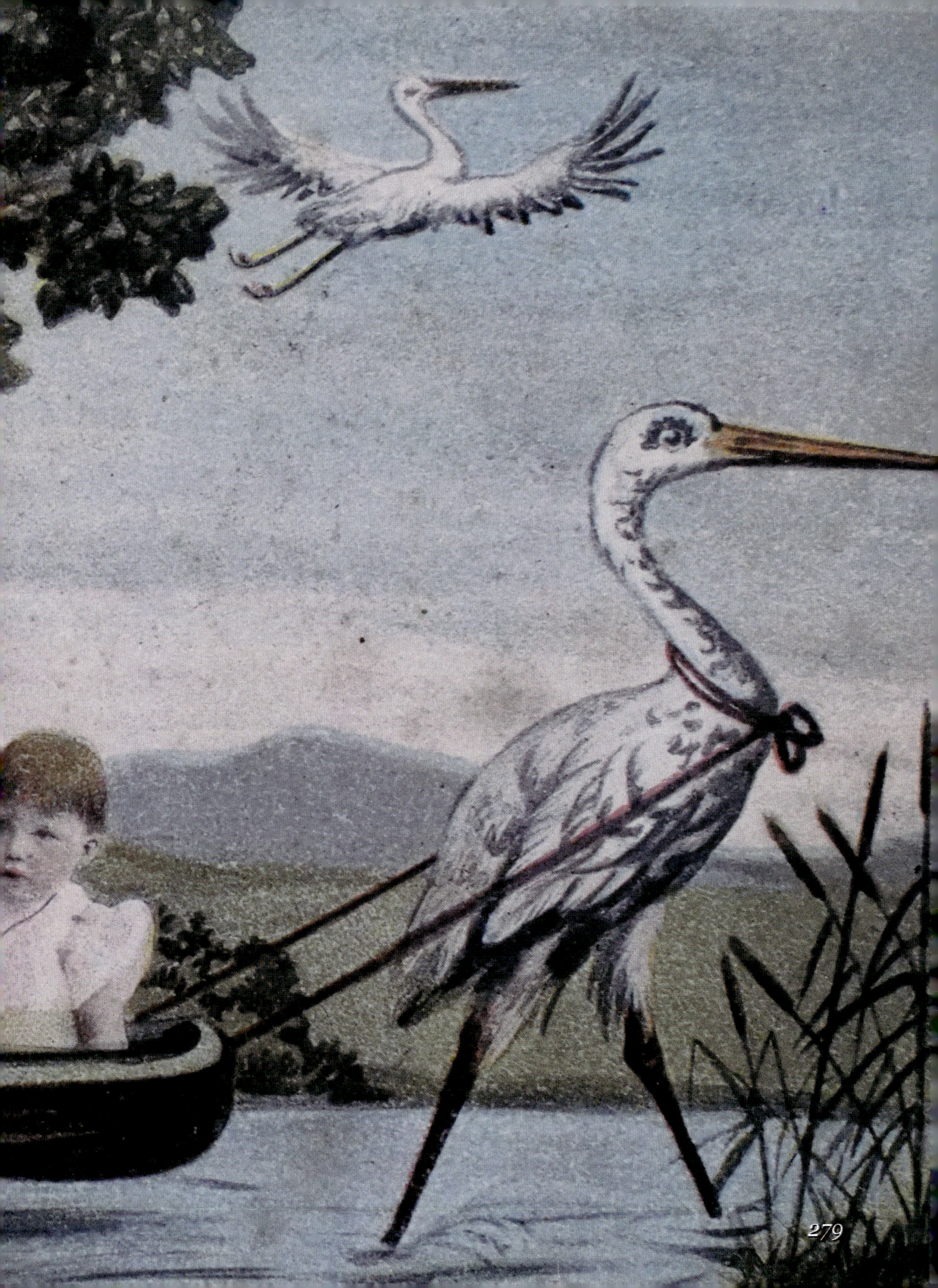

280

281

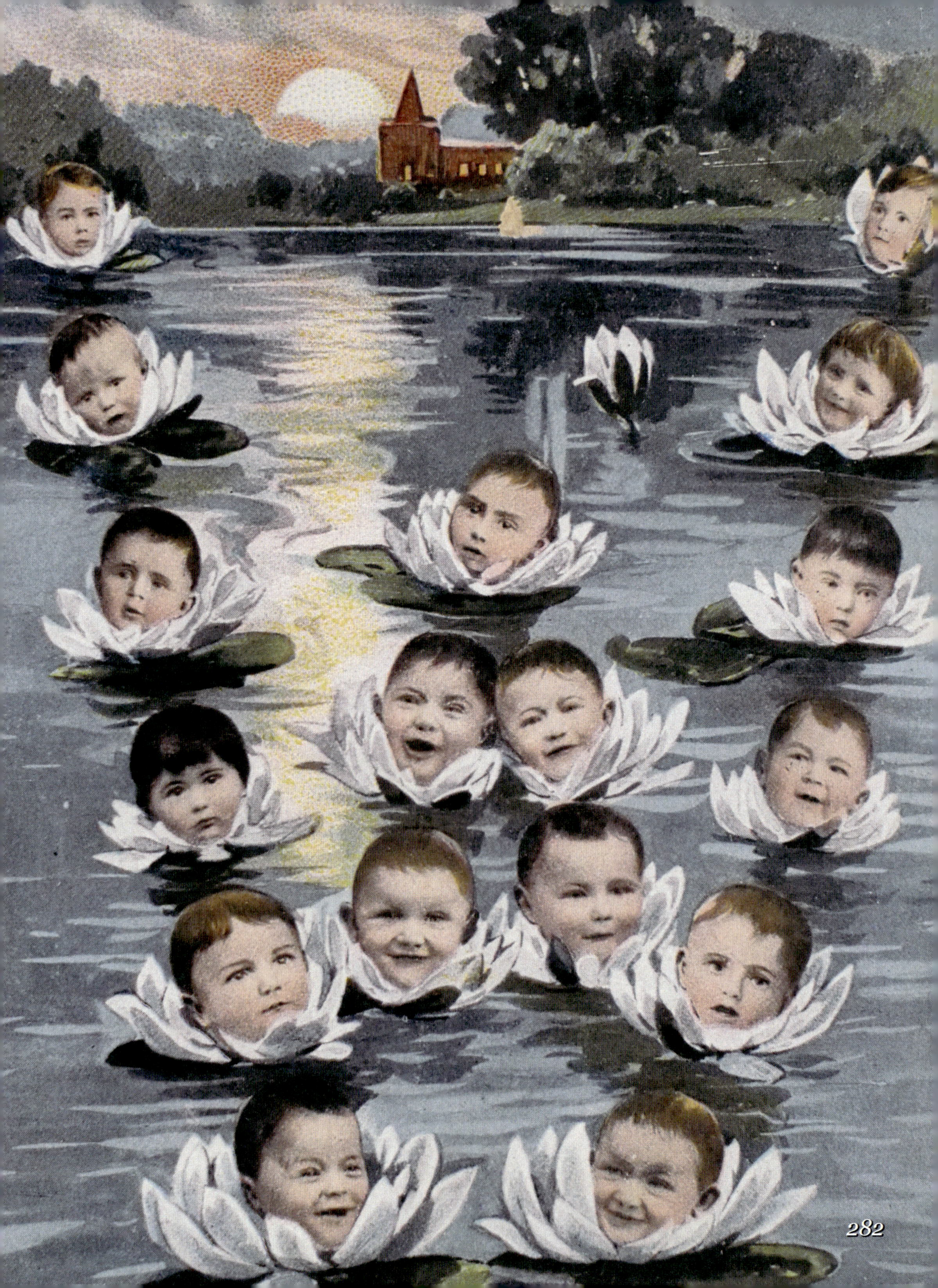

Dear Lallie,

Are you feeling brighter to day. Get out as much as you can won't you? Only one more Sunday cheer up old girl. I have got your "W" at last after going all over the town for it. When do you propose having your holiday. Shall we talk it over at Whitsun.

much love Yrs as ever
Will

Les 2 élèves du papa sont reçus
et la tante
Le papa arriveront demain matin
à Poligny par
le train

285

286

BÉBÉS à VENDRE
Choisissez !

Chacun de ces choux mignons
Contient de l'affection.

THE END

Works Cited

Wikimedia Commons

    https://commons.wikimedia.org/wiki/File:Arms_of_the_Foundling_Hospital_with_an_admission_ticket_(BM_1858,0417.578).jpg.

Arnaud, Étienne, and Lucien Boisyvon. "Le cinéma pour tous." *Libr. Garnier*, 1922, p. 42.

"The baker of Eeklo." *Muiderslot*, https://muiderslot.nl/en/featured_item/the-baker-of-eeklo/.

Barry, Rebecca R. "Coney Island's Incubator Babies." JSTOR Daily, 15 August 2018, https://daily.jstor.org/coney-islands-incubator-babies/.

Birch, James. *Babylon: Surreal Babies*. Edited by George Melly, Dewi Lewis, 2010.

Creagh, Dianne. "The Baby Trains: Catholic Foster Care and Western Migration, 1873-1929." *Journal of Social History* Vol. 46, No. 1 (Fall 2012), pp. 197-218 (22 pages).

Dargis, Manohla. "Overlooked No More: Alice Guy Blaché, the World's First Female Filmmaker (Published 2019)." *The New York Times*, 9 September 2019, https://www.nytimes.com/2019/09/06/obituaries/alice-guy-blache-overlooked.html.

Denoël/Gonthie. *Autobiographie d'une pionnière du cinéma, 1873-1968*. Paris, 1976.

Dietrick, Janelle. *La Fée Aux Choux, Alice Guy's Garden of Dreams*. Paradis Perdu Press, 2022. Chapters 17-26.

Dunn, P. M. "Stéphane Tarnier (1828–1897), the architect of perinatology in France." *Arch Dis Child Fetal Neonatal Ed.*, vol. 86, no. 2, 2002, pp. F137–F139.

Elderkin, G.W. "The Bee of Artemis." 2 ed., vol. 60, The American Journal of Philology, 1939, pg 203-213.

Encyclopedia.com. "Incubator." https://www.encyclopedia.com/plants-and-animals/agriculture-and-horticulture/agriculture-general/incubator. Accessed 27 June 2023.

Entre & Lumière. "Trois questions a la petite fille de Alice Guy: Regine Blaché-Bolton." 2012.

Foreman, Amanda. "The Amazon Women: Is There Any Truth Behind the Myth?" *Smithsonian Magazine*, 2014, https://www.smithsonianmag.com/history/amazon-women-there-any-truth-behind-myth-180950188/.

Fulton, J. "Baby Incubators." *Canada Lancet*, vol. 15, 1883, pp. 250-251. https://www.google.com/books/edition/Canada_Lancet/8Z5XAAAAMAAJ.

"Goddesses of Liberty: Statues, State Seals of Minerva, Athena, Plenty | Pagan U.S." *Coven Oldenwilde*, 29 January 2011, http://www.oldenwilde.org/oldenwilde/gen_info/pagan_us/goddesses_us.html.

Guy, Alice. *The memoirs of Alice Guy Blaché*. Scarecrow press, 1996.

Guy, Alice. "Sage-femme de premire classe AKA Midwife to the Upper Classes : Alice Guy." *Internet Archive*, 4 December 2020, https://archive.org/details/silent-sage-femme-de-premire-classe-aka-midwife-to-the-upper-classes.

Han, Yoonji. "The True Story Behind the Black Jockey in Jordan Peele's 'Nope.'" *Insider*, 2 August 2022, https://www.insider.com/nope-black-jockey-pictures-muybridge-horse-in-motion-history-2022-8.

"Het Groote Tafereel der Dwaasheid [The Great Picture (or Scene) of Folly]." *CURIOSity Digital Collections*, https://curiosity.lib.harvard.edu/south-sea-bubble/feature/het-groote-tafereel-der-dwaasheid-the-great-picture-or-scene-of-folly.

Holt, Marilyn Irvin. *The orphan trains : placing out in America*. University of Nebraska Press, 1992.

IMDb. "Les méfaits d'une tête de veau (Short 1899)." https://www.imdb.com/title/tt0351391/.

Jordanes. *The Origin and Deeds of the Goths*. Princeton University Press, 1908.

Kornoes, Sheldon B. ""An Encapsulated History of Thermoregulation in the Neonate,."" *MD, NeoReviews*, vol. 5, no. 3, 2004.

"The Legend Cabbage Patch Kids." *Cabbage Patch Kids*, https://cabbagepatchkids.com/pages/the-legend.

Miller, Julie. *Abandoned: Foundlings in Nineteenth-Century New York City*. NYU Press, 2008.

Mitchell, Kerrie. "San Francisco is a Ghost Town: The Story Behind Eadweard Muybridge's Spooky Panorama." *New-York Historical Society*, 11 September 2019, https://www.nyhistory.org/blogs/san-francisco-is-a-ghost-town-the-story-behind-eadweard-muybridges-spooky-panorama.

Morton, Ella. "The Birth of the Baby Hatch, for Surrendering Infants Safely." Atlas Obscura, 10 July 2014, https://www.slate.com/blogs/atlas_obscura/2014/07/10/ospedale_degli_innocenti_or_hospital_of_the_innocents_and_its_foundling.html.

"Oeuvre Maternelle Des Couveuses d'Enfants." *Neonatology on the Web*, 27 February 2011, https://neonatology.net/classics/lion/LionParisBooklet.html.

Pierre Laroche. "Du Cinéma Parlant au Cinéma Muet." *Naissance du Cinéma, Les Cahiers de Radio-Paris, Conférences données dans l'auditorium du Poste National Radio-Paris*, 1939, p. 922.

"Reader criticizes Statue of Liberty's shadowy past." *Great Falls Tribune*, 30 June 2016, https://www.greatfallstribune.com/story/opinion/letters-to-the-editor/2016/06/30/reader-criticizes-statue-libertys-shadowy-past/86578432/.

Rebovich, Kelsey. "The Infant Incubator in Europe (1860-1890) | The Embryo Project Encyclopedia." 11 February 2017, https://embryo.asu.edu/pages/infant-incubator-europe-1860-1890.

Ryan, J. A. "CATHOLIC ENCYCLOPEDIA: Foundling Asylums." *New Advent*, https://www.newadvent.org/cathen/06159a.htm.

Schlott, Rikki. "Orphan Trains: A Brief History and Research How-to." *New York Genealogical & Biographical Society |*, 13 November 2020, https://www.newyorkfamilyhistory.org/blog/orphan-trains-brief-history-and-research-how.

Strelan, Rick. *Paul, Artemis, and the Jews in Ephesus*. De Gruyter, 2014.

su grimh.org. "Les Méfaits d'une tête de veau."

Tanne, J. H., and FDA. "FDA approves use of cloned animals for food." *NCBI*, https://www.ncbi.nlm.nih.gov/pmc/articles/PMC2213849/.

Tsarion, Michael. *Atlantis, Alien Visitation, and Genetic Manipulation*. Angels at Work Publishing, 2003.

Warren, Andrea. *Orphan Train Rider: One Boy's True Story*. Houghton Mifflin, 1996.

Wikimedia. https://commons.wikimedia.org/wiki/File:Panorama_of_San_Francisco_by_Eadweard_Muybridge,_1878.jpg.

Wikipedia. "Babyland General Hospital." https://en.wikipedia.org/wiki/Babyland_General_Hospital.

Wikipedia. "Foundling Hospital." https://en.wikipedia.org/wiki/Foundling_Hospital.

Wikipedia. "Ibn al-Haytham." https://en.wikipedia.org/wiki/Ibn_al-Haytham.

Wikipedia. "La Fée aux Choux." https://en.wikipedia.org/wiki/La_F%C3%A9e_aux_Choux.

Wikipedia. "Les méfaits d'une tête de veau."

Wikipedia. "Levinus Vincent." https://en.wikipedia.org/wiki/Levinus_Vincent.

Wikipedia. "Orphan Train." *Wikipedia*, https://en.wikipedia.org/wiki/Orphan_Train.

IMAGES USED

Fig 1.1. Scheiner's helioscope as illustrated in his book Rosa Ursina sive Sol (1626–30)

Fig 1.2. Muybridge's The Horse in Motion, 1878

Fig 1.3. Panorama of San Francisco by Eadweard Muybridge, 1878

Fig 1.4. Baptist railroad chapel car Glad Tidings childrens meeting 1910

Fig 3.1. Infant Incubator - Martin Couney holding two babies ,
THE NEW YORK PUBLIC LIBRARY

Fig 3.2. Pilier Est de la Tour Eiffel. Couveuse d'enfants avec Bébés vivants 1904

Fig 3.3. Exposition Universelle et Internationale de Bruxelles, 1910, Neonatology.net

Fig 3.4. Early baby incubator, 19th century

Fig 4.1. The Foundling Hospital, Holborn, London; a view of the court

Fig 4.2. William Hogarth - Arms of the Foundling Hospital

Fig 4.3. Philip Galle, after Maerten van Heemskerck, Dianae Ephesiae Templum (The Temple of Diana at Ephesus), 1572

Fig 5.1. Marching Orphans, Mennonite Church USA Archives

Fig 5.2. Orphan train flyer, 1910

Fig 5.3. Orphans at horse show - N.Y. , 1913

Fig 5.4. "Street Arabs at Night" by Jacob Riis, circa 1890, Rare Book & Manuscript Library, Columbia University

Fig 5.5. (King1893NYC) pg435 CHILDREN'S AID SOCIETY, SECOND AVENUE AND 44TH STREET

La Fée aux Choux 1900 version

Fig 6.1. Uniformed Letter Carrier with Child in Mailbag, circa 1900s

Fig 6.2. "Couveuses d'Enfants" by Adolfo Hohenstein

Fig 6.3. "Oeuvre Maternelle des Couveuses d'Enfants," from Neonatology.net"

Sage-femme de première classe, Alice Guy, 1902

Fig 7.1. Terminal Figure - Diana of Ephesus, circa 1540

Fig 7.2. Wilhelm Schubert van Ehrenberg - The Seven Wonders of the World; The Temple of Diana at Ephesus

Fig 7.3. Plato Engraving

Fig 7.4. Allaert Claesz - Naked Woman and a Dragon - 1523

Fig 7.5. La galerie agréable du monde, Van Der Aa, Pieter Boudewyn 1729

Fig 7.6. Statue of Liberty LCCN2002716183

Fig 7.7. Declaration of the Rights of Man and of the Citizen painted by Jean-Jacques-François Le Barbier in 1789

Fig 7.8. Giovanni Boccaccio - Penthésilée BnF Français 599 fol. 27v, illuminated manuscript

Fig 7.9. Frontispiece to "Las Sergas de Esplandián" by Garci Rodriguez de Montalvo

Fig 7.10. Bee-goddess, perhaps associated with Artemis above female heads. Gold plaques, 7th century BC

Fig 7.11. Copper by Salomon Kleiner (1700–1761) in: [Johann Karl Newen von Newenstein ed.]

Fig 7.12. 'La Fontane di Roma', Giovanni Battista Falda 1691

Fig 7.13. Magna Mater, 1702

Fig 7.14. 19th century engraving of Homunculus from Goethe's Faust part II

Fig 7.15. Flora's Wagon of Fools: Allegory on the Tulip mania. Painted by Hendrik Gerritsz Pot, circa 1637

Fig 7.16. Het groote tafereel der dwaasheid, 1720, pg133

Fig 7.17. Het groote tafereel der dwaasheid, 1720, pg71

Fig 7.18. Het groote tafereel der dwaasheid, 1720, pg65

Fig 7.19. Het groote tafereel der dwaasheid, 1720, pg45

Fig 7.20. Het groote tafereel der dwaasheid, 1720, pg59

Fig 7.21. De legende van de bakker van Eekloo Rijksmuseum, circa 1560

Fig 7.22. Wondertooneel der nature, 1706, pg47

Fig 7.23. Wondertooneel der nature, 1706, pg7

Copyright Disclaimer

The creators of this work have made every effort to respect copyright laws and principles of Fair Use. We have undertaken thorough research to ensure that all text and images used in this publication are either within the public domain or have been used with proper attribution.

Fair Use Assertion: We believe, in good faith, that any copyrighted content included herein has been used in a manner that qualifies as Fair Use under copyright law. Such usage has been minimal and solely for purposes that are transformative, educational, or illustrative.

Public Domain Images: Many of the images, especially those prior to 1920—including numerous postcards—are believed to be in the public domain due to their age. While efforts have been made to identify and credit original sources, the nature of public domain content means that the original copyright holder may sometimes be untraceable. Where possible, and particularly for images sourced from WikiCommons, a comprehensive list with corresponding titles can be found in the "Images Used" section.

Quotes and Citations: All textual quotes and excerpts, to the best of our knowledge, have been accurately referenced and credited to their respective authors or sources.

We respect intellectual property rights and aim to ensure all content is used appropriately. If any party believes their copyrighted content has been used without due credit or in violation of Fair Use principles, please contact us with the information provided at the end of the book. We are committed to addressing such concerns promptly and appropriately.

SPECIAL THANKS

We owe a profound debt of gratitude to our friends and family, whose unwavering love and support have been instrumental from the inception of "Mind Unveiled." Our mothers deserve a spotlight of their own—without their constant nurturing and belief in us, this journey might have remained a dream. Their influence runs deep, and we can't emphasize enough how instrumental they've been in making this endeavor possible.

Our gratitude extends to the dedicated moderators of our Discord community and the talented translators who generously contributed their time and skills. Witnessing our work translated into a myriad of languages has been nothing short of exhilarating.

To every commenter, supporter, and silent reader who engaged with our work: your enthusiasm has been our driving force. If you've made it this far, it signifies your appreciation for our explorations and musings. Your very engagement is a testament to the value you find in our content, which in turn inspires us to forge ahead.

For us, it's not about cementing a universal truth but rather sparking a shift in perspective, igniting the flame of curiosity, and encouraging continuous questioning. If we've played even a small role in influencing such an outlook, then we believe our mission has been a success. From the depths of our hearts, thank you.

If you would like to contact us please email us at *mindunveiled@gmail.com* or visit our website at *www.mindunveiled.com*. Share your thoughts, let us know if there is anything we missed and again thank you...

All we can hope is that our MINDS... may be unveiled...

Made in the USA
Las Vegas, NV
27 September 2023

78220920R00178